A READING APPROACH TO COLLEGE *WRITING*

A READING APPROACH TO COLLEGE

WRITING

1971 Edition

Edited by

Martha Heasley Cox

San Jose State College

CHANDLER PUBLISHING COMPANY

An Intext Publisher • Scranton / London / Toronto

Book and Cover Designed by Joseph M. Roter

PRINTED IN THE UNITED STATES OF AMERICA.
LIBRARY OF CONGRESS CATALOG CARD NO. 77-139488
INTERNATIONAL STANDARD BOOK NUMBER 0-8102-0411-8

Contents

**Selections thus identified are newly included since the preceding (1969) edition.*

10. COHERENCE 317

11. REVIEW OF RHETORICAL PRINCIPLES 347

12. FOR FURTHER STUDY 359

APPENDICES 369

Pictures

Preface

In this 1971 edition of *A Reading Approach to College Writing,* as in the eleven previous editions, I have attempted to collect material of literary value which will stimulate and challenge. Naturally, not all of the essays are of equal quality, but I have made an effort to avoid the dated, the tired, the maudlin, the banal, the immature, and to select only complete, current, relatively short, chiefly expository essays.

Although realizing that the student may need drill in grammar, sentence structure, spelling, and punctuation, I have made no effort to treat these matters as such, here, but anticipate that this book will be used in conjunction with one of several excellent texts already available for these purposes. I have found that duplication of such materials is not only time-consuming, but also frequently confusing to the student because of inevitable differences in terminology and approach.

My primary concern has been to supply provocative reading material which suggests numerous worthwhile writing assignments. The exercises following each essay contain questions aimed at developing some of the ideas inherent in the essay, and at analyzing the method or form through which the author developed those ideas as well as vocabulary studies and suggested topics for both paragraph and full theme development.

In introductory sections preceding the essays I have discussed briefly such rhetorical principles as the thesis statement, good diction, effective sentences, purpose statements, topic sentences, introductions and conclusions, simple patterns of development, and transitional words and linking devices. In addition, I have called the student's attention to the effective use of these principles by the authors represented here.

Essays which will readily arouse the student's interest and best exemplify those principles of composition he needs to know immediately are placed first. Continuity in content within the chapters is provided by the selection of essays with similar subject matter or theme. In this revision I have attempted to supply a progression of ideas from chapter to chapter, too, concentrating on six major themes; (1) the historical, current, and prospective problems of man and his environment, with especial attention to the automobile; (2) education and its changing importance in time, place, and race; (3) drug use and abuse, present and past; (4) woman and her changing relationships and dilemmas; (5) discrimination and civil rights, with particular reference to Blacks, Indians, and Chicanos; and (6) symbols and values and their eternal or ephemeral significance.

Finally, the appendices contain thought-provoking statements and two essays on writing: Paul Roberts's timeless advice on how to write a paper and Rudolph Flesch's hints for improving spelling.

It is my hope that this collection will provide students with subject matter, patterns, and incentive for developing their own ideas effectively.

Revisions in the 1971 Edition

In this fifth revision of the 1960 Alternate Edition of *A Reading Approach to College Writing,* I have omitted fifteen essays which were included in the 1969 revision and have added twenty-two new selections. Some of the essays omitted had become dated, the inevitable fate of much material dealing with contemporary issues and collected from current books and periodicals, and some had proved less successful than others in my own classes and in those of my colleagues who have used the text. In fact, this edition contains only four essays from the original, the 1960, version. These articles as well as those retained from the other editions have proved particularly stimulating and beneficial in supplying both ideas and patterns for student writing. My aim in both the selection of new essays and in the retention of old ones was the same as in the first edition.

M.H.C.

The Editions of *A Reading Approach to College Writing*

Original Edition, published 1959	Alternate Edition, published 1960
1961 Edition	1962 Edition
1964 Edition	1965 Edition
1966 Edition	1967 Edition
1968 Edition	1969 Edition
1970 Edition	1971 Edition

The 1961, 1964, 1966, 1968, and 1970 Editions are based on the selection of essays in the Original Edition. There have been some substitutions and additions to keep the content of current and stimulating character; there have been some changes in the expository material to achieve greater clarity and improved teaching quality.

The Alternate Edition contained an entirely different selection of essays from that in the Original Edition, but the expository material was essentially the same.

The 1962, 1965, 1967, 1969, and 1971 Editions are based on the selection of essays in the Alternate Edition. Changes and additions among the essays have been made in order to maintain currency and interest; expository material has been revised to achieve greater clarity and improved teaching quality.

A READING APPROACH TO COLLEGE ***WRITING***

Much of the dreariness and drudgery which too often accompany compulsory writing result from having nothing to say and, consequently, no desire to say it. Selections in this text are offered to help remedy both ills by providing provocative ideas you will wish to discuss. Since the selections are also models of good writing, studying their authors' methods of expressing their thoughts will help you to express your own more satisfactorily.

You will find two readings of each essay helpful: the first time through, concentrate only on what the author says; the next time, study his technique carefully. Questions at the end of each selection will help guide your study, and a quick glance through them before your second reading should prove beneficial.

Before you write a paper based on any of the essays, read through the writing suggestions offered. You will find some amusing, some boring, some irritating, some challenging, some easy, some hard. Some you will eliminate immediately as possibilities for your paper, either because you find them uninteresting or because you know too little about the topics to make worthwhile comments on them. Some you may wish to limit further or to make more precise or unified. Remember that the suggestions are intended only as springboards for your writing. An effort has been made to include a sufficient variety for every selection so that you will find at least one you want to write on and can discuss intelligently.

After you have selected your topic, formulate your thesis statement. This thesis statement or statement of intention should be more than just the subject of your paper. It should also state your main idea and show your purpose in writing.

The first selection in this collection, for example, describes God's creation of man and preparation of a place for him to live. In the second essay, the author's subject or main idea is that man has turned his world into a wasteland; the author's purpose is to describe the desolation so vividly as to shame and shock her readers into action. The thesis statement should be restricted enough to allow you to discuss it adequately in the time and space allowed; otherwise you may have the all too common student experience of turning in a paper at the end of the class hour with the hastily added excuse or plea, "I'm sorry, but I didn't have time to finish," as your only conclusion. The thesis statement should be precise enough to prevent your writing a mass of vague generalizations; otherwise your paper may come home to you with such comments as "why?" "when?" "how?" "support," "illustrate," and "prove" scattered profusely throughout its margins. Your thesis statement should be unified enough to force you to place the emphasis on one major idea; otherwise you may write a meandering paper with little connection between its parts and no logical organization.

Formulating a statement of intention before you start will force you to ascertain whether you actually have something to say, and will make you determine your purpose in saying it. It will, furthermore, act as a guide, helping you to organize your supporting ideas and illustrations, to place together those that have affinity, and to delete those that—no matter how much you would like to include them—have no relation to your subject or purpose.

One usually writes either to inform, to persuade, to entertain, to amuse, to satirize, or to convince. But you may, of course, have more than one purpose in any assignment. You may wish primarily to inform, that is, to convey information, yet hope to be moderately entertaining in doing so—or, at least to escape boredom and dullness. If your primary purpose is to entertain, you may also hope to be informative and perhaps, even, persuasive or convincing in the process. If you write satire, you desire to bring about reform; through satire you attempt to convince or persuade and, often, also to entertain. Usually, however, you have one basic purpose in writing which is more powerful than any other purpose or combination of purposes. Always determine what it is before you write even the first word. Then marshall your ideas, facts, and illustrations, and put them into the words, sentences, and paragraphs which will make up your paper.

Throughout this text, you will have the opportunity, as you read and write, to respond to the ideas of intelligent and interesting people on subjects of concern in our time. As you read, your attention will be called to the principles these writers use which you may profitably emulate. In the first essays, note particularly how the authors convey their main ideas and purposes to you.

ADAM AND EVE (Albert Dürer)

Achenbach Foundation for Graphic Arts, California Palace of the Legion of Honor, Lincoln Park, San Francisco, California 94121

The Garden of Eden

The Book of Genesis

And the Lord God formed man of the dust of the ground, and breathed into his nostrils the breath of life; and man became a living soul.

And the Lord God planted a garden eastward in Eden; and there he put the man whom he had formed. And out of the ground made the Lord God to grow every tree that is pleasant to the sight, and good for food; the tree of life also in the midst of the garden, and the tree of knowledge of good and evil. And a river went out of Eden to water the garden; and from thence it was parted, and became into four heads. The name of the first is Pison: that is it which compasseth the whole land of Havilah, where there is gold; and the gold of that land is good: there is bdellium and the onyx stone. And the name of the second river is Gihon: the same is it that compasseth the whole land of Ethiopia. And the name of the third river is Hiddekel: that is it which goeth toward the east of Assyria. And the fourth river is Euphrates. And the Lord God took the man, and put him into the garden

☐ Genesis 2:7-3:24.

of Eden to dress it and to keep it. And the Lord God commanded the man, saying, "Of every tree of the garden thou mayest freely eat: But of the tree of the knowledge of good and evil, thou shalt not eat of it: for in the day that thou eatest thereof thou shalt surely die."

And the Lord God said, "It is not good that the man should be alone; I will make him an help meet for him." And out of the ground the Lord God formed every beast of the field, and every fowl of the air; and brought them unto Adam to see what he would call them: and whatsoever Adam called every living creature, that was the name thereof. And Adam gave names to all cattle, and to the fowl of the air, and to every beast of the field; but for Adam there was not found an help meet for him.

And the Lord God caused a deep sleep to fall upon Adam, and he slept: and he took one of his ribs, and closed up the flesh instead thereof; and the rib, which the Lord God had taken from man, made he a woman, and brought her unto the man. And Adam said, "This is now bone of my bones, and flesh of my flesh: she shall be called Woman, because she was taken out of Man." Therefore shall a man leave his father and his mother, and shall cleave unto his wife: and they shall be one flesh.

And they were both naked, the man and his wife, and were not ashamed.

Now the serpent was more subtil than any beast of the field which the Lord God had made. And he said unto the woman, "Yea, hath God said, 'Ye shall not eat of every tree of the Garden'?"

And the woman said unto the serpent, "We may eat of the fruit of the trees of the garden: But of the fruit of the tree which is in the midst of the garden, God hath said, 'Ye shall not eat of it, neither shall ye touch it, lest ye die.' "

And the serpent said unto the woman, "Ye shall not surely die: For God doth know that in the day ye eat thereof, then your eyes shall be opened, and ye shall be as gods, knowing good and evil."

And when the woman saw that the tree was good for food, and that it was pleasant to the eyes, and a tree to be desired to make one wise, she took of the fruit thereof, and did eat, and gave also unto her husband with her; and he did eat. And the eyes of them both were opened, and they knew that they were naked; and they sewed fig leaves together, and made themselves aprons. And they heard the voice of the Lord God walking in the garden in the cool of the day: and Adam and his wife hid themselves from the presence of the Lord God amongst the trees of the garden.

And the Lord God called unto Adam, and said unto him, "Where art thou?"

And he said, "I heard thy voice in the garden, and I was afraid, because I was naked; and I hid myself."

And he said, "Who told thee that thou wast naked? Hast thou eaten of the tree, whereof I commanded thee that thou shouldest not eat?"

And the man said, "The woman whom thou gavest to be with me, she gave me of the tree, and I did eat."

And the Lord God said unto the woman, "What is this that thou hast done?"

And the woman said, "The serpent beguiled me, and I did eat."

And the Lord God said unto the serpent, "Because thou hast done this, thou art cursed above all cattle, and above every beast of the field; upon thy belly shalt thou go, and dust shalt thou eat all the days of thy life: And I will put enmity between thee and the woman, and between thy seed and her seed; it shall bruise thy head, and thou shalt bruise his heel."

Unto the woman he said, "I will greatly multiply thy sorrow and thy conception; in sorrow thou shalt bring forth children; and thy desire shall be to thy husband, and he shall rule over thee."

And unto Adam he said, "Because thou hast hearkened unto the voice of thy wife, and hast eaten of the tree of which I commanded thee, saying, 'Thou shalt not eat of it': cursed is the ground for thy sake; in sorrow shalt thou eat of it all the days of thy life; thorns also and thistles shall it bring forth to thee; and thou shalt eat the herb of the field; in the sweat of thy face shalt thou eat bread, till thou return unto the ground; for out of it wast thou taken: for dust thou art, and unto dust shalt thou return."

And Adam called his wife's name Eve; because she was the mother of all living.

Unto Adam also and to his wife did the Lord God make coats of skins, and clothed them.

And the Lord God said, "Behold, the man is become as one of us, to know good and evil: and now, lest he put forth his hand, and take also of the tree of life, and eat, and live for ever": Therefore the Lord God sent him forth from the garden of Eden, to till the ground from whence he was taken. So he drove out the man; and he placed at the east of the garden of Eden Cherubims, and a flaming sword which turned every way, to keep the way of the tree of life.

THE CREATION of man and woman and the story of their brief sojourn in the Garden of Eden, which God prepared for them, is recounted in this excerpt from the first Book of the Bible, called Genesis or "of the beginning." These ancient oral accounts may have been put into writing as early as the twelfth century before Christ. About the third century B.C., the Old Testament books were fixed in substantially their present form. During the next century they were translated from the Semitic tongues into Greek; since then they have been translated many times and into most languages known to man. This English text is from the King James Bible of 1611, the Authorized Version prepared by scholars of the Church of England.

Vocabulary Study

A. The word *Eden* means "delight" or "enjoyment" in Hebrew. It is a garden of God or a divine park. What other term is frequently used for the Garden of Eden today?

B. The word *Adam* is usually translated in Hebrew as "man" or "mankind." Why, according to Adam, did he call his help meet "woman"?

C. The walking and talking serpent was, we are told, "more subtil than any beast of the field." How is the word *subtil* more frequently spelled now? What similar or synonymous terms could you use to describe this serpent?

D. Eve told God that the serpent *beguiled* her. What words might be substituted for *beguiled?*

E. *Cherubim* (a plural; other plurals, *cherubs, cherubims;* singular, *cherub*) are variously described in the Bible. Ezekiel 1 says, in part, that "they had the likeness of a man. And every one had four faces, and every one had four wings. . . . the face of a man, and the face of a lion, on the right side: . . . the face of an ox on the left side; they . . . also had the face of an eagle." What is the usual meaning of the word *cherub* today?

Questions on Form and Content

A. What is the subject or main idea of this portion of the book of Genesis?

B. What, in this account, is the order of creation?

C. What did God plant in the Garden?

D. What task did God assign man there?

E. God granted Adam the right to full enjoyment of the Garden of Eden with one exception. What was he forbidden?

F. Eve was created as a help meet for Adam, a partner suitable for him. From what we are told, what was the first thing she helped him to do? With what result?

G. Do the actions of Adam and Eve after they have partaken of the fruit of the tree of the knowledge of good and evil seem to indicate the predominance of the latter knowledge over the former? What, if any, of their actions shows that they attained knowledge of good from the forbidden fruit? What actions seem to be the result of the knowledge of evil?

H. How gallant or gentlemanly do you consider Adam's reactions after he has partaken of the fruit? Is there any indication that he holds God as well as Eve partly responsible for his transgression?

I. Adam blames Eve for his disobedience; Eve blames the serpent. Whom does the serpent charge?

J. Which of the three punishments meted out by God seems to you the most severe: the serpent's, the woman's, or the man's? Why?

K. What significance do you attach to the fact that God, instead of beginning afresh in making woman, made her from man's rib?

L. Is there any indication in this account that man was destined to be immortal before his fall?

M. The tree of life was believed to grant eternal life; the tree of the knowledge of good and evil conferred wisdom. The tree of life does not figure in the temptation story, presumably because man was originally conceived as mortal. What, then, is the significance of the death sentence: "in the day that thou eatest thereof [the forbidden fruit] thou shalt surely die"?

Suggestions for Writing

A. Bernhard W. Anderson, in his *Understanding the Old Testament,* says of the Paradise story: "Taken by itself, the story is filled with images —like the Tree of Life and the cunning serpent—which are found in ancient folklore." Write a paper on the images in the story.

B. Mr. Anderson continues: "Indeed, the story evidently once circulated as the story teller's answer to several questions: Why are man and woman attracted to each other? Why does social propriety demand the wearing of clothes? Why must there be the pain of childbirth and the misery of hard work? Why is the serpent hated by man? These, and other questions, were answered in the story that bears even yet the marks of an ancient popular tradition." With or without reference to the story, answer one of the questions Mr. Anderson poses.

C. Isaac Asimov, in Volume I of *Asimov's Guide to the Bible,* says "the tale of the serpent is quite un-Biblical in atmosphere. Only here and in one other case (that of Balaam's ass) do the Hebrew scriptures mention talking animals. It seems quite likely that the tale of the serpent is extremely primitive and represents a remnant of nature myth." Write a paper on the nature of the serpent. How do you picture him before and after the curse? What seems to be the motive for his mischief? As seed of woman, do you still feel enmity toward him?

D. God gave to Adam the right and the responsibility to name all cattle, fowl, and beasts. Adam names Eve, too, either through divine direction or his own initiative. Naming the animals, according to Biblical scholars, signifies man's dominion over them. What animal names seem particularly appropriate to you? Which, inappropriate? In other words, how good a job did Adam do?

E. In your own words, write a description of the Garden of Eden as it is pictured in the Bible. Discuss its topography, location, and inhabitants. What would make it seem a garden of delight?

F. The serpent is often equated with Satan. What other symbols can you find in the story?

G. Discuss the temptation. What part do doubt, suspicion, and promise play in it?

H. God provides Adam and Eve with coats of skins, thus protecting them even in the time of banishmant. What precedent did He set? How has man subsequently used animal skins for his attire? With what results today?

I. "Sin, according to this story, is an act of the will in revolt against God. It is occasioned by man's ambition to overstep his status as a creature, to become like God . . . ," says Mr. Anderson. "In Adam's fall, we sinned all," the Puritan readers began. How would you define sin today? What acts are regarded—and punished—as sinful in our time and place?

J. Discuss Eve as a progenitor of modern woman. She talks, gathers food, and sews. Would you consider her enslaved or liberated?

K. Discuss the questions of guilt and judgment as they appear in the story.

L. Mr. Anderson says "the story deals with the question of why man, God's creature, refuses to acknowledge the sovereignty of his Creator, with the result that history is a tragic story of man's banishment from the life for which he was intended." Comment.

Wasteland *Marya Mannes*

Cans. Beer cans. Glinting on the verges of a million miles of roadways, lying in scrub, grass, dirt, leaves, sand, mud, but never hidden. Piels, Rheingold, Ballantine, Schaefer, Schlitz, shining in the sun or picked by moon or the beams of headlights at night; washed by rain or flattened by wheels, but never dulled, never buried, never destroyed. Here is the mark of savages, the testament of wasters, the stain of prosperity.

Who are these men who defile the grassy borders of our roads and lanes, who pollute our ponds, who spoil the purity of our ocean benches with the empty vessels of their thirst? Who are the men who make these vessels in millions and then say, "Drink—and discard"? What society is this that can afford to cast away a million tons of metal and to make of wild and fruitful land a garbage heap?

What manner of men and women need thirty feet of steel and two hundred horsepower to take them, singly, to their small destinations? Who demand that

□ Marya Mannes, "Wasteland," from *More in Anger* (Philadelphia and New York, 1958), pp. 40-41.

WASTELAND

R. Keith Richardson

what they eat is wrapped so that forests are cut down to make the paper that is thrown away, and what they smoke and chew is sealed so that the sealers can be tossed in gutters and caught in twigs and grass?

What kind of men can afford to make the streets of their towns and cities hideous with neon at night, and their roadways hideous with signs by day, wasting beauty; who leave the carcasses of cars to rot in heaps; who spill their trash into ravines and make smoking mountains of refuse for the town's rats? What manner of men choke off the life in rivers, streams and lakes with the waste of their produce, making poison of water?

Who is as rich as that? Slowly the wasters and despoilers are impoverishing our land, our nature, and our beauty, so that there will not be one beach, one hill, one lane, one meadow, one forest free from the debris of man and the stigma of his improvidence.

Who is so rich that he can squander forever the wealth of earth and water for the trivial needs of vanity or the compulsive demands of greed; or so prosperous in land that he can sacrifice nature for unnatural desires? The earth we abuse and the living things we kill will, in the end, take their revenge; for in exploiting their presence we are diminishing our future.

And what will we leave behind us when we are long dead? Temples? Amphorae? Sunken treasure?

Or mountains of twisted, rusted steel, canyons of plastic containers, and a million miles of shores garlanded, not with the lovely wrack of the sea, but with the cans and bottles and light-bulbs and boxes of a people who conserved their convenience at the expense of their heritage, and whose ephemeral prosperity was built on waste.

Marya Mannes was born in New York City, where she was graduated from Miss Veltin's School for Girls. In 1961 she was awarded an honorary Doctor of Hebrew Literature degree at Hood College. Miss Mannes has been a feature editor for *Vogue* and *Glamour,* and a staff writer for *The Reporter.* In addition, she has served as an intelligence analyst for the United States government and made numerous television appearances. In 1958 she received the George Polk Memorial Award for Magazine Writing. She is the author of a novel, *Message from a Stranger;* two books of essays, *More in Anger,* from which the preceding essay is taken, and *But Will It Sell?;* and two books of satiric verse, *Subverse* and *The New York I Know.*

Vocabulary Study

The context will often give the meaning of a word, even if it is unfamiliar to you. Study each italicized word in these excerpts from "Wasteland"; then, from the list below, select the word or phrase nearest in meaning to the italicized word. The list contains extra words.

A. men who *defile* the grassy borders of our roads
B. one forest free from the *debris* of man and the *stigma* of his *improvidence.*
C. *squander* forever the wealth of earth
D. we are *diminishing* our future.
E. the lovely *wrack* of the sea
F. whose *ephemeral* prosperity was built on waste.

mark of disgrace or reproach	seaweed or other marine life cast on shore
lessening	spend wastefully
disparaging	lack of foresight or thrift
contaminate	endangering
unexcelled	badge of merit
rubbish	transitory

Questions on Form and Content

A. What is Miss Mannes's main idea? What is her purpose?
B. How would you describe the style of her essay? the tone?
C. What specific practices does Miss Mannes deplore?
D. Miss Mannes asks what we will leave behind us when we are long dead? How does she answer her question?
E. Miss Mannes wrote this essay in 1956, long before such terms as ecology and environmental control and Earth Day became familiar expressions and popular causes. How timely does the article now appear? What have we done to rescue our land from its wasters and despoilers?

Suggestions for Writing

A. Some companies and some municipalities have waged campaigns recently to collect discarded beer cans and bottles. If you have participated in such an experiment, describe it. How effective was it? Of how much lasting value?
B. In the fall of 1969, students on the San Jose State College campus purchased and buried a new automobile. In the summer of 1970 eight

young people burned their drivers' licenses in San Francisco. Do you consider either act justified? Why or why not?

C. Have there been drives on your campus to improve your environment? If so, describe one or more of them.

D. Do you have a personal ecology program? If so, what is it?

E. Miss Mannes speaks of polluted ponds and poisoned waters. Can you discuss specific examples?

F. Discuss some current moves to save our forests, such as recycling newspapers.

G. Miss Mannes says that neon makes the streets of our towns and cities hideous at night and that signs make our roadways hideous by day. Do you agree? If so, why? If not, why not?

H. "The earth we abuse and the living things we kill will, in the end, take their revenge; for in exploiting their presence we are diminishing our future," says Miss Mannes. Develop her thesis, using one or more examples or illustrations. You might consider dead lakes; or disappearing species, such as whales, crocodiles, or leopards; and some of the reasons for their scarcity.

I. Miss Mannes asks: "And what will we leave behind us when we are long dead? Temples? Amphorae? Sunken treasure?" Discuss a temple which is a part of our heritage from antiquity.

J. An amphora is a large two-handled earthenware vessel which was used by the Greeks and Romans to hold liquids, as a standard unit of capacity, and as an ornament. In Athenian games and festivals, decorated amphorae were presented as prizes to victors. What is their counterpart in our civilization: beer cans, plastic measuring cups, gold-plated trophies —or do we have corresponding treasures that might become heirlooms?

K. Relate the story of a famous sunken treasure.

L. How would you answer the question: "And what will we leave behind us when we are long dead?" What, in the United States or the world, seems to you worthy of preservation?

M. Compare and contrast the Garden of Eden with the Wasteland.

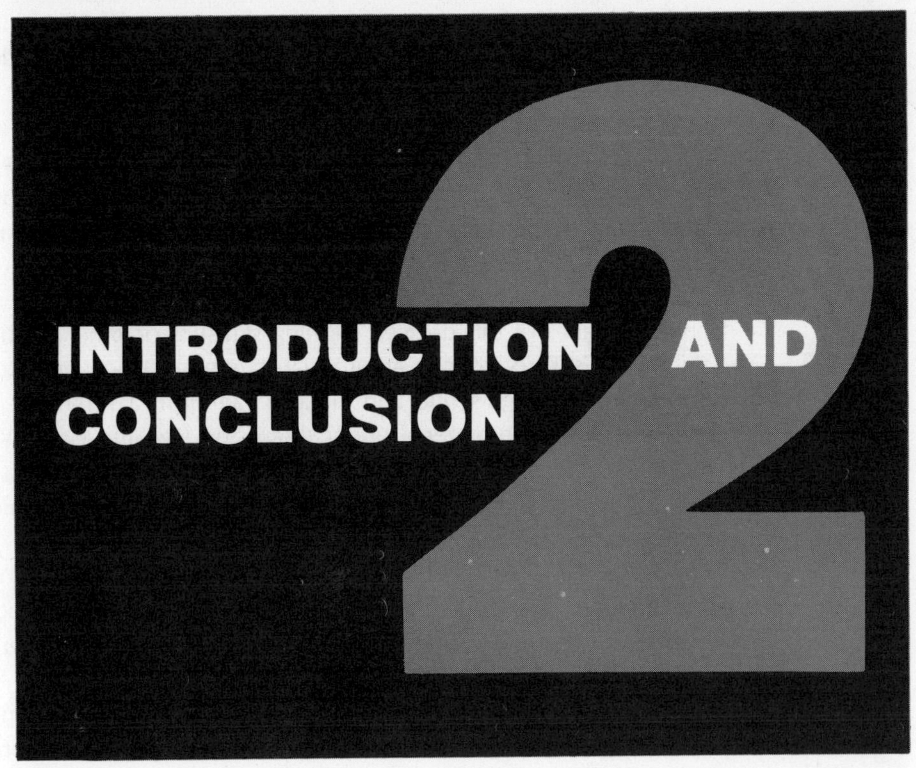

2 INTRODUCTION AND CONCLUSION

Every paper consists of three parts—introduction, body, and conclusion or, if you prefer, beginning, middle, and end.

Often the introduction of the paper is the most difficult part to write. It is also one of the most important parts, as it makes the initial and probably lasting impression on the reader, interests or bores him at the very outset. Furthermore it sets the tone or feeling of the paper or reveals the writer's attitude toward his reader, his subject, and himself. The tone may be, for instance, formal or informal, serious or humorous, condescending or respectful, belligerent or friendly, sincere or insincere, pompous or simple, enthusiastic or indifferent, ironic, emotional, dogmatic, questioning. And the introduction is of primary importance in establishing this feeling.

But no student should be so concerned about an effective opening paragraph that he wastes half his allotted writing period staring at a blank sheet of paper. If you have trouble beginning, try writing the main body of your paper, then write the introduction last. You may find that you have thought of a good idea for an opening paragraph as you wrote the rest of your paper, or you may feel that you actually wrote a sufficient introduction as you developed your ideas in the body of your paper.

A direct statement of the central idea of purpose of the paper is often the best beginning. When the central idea is given in the title, however, as is the case with both essays in this chapter, other beginnings are usually preferable. Further possibilities for a good beginning are an interesting experience or anecdote which is relevant to the material to be discussed (Arthur C. Clarke uses this approach); a challenging question which may be answered in the article (note the use Edith Hamilton makes of this device); startling statistics or other factual data (look at Ralph Nader's introduction); an unusual statement which will interest the reader (see Ashley Montagu's title and initial paragraph); a reference to the writer's experience with the material under discussion (see the E. B. White and James Thurber selections); a definition of the subject (as used by Russell Lynes in "Is There a Gentleman in the House?"); or background material which might prove helpful to the reader (look at "The Obsolescence of Man").

You should not begin your paper with an apology, such as "I don't know much about foreign cars, but. . . ." You should not make your introduction a mere repetition of the title, as the student did who began his paper entitled "I Prefer Foreign Cars" with the sentence "I like foreign cars better than American cars." Nor should you make the first sentence of your paper dependent upon the title for meaning, as you would if you started a composition called "Foreign Cars" with a sentence beginning "These cars are. . . ."

Many students come to college with the firm belief that a paper may be ended in one way only—with a summary of what has already been said. Actually, most short papers require no summary at all, but if you feel one is essential, do not merely repeat in the same words what you have just said once, or twice, or thrice! If you want to restate your main idea, try to do so in different words and with more force than you used elsewhere in your paper. If your paper is of sufficient length and complexity to justify a summary, by all means use one. Make it concise and forceful and be certain that it does actually summarize the chief parts of your paper.

Sometimes a warning to your readers or a plea for an attitude or for action is an effective conclusion if either is relevant to your purpose. Remember how skillfully Marya Mannes employed this method in the last chapter. Note how Loren Eiseley uses the same approach in the next essay. An interesting anecdote or a striking example or illustration which emphasizes your topic can also be used. Arthur C. Clarke uses this type of conclusion in "The Obsolescence of Man."

But whatever method you choose, the final section of your paper should be logical in that it should be justified by the rest of your paper. It should reinforce the central idea of your whole paper and contain no inappropriate details which distract the reader's interest from your purpose in your composition. It should always be something other than vague generalities, as they are of no more value than repetitious summaries. It should not be an apology, nor a bid for sympathy because you lack knowledge of the subject or lack ability to write outstandingly well on it—neither of these is any more effective here than at the beginning. Your conclusion should actually conclude your ideas and not leave the reader with the feeling that the bell rang or that you reached your five-hundred-word limit or that you came to the end of the page and decided to stop writing.

It is also quite unnecessary to write "The end," "Finis," or "Thirty" after your last sentence. Your reader, who is, of course, usually your instructor, is able to see that the rest of the page is blank or that there are no other pages following.

An Evolutionist Looks at Modern Man

Loren C. Eiseley

In the age of technology which now surrounds us, and which boasts of its triumphs over nature, one thing is ever more apparent to the anthropologist—the student of man. We have not really conquered nature because we have not conquered ourselves. It is modern man, *Homo sapiens*, "the wise" as he styles himself, who is now the secret nightmare of man. It is his own long shadow that falls across his restless nights and that follows soundlessly after the pacing feet of statesmen.

Not long ago I chanced to walk through the Hall of Man in one of the country's large museums. Persons of great learning have been instrumental in erecting those exhibits, and I hoped to find there some clue as to human destiny, some key that might unlock in a few succinct sentences the nature of man. The exhibit ended in a question mark before an atomic machine and a graph showing the almost incredible energy that now lay open to the hand of man. Needless to say, I agreed

☐ Loren C. Eiseley, "An Evolutionist Looks at Modern Man," from *Adventures of the Mind,* First Series, ed. Richard Thruelsen and John Kobler (New York, 1959), pp. 3-18.

with the question mark which ended the history of humanity within that hall.

But as I turned and went in the other direction, step by step, eon by eon, back into the past, I came to a scarcely human thing crouched over a little fire of sticks and peering up at me under shaggy brows. The caption read: "Man begins his technological climb up the energy ladder. He discovers fire." I walked a short way backward and forward. I read the captions. I looked again at the creatures huddled over a fire of sticks—at the woman clutching a child to her breast. Again I searched the hall. This was the sum total of all that science had here seen fit to emphasize graphically as important to the human story. The hunters' tools were there, the economic revolution effected by agriculture was ably presented. Summarized before my eyes, populations grew, cities and empires rose and fell, and still man's energy accumulated.

One saw another thing. One saw the armored legions grow and grow until at last continent confronted continent and the powers of death to a world lay in the hands of the descendants of that maned woman and her consort by the fire of sticks.

I hesitated again before those forgotten engines of the past, for it seemed to me that there was lacking here some clue, some vital essence of the creature man, and that I was looking upon stone and polished sword and catapult from some place just a little remote and distorted. "This is the history of man," the caption ran through my head, and at that moment, finally, I knew I was looking at the past through the eyes of a modern twentieth-century American, or for that matter, a Russian. There was no basic difference.

In that whole exhibit were ranged the energies of wheat and fire and oil, but of what man had dreamed in his relations with other men, there was little trace. Yet it is only on paper, or, in human heads, we might say in paraphrase of Shaw, that man has sought successfully to transcend himself, his appetites and his desires. In that great room was scarcely a hint of the most remarkable story of all, the rise of a value-creating animal and the way in which his intangible dreams had been modified and transformed to bring him to the world he faces today.

The educated public has come to accept the verdict of science that man, along with the plant and animal world about us, is the product of endless evolutionary divergence and change. In accepting this verdict of science, however, men have frequently failed to inquire in what way human evolution may differ from that of other animals, or by what extra dangers and responsibilities the human brain may be haunted. In the revolt from the fanatical religiosity of past centuries we have too often welcomed with open arms a dogmatic scientific naturalism which, like the devil with Faust, seemed to offer unlimited material power over nature while, at the same time, assuring us that our moral responsibilities were limited and excusable since we were, after all, only the natural evolutionary culmination of a line of apes that chanced to descend upon the ground.

Darwin and his compatriots, struggling to establish for their day a new and quite amazing interpretation of human history, placed great emphasis upon man's relationship to the animal world about him. Indeed, at times they overemphasized man's kinship with the existing apes, partly because of their anxiety to prove the reality of man's descent from lower forms of life, partly because in their lifetime the course of human evolution was very imperfectly known from fossils. The result was that Darwin's own interpretation of the early stages of human evolution wavered between a theory involving an early and Edenlike seclusion on some oceanic island, to a later more ferocious and competitive existence on one of the major continents.

These extremes of interpretation need not concern us now except to illustrate the hesitancy with which Darwin attempted to account for some of the peculiar qualities of man. Today we are well convinced of the general course of man's rise from some ancient anthropoid line. Each year new fossil evidence of this fact is brought to our attention. Each year the public grows more accustomed to this history, feels more at home in the natural world which it casually assumes to be dominated by struggle, by a dog-eat-dog interpretation of existence which descends to us from the Darwinian period.

Some time ago I had a letter from a professional friend of mine commenting upon the education his daughter was receiving at a polite finishing school. "She has been taught," he wrote to me a little sadly, "that there are two kinds of people, the tough- and the tender-minded. Her professor, whose science I will not name, informed her that the tough-minded would survive."

This archaic remark shook me. I knew it was not the product of the great selfless masters of the field, but it betrayed an attitude which demanded an answer. In that answer is contained the whole uniqueness of man. Man has not really survived by toughness in a major sense—even the great evolutionists Darwin and Wallace had had trouble with that aspect of man—instead, he has survived through tenderness. Man in his arrogance may boast that the battle is to the strong, that pity and affection are signs of weakness. Nevertheless, in spite of the widespread popularity of such ideas, the truth is that if man at heart were not a tender creature toward his kind, a loving creature in a peculiarly special way, he would long since have left his bones to the wild dogs that roved the African grasslands where he first essayed the great adventure of becoming human.

The professor who growled to his class of future mothers about being tough-minded spent a childhood which is among the most helpless and prolonged of any living creature. If our parents had actually practiced certain of the philosophies that now flourish among us, or if our remote ancestors had achieved that degree of sophistication which would have enabled them to discount their social responsibilities for the day's pleasure, we—you and I and all of us—would never have enjoyed the experience of living.

Man, in the achievement of a unique gift—a thinking brain capable of weighing stars or atoms—cannot grow that brain in the nine months before birth. It is, moreover, a peculiarly plastic brain, intended to receive impressions from the social world around it. Instinct, unlike the case in the world of animals, is here reduced to a minimum. This brain must grow and learn, be able to profit by experience. In man much of that growth and learning comes after birth. The result is that the human infant enters the world in a peculiarly helpless and undeveloped condition. His childhood is lengthy because his developing brain must receive a large store of information and ways of behavior from the social group into which it is born. It must acquire the complicated tool of speech.

The demands of learning thus placed upon the human offspring are greater than in any other animal. They have made necessary the existence of a continued family, rather than the casual sex life of many of the lower animals. Although the family differs in many of its minor features in distinct societies, it is always and everywhere marked by its tender and continuing care of the human offspring through the lengthened period of childhood.

The social regulations of all human groups promote the welfare of the young. Man's first normal experience of life involves maternal and paternal care and affection. It continues over the years of childhood. Thus the creature who strives at times to deny the love within himself, to reject the responsibilities to which he owes his own existence, who grows vocal about "tough-mindedness" and "the struggle for existence," is striving to reject his own human heritage. For without the mysteriously increased growth rate of the brain and the correlated willingness of fallible, loving adults to spend years in nursing the helpless offspring they have produced, man would long since have vanished from the earth.

We take the simple facts of human life too much for granted. To the student of human evolution this remarkable and unique adjustment of our peculiar infancy to a lengthened family relationship between adults is one of the more mysterious episodes in the history of life. It is so strange, in fact, that only in one group of creatures—that giving rise to man—has it been successfully developed in the three billion years or so that life has existed on the planet. Family life is a fact that underlies everything else about man—his capacity for absorbing culture, his ability to learn—everything, in short, that enables us to call him human. He is born of love and he exists by reason of a love more continuous than in any other form of life. Yet this, in all irony, is the creature who professes to pierce the shams of life and to live by tough-mindedness!

Let us see how this nascent and once-aspiring creature now lives in great danger of re-entering the specialized trap that his ancestors escaped from ages ago when they evolved a brain capable of abstract thought. "Man is the dwarf of himself," Emerson once wrote, and never, perhaps, has he been more of a dwarf than in this age where he appears to wield so much power. The only sign of health remaining to him is the fact that he is still capable of creeping out of the interior of his thickening crust of technological accomplishment to gaze around him with a sense of dissatisfaction and unease.

He has every reason to feel this way. For man has never lived before in so great an age of exterior accomplishment, so tremendous a projection of himself into his machines, nor yet so disheartening a period in all that stands for the nobler aspects of the human dream. His spiritual yearnings to transcend his own evil qualities are dimming as he is constantly reminded of his animal past. His desire to fly away to Mars, still warring, still haunted by his own black shadow, is the adolescent escape mechanism of a creature who would prefer to infect the outer planets with his problems than to master them at home.

Even now in the enthusiasm for new discoveries, reported public interviews with scientists tend to run increasingly toward a future replete with more inventions, stores of energy, babies in bottles, deadlier weapons. Relatively few have spoken of values, ethics, art, religion—all those intangible aspects of life which set the tone of a civilization and determine, in the end, whether it will be cruel or humane; whether, in other words, the modern world, so far as its interior spiritual life is concerned, will be stainless steel like its exterior, or display the rich fabric of genuine human experience. The very indifference of many scientists to such matters reveals how far man has already gone toward the world of the "outside," of no memory, of contempt toward all that makes up the human tradition.

"Wars will be fought in space," prophesied a high military authority recently. "Teach children the hard things first." "Ah, but what hard things?" the teacher asks, because youth is shaped in the teaching and becomes what he is taught. Without spiritual insight and generosity, without the ability to rise beyond power and mechanical extensions, man will encounter in place of the nature which gave him birth only that vast, expanding genie rising from his own brain—himself. Nothing more terrible threatens to confront him in his final hour.

It is increasingly plain that if we read the past as a justification for a kind of moral complacency, an animal limit which justifies military remarks such as "man will always fight," we have not read it well. Until man came, it is true, the evolution of life had been an evolution of parts. It had been hook and clutching bur and fang, struggling upward in an agelong effort. Life had been shaped by the blind forces of the inanimate world. All it had that was different was the will to crawl, the will to find the crevice, the niche, the foothold in this mountain of inanimate matter, and to hold its place against the forces which ever seek to disperse and destroy the substance of life. In all that prehuman world there had been no animal capable of looking back or forward. No living creature had wept above another's grave. There had been nothing to comprehend the whole.

For three billion years that rule remained unbroken. At the end of that time there occurred a small soundless concussion. In a sense it was the most terrible explosion in the world, because it forecast and contained all the rest. The coruscating heat of atomic fission, the red depths of the hydrogen bomb—all were potentially contained in a little packet of gray matter that, somewhere between about a million and 600,000 years ago, quite suddenly appears to have begun to multiply itself in the thick-walled cranium of a ground-dwelling ape.

The event itself took place in silence, the silence of cells multiplying at an enormous pace under a small bone roof, the silence of some great fungus coming up at night in a forest glade. The eruption had about it the utter unpredictability of nature when she chooses to bypass her accepted laws and to hurtle headlong into some new and unguessed experiment. Even the solar system has now felt the impact of that tiny, soundless explosion. The fact that it was the product of evolutionary forces does not lessen its remarkable quality.

For three billion years, until an ageless watcher might have turned away in weariness, nothing had moved but the slime and its creations. Toward the end of that time a small, unprepossessing animal sat on his haunches by a rock pile on a waste of open ground. He clutched a stick and chewed the end of it meditatively. He was setting the fuse of the great explosion. In his head was the first twinkle of that tenuous rainbow bridge which stretches between earth and the city of the gods.

At that moment the ancestor of man had become the molder of things, rather than their victim, but he had, at the same time, suffered a major loss of instinctive adjustments to life. As the psychologist Jung very aptly remarks: "The forlornness of consciousness in our world is due primarily to the loss of instinct, and the reason for this lies in the development of the human mind over the past eon."

In a recent paper given before the Research Conference on Growth and Aging, my colleague, Dr. W. M. Krogman, remarked that "The mind of man, the learning potential of an evolved cerebral cortex, enabled him to focus upon the *quality* of things rather than mere quantity." Man has become, in other words, a value-creating animal. He sets his own goals and more and more exerts his own will upon recalcitrant matter and the natural forces of the universe. In this activity he has passed from the specialized evolution of the parts of the body to a projection of such "part" evolution upon his machines and implements. In this respect man is a unique being. Having achieved high intellectual ability, he may remain comparatively unchanged in structure while all around him other animals are still subjected to the old laws of specialized selection. His brain evolves parts and replaces them, but only upon man's mechanical inventions: his tools. This fact gives man a kind of freedom which none of the crawlers-up-the-mountain ever had. He is, as the philosopher Henri Bergson once remarked, a reservoir of indetermination; his power of choice for good or evil is enormous.

It is here that we come upon what I choose to call the "unnatural" aspect of man; unnatural, that is, in the sense that there is nothing else like it on the planet. Even Darwin confessed that his principle of limited perfection—that is, the conception that life would evolve only sufficiently to maintain itself in competition with other life or to adjust to changes in its environment—had been upset in the case of man. A part, such as a tooth or an eye, could reach perfection only for a given purpose in a particular environment. With man, however, Darwin professed to observe no foreseeable limit to the development of the mental faculties.

Psychology had once regarded human nature as something consisting of separate abilities given to man at the time of creation. Mind was a fixed, unchanging thing that molded history. Now it was to be seen as malleable and moving, subject like the body, though in a different and more mysterious way, to change. Perhaps, indeed, there was no such thing as human nature in the old fixed sense, except the human ability to become what it most desired in terms of the social world in which it existed. As we have seen, the mind's power of choice has opened to man a tremendous freedom, but it is a freedom whose moral implications only a few great spiritual leaders have fully grasped.

Increasingly, at the very height of the human achievement, there loom two obstacles which threaten to cast man back into the world of parts, tools and processes, in a way he has scarcely imagined. In fact there are times when it appears man is so occupied with the world he is now creating that he has already lost a sense for what may be missing in his society. He is deeply influenced by his knowledge of the past and the animal limitations which it seems to place upon his earlier spiritual aspirations. Equally, he confuses "progress" with his mechanical extensions which represent his triumph over the caprices of biological selection. Man, in a new way, shows formidable signs of taking the road of the dinosaurs, though by quite another track.

On a night during the period of the Korean War I sat with an old hunter at a campfire in the wilds of Wyoming. Around us in the mountain dark were geological strata that contained the remains of dinosaurs. My companion threw a log upon the fire. As the flames rose upward, I could see the bronzed old American face looking at me across the fire. It could have been a face from any period out of the frontier past. And it was the frontier that spoke to me from the man who had two sons in Korea.

"America," he said, "needs a strong enemy. It will keep her from getting fat and make her strong."

I nodded dubiously. It was a philosophy of the frontier, of the woods. But I saw in my mind's eye the fate of the colossi that lay about us in the stone. They had warred and thundered, shaken the earth with their tread, grown larger, armored themselves with great shields of bone, and teeth like bear traps. Spikes had glistened on their tails and foreheads. In the end they had vanished with their monstrous tumult, and some small, ratlike mammals and a few birds had come hesitantly into the arena they had vacated. It had been a war of parts, won, not by the participants, but by some small, relatively intelligent creatures that had hidden in the trees.

"We need a strong enemy," my friend repeated. I did not doubt it was being said also in the Siberian forests and on the Manchurian plains. Faster and faster labor the technicians, the scientists of parts. They labor so today. The pace grows ever swifter. Already, and I quote from one recent industrial report, "scientists and engineers can be utilized more effectively by confining their work almost entirely to the field of their specialization." This remark indicates the re-emergence of the war of parts, and if continued, it forecasts the death of all we claim as human. Such statements convey a failure to grasp that it is the creative thinker capable of using his brain out of the immediate context of his surroundings who is the innovator, the religious leader, the artist, the man who in all ages has been, in the words of Lancelot Whyte, "the very creator of humanity."

"Man," John Burroughs once remarked, "is like the trainer of wild beasts who, at his peril, for one instant relaxes his mastery over them. Gravity, electricity, fire, flood, hurricane, will crush or consume him if his hands are unsteady or his wits tardy." It is true that man has been badly knocked about by raw nature, but that nature has never organized her powers for the deliberate purpose of destroying man. He has even benefited and had his wits sharpened by her vagaries. Man has survived the long inexorable marchings of the glacial ice that pressed him back upon the Mediterranean and threatened his annihilation in Europe. He has left his bones under the boiling mud of volcanic upheavals. He has known drought and famine—the careless buffets of the storm that blows unceasingly through nature. He has seen cities go down, cities full of adept artisans and clever technicians, cities fallen to the sands when an old enemy cut off the water supply.

Who was that enemy? It was man. He is the other face of that nature man has feared. Now, in an age when man lays his hands upon the lightning, and heat in millions of degrees shudders in his confining mechanisms, an old shadow, a monstrous growing shadow, falls across the doorway of all the world's laboratories. It is merely man, merely the creature of the fire of sticks, merely the museum wielder of the sling and spear, but now grown large enough to shadow the sun. This creature thinks with all the malignant concentration that man has so far escaped in nature, and it thinks toward just one purpose—the creation of the ultimate weapon. Ultimate, ultimate, and still more ultimate, as if there were a growing secret zero in its mind.

So terrible is the fascination of that zero, so much does it appeal to some ancient power-loving streak in our still primitive natures, that whether men plan aggression or defense from it, they are, in degree, corrupted. At heart they know the word "neutral" has lost its meaning; that the blow, if it falls, will mean what the ultimate weapon means—death to green grass and singing bird, death to a world.

Nevertheless, as I have said, no creature in the world demands more love than man; no creature is less adapted to survive without it. Man is a paradox. Individually most men hate and fear war in spite of much of the talk of professional militarists about instinct. Men have to be drummed to war, propagandized to war, assured their cause is righteous. Even dictators have to render lip service to humanitarian principles. None of this sounds particularly as though an "instinct" for war existed. There are, instead, things from the old dark midnight of the past that suffice as well for evil purposes. Fear of the stranger, when the stranger was two eyes in the dark beyond the fire at a cave mouth; aggressive hungers that were stoked to a high pitch by nature in the million years of man's wandering across the wastes of an open world. Man is not completed—that is the secret of his paradoxical behavior. He is not made. He is, perhaps about to be. Once long ago in the Middle Ages he was called *Homo duplex*—a thing half of dust and half of spirit. The term well expresses his predicament.

Today we know a great deal about human evolution, but as scientists we have failed, I sometimes think, to convey successfully to the public the marvel of the human transformation. We have shown man the anthropoidal skulls of his ancestors. We have convinced him that the human brain is an instrument of ancient origin which has not sprung full blown into being, but rather partakes of both the old and the new; that it includes the imperfections which are written into the substance of all moving and growing life. The vestigial organs that are concealed here and there in our bodies and which tell tales of the long past—of trees and waters in our lost ancestral world—have their corollary in the mind of man. His flashes of unreasoning temper, his frustrations, his occasional irrationalities are, some of them, echoes out of an older, more primitive machine. Yet signs of affection and mutual co-operation, love of beauty, dreams of a future life, can be traced into forms of man physically more primitive than ourselves.

Now, however, it is the present which concerns us—the present that creates tomorrow. Who contends for it—the rocket century with its vast zero looming over the future? The now is *our* responsibility, not that of the hoarse-voiced animal that came from the wood in a dream and made our today. Nor can we call to those pleasant, wide-browed people whom we strive to conjure up as inhabiting the comfortable future of our novels and dreams. They are lost in the unfathomable, formless future which we are engaged in shaping. Do we want them deeply? Do we want them enough, in the heavy-handed violence of this day, to live toward them at all cost, to struggle once more against the destructive forces of nature? To stand up and face, as every man must face, that ancient lurking shadow of himself? Is the price of acquiring brains, brains to look before and after in the universe, only to mean subservience to man after escaping subservience to nature that has lasted for a million years? Is it to mean acquiescence in the plans of those clever intellects who talk glibly of psychological "break-throughs" and the subliminal control of nations? Is it for this that men have labored up the dark pathway behind us and died often and blindly for some vision they could scarcely see?

A society has an image of itself, its way of life. This image is a wavering, composite picture reflected from millions of minds. If the image is largely compounded of the events of the present; if tradition is weak, the past forgotten, that image can alter by subtle degrees. A "cold war" such as we are fighting demands great tenacity in democratic institutions. Secrecy grows, technicians multiply, two great societies shoulder each other down a road that may look increasingly alike to both. The humane tradition—arts, letters, philosophy, the social sciences—threatens to be ignored as unrealistic in what has become a technological race for survival.

Man was a social animal long before he was man. But when he created huge societies and elaborated the world of culture that surrounds him today, he was acting, in some degree, consciously. Man, unlike the animal, is aware of the nature of his society. His conscious image of it is tremendously important in shaping what it will become. It is this that helps to build the human future, and why the future must be fought for day by day in the lives of innumerable and humble men.

Man, whether he engaged in war or not, is in a pyramiding technological society whose values are largely directed outward upon things. The important fact in such a material age is that we do not abandon or forget that man has always sought to transcend himself spiritually, and that this is part of his strange heritage. It is a heritage which must be preserved in our schools and churches, for in a society without deep historical memory, the future ceases to exist and the present becomes a meaningless cacophony. A future worth contemplating will not be achieved solely by flights to the far side of the moon. It will not be found in space. It will be achieved, if it is achieved at all, only in our individual hearts. This is the choice that has been presented man, as a free agent, as one who can look before and after in the cosmos.

And if indeed men do achieve that victory, they will know, with the greater insight they will then possess, that it is not a human victory, but nature's new and final triumph in the human heart—perhaps that nature which is also God. "The rationality of man," a great theologian once wrote, "is the little telltale rift in Nature which shows there is something beyond or behind her." It remains for man, in his moral freedom, to prove that statement true.

LOREN C. EISELEY, anthropologist and university professor, received his Bachelor of Arts degree at the University of Nebraska and his Master of Arts and Doctor of Philosophy degrees at the University of Pennsylvania. He has also been a postdoctoral fellow at Columbia University and at the American Museum of Natural History. Now an anthropology professor at the University of Pennsylvania, he has written numerous articles for both literary and scientific journals on human evolution and natural history. Three of his books, *The Immense Journey, Darwin's Century,* and *The Firmament of Time,* have won important literary awards. His most recent books are *Francis Bacon and the Modern Dilemma, The Mind as Nature, The Unexpected Universe,* and *The Invisible Pyramid.*

Vocabulary Study

From the list provided below, select the word or phrase nearest in meaning to the word italicized in the following excerpts from "An Evolutionist Looks at Modern Man." The list contains extra words.

A. in a few *succinct* sentences
B. in *paraphrase* of Shaw
C. his *intangible* dreams
D. man in his *arrogance* may boast
E. *coruscating* heat of atomic fission

F. exerts his own will upon *recalcitrant* matter

G. his wits sharpened by her *vagaries*

H. all the *malignant* concentration that man has so far escaped in nature

I. the creation of the *ultimate* weapon.

J. the present becomes a meaningless *cacophony.*

outrageous	final or maximum
caprices	evil
glittering	haughtiness
impalpable	discord
arsenal	mandate
stubbornly defiant	rewording
concise	

Questions on Form and Content

A. How does Mr. Eiseley begin his essay?

B. What, according to Mr. Eiseley, does *Homo sapiens* mean? What, in the essay, would show that man deserves the name?

C. After his initial paragraph, Mr. Eiseley tells of his recent visit to the Hall of Man in a large museum. What is his purpose in relating this visit?

D. Mr. Eiseley says that in that exhibit he found little trace of the most remarkable story of all. What is that story?

E. Mr. Eiseley concludes that, contrary to the popular notion, man owes his survival to tenderness rather than to toughness. How important has family life been in the development of man?

F. Man, says the author, shows formidable signs of taking the road of the dinosaurs, though by quite another track. At the very height of human achievement, what two obstacles, according to Mr. Eiseley, threaten to cast man back into the world of parts, tools, and processes?

G. What danger does Mr. Eiseley see in excessive specialization?

H. What reason does Mr. Eiseley give for man's paradoxical behavior?

I. Man, Mr. Eiseley tells us, was once called *Home duplex.* What does the term mean? How is it still applicable?

J. How does Mr. Eiseley conclude the essay?

Suggestions for Writing

A. "The age of technology," says Mr. Eiseley, "boasts of its triumphs over nature." Discuss one such triumph, or several.

B. "I knew I was looking at the past through the eyes of a modern twentieth-century American, or for that matter, a Russian. There was no basic difference," writes Mr. Eiseley. How are modern Americans and Russians alike? Why would Mr. Eiseley not consider their differences basic? With whom is he contrasting them?

C. "Man has not really survived by toughness in a major sense . . . instead, he has survived through tenderness," Mr. Eiseley contends. Comment and exemplify.

D. Discuss and evaluate Mr. Eiseley's comments regarding the family: "Family life is a fact that underlies everything else about man—his capacity for absorbing culture, his ability to learn—everything, in short, that enables us to call him human."

E. Do any of the lower animals have what could be called a family life? If so, select one or more examples and compare their familial pattern with that of man.

F. "We take simple facts of human life too much for granted," says Mr. Eiseley. Comment.

G. According to the author, "man has never lived before in so great an age of exterior accomplishment, so tremendous a projection of himself into his machines, nor yet so disheartening a period in all that stands for the nobler aspects of the human dream." Comment on one of the questions suggested by this view: What are some of modern man's most noteworthy exterior accomplishments? How has man projected himself into his machines? What do you consider most disheartening in this period of time? What are some of the nobler aspects of the human dream?

H. Mr. Eiseley says that man's "desire to fly away to Mars, still warring, still haunted by his own black shadow, is the adolescent escape mechanism of a creature who would prefer to infect the outer planets with his problems than to master them at home." Comment.

I. Discuss one of the following comments Mr. Eiseley makes on war:

> It is increasingly plain that if we read the past as a justification for a kind of moral complacency, an animal limit which justifies military remarks such as "man will always fight," we have not read it well.

> Individually most men hate and fear war in spite of much of the talk of professional militarists about instinct. Men have to be drummed to war, propagandized to war, assured their cause is righteous.

J. How would you have replied to the old hunter at the Wyoming campfire who said, "America needs a strong enemy. It will keep her from getting fat and make her strong"?

K. Mr. Eiseley says that man is in danger of "taking the road of the dinosaurs, though by a different track." Where did the dinosaurs go? On what track?

L. "In all that prehuman world there had been no animal capable of looking back or forward. No living creature had wept above another's grave. There had been nothing to comprehend the whole," writes Mr. Eiseley. Comment.

M. "Man is a paradox. . . . Man is not completed—that is the secret of his paradoxical behavior. He is not made. He is, perhaps, about to be." Comment.

N. Discuss "An Evolutionist Looks at Modern Man" in the light of the Biblical account of the creation in the Book of Genesis.

The Obsolescence of Man

Arthur C. Clarke

About a million years ago, an unprepossessing primate discovered that his forelimbs could be used for other purposes besides locomotion. Objects like sticks and stones could be grasped—and, once grasped, were useful for killing game, digging up roots, defending or attacking, and a hundred other jobs. On the third planet of the Sun, tools had appeared; and the place would never be the same again.

The first users of tools were *not* men—a fact appreciated only in the last year or two—but prehuman anthropoids; and by their discovery they doomed themselves. For even the most primitive of tools, such as a naturally pointed stone that happens to fit the hand, provides a tremendous physical and mental stimulus to the user. He has to walk erect; he no longer needs huge canine teeth—since sharp flints can do a better job—and he must develop manual dexterity of a high order. These are the specifications of Homo sapiens; as soon as they start to be filled,

□ Arthur C. Clarke, "The Obsolescence of Man," from *Profiles of the Future* (New York, 1963), pp. 212-227.

all earlier models are headed for rapid obsolescence. To quote Professor Sherwood Washburn of the University of California's anthropology department: "It was the success of the simplest tools that started the whole trend of human evolution and led to the civilizations of today."

Note that phrase—"the whole trend of human evolution." The old idea that man invented tools is therefore a misleading half-truth; it would be more accurate to say that *tools invented man.* They were very primitive tools, in the hands of creatures who were little more than apes. Yet they led to us—and to the eventual extinction of the ape-men who first wielded them.

Now the cycle is about to begin again; but neither history nor prehistory ever exactly repeats itself, and this time there will be a fascinating twist in the plot. The tools the ape-men invented caused them to evolve into their successor, Homo sapiens. The tool we have invented *is* our successor. Biological evolution has given way to a far more rapid process—technological evolution. To put it bluntly and brutally, the machine is going to take over.

This, of course, is hardly an original idea. That the creations of man's brain might one day threaten and perhaps destroy him is such a tired old *cliché* that no self-respecting science-fiction writer would dare to use it. It goes back, through Čapek's R.U.R., Samuel Butler's *Erewhon,* Mary Shelley's *Frankenstein* and the Faust legend to the mysterious but perhaps not wholly mythical figure of Daedalus, King Minos' one-man office of scientific research. For at least three thousand years, therefore, a vocal minority of mankind has had grave doubts about the ultimate outcome of technology. From the self-centered, human point of view, these doubts are justified. But that, I submit, will not be the only—or even the most important—point of view for much longer.

When the first large-scale electronic computers appeared some fifteen years ago, they were promptly nicknamed "Giant Brains"—and the scientific community, as a whole, took a poor view of the designation. But the scientists objected to the wrong word. The electronic computers were not *giant* brains; they were dwarf brains, and they still are, though they have grown a hundredfold within less than one generation of mankind. Yet even in their present flint-ax stage of evolution, they have done things which not long ago almost everyone would have claimed to be impossible—such as translating from one language to another, composing music, and playing a fair game of chess. And much more important than any of these infant *jeux d'esprit* is the fact that they have breached the barrier between brain and machine.

This is one of the greatest—and perhaps one of the last—breakthroughs in the history of human thought, like the discovery that the Earth moves round the Sun, or that man is part of the animal kingdom, or that $E = mc^2$. All these ideas took time to sink in, and were frantically denied when first put forward. In the same way it will take a little while for men to realize that machines can not only think, but may one day think them off the face of the Earth.

At this point you may reasonably ask: "Yes—but what do you mean by *think?*" I propose to sidestep that question, using a neat device for which I am indebted to the English mathematician A. M. Turing. Turing imagined a game played by two teleprinter operators in separate rooms—this impersonal link being used to remove all clues given by voice, appearance, and so forth. Suppose one operator was able to ask the other any questions he wished, and the other had to make suitable replies. If, after some hours or days of this conversation, the questioner could not decide whether his telegraphic acquaintance was human or purely mechanical, then he could hardly deny that he/it was capable of thought. An electronic brain that passed this test would, surely, have to be regarded as an intelligent entity. Anyone who argued otherwise would merely prove that he was less intelligent than the machine; he would be a splitter of nonexistent hairs, like the scholar who proved that the *Odyssey* was not written by Homer, but by another man of the same name.

We are still decades—but not centuries—from building such a machine, yet already we are sure that it could be done. If Turing's experiment is never carried out, it will merely be because the intelligent machines of the future will have better things to do with their time than conduct extended conversations with men. I often talk with my dog, but I don't keep it up for long.

The fact that the great computers of today are still high-speed morons, capable of doing nothing beyond the scope of the instructions carefully programmed into them, has given many people a spurious sense of security. No machine, they argue, can possibly be more intelligent than its makers—the men who designed it, and planned its functions. It may be a million times faster in operation, but that is quite irrelevant. Anything and everything that an electronic brain can do must also be within the scope of a human brain, if it had sufficient time and patience. Above all, it is maintained, no machine can show originality or creative power or the other attributes which are fondly labeled "human."

The argument is wholly fallacious; those who still bring it forth are like the buggy-whip makers who used to poke fun at stranded Model T's. Even if it were true, it could give no comfort, as a careful reading of these remarks by Dr. Norbert Wiener will show:

> This attitude (the assumption that machines cannot possess any degree of originality) in my opinion should be rejected entirely. . . . It is my thesis that machines can and do transcend some of the limitations of their designers. . . . It may well be that

> in principle we cannot make any machine, the elements of whose behaviour we cannot comprehend sooner or later. This does not mean in any way that we shall be able to comprehend them in substantially less time than the operation of the machine, nor even within any given number of years or generations. . . . This means that though they are theoretically subject to human criticism, such criticism may be ineffective until a time long after it is relevant.

In other words, even machines *less* intelligent than men might escape from our control by sheer speed of operation. And in fact, there is every reason to suppose that machines will become much more intelligent than their builders, as well as incomparably faster.

There are still a few authorities who refuse to grant any degree of intelligence to machines, now or in the future. This attitude shows a striking parallel to that adopted by the chemists of the early nineteenth century. It was known then that all living organisms are formed from a few common elements—mostly carbon, hydrogen, oxygen, and nitrogen—but it was firmly believed that the materials of life could not be made from "mere" chemicals alone. There must be some other ingredient—some essence or vital principle, forever unknowable to man. No chemist could ever take carbon, hydrogen, and so forth and combine them to form any of the substances upon which life was based. There was an impassable barrier between the worlds of "inorganic" and "organic" chemistry.

This *mystique* was destroyed in 1828, when Wöhler synthesized urea, and showed that there was no difference at all between the chemical reactions taking place in the body and those taking place inside a retort. It was a terrible shock to those pious souls who believed that the mechanics of life must always be beyond human understanding or imitation. Many people are equally shocked today by the suggestion that machines can think, but their dislike of the situation will not alter it in the least.

Since this is not a treatise on computer design, you will not expect me to explain how to build a thinking machine. In fact, it is doubtful if any human being will ever be able to do this in detail, but one can indicate the sequence of events that will lead from H. sapiens to M. sapiens. The first two or three steps on the road have already been taken; machines now exist that can learn by experience, profiting from their mistakes and—unlike human beings—never repeating them. Machines have been built which do not sit passively waiting for instructions, but which explore the world around them in a manner which can only be called inquisitive. Others look for proofs of theorems in mathematics or logic, and sometimes come up with surprising solutions that had never occurred to their makers.

These faint glimmerings of original intelligence are confined at the moment to a few laboratory models; they are wholly lacking in the giant computers that can now be bought by anyone who happens to have a few hundred thousand dollars to spare. But machine intelligence will grow, and it will start to range beyond the bounds of human thought as soon as the second generation of computers appears—the generation that has been designed, not by men, but by other, "almost intelligent" computers. And not only designed, but also built—for they will have far too many components for manual assembly.

It is even possible that the first genuine thinking machines may be *grown* rather than constructed; already some crude but very stimulating experiments have been carried out along these lines. Several artificial organisms have been built which are capable of rewiring themselves to adapt to changing circumstances. Beyond this there is the possibility of computers which will start from relatively simple beginnings, be programmed to aim at specific goals, and search for them by constructing their own circuits, perhaps by growing networks of threads in a conducting medium. Such a growth may be no more than a mechanical analogy of what happens to every one of us in the first nine months of our existence.

All speculations about intelligent machines are inevitably conditioned—indeed, inspired—by our knowledge of the human brain, the only thinking device currently on the market. No one, of course, pretends to understand the full workings of the brain, or expects that such knowledge will be available in any foreseeable future. (It is a nice philosophical point as to whether the brain can ever, even in principle, understand itself.) But we do know enough about its physical structure to draw many conclusions about the limitations of "brains"—whether organic or inorganic.

There are approximately ten billion separate switches—or neurons—inside your skull, "wired" together in circuits of unimaginable complexity. Ten billion is such a large number that, until recently, it could be used as an argument against the achievement of mechanical intelligence. About ten years ago a famous neurophysiologist made a statement (still produced like some protective incantation by the advocates of cerebral supremacy) to the effect that an electronic model of the human brain would have to be as large as the Empire State Building, and would need Niagara Falls to keep it cool when it was running.

This must now be classed with such interesting pronouncements as, "No heavier than air machine will ever be able to fly." For the calculation was made in the days of the vacuum tube (remember it?), and the transistor has now completely altered the picture. Indeed—such is the rate of technological progress today—the transistor itself is being replaced by still smaller and faster devices, based upon abstruse principles of quantum physics. If the problem was merely one of space, today's electronic techniques would allow us to pack a computer as complex as the human brain on to a single floor of the Empire State Building.

Interlude for agonizing reappraisal. It's a tough job keeping up with science, and since I wrote that last paragraph the Marquardt Corporation's Astro Division has announced a new memory device which could store inside a six-foot cube *all information recorded during the last 10,000 years.* This means, of course, not only every book ever printed, but *everything* ever written in *any* language on paper, papyrus, parchment, or stone. It represents a capacity untold millions of times greater than that of a single human memory, and though there is a mighty gulf between merely storing information and thinking creatively—the Library of Congress has never written a book—it does indicate that mechanical brains of enormous power could be quite small in physical size.

This should not surprise anyone who remembers how radios have shrunk from the bulky cabinet models of the thirties to the vest-pocket (yet much more sophisticated) transistor sets of today. And the shrinkage is just gaining momentum, if I may employ such a mind-boggling phrase. Radio receivers the size of lumps of sugar have now been built; before long, they will be the size not of lumps but of grains, for the slogan of the micro-miniaturization experts is "If you can see it, it's too big."

Just to prove that I am not exaggerating, here are some statistics you can use on the next hi-fi fanatic who takes you on a tour of his wall-to-wall installation. During the 1950's, the electronic engineers learned to pack up to a hundred thousand components into one cubic foot. (To give a basis of comparison, a good hi-fi set may contain two or three hundred components, a domestic radio about a hundred.) Here at the beginning of the sixties, the attainable figure is around a million components per cubic foot; by 1970, when today's experimental techniques of microscopic engineering have begun to pay off, it may reach a hundred million.

Fantastic though this last figure is, the human brain surpasses it by a thousandfold, packing its ten billion neurons into a *tenth* of a cubic foot. And although smallness is not necessarily a virtue, even this may be nowhere near the limit of possible compactness.

For the cells composing our brains are slow-acting, bulky, and wasteful of energy—compared with the scarcely more than atom-sized computer elements that are theoretically possible. The mathematician John von Neumann once calculated that electronic cells could be ten billion times more efficient than protoplasmic ones; already they are a million times swifter in operation, and speed can often be traded for size. If we take these ideas to their ultimate conclusion, it appears that a computer equivalent in power to one human brain need be no bigger than a matchbox.

This slightly shattering thought becomes more reasonable when we take a critical look at flesh and blood and bone as engineering materials. All living creatures are marvelous, but let us keep our sense of proportion. Perhaps the most wonderful thing about Life is that it works at all, when it has to employ such extraordinary materials, and has to tackle its problems in such roundabout ways.

As a perfect example of this, consider the eye. Suppose *you* were given the problem of designing a camera—for that, of course, is what the eye is—which *has to be constructed entirely of water and jelly,* without using a scrap of glass, metal, or plastic. Obviously, it can't be done.

You're quite right; the feat is impossible. The eye is an evolutionary miracle, but it's a lousy camera. You can prove this while you're reading the next sentence.

Here's a medium-length word:—photography. Close one eye and keep the other fixed—repeat, *fixed*—on that center "g". You may be surprised to discover that—unless you cheat by altering the direction of your gaze—you cannot see the whole word clearly. It fades out three or four letters to the right and left.

No camera ever built—even the cheapest—has as poor an optical performance as this. For color vision also the human eye is nothing to boast about; it can operate only over a small band of the spectrum. To the worlds of the infrared and ultraviolet, visible to bees and other insects, it is completely blind.

We are not conscious of these limitations because we have grown up with them, and indeed if they were corrected the brain would be quite unable to handle the vastly increased flood of information. But let us not make a virtue of a necessity; if our eyes had the optical performance of even the cheapest miniature camera, we would live in an unimaginably richer and more colorful world.

These defects are due to the fact that precision scientific instruments simply cannot be manufactured from living materials. With the eye, the ear, the nose—indeed, all the sense organs—evolution has performed a truly incredible job against fantastic odds. But it will not be good enough for the future; indeed, it is not good enough for the present.

There are some senses that do not exist, that can probably never be provided by living structures, and that we need in a hurry. On this planet, to the best of our knowledge, no creature has ever developed organs that can detect radio waves or radioactivity. Though I would hate to lay down the law and claim that nowhere in the universe can there be organic Geiger counters or living TV sets, I think it highly improbable. There are some jobs that can be done only by vacuum tubes or magnetic fields or electron beams, and are therefore beyond the capability of purely organic structures.

There is another fundamental reason living machines such as you and I cannot hope to compete with nonliving ones. Quite apart from our poor materials, we are handicapped by one of the toughest engineering specifications ever issued.

What sort of performance would you expect from a machine which has to grow several billionfold during the course of manufacture—and which has to be completely and continuously rebuilt, molecule by molecule, every few weeks? This is what happens to all of us, all the time; you are not the man you were last year, in the most literal sense of the expression.

Most of the energy and effort required to run the body goes into its perpetual tearing down and rebuilding—a cycle completed every few weeks. New York City, which is a very much simpler structure than a man, takes hundreds of times longer to remake itself. When one tries to picture the body's myriads of building contractors and utility companies all furiously at work, tearing up arteries and nerves and even bones, it is astonishing that there is any energy left over for the business of thinking.

Now I am perfectly well aware that many of the "limitations" and "defects" just mentioned are nothing of the sort, looked at from another point of view. Living creatures, because of their very nature, can evolve from simple to complex organisms. They may well be the only path by which intelligence can be obtained, for it is a little difficult to see how a lifeless planet can progress directly from metal ores and mineral deposits to electronic computers by its own unaided efforts.

Though intelligence can arise only from life, it may then discard it. Perhaps at a later stage, as the mystics have suggested, it may also discard matter; but this leads us in realms of speculations which an unimaginative person like myself would prefer to avoid.

One often-stressed advantage of living creatures is that they are self-repairing and reproduce themselves with ease—indeed, with enthusiasm. This superiority over machines will be short-lived; the general principles underlying the construction of self-repairing and self-reproducing machines have already been worked out. There is, incidentally, something ironically appropriate in the fact that A. M. Turing, the brilliant mathematician who pioneered in this field and first indicated how thinking machines might be built, shot himself a few years after publishing his results. It is very hard not to draw a moral from this.

The greatest single stimulus to the evolution of mechanical—as opposed to organic—intelligence is the challenge of space. Only a vanishingly small fraction of the universe is directly accessible to mankind, in the sense that we can live there without elaborate protection or mechanical aids. If we generously assume that humanity's potential *Lebensraum* extends from sea level to a height of three miles, over the whole Earth, that gives us a total of some half billion cubic miles. At first sight this is an impressive figure, especially when you remember that the entire human race could be packaged into a one-mile cube. But it is absolutely nothing, when set against Space with a capital "S." Our present telescopes, which are certainly not the last word on the subject, sweep a volume at least a million million million million million million million million million million times greater.

Though such a number is, of course, utterly beyond conception, it can be given a vivid meaning. If we reduced the known universe to the size of the Earth, then the portion in which *we* can live without space suits and pressure cabins is about the size of a single atom.

It is true that, one day, we are going to explore and colonize many other atoms in this Earth-sized volume, but it will be at the cost of tremendous technical efforts, for most of our energies will be devoted to protecting our frail and sensitive bodies against the extremes of temperature, pressure, or gravity found in space and on other worlds. Within very wide limits, machines are indifferent to these extremes. Even more important, they can wait patiently through the years and the centuries that will be needed for travel to the far reaches of the universe.

Creatures of flesh and blood such as ourselves can explore space and win control over infinitesimal fractions of it. But only creatures of metal and plastic can ever really conquer it, as indeed they have already started to do. The tiny brains of our Prospectors and Rangers barely hint at the mechanical intelligence that will one day be launched at the stars.

It may well be that only in space, confronted with environments fiercer and more complex than any to be found upon this planet, will intelligence be able to reach its fullest stature. Like other qualities, intelligence is developed by struggle and conflict; in the ages to come, the dullards may remain on placid Earth, and real genius will flourish only in space—the realm of the machine, not of flesh and blood.

A striking parallel to this situation can already be found on our planet. Some millions of years ago, the most intelligent of the mammals withdrew from the battle of the dry land and returned to their ancestral home, the sea. They are still there, with brains larger and potentially more powerful than ours. But (as far as we know) they do not use them; the static environment of the sea makes little call upon intelligence. The porpoises and whales, which might have been our equals and perhaps our superiors had they remained on land, now race in simpleminded and innocent ecstasy beside the new sea monsters carrying sixteen megatons of death. Perhaps they, not we, made the right choice; but it is too late to join them now.

If you have followed me so far, the protoplasmic computer inside your skull should now be programmed to accept the idea—at least for the sake of argument—that machines can be both more intelligent and more versatile than men, and may well be so in the very near future. So it is time to face the question: Where does that leave man?

I suspect that this is not a question of very great importance—except, of course, to man. Perhaps the Neanderthalers made similar plaintive noises, around 100,-000 B.C., when H. sapiens appeared on the scene, with his ugly vertical forehead and ridiculous protruding chin. Any Paleolithic philosopher who gave his colleagues the right answer would probably have ended up in the cooking pot; I am prepared to take that risk.

The short-term answer may indeed be cheerful rather than depressing. There may be a brief golden age when men will glory in the power and range of their new partners. Barring war this age lies directly ahead of us. As Dr. Simon Remo put it recently: "The extension of the human intellect by electronics will become our greatest occupation within a decade." That is undoubtedly true, if we bear in mind that at a somewhat later date the word "extension" may be replaced by "extinction."

One of the ways in which thinking machines will be able to help us is by taking over the humbler tasks of life, leaving the human brain free to concentrate on higher things. (Not, of course, that this is any guarantee that it will do so.) For a few generations, perhaps, every man will go through life with an electronic companion, which may be no bigger than today's transistor radios. It will "grow up" with him from infancy, learning his habits, his business affairs, taking over all the minor chores like routine correspondence and income-tax returns and engagements. On occasion it could even take its master's place, keeping appointments he preferred to miss, and then reporting back in as much detail as he desired. It could substitute for him over the telephone so completely that no one would be able to tell whether man or machine was speaking; a century from now, Turing's "game" may be an integral part of our social lives, with complications and possibilities which I leave to the imagination.

You may remember that delightful robot, Robbie, from the movie *Forbidden Planet.* (One of the three or four movies so far made that anyone interested in science fiction can point to without blushing; the fact that the plot was Shakespeare's doubtless helped.) I submit, in all seriousness, that most of Robbie's abilities—together with those of a better known character, Jeeves—will one day be incorporated in a kind of electronic companion-secretary-valet. It will be much smaller and neater than the walking jukeboxes or mechanized suits of armor which Hollywood presents, with typical lack of imagination, when it wants to portray a robot. And it will be extremely talented, with quick-release connectors allowing it to be coupled to an unlimited variety of sense organs and limbs. It would, in fact, be a kind of general purpose, disembodied intelligence that could attach itself to whatever tools were needed for any particular occasion. One day it might be using microphones or electric typewriters or TV cameras; on another, automobiles or airplanes—or the bodies of men and animals.

And this is, perhaps the moment to deal with a conception which many people find even more horrifying than the idea that machines will replace or supersede us. It is the idea . . . that they may combine with us.

I do not know who first thought of this; probably the physicist J. D. Bernal, who in 1929 published an extraordinary book of scientific predictions called *The World, the Flesh and the Devil.* In this slim and long out-of-print volume (I sometimes wonder what the sixty-year-old Fellow of the Royal Society now thinks of his youthful indiscretion, if he ever remembers it) Bernal decided that the numerous limitations of the human body could be overcome only by the use of mechanical attachments or substitutes—until, eventually, all that might be left of man's original organic body would be the brain.

This idea is already far more plausible than when Bernal advanced it, for in the last few decades we have seen the development of mechanical hearts, kidneys, lungs, and other organs, and the wiring of electronic devices directly into the human nervous system.

Olaf Stapledon developed this theme in his wonderful history of the future, *Last and First Men,* imagining an age of immortal "giant brains," many yards across, living in beehive-shaped cells, sustained by pumps and chemical plants. Though completely immobile, their sense organs could be wherever they wished, so their center of awareness—or consciousness, if you like—could be anywhere on Earth or in the space above it. This is an important point which we—who carry our brains around in the same fragile structure as our eyes, ears, and other sense organs, often with disastrous results—may easily fail to appreciate. Given perfected telecommunications, a fixed brain is no handicap, but rather the reverse. Your present brain, totally imprisoned behind its walls of bone, communicates with the outer world and receives its impressions of it over the telephone wires of the central nervous system—wires varying in length from a fraction of an inch to several feet. *You would never know the difference if those "wires" were actually hundreds or thousands of miles long, or included mobile radio links, and your brain never moved at all.*

In a crude way—yet one that may accurately foreshadow the future—we have already extended our visual and tactile senses away from our bodies. The men who now work with radio isotopes, handling them with remotely controlled mechanical fingers and observing them by television, have achieved a partial separation between brain and sense organs. They are in one place; their minds effectively in another.

Recently the word "Cyborg" (cybernetic organism) has been coined to describe the machine-animal of the type we have been discussing. Doctors Manfred Clynes and Nathan Kline of Rockland State Hospital, Orangeburg, New York, who invented the name, define a Cyborg in these stirring words: "an exogenously extended organizational complex functioning as a homeostatic system." To translate, this means a body which has machines hitched to it, or built into it, to take over or modify some of its functions.

I suppose one could call a man in an iron lung a Cyborg, but the concept has far wider implications than this. One day we may be able to enter into temporary unions with any sufficiently sophisticated machines, thus being able not merely to control but to *become* a space-ship or a submarine or a TV network. This would give far more than purely intellectual satisfaction; the thrill that can be obtained from driving a racing car or flying an airplane may be only a pale ghost of the excitement our great-grandchildren may know, when the individual human consciousness is free to roam at will from machine to machine, through all the reaches of sea and sky and space.

But how long will this partnership last? Can the synthesis of man and machine ever be stable, or will the purely organic component become such a hindrance that it has to be discarded? If this eventually happens—and I have given good reasons for thinking that it must—we have nothing to regret, and certainly nothing to fear.

The popular idea, fostered by comic strips and the cheaper forms of science fiction, that intelligent machines must be malevolent entities hostile to man, is so absurd that it is hardly worth wasting energy to refute it. I am almost tempted to argue that only *un*intelligent machines can be malevolent; anyone who has tried to start a balky outboard will probably agree. Those who picture machines as active enemies are merely projecting their own aggressive instincts, inherited from the jungle, into a world where such things do not exist. The higher the intelligence, the greater the degree of cooperativeness. If there is ever a war between men and machines, it is easy to guess who will start it.

Yet however friendly and helpful the machines of the future may be, most people will feel that it is a rather bleak prospect for humanity if it ends up as a pampered specimen in some biological museum—even if that museum is the whole planet Earth. This, however, is an attitude I find impossible to share.

No individual exists forever; why should we expect our species to be immortal? Man, said Nietzsche, is a rope stretched between the animal and the superhuman—a rope across the abyss. That will be a noble purpose to have served.

Arthur Charles Clarke, internationally known science-fiction writer and winner of the United States Space Writer Award, was born in Minehead, England, in 1917. He received the Bachelor of Science Degree with First Class Honors from King's College in London in 1948. After serving in the Royal Air Force from 1941 to 1946, he has been an auditor, an editor, and an underseas photographer. He has also made numerous radio and television appearances, acting as a consultant during lunar expeditions. With Stanley Kubrick, he wrote the screen play for the MGM film *2001: A Space Odyssey* and, later, a novel of the same title based on the screenplay. Among his nonfiction works are *Interplanetary Flight, The Exploration of Space, Going into Space, The Challenge of the Space Ship, The Challenge of the Sea, Voices from the Sky, Profiles of the Future,* from which "The Obsolence of Man" is taken, and *The Nine Billion Names of God.*

Vocabulary Study

From the list below, select the word or phrase nearest in meaning to the italicized word in the excerpts from "The Obsolescence of Man." The list contains extra words.

A. A *spurious* sense of security
B. that is quite *irrelevant*
C. The argument is wholly *fallacious*
D. a manner which can only be called *inquisitive*
E. like some protective *incantation*
F. based upon *abstruse* principles
G. brains larger and *potentially* more powerful
H. more *versatile* than men
I. the word *extension* may be replaced by *extinction*
J. machines will replace or *supersede* us
K. machines must be *malevolent entities* hostile to man

impertinent
curious
possibly
incumbent
malicious
erroneous
iconoclast
chant
false *or* counterfeit
many-sided
annihilation
benevolent
invidious
recondite
abstinent
continuation
supplant
beings

Questions on Form and Content

A. At what period in time does Mr. Clarke begin his essay? In what age does he conclude it? Why, in each case?

B. What is the tone and mood of the conclusion? Do you concur with Mr. Clarke's appraisal of and attitude toward the destiny he projects for humanity in his final remarks?

C. In Mr. Clarke's view, what role have tools played in man's progression?

D. What have computers already accomplished, which, not so long ago, would have been considered impossible?

E. What even more remarkable traits have laboratory computers exhibited?

F. What almost incredible activities does Mr. Clarke predict for second-generation computers?

G. What, according to Mr. Clarke, is the "greatest single stimulus to the evolution of mechanical—as opposed to organic—intelligence"? Why?

H. If machines can be both more intelligent and more versatile than man, where does that leave man? What "golden age" does Mr. Clark predict for him in the interim?

Suggestions for Writing

A. In Melbourne, Australia, in July, 1970, demonstrators shot a computer. Four men were arrested after emptying a double-barreled shotgun into a local office of Honeywell, Inc. Honeywell manufactures fragmentation bombs. In the light of Mr. Clarke's article, comment on the men's action. Consider, particularly, his statement: "If there is ever a war between men and machines, it is easy to guess who will start it."

B. "The old idea that man invented tools is therefore a misleading half-truth; it would be more accurate to say that *tools invented man,*" says Mr. Clarke. Comment.

C. Mr. Clark mentions several literary works in which the creations of man's brains threaten to destroy him: Karl Čapek's play *R.U.R.* (Rossom's Universal Robots), Samuel Butler's *Erewhon,* Mary Shelley's *Frankenstein,* various treatments of the Faust legend, and the story of Daedalus, "King Minos' one-man office of scientific research." Write a paper based on one of these works, using it to support—or refute—Mr. Clarke's thesis.

D. Mr. Clarke says: "Some millions of years ago, the most intelligent of the mammals withdrew from the battle of the dry land and returned to their ancestral home, the sea. They are still there, with brains larger and potentially more powerful than ours." Write a paper on one of these land dropouts, perhaps the porpoise or the whale, who "now race in simpleminded and innocent ecstasy beside the new sea monsters carrying sixteen megatons of death."

E. Mr. Clarke says that, for a brief golden age, "thinking machines will be able to help us . . . by taking over the humbler tasks of life." He adds that one "could even take over its master's place, keeping appointments he preferred to miss, and then reporting back in as much detail as he desired." What tasks and appointments would you like to assign to an electronic companion-secretary-valet?

F. If, some day, as Mr. Clarke suggests, you have the opportunity to combine with a machine, or—more likely—it decides to combine with you, do you have any preference as to the kind of machine, should you have the alternative of accepting or rejecting a proposal? Discuss the advantages and disadvantages of sharing the life of some particular machine you know.

G. In July, 1970, a history professor at New York University and a former teaching aide held a multimillion dollar computer as ransom, threatening to destroy the computer unless the University gave them $100,000 to use for bail for a Black Panther facing trial on bomb-conspiracy charges. Discuss their strange extortion plot in the light of Mr. Clarke's article.

H. In 1929, according to Mr. Clarke, the physicist J. D. Bernal decided that "the numerous limitations of the human body could be overcome only by the use of mechanical attachments or substitutes—until, eventually, all that might be left of man's original organic body would be the brain." If Mr. Bernal was right, what developments can you envision for such a society? You might consider such possibilities as the market for new and used parts—or whole bodies, the opportunities for mechanics, planned obsolescence, new models, the two- or three-body man, the pollution and disposal problems.

I. As Mr. Clarke notes, Mr. Bernal was prophetic in that we have recently seen the development and use of mechanical hearts, kidneys, lungs, and other organs, and the wiring of electronic devices directly into the human nervous system. Write a paper on a current development in this field.

J. "One day we may be able to enter into temporary unions with any sufficiently sophisticated machines, thus being able not merely to control but to *become* a space-ship or a submarine or a TV network. This would give far more than purely intellectual satisfaction; the thrill that can be obtained from driving a racing car or flying an airplane may be only a pale ghost of the excitement our great-grandchildren may know, when the individual human consciousness is free to roam at will from machine to machine, through all the reaches of sea and sky and space," says Mr. Clarke. Do you find the prospect of *being* a space-ship or a submarine or a television network thrilling? Why or why not?

K. Mr. Clarke says "the higher the intelligence, the greater the degree of cooperativeness." Comment.

L. Mr. Clark concludes: "No individual exists forever; why should we expect our species to be immortal?" How would you reply?

M. *The New York Times* in September, 1970, reported that a team of scientists at Yale University had successfully interconnected a computer with a chimpanzee's brain. The same story contained a discussion of work by Dr. Jose Delgado on brain signals at the University of California Medical Center in San Francisco. Investigate this story and discuss it in the light of Mr. Clarke's suggestions.

N. The poem that follows is a concrete poem, a poem that appeals to sight as well as to sound and sense. What is its visual image? Does the lack of punctuation add or detract? Why, in either case? Does the rhythm accelerate as the poem progresses? If so, with what effect? How does the author work his name and the occasion for the poem into the poem itself? How does the subject matter of the poem reflect the ideas of all four prose selections which have appeared in the first two chapters of this text? In what way is the ending itself circular in nature? How does the form of the poem match the content?

Video Statement

Aldo Tambellini

[*The poem appears on the facing page, as it was originally printed.*]

□Aldo Tambellini, "Simultaneous Video Statements," from *Radical Software* (Summer 1970), p. 17.

america
once tested the atom bomb in
hiroshima and the atomic age began the
industrial revolution was a world of machines
the fabrications of objects the atomic space age is a
world of matter of non physical forces of energy arms and
legs of machines are controlled by nervous systems and brains of
the computer we are the primitives of a new era the fetus is cond
itioned to the simultaneous beat of our period the instantaneous chang
es the child born to a world of radiation of ultrasonic sound of superson
ic speed will float with the weightlessness of astronauts in the midst of to
days totalitarian system there is the struggle of man to expand his senses in
attempting to become organic with his scientific environment his newly disc
overed nature the rebellion is against man as an exploited economic commodi
ty man as a specialized entity we have witnessed the explosion of the black
man and the apathy of the artist the specialization of the picture maker the
writer the music maker is challenged by programmed computers able to produce
the same act of specialization the computer age places a higher demand on
the creative artist the octopus spreads in many directions under one core
the concept of art has disappeared electromedia is our era we must get
to the heart of the medium to its tube its filament its energy we must
produce visions from the stuff which media are made of it is from
blackness that we begin to be resensitized for blackness is like
the womb where light was first felt perceived but not yet
seen aldo tambellini electromedia a movement a r t s
canada november 1967 . . .and before the beginning was
black before the b e g i n n i n g and b e f o r e
the beginning was black before the
beginning and before the
beginning

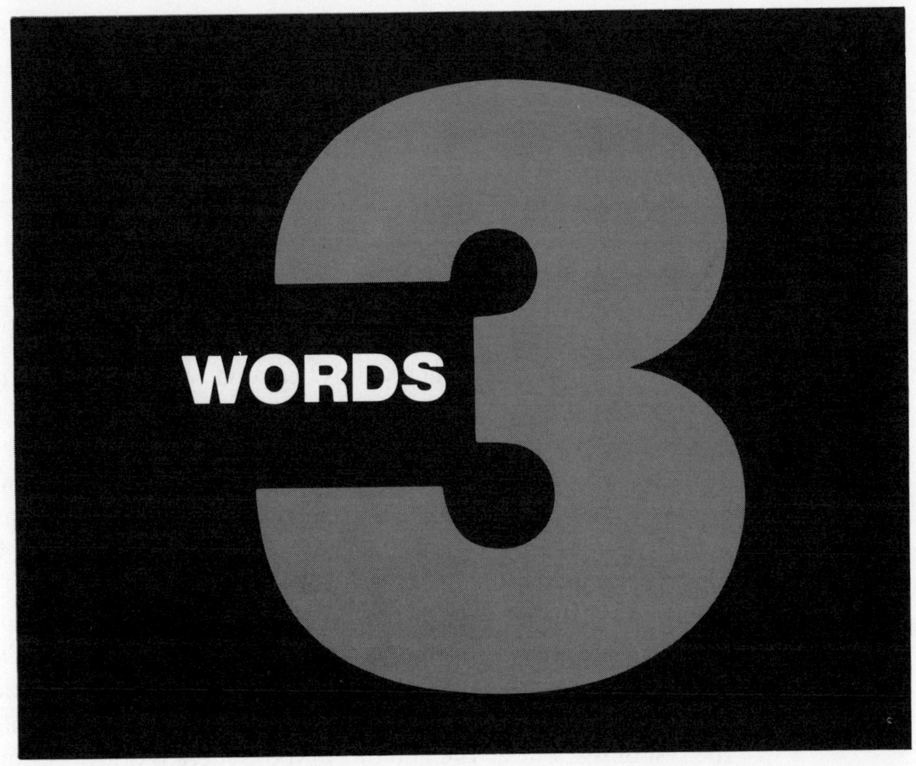

Every writer is concerned with the wise choice and judicious manipulation of words into the sentences and paragraphs which comprise communication. Words are classified in many ways: formal, informal, colloquial; standard, nonstandard; learned, popular, illiterate; specific, general; connotative, denotative; trite, hackneyed. You have, no doubt, heard of these classifications in English courses. At this time, however, you should be concerned with such terms only as they help you to recognize and use the proper word in the right place. To be able to do this, you must acquire a knowledge of and feeling for good diction, that is, for a good choice of language.

In general, good diction is accurate, appropriate to its context (formal, informal, or colloquial) and as specific as possible. It may be connotative or figurative, but it is never trite or hackneyed and almost never nonstandard. The accurate word must be exact, not one that sounds or looks similar to, or means nearly the same as the one desired. Students frequently have difficulty with such words as *effect-affect, accept-except,* and *disinterested-uninterested.* The vocabulary exercise on "So You Want to Be a Dropout" in the next chapter should help you to see how much trouble you have with this problem. If it is considerable, you will do well to read carefully Rudolf Flesch's article "How to Be a Perfect Speller," Appendix B of this book, as he offers several helpful suggestions for differentiating between such words.

The accurate word has the right *denotation,* the primary or actual meaning, and the right *connotation,* the implication it suggests in addition to its meaning. For example, the words *kittenish* and *catty* denote feline characteristics, but there is a vast difference in the circumstances under which you can safely apply the two to a member of the human race. In his essay which is Appendix A of this book, Paul Roberts calls such words "colored words," because they are loaded with associations, either good or bad. He notes that *mother, liberty,* and *manly* have agreeable associations for most people, while *mother-in-law, radical,* and *reactionary* have unpleasant overtones or echoes and are sometimes used to convey contempt. Equally strong connotations are attached to many words in our language, and your choice of the right words depends in part on your awareness of their connotations.

To recognize and choose the correct word in context, you must be able to differentiate between *levels of usage.* In "So You Want to Be a Dropout," in the next chapter, the student uses a markedly different vocabulary in his conversations with his adviser, the dean, and his parents from that he employs throughout the rest of the article. The author's purpose there is primarily humorous but the student does recognize that some words are acceptable on any level; others are not. We clothe our thoughts in words to suit the appropriate occasions much as we wear bermudas to a barbecue, but not to a candlelight dinner. For formal literary English we use an extensive vocabulary of learned words in suitable structures and avoid abbreviations, contractions, and colloquialisms. In informal and colloquial English we use the words and expressions that educated, cultivated people use when speaking and writing informally to each other. Nonstandard or illiterate English consists of the words and structures of the uneducated. Unless there is a special assignment in which you want to represent uneducated speech, illiterate English has no place in the writing of college students. Of course, it is important to remember that much of our vocabulary consists of so-called popular words, words used by both the educated and uneducated and acceptable at all stylistic levels.

Good diction must be specific in order to be colorful and vivid. A specific word points to a particular person, place, or thing while a general word refers to a group or class. There are, of course, degrees of being general and specific. The general word *food* is less specific than *dessert,* but *lemon chiffon pie* is more specific still. The use of specific words will help you to avoid the dullness and ineffectuality of abstractions. Follow Paul Roberts' advice: "Don't say, 'I like certain kinds of popular music very much.' Say, 'Whenever I hear Gerber Sprinklittle play "Mississippi Man" on the trombone, my socks creep up my ankles.' "

In *figurative language* one thing is likened to another through comparison or analogy. The most commonly used figures of speech are called metaphor, simile, and personification. The *metaphor* ascribes to one thing the qualities of another ("Spelling is the stepchild of our scientific age," from "How to Be a Perfect Speller"; "the tender heart became stone," from Frederick Douglass's "Narrative"), while the simile says that one thing is like another ("the lamblike disposition gave way to one of tiger-like fierceness," from Frederick Douglass's "Narrative"). Personification endows inanimate objects or abstract ideas with human qualities ("Sometimes History seems to me Fate, graven-faced and ineluctable, marching everything down some long-prescribed path," from "The Oppressed Emancipated Woman").

If you are to use good diction, you must avoid the overused expression that has become trite and hackneyed. Most slang was once perceptive and colorful, but through overuse it has become worn and stale. As Mr. Roberts says, "Slang adjectives like *cool* ('That's real cool') tend to explode all over the language. They are applied to everything, lose their original force, and quickly die." The use of trite expressions or clichés, such as, "just between you and me," "it's the pure and simple truth," and "she gave him the best years of her life," shows that the writer has not been willing to spend the time necessary for choosing clear and specific words.

As you read the essays in this book, study carefully the use of words. Go to your dictionary at any time you are unsure of either the meaning or standing of a word. It can help you decide correct levels of usage if it labels words as colloquial, slang, technical, or the like. However, you will have to get a feeling for words chiefly through your own direct contact with them—through listening to the speech of educated people, through wide reading, and through your attempts to find the accurate words to express your ideas.

From
Narrative of the Life of Frederick Douglass, an American

Frederick Douglass

I lived in Master Hugh's family about seven years. During this time, I succeeded in learning to read and write. In accomplishing this, I was compelled to resort to various stratagems. I had no regular teacher. My mistress, who had kindly commenced to instruct me, had, in compliance with the advice and direction of her husband, not only ceased to instruct, but had set her face against my being instructed by any one else. It is due, however, to my mistress to say of her, that she did not adopt this course of treatment immediately. She at first lacked the depravity indispensable to shutting me up in mental darkness. It was at least necessary for her to have some training in the exercise of irresponsible power, to make her equal to the task of treating me as though I were a brute.

My mistress was, as I have said, a kind and tender-hearted woman; and in the simplicity of her soul she commenced, when I first went to live with her, to treat me as she supposed one human being ought to treat another. In entering upon

□ Frederick Douglass, *Narrative of the Life of Frederick Douglass, An American Slave* (Boston, 1845), Chapter VII.

the duties of a slaveholder, she did not seem to perceive that I sustained to her the relation of a mere chattel, and that for her to treat me as a human being was not only wrong, but dangerously so. Slavery proved as injurious to her as it did to me. When I went there, she was a pious, warm, and tender-hearted woman. There was no sorrow or suffering for which she had not a tear. She had bread for the hungry, clothes for the naked, and comfort for every mourner that came within her reach. Slavery soon proved its ability to divest her of these heavenly qualities. Under its influence, the tender heart became stone, and the lamblike disposition gave way to one of tiger-like fierceness. The first step in her downward course was in her ceasing to instruct me. She now commenced to practise her husband's precepts. She finally became even more violent in her opposition than her husband himself. She was not satisfied with simply doing as well as he had commanded; she seemed anxious to do better. Nothing seemed to make her more angry than to see me with a newspaper. She seemed to think that here lay the danger. I have had her rush at me with a face made all up of fury, and snatch from me a newspaper, in a manner that fully revealed her apprehension. She was an apt woman; and a little experience soon demonstrated, to her satisfaction, that education and slavery were incompatible with each other.

From this time I was most narrowly watched. If I was in a separate room any considerable length of time, I was sure to be suspected of having a book, and was at once called to give an account of myself. All this, however, was too late. The first step had been taken. Mistress, in teaching me the alphabet, had given me the *inch,* and no precaution could prevent me from taking the *ell.*

The plan which I adopted, and the one by which I was most successful, was that of making friends of all the little white boys whom I met in the street. As many of these as I could, I converted into teachers. With their kindly aid, obtained at different times and in different places, I finally succeeded in learning to read. When I was sent on errands, I always took my book with me, and by doing one part of my errand quickly, I found time to get a lesson before my return. I used also to carry bread with me, enough of which was always in the house, and to which I was always welcome; for I was much better off in this regard than many of the poor white children in our neighborhood. This bread I used to bestow upon the hungry little urchins, who, in return, would give me that more valuable bread of knowledge. I am strongly tempted to give the names of two or three of those little boys, as a testimonial of the gratitude and affection I bear them; but prudence forbids;—not that it would injure me, but it might embarrass them; for it is almost an unpardonable offence to teach slaves to read in this Christian country. It is enough to say of the dear little fellows, that they lived on Philpot Street, very near Durgin and Bailey's ship-yard. I used to talk this matter of slavery over with them. I would sometimes say to them, I wished I could be as free as they would be when they got to be men. "You will be free as soon as you are twenty-one, *but I am a slave for life!* Have not I as good a right to be free as you have?" These words used to trouble them; they would express for me the liveliest sympathy, and console me with the hope that something would occur by which I might be free.

I was now about twelve years old, and the thought of being *a slave for life* began to bear heavily upon my heart. Just about this time, I got hold of a book entitled "The Columbian Orator." Every opportunity I got, I used to read this book. Among much of other interesting matter, I found in it a dialogue between a master and his slave. The slave was represented as having run away from his master three times. The dialogue represented the conversation which took place between them, when the slave was retaken the third time. In this dialogue, the whole argument in behalf of slavery was brought forward by the master, all of which was disposed of by the slave. The slave was made to say some very smart as well as impressive things in reply to his master—things which had the desired though unexpected effect; for the conversation resulted in the voluntary emancipation of the slave on the part of the master.

In the same book, I met with one of Sheridan's mighty speeches on and in behalf of Catholic emancipation. These were choice documents to me. I read them over and over again with unabated interest. They gave tongue to interesting thoughts of my own soul, which had frequently flashed through my mind, and died away for want of utterance. The moral which I gained from the dialogue was the power of truth over the conscience of even a slaveholder. What I got from Sheridan was a bold denunciation of slavery, and a powerful vindication of human rights. The reading of these documents enabled me to utter my thoughts, and to meet the arguments brought forward to sustain slavery; but while they relieved me of one difficulty, they brought on another even more painful than the one of which I was relieved. The more I read, the more I was led to abhor and detest my enslavers. I could regard them in no other light than a band of successful robbers, who had left their homes, and gone to Africa, and stolen us from our homes, and in a strange land reduced us to slavery. I loathed them as being the meanest as well as the most wicked of men. As I read and contemplated the subject, behold! that very discontentment which Master Hugh had predicted would follow my learning to read had already come, to torment and sting my soul to unutterable anguish. As I writhed under it, I would at times feel that learning to read had been a curse rather than a blessing. It had given me a view of my wretched condition, without the remedy. It opened my eyes to the horrible pit, but to no ladder upon which to get out. In moments of agony, I envied my fellow-slaves for their stupidity. I have often wished myself a beast. I preferred the condition of the meanest reptile to my own. Any thing, no matter what, to get rid of thinking! It was this everlasting thinking of my condition that tormented me. There was no getting rid of it. It was pressed upon me by every object within sight or hearing, animate or inanimate. The silver trump of freedom had roused my soul to eternal wakefulness. Freedom now appeared, to disappear no more forever. It was heard in every sound, and seen in every thing. It was ever present to torment me with a sense of my wretched condition. I saw nothing without seeing it, I heard nothing without hearing it, and felt nothing without feeling it. It looked from every star, it smiled in every calm, breathed in every wind, and moved in every storm.

I often found myself regretting my own existence, and wishing myself dead; and but for the hope of being free, I have no doubt but that I should have killed myself, or done something for which I should have been killed. While in this state of mind, I was eager to hear any one speak of slavery. I was a ready listener. Every little while, I could hear something about the abolitionists. It was some time before I found what the word meant. It was always used in such connections as to make it an interesting word to me. If a slave ran away and succeeded in getting clear, or if a slave killed his master, set fire to a barn, or did any thing very wrong in the mind of a slaveholder, it was spoken of as the fruit of *abolition.* Hearing the word in this connection very often, I set about learning what it meant. The dictionary afforded me little or no help. I found it was "the act of abolishing"; but then I did not know what was to be abolished. Here I was perplexed. I did not dare to ask any one about its meaning, for I was satisfied that it was something they wanted me to know very little about. After a patient waiting, I got one of our city papers, containing an account of the number of petitions from the north, praying for the abolition of slavery in the District of Columbia, and of the slave trade between the States. From this time I understood the words *abolition* and *abolitionist,* and always drew near when that word was spoken, expecting to hear something of importance to myself and fellow-slaves. The light broke in upon me by degrees. I went one day down on the wharf of Mr. Waters; and seeing two Irishmen unloading a scow of stone, I went, unasked, and helped them. When we had finished, one of them came to me and asked, "Are ye a slave for life?" I told him that I was. The good Irishman seemed to be deeply affected by the statement. He said to the other that it was a pity so fine a little fellow as myself should be a slave for life. He said it was a shame to hold me. They both advised me to run away to the north; that I should find friends there, and that I should be free. I pretended not to be interested in what they said, and treated them as if I did not understand them; for I feared they might be treacherous. White men have been known to encourage slaves to escape, and then, to get the reward, catch them and return them to their masters. I was afraid that these seemingly good men might use me so; but I nevertheless remembered their advice, and from that time I resolved to run away. I looked forward to a time at which it would be safe for me to escape. I was too young to think of doing so immediately; besides, I wished to learn how to write, as I might have occasion to write my own pass. I consoled myself with the hope that I should one day find a good chance. Meanwhile, I would learn to write.

The idea as to how I might learn to write was suggested to me by being in Durgin and Bailey's ship-yard, and frequently seeing the ship carpenters, after hewing, and getting a piece of timber ready for use, write on the timber the name of that part of the ship for which it was intended. When a piece of timber was intended for the larboard side, it would be marked thus—"L." When a piece was for the starboard side, it would be marked thus—"S." A piece for the larboard side forward, would be marked thus—"L. F." When a piece was for starboard side forward, it would be marked thus—"S. F." For larboard aft, it would be marked thus—"L. A." For starboard aft, it would be marked thus—"S. A." I soon learned the names of these letters, and for what they were intended when placed upon a piece of timber in the ship-yard. I immediately commenced copying them, and in a short time was able to make the four letters named. After that, when I met with any boy who I knew could write, I would tell him I could write as well as he. The next word would be, "I don't believe you. Let me see you try it." I would then make the letters which I had been so fortunate as to learn, and ask him to beat that. In this way I got a good many lessons in writing, which it is quite possible I should never have gotten in any other way. During this time, my copy-book was the board fence, brick wall, and pavement; my pen and ink was a lump of chalk. With these, I learned mainly how to write. I then commenced and continued copying the Italics in Webster's Spelling Book, until I could make them all without looking on the book. By this time, my little Master Thomas had gone to school, and learned how to write, and had written over a number of copy-books. These had been brought home, and shown to some of our near neighbors, and then laid aside. My mistress used to go to class meeting at the Wilk Street meetinghouse every Monday afternoon, and leave me to take care of the house. When left thus, I used to spend this time writing in the spaces left in Master Thomas's copy-book, copying what he had written. I continued to do this until I could write a hand very similar to that of Master Thomas. Thus, after a long, tedious effort for years, I finally succeeded in learning how to write.

Frederick Douglass, born a slave in Talbot County, Maryland, escaped from bondage in 1838. He became the leading Negro in the antislavery movement and after the Civil War emerged as the chief spokesman for the Negro cause. He wrote three autobiographies: *Narrative of the Life of Frederick Douglass, An American Slave* (1845); *My Bondage and My Freedom* (1855); *Life and Times of Frederick Douglass* (1881). A famous orator, Douglass helped to recruit Negro soldiers for the 54th and 55th Massachusetts Regiments during the Civil War. Later he became Secretary of the Santa Domingo Commission, Marshall and Recorder of Deeds of the District of Columbia, and Minister of the United States to Haiti.

Vocabulary Study

A. Mr. Douglass's love of words, undoubtedly born from his struggle to acquire them, is reflected in his writing. The following words are ones you should learn. Select from the list at the end of this section the word closest in meaning to that italicized in each excerpt.

1. I was compelled to resort to various *stratagems.*
2. My mistress, who had kindly commenced to instruct me, had, in *compliance* with the advice and direction of her husband
3. She at first lacked the *depravity* indispensable to shutting me up in mental darkness.
4. I sustained to her the relation of a mere *chattel*
5. Slavery proved as *injurious* to her as it did to me.
6. the hungry little *urchins*
7. but *prudence* forbids
8. a powerful *vindication* of human rights
9. a bold *denunciation* of slavery
10. I was led to *abhor* and detest my enslavers.
11. I feared they might be *treacherous.*
12. in a manner that fully revealed her *apprehension*
13. I read them over and over again with *unabated* interest.

unnatural	baggage	undertook	undiminished	traitorous
begun	tricks	acquiescence	youngsters	fear
concluded	corruption	hate	harmful	understanding
meaningless	property	justification	caution	condemnation

B. Mr. Douglass relies heavily on *figurative language.* His words paint pictures. Comment on the appropriateness of each of these "word pictures" to the context which frames it.

1. The tender heart became stone, and the lamblike disposition gave way to tiger-like fierceness.
2. a face made all up of fury
3. valuable bread of knowledge
4. The silver trump of freedom
5. they gave tongue to interesting thoughts
6. I opened my eyes to the horrible pit, but had no ladder upon which to get out.
7. The light broke in upon me by degrees.

Questions on Form and Content

A. Mr. Douglass states early in his essay that slavery had an extremely negative effect on his mistress. What was that effect?

B. How did Mr. Douglass's attitude after he had learned to read support his master's initial fears about an educated slave?

C. Mr. Douglass claims that the dictionary was of little practical use. What did he substitute for the dictionary as a learning device?

D. Mr. Douglass says, "Mistress, in teaching me the alphabet, had given me the *inch,* and no precaution could prevent me from taking the *ell.*" What does he mean? How does the rest of the essay develop this concept?

E. What does Mr. Douglass mean when he says that it was dangerously wrong for his mistress to treat him as a human being?

F. Why does Mr. Douglass include reference to what he read as a child?

G. In what way do Mr. Douglass's actions as a boy reflect his native intelligence?

H. What is Mr. Douglass's attitude toward the white people he knew as a child?

I. For what kind of reader do you think this essay was written? Why?

Suggestions for Writing

A. In the first half of the nineteenth century, Mr. Douglass wrote that it "is an almost unpardonable offence to teach slaves to read in this Christian country." In the latter half of the twentieth century this country still is struggling with the problems of equal education for all. What are some recent developments in that struggle?

B. Frederick Douglass, when about twelve years old, said to his young white friends: "You will be free as soon as you are twenty-one, *but I am a slave for life!* Have not I as good a right to be free as you have?" Had you had the opportunity, how would you have liked to answer?

C. Should *everyone* be free before twenty-one? If you have not reached that age, what, if anything, inhibits your freedom? With what, if any, justification?

D. If you feel that a human being must be held responsible for his acts, when does he reach the age of accountability?

E. Mr. Douglass writes: "I was now about twelve years old, and the thought of being *a slave for life* began to bear heavily upon my heart." He then found a book with a dialogue containing "the whole argument in behalf of slavery." What argument could you make for its existence? For its abolition?

F. Mr. Douglass tells us how he used his ingenuity to learn to write. His method shows that he also knew a great deal about the motivations of other boys. What?

G. How did Tom Sawyer or Benjamin Franklin or some other youth, either fictional or real, accomplish his aims in a similar fashion?

H. Henry Clay maintained that, "Slavery is a curse to the master and a wrong to the slave." Support this statement using Mr. Douglass's essay as a basis for your discussion.

I. Write a logical explanation of the slaveholder's position (as expressed by Master Hugh) on the education of slaves. Show how the incident between the Irish dock workers and young Douglass illustrates the effect of this position on the slaves themselves.

J. Jose Ortega y Gasset, a noted philosopher, in trying to describe what it is that makes man *man*, distinct from animals, says: "We do not live to think, but the other way round: we think in order that we may succeed in surviving . . . for unlike all other entities in the universe, man is not and can never be sure that he is, in fact, man, as the tiger is sure of being a tiger and the fish of being a fish." Mr. Douglass records his response to himself as a thinking being thus: "I have often wished myself a beast. I preferred the condition of the meanest reptile to my own. Any thing, no matter what, to get rid of thinking!" Write an essay in which you attack or defend the concept (as expressed by Ortega y Gasset) of man as necessarily a thinking being. Is thinking a blessing or a curse?

What light does Mr. Douglass's essay shed on the subject? How is the whole question of man's ability to think related to what happened in the Garden of Eden?

K. Compare Douglass's writing style with contemporary black militant writings. What difference in technique and language do you note? To what kind of audience does each write? For what purpose? Which is more effective and why?

L. Write an essay in which you discuss Mr. Douglass's attitudes toward whites. Do his statements display maturity and understanding?

M. In the Funk and Wagnalls College Dictionary, intelligence is defined as: "1. The faculty of perceiving and comprehending meaning; mental quickness; active intellect; understanding. 2. The ability to adapt to new situations and to learn from experience. 3. The inherent ability to seize the essential factors of a complex matter." Which of these definitions does Mr. Douglass exemplify? Support with examples from his essay.

N. Throughout his essay, Mr. Douglass uses figurative language to describe his situation. Another Negro slave, Patsy Michener, also used figurative language in order to talk about slavery. Write an essay in which you develop, in your own words, the basic concept she attempts to communicate in this passage:

> Two snakes full of poison. One lying with his head pointing North, the other with his head pointing South. Their names was Slavery and Freedom. The snake called Slavery lay with his head pointed South and the snake called Freedom pointed North. Both bit the nigger and they was both bad.—Library of Congress records

O. How would you describe your own intellectual ability? What are its strengths and weaknesses?

P. Langston Hughes (1902-1967) poet, dramatist, lecturer, columnist, and translator, was born in Joplin, Missouri, and attended Columbia University during 1921-1922. The following poem, "Theme for English B," may have reference to his experiences there. Study the poem: then answer one or more of the following questions:

1. Who is the speaker in the poem and from what kind of environment does he come?

2. What does the line, "So will my page be colored that I write?" mean?

3. What is the basis for the claim, "But it will be a part of you, instructor"?

4. Has the speaker completed the assignment? How does he expect the teacher to react?

5. How are words used in this poem in such a way that they contribute to the informality of tone and style?

The instructor said,

> *Go home and write*
> *a page tonight.*
> *And let that page come out of you——*
> *Then, it will be true.*

I wonder if it's that simple?

I am twenty-two, colored, born in Winston-Salem.
I went to school there, then Durham, then here
to this college on the hill above Harlem.
I am the only colored student in my class.

☐ Langston Hughes, "Theme for English B," from *Montage of a Dream Deferred* (New York, 1951), pp. 39-40.

The steps from the hill lead down into Harlem,
through a park, then I cross St. Nicholas,
Eighth Avenue, Seventh, and I come to the Y,
the Harlem Branch Y, where I take the elevator
up to my room, sit down, and write this page:

It's not easy to know what is true for you or me
at twenty-two, my age. But I guess I'm what
I feel and see and hear. Harlem, I hear you:
hear you, hear me—we two—you, me, talk on this page.
(I hear New York, too.) Me—who?

Well, I like to eat, sleep, drink, and be in love.
I like to work, read, learn, and understand life.
I like a pipe for a Christmas present,
or records—Bessie, bop, or Bach.
I guess being colored doesn't make me *not* like
the same things other folks like who are other races.

So will my page be colored that I write?
Being me, it will not be white.
But it will be
a part of you, instructor.
You are white——
yet a part of me, as I am a part of you.
That's American.
Sometimes perhaps you don't want to be a part of me.
Nor do I often want to be a part of you.
But we are, that's true!
As I learn from you,
I guess you learn from me——
although you're older—and white——
and somewhat more free.

This is my page for English B.

From *Black Elk Speaks*

As told through John G. Neihardt

I am a Lakota of the Ogalala band. My father's name was Black Elk, and his father before him bore the name, and the father of his father, so that I am the fourth to bear it. He was a medicine man and so were several of his brothers. Also, he and the great Crazy Horse's father were cousins, having the same grandfather. My mother's name was White Cow Sees; her father was called Refuse-to-Go, and her mother, Plenty Eagle Feathers. I can remember my mother's mother and her father. My father's father was killed by the Pawnees when I was too little to know, and his mother, Red Eagle Woman, died soon after.

I was born in the Moon of the Popping Trees (December) on the Little Powder River in the Winter When the Four Crows Were Killed (1863), and I was three years old when my father's right leg was broken in the Battle of the Hundred

□ John G. Neihardt, *Black Elk Speaks,* Chapter II, "Early Boyhood" (New York, 1932; Lincoln, Nebraska, 1961), pp. 7-19. A publisher's note in the 1961 edition explains that Mr. Neihardt prefers to have the authorship given "as told through" rather than "as told to," also that "Oglala" is the modern preference rather than "Ogalala."

Slain.[1] From that wound he limped until the day he died, which was about the time when Big Foot's band was butchered on Wounded Knee (1890). He is buried here in these hills.

I can remember that Winter of the Hundred Slain as a man may remember some bad dream he dreamed when he was little, but I can not tell just how much I heard when I was bigger and how much I understood when I was little. It is like some fearful thing in a fog, for it was a time when everything seemed troubled and afraid.

I had never seen a Wasichu[2] then, and did not know what one looked like; but every one was saying that the Wasichus were coming and that they were going to take our country and rub us all out and that we should all have to die fighting. It was the Wasichus who got rubbed out in that battle, and all the people were talking about it for a long while; but a hundred Wasichus was not much if there were others and others without number where those came from.

I remember once that I asked my grandfather about this. I said: "When the scouts come back from seeing the prairie full of bison somewhere, the people say the Wasichus are coming; and when strange men are coming to kill us all, they say the Wasichus are coming. What does it mean?" And he said, "That they are many."

When I was older, I learned what the fighting was about that winter and the next summer. Up on the Madison Fork the Wasichus had found much of the yellow metal that they worship and that makes them crazy, and they wanted to have a road up through our country to the place where the yellow metal was; but my people did not want the road. It would scare the bison and make them go away, and also it would let the other Wasichus come in like a river. They told us that they wanted only to use a little land, as much as a wagon would take between the wheels; but our people knew better. And when you look about you now, you can see what it was they wanted.

Once we were happy in our own country and we were seldom hungry, for then the two-leggeds and the four-leggeds lived together like relatives, and there was plenty for them and for us. But the Wasichus came, and they have made little islands for us and other little islands for the four-leggeds, and always these islands are becoming smaller, for around them surges the gnawing flood of the Wasichu; and it is dirty with lies and greed.

A long time ago my father told me what his father told him, that there was once

[1]The Fetterman Fight, commonly described as a "massacre," in which Captain Fetterman and 81 men were wiped out on Peno Creek near Fort Phil Kearney, December 21, 1866.

[2]A term used to designate the white man, but having no reference to the color of his skin. [Later in the book the expression "black Wasichu soldiers" occurs.]

a Lakota holy man, called Drinks Water, who dreamed what was to be; and this was long before the coming of the Wasichus. He dreamed that the four-leggeds were going back into the earth and that a strange race had woven a spider's web all around the Lakotas. And he said: "When this happens, you shall live in square gray houses, in a barren land, and beside those square gray houses you shall starve." They say he went back to Mother Earth soon after he saw this vision, and it was sorrow that killed him. You can look about you now and see that he meant these dirt-roofed houses we are living in, and that all the rest was true. Sometimes dreams are wiser than waking.

And so when the soldiers came and built themselves a town of logs there on the Piney Fork of the Powder, my people knew they meant to have their road and take our country and maybe kill us all when they were strong enough. Crazy Horse was only about 19 years old then, and Red Cloud was still our great chief. In the Moon of the Changing Season (October) he called together all the scattered bands of the Lakota for a big council on the Powder River, and when we went on the warpath against the soldiers, a horseback could ride through our village from sunrise until the day was above his head, so far did our camp stretch along the valley of the river; for many of our friends, the Shyela[3] and the Blue Clouds,[4] had come to help us fight.

And it was about when the bitten moon was delayed (last quarter) in the Time of the Popping Trees when the hundred were rubbed out. My friend, Fire Thunder here, who is older than I, was in that fight and he can tell you how it was.

Fire Thunder Speaks:

I was 16 years old when this happened, and after the big council on the Powder we had moved over to the Tongue River where were were camping at the mouth of Peno Creek. There were many of us there. Red Cloud was over all of us, but the chief of our band was Big Road. We started out on horseback just about sunrise, riding up the creek toward the soldier's town on the Piney, for we were going to attack it. The sun was about half way up when we stopped at the place where the Wasichu's road came down a steep, narrow ridge and crossed the creek. It was a good place to fight, so we sent some men ahead to coax the soldiers out. While they were gone, we divided into two parts and hid in the gullies on both sides of the ridge and waited. After a long while we heard a shot up over the hill, and we knew the soldiers were coming. So we held the noses of our ponies that they might not whinny at the soldiers' horses. Soon we saw our men coming back,

[3]Cheyennes.
[4]Arapahoes.

and some of them were walking and leading their horses, so that the soldiers would think they were worn out. Then the men we had sent ahead came running down the road between us, and the soldiers on horseback followed, shooting. When they came to the flat at the bottom of the hill, the fighting began all at once. I had a sorrel horse, and just as I was going to get on him, the soldiers turned around and began to fight their way back up the hill. I had a six-shooter that I had traded for, and also a bow and arrows. When the soldiers started back, I held my sorrel with one hand and began killing them with the six-shooter, for they came close to me. There were many bullets, but there were more arrows—so many that it was like a cloud of grasshoppers all above and around the soldiers; and our people, shooting across, hit each other. The soldiers were falling all the while they were fighting back up the hill, and their horses got loose. Many of our people chased the horses, but I was not after horses; I was after Wasichus. When the soldiers got on top, there were not many of them left and they had no place to hide. They were fighting hard. We were told to crawl up on them, and we did. When we were close, someone yelled: "Let us go! This is a good day to die. Think of the helpless ones at home!" Then we all cried, "Hoka hey!" and rushed at them. I was young then and quick on my feet, and I was one of the first to get in among the soldiers. They got up and fought very hard until not one of them was alive. They had a dog with them, and he started back up the road for the soldiers' town, howling as he ran. He was the only one left. I did not shoot at him because he looked too sweet;[5] but many did shoot, and he died full of arrows. So there was nobody left of the soldiers. Dead men and horses and wounded Indians were scattered all the way up the hill, and their blood was frozen, for a storm had come up and it was very cold and getting colder all the time. We left all the dead lying there, for the ground was solid, and we picked up our wounded and started back; but we lost most of them before we reached our camp at the mouth of the Peno. There was a big blizzard that night; and some of the wounded who did not die on the way, died after we got home. This was the time when Black Elk's father had his leg broken.

Black Elk Continues:

I am quite sure that I remember the time when my father came home with a broken leg that he got from killing so many Wasichus, and it seems that I can remember all about the battle too, but I think I could not. It must be the fear that I remember most. All this time I was not allowed to play very far away from our

[5]Because of its current colloquial usage as a vapid sentimentalism, the expression may well seem off key in the mouth of the grizzled old warrior.

tepee, and my mother would say, "If you are not good the Wasichus will get you."

We must have broken camp at the mouth of the Peno soon after the battle, for I can remember my father lying on a pony drag with bison robes all around him, like a baby, and my mother riding the pony. The snow was deep and it was very cold, and I remember sitting in another pony drag beside my father and mother, all wrapped up in fur. We were going away from where the soldiers were, and I do not know where we went, but it was west.

It was a hungry winter, for the deep snow made it hard to find the elk; and also many of the people went snowblind. We wandered a long time, and some of the bands got lost from each other. Then at last we were camping in the woods beside a creek somewhere, and the hunters came back with meat.

I think it was this same winter when a medicine man, by the name of Creeping, went around among the people curing snowblinds. He would put snow upon their eyes, and after he had sung a certain sacred song that he had heard in a dream, he would blow on the backs of their heads and they would see again, so I have heard. It was about the dragonfly that he sang, for that was where he got his power, they say.

When it was summer again we were camping on the Rosebud, and I did not feel so much afraid, because the Wasichus seemed farther away and there was peace there in the valley and there was plenty of meat. But all the boys from five or six years up were playing war. The little boys would gather together from the different bands of the tribe and fight each other with mud balls that they threw with willow sticks. And the big boys played the game called Throwing-Them-Off-Their-Horses, which is a battle all but the killing; and sometimes they got hurt. The horsebacks from the different bands would line up and charge upon each other, yelling; and when the ponies came together on the run, they would rear and flounder and scream in a big dust, and the riders would seize each other wrestling until one side had lost all its men, for those who fell upon the ground were counted dead.

When I was older, I too, often played this game. We were always naked when we played it, just as warriors are when they go into battle if it is not too cold, because they are swifter without clothes. Once I fell off on my back right in the middle of a bed of prickly pears, and it took my mother a long while to pick all the stickers out of me. I was still too little to play war that summer, but I can remember watching the other boys, and I thought that when we all grew up and were big together, maybe we could kill all the Wasichus or drive them far away from our country.

It was in the Moon When the Cherries Turn Black (August) that all the people were talking again about a battle, and our warriors came back with many wounded. It was The Attacking of the Wagons,[6] and it made me afraid again, for we did not win that battle as we did the other one, and there was much mourning for the dead. Fire Thunder was in that fight too, and he can tell you how it was that day.

Fire Thunder Speaks:

It was very bad. There is a wide flat prairie with hills around it, and in the middle of this the Wasichus had put the boxes of their wagons in a circle, so that they could keep their mules there at night. There were not many Wasichus, but they were lying behind the boxes and they shot faster than they ever shot at us before. We thought it was some new medicine of great power that they had, for they shot so fast that it was like tearing a blanket. Afterwards I learned that it was because they had new guns that they loaded from behind, and this was the first time they used these guns.[7] We came on after sunrise. There were many, many of us, and we meant to ride right over them and rub them out. But our ponies were afraid of the ring of fire the guns of the Wasichus made, and would not go over. Our women were watching us from the hills and we could hear them singing and mourning whenever the shooting stopped. We tried hard, but we could not do it, and there were dead warriors and horses piled all around the boxes and scattered over the plain. Then we left our horses in a gulch and charged on foot, but it was like green grass withering in a fire. So we picked up our wounded and went away. I do not know how many of our people were killed, but there were very many. It was bad.

Black Elk Continues:

I do not remember where we camped that winter but it must have been a time of peace and of plenty to eat.

Standing Bear Speaks:

I am four years older than Black Elk, and he and I have been good friends since boyhood. I know it was on the Powder that we camped where there were many cottonwood trees. Ponies like to eat the bark of these trees and it is good for them. That was the winter when High Shirt's mother was killed by a big tree that fell on her tepee. It was a very windy night and there were noises that 'woke me, and then I heard that an old woman had been killed, and it was High Shirt's mother.

[6]The Wagon Box Fight, which took place about six miles west of Fort Phil Kearney on August 2, 1867.

[7]Breech-loading Springfields.

Black Elk Continues:

I was four years old then, and I think it must have been the next summer that I first heard the voices. It was a happy summer and nothing was afraid, because in the Moon When the Ponies Shed (May) word came from the Wasichus that there would be peace and that they would not use the road any more and that all the soldiers would go away. The soldiers did go away and their towns were torn down; and in the Moon of Falling Leaves (November), they made a treaty with Red Cloud that said our country would be ours as long as grass should grow and water flow. You can see that it is not the grass and the water that have forgotten.

Maybe it was not this summer when I first heard the voices, but I think it was, because I know it was before I played with bows and arrows or rode a horse, and I was out playing alone when I heard them. It was like somebody calling me, and I thought it was my mother, but there was nobody there. This happened more than once, and always made me afraid, so that I ran home.

It was when I was five years old that my Grandfather made me a bow and some arrows. The grass was young and I was horseback. A thunder storm was coming from where the sun goes down, and just as I was riding into the woods along a creek, there was a kingbird sitting on a limb. This was not a dream, it happened. And I was going to shoot at the kingbird with the bow my Grandfather made, when the bird spoke and said: "The clouds all over are one-sided." Perhaps it meant that all the clouds were looking at me. And then it said: "Listen! A voice is calling you!" Then I looked up at the clouds, and two men were coming there, headfirst like arrows slanting down; and as they came, they sang a sacred song and the thunder was like drumming. I will sing it for you. The song and the drumming were like this:

> "Behold, a sacred voice is calling you;
> All over the sky a sacred voice is calling."

I sat there gazing at them, and they were coming from the place where the giant lives (north). But when they were very close to me, they wheeled about toward where the sun goes down, and suddenly they were geese. Then they were gone, and the rain came with a big wind and a roaring.

I did not tell this vision to any one. I liked to think about it, but I was afraid to tell it.

John G. Neihardt, born in Sharpsburg, Illinois, in 1881, holds degrees from Nebraska Normal College, the University of Nebraska, Creighton University, and the University of Mississippi. He lived among the Omaha Indians from 1901 to 1907, studying their character and history, and was later associated with the Oglala Sioux (Lakota). His varied occupations include the posts of Professor of Poetry at the University of Nebraska and Poet in Residence at the University of Mississippi, Fulbright lecturer in India, literary editor of the *Saint Louis-Post Dispatch,* director of information of the Office of Indian Affairs, and field representative of the Office of Indian Affairs. The recipient of numerous awards for his poetry, his books include *Lyric and Dramatic Poems, The Song of the Indian Wars, The River and I, Indian Tales and Others, A Cycle of the West,* and *Black Elk Speaks,* from which the preceding selection is taken.

Vocabulary Study

One of the most striking features of Black Elk's story is the way in which names capture the essence of people, places, and things. In the past, family names (last names) were relatively unheard of among Indians. Their existence today is largely a result of the efforts of whites to make census counts of the Indians living on reservations. Over the centuries, however, the personal names of Indians have exhibited a feel for language. Many of them are extremely descriptive; others beautiful in their combination of sounds. Examine the names given to people in this story. What do they tell you about the personality or background of the person to whom they belong? What are the similarities and differences between these names and the names (both first and last) used by other peoples? (One might think of some descriptive names like Miller, Johnson, Byrd, Priestly, White, Brown, Handy, Mandelbaum, which means "almond tree," and Dupont, "from the bridge.")

Names are important in still another sense among many Indians. It was (and in some cases still is) the practice to bestow a "secret" or "war" name upon an Indian child. This name, often given by the maternal grandmother, was to announce the presence of the child to the spirits. Unlike a "social" name, it was never used publicly (except in rare occasions, perhaps when a medicine man had to call upon the spirits to heal a sick man). If the secret name were discovered, it might be used for harmful purposes by witches seeking revenge for some offense.

Within Black Elk's narrative, Indian names appear for nearly all of the months. What are they and why do you suppose each one was chosen? Are these names more or less effective for the purposes of the Oglala tribe than our more conventional names for the months?

Places and events are also significant in this story, and the names given them attempt to convey their significance. What observations can you make about Indian names and white names given to the same place or event?

Questions on Form and Content

A. How is Black Elk's story organized?

B. What similarities in language and style do you notice between Black Elk's chapter and the selection from the Bible which appeared in Chapter 1 of this book?

C. What was the Indian's attitude toward the white man?

D. What was the reason for the many battles near Black Elk's homeland?

E. How does Black Elk's tale reveal a difference in values between the white man and the Indian?

F. Why did the Indians resist the road through their land?

G. How does the Indian's attitude toward nature, as expressed in this story, differ from the conventional attitude of the white man toward his environment?

H. Black Elk says, "Sometimes dreams are wiser than waking." How does his tale support this statement?

I. How does the picture of war given here by Fire Thunder differ from the traditional view presented in television westerns?

J. How did the trouble with the white men affect the Indian children in Black Elk's tribe?

Suggestions for Writing

A. Black Elk says: "I can remember that Winter of the Hundred Slain as a man may remember some bad dream he dreamed when he was little, but I cannot tell just how much I heard when I was bigger and how much I understood when I was little." Do you have a similar memory? If so, recount it.

B. Black Elk tells of tales he heard of the white man before he had ever seen one or even knew how one looked. Do you remember the first Indian you ever saw? Can you recount Indian stories you heard as a child?

C. What does Black Elk's account reveal about the difference in values held by his people and those held by white men?

D. Black Elk writes: "But the Wasichus came, and they have made little islands for us and other little islands for the four-leggeds, and always these islands are becoming smaller, for around them surges the gnawing flood of the Wasichu; and it is dirty with lies and greed." Discuss the justification for his remarks.

E. "Sometimes dreams are wiser than waking," says Black Elk. Comment and discuss on the basis of other observations, including perhaps your own.

F. Black Elk tells how the medicine man, Creeping, cured snowblinds through the power of a sacred song. Do you know chants or songs famed for their curative or magical power? If so, relate one and discuss its peculiar influence.

G. Black Elk says during the summer after the battle when "the hundred were rubbed out," "all the boys from five or six years up were playing war." What did the little boys use for weapons? How did the older boys play war? How do children today play the game? With what weapons? Should they be permitted to do so? Why or why not?

H. When Black Elk was four years old, the soldiers went away. Before going, "they made a treaty with Red Cloud that said our country would be ours as long as grass should grow and water flow. You can see that it is not the grass and the water that have forgotten." Who has?

I. Discuss the possible meaning of Black Elk's vision and voices.

J. Tell the story of another who has heard voices or had visions, or both: perhaps Joan of Arc, or Bernadette of Lourdes, or William Blake.

K. Use an Indian myth or legend as the basis for discussion of some major point of value distinction between Indians and whites.

L. Black Elk's story suggests that the Indians and Anglos have different attitudes toward nature. His references to nature are highly personalized; he implies that in a very important sense the four-leggeds and the two-leggeds are one. Write an essay in which you discuss the relationship between that attitude and the attitude advocated by contemporary environmentalists.

M. In his story Black Elk refers to the deeds of the medicine man, Creeping, who effectively cured snowblinds. In addition to whatever "medicine" such a healer brings to a patient (many of these simple remedies, composed largely of herbs, have been adopted by Anglos), he brings the power of song. It is still customary on the reservations to hold a "sing" for an ill person. At such times, the sick one's clan gathers—though many of the members have to travel quite a distance. They participate in the healing ceremony which often lasts for days. Such ceremonies sometimes seem to succeed in cases where medical care in a hospital has failed. What explanation can you offer? Write an essay in which you further develop this concept of the importance of the "sing" in Indian life or the function of a similar practice in another society, such as "faith healing" or a gypsy gathering.

Time Changes Things

Juan Garcia

I felt strange that morning. My eyes opened and slowly I became aware of everything. Shapes were still vague, however. The dimly lit room was keeping the new light of the day out with the help of the clouds. It was still raining. The rain pounced on the window repeatedly, endlessly, as if punishing it for some crime that had been committed. Mist had formed and drops of water rolled down the window pane, taking different paths, assuming the shapes of prison bars. I didn't know which one of us, the world outside or I, had been jailed. I didn't feel too well. I slid under the covers.

I was hot under the covers. My body was bathed in sweat. I remembered having turned up the heater full blast the night before just after my mother had come in to turn it down. I didn't want to feel the cold of the night. I liked feeling warm. I felt secure feeling warm. But somehow that morning it didn't matter as I peeked over the covers out to the world through the bars. I didn't want to get out of bed. I enjoyed the wet warmth of my sweat under the covers. At another time feeling like this would have made me feel dirty, like when a man and a woman do things under the covers at night. Besides not liking to feel cold, I despised feeling dirty. Staring out the window, the dull colors of the world forced me to think of how little I mattered. If I didn't come out I wouldn't be missed. The fence, the walk, the orange trees, the houses and the animals wouldn't miss me.

If I didn't come out everything would have to accept my absence. Everything would be forced to get along without me. How sad! I found it hard to accept that. I couldn't get along very well if I didn't know what was there when I got up every morning. The rain, my mom and dad, breakfast, school, and everything else had to be there. I couldn't get along if my everyday things were not there.

Now there was more light and I could see things around me more distinctly. I became aware of the solemn tick-tock of the old wind-up clock that had always been there on the same old table, forever, as far back as I could remember. Outside I could see the trees swaying with the wind, like pendulums. I didn't like it. All of a sudden the rain stopped and the wind slackened as if someone had turned off a switch. I got scared. I could not stand it in bed now, so I decided to try to get up. It was a long way to my clothes on the chair. Thinking it was cold, I stuck my leg out from under the covers to feel the air. No wonder I was sweating, it was hot because the heater was still on.

Usually, every morning, the fragrance of chorizo and eggs filled the kitchen air. Lots of smoke, a bright light, and the empty dishes that my dad had left after eating before going to work was what greeted me every morning when I got up. That morning as I walked into the kitchen there was no light, no dishes and no smoke. My mother and abuelita were sitting on little chairs, conversing in Spanish and not in their usual high-pitched tones. In a kind of surprised voice I asked, "Haven't you made anything yet?" I didn't wait for an answer and just kept on walking toward the bathroom. As I opened the door a gust of extremely cold air, looking for escape, paralyzed me. The bathroom had always been the coldest part of the house. The bathroom belonged to the cold and the boundaries set up were not to be violated by the warmth found elsewhere in the house. I didn't mind it though, except when I got up all warm and the cold hit me. I felt a little warmth for the cold in the house anyway. Once you get used to things they can be a source of warmth if one wants.

My father wasn't going to work that morning because it was raining. Construction workers don't work on rainy days. But now it had stopped raining and the sun was out. Strange how the clouds had disappeared so fast. Not one in sight. My mother refilled his thermos bottle with coffee. There was still no breakfast and my stomach was quickly becoming irritated with hunger pains. Then it struck me how nothing was going right. My mother was slow this morning, and I depended on her more than anyone else and she wasn't functioning right. She had been reminiscing about her past. She thought of her long deceased father who had died in her arms after being shot by a distant member of the family. And she had been seeing blood dripping from the sacred heart on the picture of Jesus Christ that hung over her bed.

My mother and abuelita talked and talked about this, trying to extract some sort of meaning from the vision. They worried about my uncle who was then in Mexico with his family, in Zacatecas. My mother and abuelita were looking sad. My father left for work and I left for school without breakfast. Funny, I wasn't sure how to cope with the situation of no breakfast. I had never been confronted with this problem before because breakfast had always been there. How many times had I ever gotten up without the usual things? Hardly ever. Everything was routine. I liked the routine, and I didn't want it changed, so I just excused the whole incident. I didn't want to have to hassle with it. No breakfast, that's all.

On the way to school I avoided my friends. This morning I didn't feel like walking with them like I usually did. I wanted to walk alone. My little brown and black dog tried to follow me. I threw him over the fence. I went through the alley to school. I asked myself why I was feeling so funny. I was acting differently and I didn't know why. I wasn't doing what I normally did. I started to run. I went splashing through all the puddles. I got soaking wet. My shoes made a funny squishing sound as I walked. It didn't matter that I wasn't doing the things that I usually did. The things around me had to accept that. I didn't look at the trees and I didn't walk with my friends. I didn't play with the animals. Everyone expected me to do what I usually did.

The teacher wouldn't let me go in the classroom all wet so I sat out in the hall by the heater to dry. The teacher had never liked me anyway. I thought that she probably felt relieved because she wouldn't have to put up with me for a whole class period. It seemed crazy for her to put herself out that way just to get rid of me. She would always catch me talking. She would always send me to the principal. That was her escape. The only thing was that I got along well with the principal. Actually, he wasn't really the principal. He was an asssistant. He was a Chicano. When he wasn't busy he would talk to me and tell me about all kinds of things. He would talk about how La Raza was a new type of people, and how we didn't have to wait long before things would change. I really wasn't aware of all the things that he was referring to. I didn't see anything that needed changing. He said that the school needed some Spanish-speaking teachers. I never asked him why. In the light of reality, I just could not see a brown face looking down at me and sending me to the principal's office all the time. I didn't even know why it was necessary to go to school. One didn't need to go to school to learn things. Still, he would talk about the reasons why Chicanos like me would get in trouble. I didn't know there were reasons for it. I always thought it just happened.

I sat there over the heater drying and I thought about why I never did what teachers told me to do. How could I, knowing that teachers were stupid. I found this out when I was in the class for the mentally retarded in the third grade. All of my friends were in that class and I wanted to be there too. All I had to do was be bad and not do any of the work, or pretend that I did not understand. The teacher would try to get us to identify objects. Every time we guessed right we would get a prize. One week she had fruit and some of us whose parents were out of work got organized. Everyday before class we would meet and decide who was going to guess the right answers. We did that so that everyone would get a chance to take some of the fruit home. Every time someone got the right answer she would give him a point. At the end of the day the one with the highest score would get the fruit. It was like taking candy from a baby. Sometimes I wondered if it wasn't really she who was mentally retarded.

The bell rang and the kids didn't come out for recess. Only the teacher came out. She told me that it was raining again and that the class was staying inside for recess. She warned me that I had better not start any trouble if I went back into the room. I was to go to the back of the class and have one of the kids in my group give me the reading assignment. I couldn't stand the teacher talking to me. She smelled. She had bad breath and I always had to turn my head a little so that I wouldn't have to confront her smell. But the trouble was that she made me face her. She insisted that I look at her when she spoke. She must have been sadistic. After that I learned to hold my breath and give her smell lots of room.

I went to the back of the room and sat with one of the pretty Chicana girls, but she moved away before I could explain. I didn't blame her though, because she always got in trouble for one reason or another when she was with me. I looked out the window at the rain. It was falling hard, nowhere in particular, just everywhere. Daydreaming, looking out the window, made time go by fast it seemed, but it didn't. The water was coming down fast and hard, like bullets coming at me and I couldn't move away in time. I fell off the chair, trying to regain my balance. The whole class turned around and stared down at me menacingly, as if I had really disturbed them. It was only recess and no one was doing anything. The water scared me. It reminded me of the hard times we had to go through when it rained.

The sky was dark. There was no light to see, and I needed to recognize the things I wanted to recognize. I couldn't see anything right. There were no bright trees. The sidewalk that I always walked on was camouflaged by that transparent liquid water that made the sidewalk look like long canals, those found near the fields and the orchards. I hated it. I didn't want to look anymore. Everything outside looked cold and I began to feel cold. I didn't feel like a part of anything. Everything was missing. My everyday things were missing. The teacher didn't care and was on my back and all the kids stayed away because they would get in trouble if they came near. I looked hard into the sky again, trying to find a bright spot like the sun. Nothing was there and there was no warmth. The trees were dancing and making fun of me because I didn't know what was going on. I wanted my mother. She would take care of me. I wanted to go home.

I told the teacher that I wanted to go home because I was sick. She grabbed me by the neck and took me to the closet. She forced me to sit. She told me to be quiet and that I wasn't going to fool her. She said that she knew me well enough and that I was only up to something. I looked at her with hate in my eyes. I turned away abruptly and just put my head to my knees and squeezed tight. Then, like a flash in my mind, I saw the sacred heart about to burst. Blood everywhere in my head. I knew something was wrong now. I got up, opened the closet door, and ripped through the classroom not caring what I hit or who I hurt. The teacher attempted to stop me at the door, but I bit into her old ugly white hand and she was forced to let go. I raced down the hallway and panicked when I saw the Chicano principal who was walking out of his office. He too tried to stop me, but I was going too fast and evaded his grasp. Finally I was out the door and ran down the middle of the canal. I looked up at the rain again and it came crashing down on my face. I never did anything to it. Why was it hitting me?

I slowed down and began to walk. I got off the canal path to walk on the big river where the cars passed. I looked into the rain and beyond it toward the sky. It was dark. There was no hope, and no light in the sky. I hadn't known that the things I usually felt and saw had so many different personalities. I didn't know that things weren't as I had seen them all the time. Things change. Time changes things. I saw my house up ahead. I broke into a run, but then I hesitated as the house began to sway back and forth with the wind. I saw it contract and expand as if panting, like when you're tired of running, or when you make love.

Juan Garcia was born in Oxnard, California, in 1949. He and his family moved to San Jose, California, in 1957. He attended San Jose State College and the University of California at Santa Cruz, where he majored in sociology.

Vocabulary Study

Juan Garcia says: "I hadn't known that the things I usually felt and saw had so many different personalities." What are some of the *personalities* he sees in each of the following? Can you discover any reason for the particular associations he makes at different points in his essay? Does his use of these words bear out his thesis that things change?

A. rain/water
B. heat
C. cold
D. wind
E. trees

Questions on Form and Content

A. How do the first few paragraphs of Juan Garcia's essay support this statement: "I couldn't get along if my everyday things were not there"?

B. What evidence does Juan give of his family's poverty?

C. How does Juan reveal his inability to cope with what is happening to him?

D. What examples does he give of racial prejudice? Are these supported?

E. How does Juan feel about La Raza?

F. Of what significance is the vision of the Sacred Heart?

G. From whose point of view is the essay written? Is it consistent?

H. Is the over-all tone of the essay optimistic or pessimistic? Support your answer with specific reference to sections of the essay.

I. Another Chicano wrote: "In our village all the neighbors call my father Don Jose. But when he left Texas and went to Michigan all the people there called him Joe." (Alfredo Vizcarra, *El Espejo,* Octavio Ignacio Romano-V., ed. Berkeley: 1969, Quinto Sol Publications, p. 95) How would this man's observation fit in with the general distinction between Anglo and Chicano societies which Juan Garcia implies in his essay?

Suggestions for Writing

A. Juan Garcia mentions that he was classified as mentally retarded in the third grade. Why? Write an essay in which you discuss the effects of racial stereotypes on education. Before you begin, you may wish to discover what provisions are made for minority groups in your state, especially in the area of testing (I.Q. and skills tests) for placement in schools.

B. A Chicano professor, at a recent convention of teachers concerned with the problems of educating Mexican-Americans, observed: "Only in the United States, where we worship knowing less and look down on knowing more, could a bilingual child be classified as disadvantaged." According to this line of thought, who are the real disadvantaged and why? Write an essay in which you discuss contemporary attitudes toward disadvantaged youth. What recommendations would you make to solve the problems you observe?

C. Juan says of his assistant principal's proposal to hire Spanish-speaking teachers, "In the light of reality, I just could not see a brown face looking down at me and sending me to the principal's office all the time." What are some of the implications of this statement? Write an essay in which you discuss the advantages and/or disadvantages of hiring minority teachers to teach minority students.

D. When Juan Garcia says, "I needed to recognize the things I wanted to recognize," he expresses a common human desire. Discuss the impact of this desire on one of these areas of perception: race; male-female relationships; man's relation to the external world; self-concept.

E. Robert Frost once said, "I could lose everything tomorrow and not be surprised." Compare this attitude toward life with Juan Garcia's? What does each reflect about the personality and maturity of its author? Which do you think is more healthy and why?

F. The poet Shelley wrote: "We—are we not formed, as notes of music are, / For one another, though dissimilar." Relate this quotation to each of the selections included in this chapter.

G. Compare or contrast the styles of each of the essays in this chapter. How does the use of language in each reflect age? race? intended audience?

H. Write a paper in which you (a) define the concept of La Raza and (b) defend or attack its basic premises.

I. The two quotations below reflect a similar attitude toward fear. What is it? Write an essay in which you present your opinion of the place of fear in man's life.

> "How can a sensitive and alive person ever feel secure? Because of the very conditions of our existence, we cannot feel secure about anything. Our thoughts and insights are at best partial truth; . . . our life and health are subject to accidents beyond our control. If we make a decision, we can never be certain of the outcome; any decision implies a risk of failure, and if it does not imply it, it has

> not been a decision in the true sense of the word. We can never be certain of the outcome of our best efforts. The result always depends on many factors which transcend our capacity of control. Just as a sensitive and alive person cannot avoid being sad, he cannot avoid feeling insecure. The psychic task which a person can and must set for himself, is not to feel secure, but to be able to tolerate insecurity, without panic and undue fear . . . : Free man is by necessity insecure; thinking man by necessity uncertain—*Erich Fromm*

> "He has not learned the lessson of life who does not every day surmount a fear.—*Ralph Waldo Emerson*

J. Discuss the attitude Juan Garcia had, as a youth, toward education. Consider, particularly, his words: "I didn't even know why it was necesssary to go to school. One didn't need to go to school to learn things."

K. Walt Whitman, who lived from 1819 to 1892, received a meager formal education, leaving school at eleven. He was later an office boy, printer's assistant, school teacher, reporter, editor, and, during the Civil War, a medical orderly. His chief literary work was *Leaves of Grass*, which he enlarged and revised throughout his life. Use his two poems, which follow, as the basis for an essay in which you discuss the ideal approach to education. What primary differences in attitude toward education are reflected in the two poems? What are the merits of each? How do the poems, considered together, condemn our formal and traditional educational system? How might Mr. Douglass react to the ideas these poems express? Mr. Hughes? Black Elk? Mr. Garcia?

Beginning My Studies

Walt Whitman

Beginning my studies the first step pleas'd me so much,
The mere fact consciousness, these forms, the power of motion,
The least insect or animal, the senses, eyesight, love,
The first step I say awed me and pleas'd me so much,
I have hardly gone and hardly wish'd to go any farther,
But stop and loiter all the time to sing it in ecstatic songs.

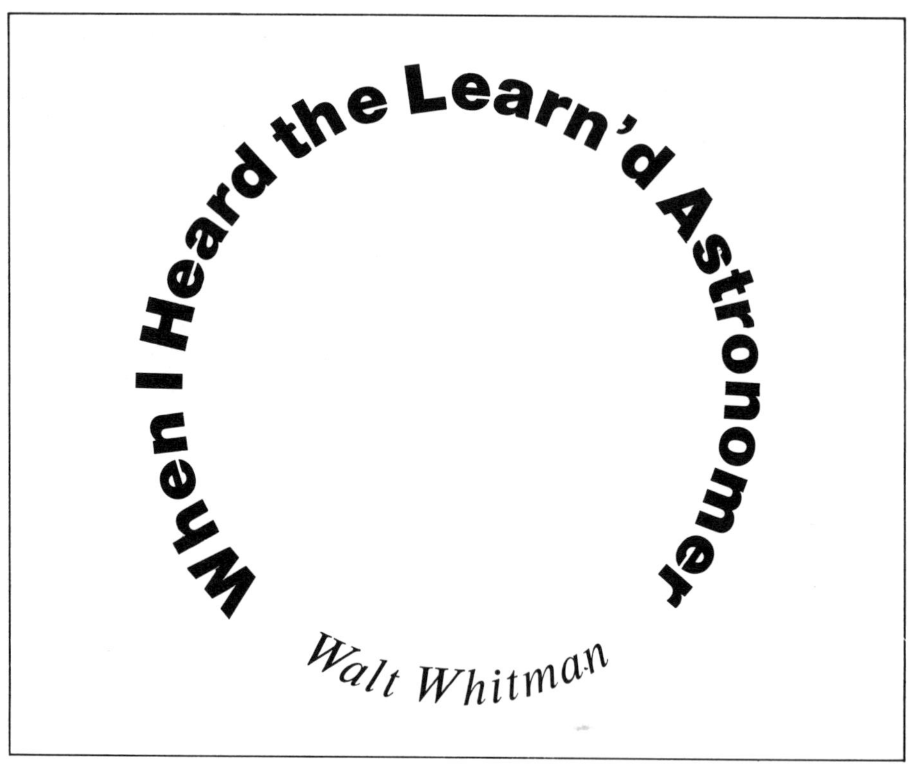

When I heard the learn'd astronomer,
When the proofs, the figures, were ranged in columns before me,
When I was shown the charts and diagrams, to add, divide, and measure them,
When I sitting heard the astronomer where he lectured with much applause in
the lecture-room,
How soon unaccountable I became tired and sick,
Till rising and gliding out I wander'd off by myself,
In the mystical moist night-air, and from time to time,
Look'd up in perfect silence at the stars.

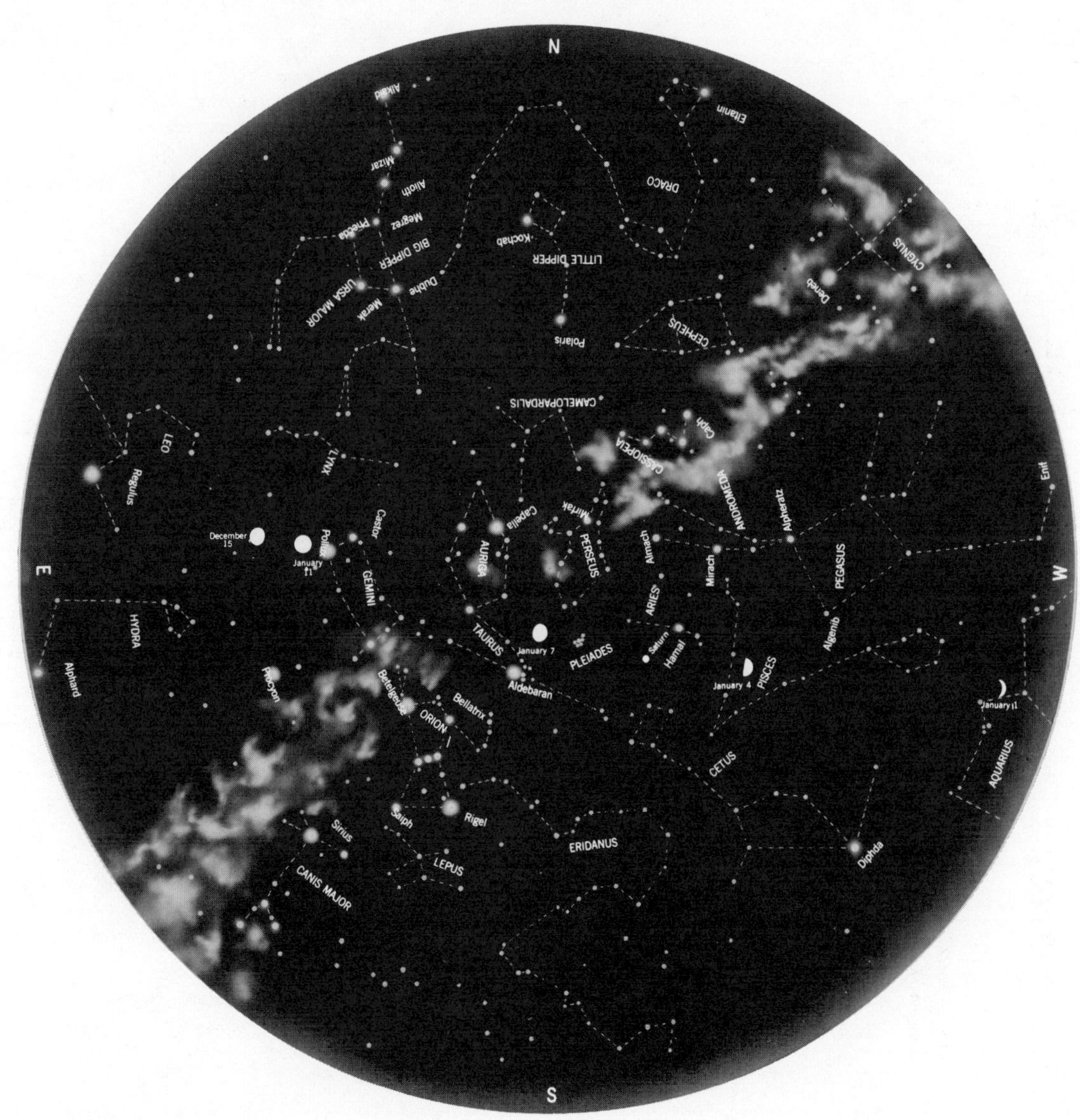

CELESTIAL EVENTS

American Museum of Natural History

Sentences, first, must be clear. No one has a right to puzzle his reader over his intended meaning. Next, sentences should be concise in that the writer should avoid unnecessary wordiness, one of the worst weaknesses in student writing. Effective sentences must have variety, both in length and in pattern. The subject-verb-complement order is the favorite and simplest structure in English, but its constant repetition can become monotonous. Varying the placement of modifiers and using inversion and subordination give needed diversity. Sentence structure can be varied too by the use of loose and periodic sentences. Sentences are called periodic if the main thought is not completed until the end, loose if the main thought is completed before the end.

Sentences must, of course, be grammatically correct; tenses must be consistent, subjects and verbs and pronouns and antecedents must agree, pronoun references must be clear and accurate, parallel constructions must be kept parallel, and elements of like meaning should be co-ordinated. Repetition of either words or sounds, when pointless, should be avoided.

Any good grammar workbook or handbook will give you explanations and examples illustrating parallelism, subordination, inversion, loose and periodic sentences, and the various other patterns of sentence structure. Your own teacher will point out errors and lapses in your papers. We call your attention to the differing sentence structures as they appear in this text, with the hope that you will be able to incorporate some of them into your own writing.

As an example of these elements study the second paragraph of the following essay. Mr. Mayer's sentences here are clear, concise, and varied both in length and in pattern. He uses no unnecessary words or phrases and never makes the reader puzzle over the meaning of a sentence.

The sentences vary in length from three words in the shortest sentence, the last one (a fragment), to fifty-two words in the longest sentence, the second one. The eight sentences of the paragraph vary in pattern too.

The author gains variety through using inversion and subordination and through varying the placement of modifiers. Sentences 2 and 5 have inverted elements. In sentences 2, 5, and 6 subordinate ideas are placed in dependent clauses.

Modifiers occur in varying positions throughout the paragraph, too. Some precede the words they modify, as *razor, dirty, red, lacrosse,* and *rival* all precede the words they describe; some modifiers are phrases which follow the words they modify, as *in a red Mustang with a lacrosse player from a rival fraternity* follows *necking* in sentence 2. Others are dependent clauses either preceding the elements they modify ("If you look at five more rocks" in sentence 5) or following the modified elements ("they'll never be able to put you back together" in sentence 6).

Such an analysis of a paragraph you have written should help you to determine whether or not you are using sufficient variety in your sentence structure. Of course, you must be sure that your sentences are clear and concise too.

So You Want to Be a Dropout

Tom Mayer

You are in the middle of a pre-exam-period dead week frantically studying rocks for the imminent five-hour identification final in elementary geology, when suddenly you decide you don't give a damn any more. It simply isn't worth the effort; you're going to fail no matter what you do. You haven't studied all term because the course was dull and the professor a fraud, and now it's too late.

But geology isn't your only problem. Recently you've decided that your friends are shallow, juvenile, and phony; your roommate snores, steals your razor blades, and leaves his dirty underwear on the armchair; and to cap it all, your girlfriend, Cynthia, has been seen repeatedly necking in a red Mustang with a lacrosse player from a rival fraternity. You feel hemmed in, harried, harassed; you haven't shaved for a month, bathed for ten days, eaten anything but Dexamil since day before yesterday, or slept in a week. You need peace and quiet and lots of it. If you look

□ Tom Mayer, "So You Want to Be a Dropout," in *The Troubled Campus* (Boston, 1966), pp. 42-49.

at five more rocks, you'll snap. They'll put you in the nut house, but you'll be so far gone they'll never be able to put you back together. You've got to get out. Out, out, OUT.

But how? Your mind churns wildly. Then, in a moment of revelation, you remember that the mechanics of dropping out are simple. Nothing to it. Most colleges are glad to be rid of you. Overcrowded classes, lack of dormitory space, not enough laboratory equipment. At the big state universities you're nothing but a number anyway. All you have to do is tell your adviser you want to take some time off to think it over. But tell him you're going to be gone only a year, or a semester, even though at the moment you're planning to emigrate to Zululand. Never burn bridges.

If your grades are in shape, there shouldn't be any problem. The worst that could happen is that you'd have to talk to a junior dean, explain to him that classwork has lost its kinetic excitement, that you feel under intense pressure and want your life to be inner-directed. You don't feel that you're doing the college experience justice, so you want to take some time out to reexamine your values.

The dean brushes a graying but boyish shock of hair off his forehead, taps his mahogany desk with his fingernails, fills his pipe, sucks on it a few times, lights it, and tells you that your problem is fairly common. Many students suffer from your brand of malaise; it's become an integral aspect of higher education; the university understands and sympathizes. You're welcome to take off as much time as you want; the only things you should do are tell your draft board and let the university know when you want to come back. You thank the dean, shake his hand, and leave his office dwelling happily on your forthcoming year in Europe, African safari, beach shack at Malibu, or muscle-building job among the colorful he-men on a pulling unit in the West Texas oilfields.

The real problems of dropping out are not, you reflect, connected with university rules or administration attitudes. As a matter of fact, the university has been surprisingly understanding. Perhaps you've been doing it an injustice all along. But your parents are going to be quite something else. If they're liberal, urban, well-educated, psychiatry-oriented, reasonably hip, relatively modern types—people who read the *New Republic,* have a family psychoanalyst, and worked as volunteers for Adlai Stevenson—the chances are you won't have much trouble when you break the news. A sigh from Mother, a suppressed grunt from Dad. They want you to be sure you know what you're doing, in much the same way that they wanted you to be sure you knew what you were doing last summer when you went to Mississippi, but once you convince them your head's screwed on right, that you merely want some time to find yourself, Dad says he's with you all the way and Mother nods agreement.

But God help you if Dad's a dirt farmer, insurance salesman, bean picker, truck driver, Republican, corporation executive, or mechanical engineer. He'll probably hit the ceiling. He's been spending a lot of money, maybe as much as three thousand dollars a year, to keep you in school; he's given you every opportunity, and you turn around and throw it in his face. You try to reason with him by saying that you only want some time to think. That, he replies, is what you go to college for. But, you say, I couldn't do any constructive thinking at college because there were too many pressures. I want to be inner-directed. Pressures, says your father. You think a corporation executive doesn't have pressures? Hell, yes, he has pressures. You gotta *live* with pressures.

Or Dad and Mother may be deeply hurt. They genuinely don't understand. They both came from poor families; they never went to college themselves; it's been a financial handicap all their lives. They've worked so desperately to put you in a position where you'll have some choice in life. They can't understand what went wrong. They drink nothing stronger than beer; they took you to church when you were young; Dad spent all his spare time with you—remember that fishing trip to Lake Chicahoocha when you were eight?—they've loved you more than anything else in the world: where did they make their mistake? But, you say, I'm only planning to take a year off, not turn Communist or something. But why? cries your mother. Yes, says your father, why? Don't we have a right to know?

So you try to explain that at college you were spinning your wheels. College ought to be a place where you do creative things with your abilities, not just dreary routines. There wasn't time to think or pursue your own interests.

Your father says he doesn't know anything about dreary routines, only that when he was a kid growing up back in the thirties, when things were really tough, a kid was lucky to be in college at all. A college kid had a job, a good job, waiting for him when he got out. Aha, you say. But not any more. Now you've got to go on to graduate school, to business school, or medical school, or law school, or veterinary school. You've got to have an M.A. or a Ph.D. to teach even. You have to be sure before you get in so deeply. Your father says he hadn't thought of it that way, and you think maybe you're getting somewhere; however, your mother begins to cry hysterically, and that ends the conversation.

As always, arguing with your parents leaves you in a state of fist-clenched frustration. You are never able to express yourself fully to them. How do you explain motivations that are so subtle and deeply rooted that often you are not clearly aware of them yourself?

Dropping out probably reflects a good deal more than mere distaste for routines, slovenly roommates, and elementary geology; in reality, it may be a manifestation of some such psychological problem as a lifelong struggle to break out of a family pattern—perhaps you were forced to go to Dad's prep school, and Dad's college, and the prospect of graduation and living at home and going into the family investment firm or dry-goods business or grocery-store chain or optical company is more than you can stand. Possibly you went to an inadequate public high school, and in your freshman year at an Ivy League college you found yourself so ill-prepared, overworked, socially inept, and plain scared that you developed a serious sense of inferiority. Everyone seemed wittier and more intelligent and better adjusted than you, so that life at college evolved into an infinite series of real and imagined humiliations. Or perhaps you came to college after four or more years at prep school and found that nothing stimulated you, that on the whole your college teachers were inferior to prep-school masters, and that, since college courses tended to be dull and superficial, the excitement and purpose had gone out of learning. Or you might be in love and get married, but either because you are poor or because your parents refuse to support you, you have to leave school and begin to earn a living. Or, sadly, you may have gotten a girl pregnant. Or perhaps you are dead earnest about pursuing a career in which a college education is of no substantial value. Professional athletes, entertainers, actors, musicians might fall into this category.

The point is that beneath your irritation with the surfaces of college life, you suspect some flaw in your own personality or background, or else you feel that attending college is essentially a frivolous and time-wasting undertaking. For you, even if you don't plan to depart college permanently, dropping out is a serious business; it seems a sharp and fateful departure from the norm of your generation, and it involves a major decision, arrived at by you, and by you alone, after a great deal of self-examination.

Finally, however, no matter why you left, or say you left, you get settled into your new job or apartment or marriage and begin life on the outside. Your parents have been reconciled to the inevitable or have disowned you; the draft board is breathing down your neck, but you're stalling them; in short, you ought to be happier than ever before. No papers, no classes, no pressures. Time to think. Time to set your life in order, decide what you really think about Zen, what ought to be done in Vietnam, how to handle de Gaulle, how to stop police brutality in New York.

You sink into a pattern of sleep and independent study, or travel, or begin an exciting relevant job, and everything ought to be fine, but predictably enough, it isn't. Rough-necking turns out to be much harder than studying rocks, your African safari didn't pan out, or your year in Europe is off because your father won't finance it. He says he'll be glad to teach you the glue business from the bottom up, but he'll be damned if he'll ante up good dollars for you to waste playing around with a bunch of screwballs and perverts in a lousy city like Paris. He's only been to Europe once, as a guest of the goddamn government, but you can take it from him, there's nothing there but a bunch of perverts and bedbugs.

Even your social life is awful. You've been away from home for a while; you've lost contact with most of your old friends from high school, and those you still know seem changed. Or maybe you've changed, but anyway, there's nobody to talk to, you never have interesting discussions, and the girls are strictly bad news. They wear too much makeup, and most of the good-looking ones are married or have moved away or are in college. You remember faithless Cynthia longingly.

Time drags. You are not so innocent as to think that college will be a bed of roses when you get back, but at least things happened there. Or perhaps you've become intrigued with the glue business but realize you need more chemistry before you can come up with any significant innovations. Several nights you've stayed late down in the vat room fooling around with a new formula for heat-resistant, cold-resistant, spit-resistant, sweet-and-sour-tasting, water-repellent stamp stickum, but after several explosions and one fire, you're modest enough and sufficiently objective to admit that you simply haven't got the background.

Of course there's always the possibility that you'll be one of the dropouts who stays out, in which case you may become a plumber or electrician or mechanic or brush salesman, or you might join the Army, or start a window-washing service. You might even make good. Perhaps you'll be like Dr. Edwin Land, who left Harvard, invented the Polaroid camera, and made about forty million dollars in the process. Or Sandy Koufax, who left the University of Cincinnati, went into the major leagues, and improved the curve ball. Or perhaps you'll be a writer or a painter. You always thought you were deeper, more talented, more given to reflection and philosophy than your contemporaries, and when you write your first short story—a delicate and melancholy tale about the time your great-aunt Gertrude had hepatitis—and sell it to the *New Yorker* for $462.15, you feel that truly you have a future in the arts. The social stigma attached to spending your life without a degree is something you are sure you can overcome; in fact, if you are at all successful, being a dropout has considerable reverse snob appeal.

But the chances are that out of boredom or fresh enthusiasm or new interests or the blunt realization that degrees mean more money, you'll return to college willingly. You'll go back with reservations and misgivings: you'll know that college hasn't changed, and perhaps in your heart of hearts you'll still believe that you could and should be doing something better, something less nebulous and more important—but you will go back. Your friends will be pleased, your parents will be ecstatic. Soon you'll be settled back in the old groove: classes, labs, fraternity parties, exams, rushing, football games, quizzes, papers, and Cynthia, or someone like her. It will be almost as if you'd never been away, except that late in those all-night bull sessions, when the jocks have gone to bed and you're tired of talking girls and the conversation turns to serious topics like values and meaning and significance, you'll be a man of experience, an intellect to be reckoned with.

Tom Mayer was born in Chicago in 1943, attended Harvard University for two years before dropping out, and Stanford University on a Stegner fellowship. He has worked in the oil fields, for the Santa Fe opera, and for five years as a life guard and swimming coach. A contributor to *The New Yorker, Story, Harper's Magazine,* and *The Atlantic,* he is also the author of a book of short stories entitled *Bubble Gum and Kipling.*

Vocabulary Study

One of the vocabulary problems that plagues students is the confusion of words that are pronounced alike and spelled similarly. In the following excerpts from the preceding essay, you have a choice between the correct form and the one often confused with it. Select the form which is correct in context.

A. The (*imminent, eminent*) five-hour identification final in elementary geology.

B. You haven't studied all term because the *(coarse, course)* was dull and the professor a fraud, and now *(its, it's) (to, too, two)* late.

C. You need *(piece, peace)* and *(quite, quiet)* and lots of it.

D. Even though at the moment you're planning to *(immigrate, emigrate)* to Zululand.

E. But your parents are going to be *(quite, quiet)* something else.

F. If *(they're, their)* liberal, urban, well-educated

G. Once you convince them your head's screwed on *(rite, write, right)*

H. There were *(too, to, two)* many pressures.

I. Don't we have a *(rite, write, right)* to know?

J. The draft board is breathing down *(you're, your)* neck, but *(you're, your)* stalling them

K. Begin an exciting *(relevant, reverent)* job

Questions on Form and Content

A. Locate the topic sentence in each paragraph in the essay.

B. Analyze the sentence structure in the third paragraph of the essay.

C. From whose viewpoint is the article written? How does the style change when the student meets with the dean, with his parents?

D. The student says that the mechanics of dropout are simple. What are they, as he describes them?

E. What two things does the junior dean tell the student to do?

F. What kind of parents are likely to give the least trouble when their son announces his decision to withdraw from college?

G. Which type may be deeply hurt?

H. What reasons for dropping out of college, other than a distaste for routines, slovenly roommates, and elementary geology, does the author discuss?

I. What is wrong with the student's life after he has withdrawn from college?

J. The author says that the student will probably return to college willingly. Why?

Suggestions for Writing

A. "For you, even if you don't plan to depart college permanently, dropping out is a serious business; it seems a sharp and fateful departure from the norm of your generation, and it involves a major decision, arrived at by you, and by you alone, after a great deal of self-examination," writes Mr. Mayer. Have you ever been a dropout? If so, why? Why did you decide to return to school?

B. Statistics show that only fifty percent of freshmen enrolled in college graduate. Have you ever considered withdrawing from college? If so, why? Why did you change your mind?

C. How realistic and valid does the author's portrayal of a student dropout seem to you? Have you ever felt, looked, and acted as this student did? Have you observed others who behaved similarly? Illustrate your comments with specific instances from your own observations.

D. Have you ever visited a dean? If so, describe the reasons for, and results of, your visit. Did you notice that the dean's vocabulary and sentence structure differed markedly from your own? If so, try to illustrate that difference as you describe your visit.

E. How do you think your parents would react if you told them that you had decided to withdraw from college? Could you place them among the types Mr. Mayer describes? Write a description of an imaginary interview with them in which you announce that you are about to become a dropout.

F. The author writes: "As always, arguing with your parents leaves you in a state of fist-clenched frustration." Comment.

G. After you've been away from home for a while and returned, have you found your old friends changed and your social life awful? If so, how and why? If not, why not?

H. Write a paper in which you discuss one or more dropouts who have made good.

I. Will college be of substantial value in the career you intend to pursue? If so, how and why?

J. Discuss the social stigma attached to life without a college degree.

K. Discuss the reverse snob appeal of being a dropout.

L. In your "heart of hearts," do you "believe that you could and should be doing something better, something less nebulous and more important" than going to college? If so, why and what?

M. Why are you going to college?

N. The term "dropout" is usually used to refer to students who do not finish high school. In 1964, the United States Office of Education spent a quarter of a million dollars in twenty large cities in an attempt to identify such dropouts and to persuade them to return to school. Of 30,411 dropouts, 10,015 agreed to come back. No one knows how many of that ten thousand stayed until graduation. Should every young man or woman complete twelve years of school? Why or why not?

O. In many major cities, bus placards urge marginal students to stay in school with such warnings as those shown on the facing page. Comment on the values to which such cards appeal.

Education is for the birds.

(The birds who want to get ahead.)

To get a good job, get a good education

A Public Service of Outdoor Advertising

BOY.

Drop out of school now and that's what they'll call you all your working life.

To get a good job, get a good education.

Educated Dropouts

Henry Elliot Weinstein

COLLEGE TRAINED YOUTHS SHUN THE PROFESSIONS FOR A FREE-FORM LIFE — JOHN SPITZER OF HARVARD IS CABBIE; CLARA PERKINSON, SMITH, CARRIES THE MAIL — OPTING OUT OF "THE SYSTEM"

SAN FRANCISCO—At four o'clock on a Saturday morning, John Spitzer's alarm rings and he rolls out of bed to drive a taxi until 1:30 in the afternoon. He has had less than two hours' sleep because he tends bar Friday nights until 2 a.m. at Andre's bistro in the North Beach district.

Across the bay in Berkeley, John Simmons is winding up his graveyard shift as a letter-sorter at the post office. Some of the mail he processes may be delivered by Clara Perkinson, who covers several miles a day as a letter-carrier in Berkeley.

For Chip Oliver, the day will be spent cooking and cleaning at the Mustard Seed, a natural foods restaurant in Mill Valley in suburban San Francisco.

□ "Educated Dropouts," Henry Elliot Weinstein, *Wall Street Journal,* Pacific Coast Edition, 82:123 (June 24, 1970), pp. 1, 19.

The jobs are all mundane by most people's standards. But the four people filling them aren't. All are college educated but chose to drop out of conventional society and the careers they were pursuing. An apparently growing number of young, white and affluent college graduates are doing the same, providing one more indication of the pervasiveness of youthful revolt in the U.S.

Impressive Credentials

Cab-driver Spitzer, who speaks three foreign languages, graduated from Harvard with highest honors and once helped edit *Ramparts* magazine. Mr. Simmons, the mail-sorter, attended Harvard law school after receiving a degree from the University of California at Berkeley, where he was a student senator. Miss Perkinson, the mail carrier, graduated from Smith College, where she majored in government. Mr. Oliver, the cook, was better known as starting guard on two Rose Bowl teams at the University of Southern California and as a left linebacker for the Oakland Raiders. He quit pro football (annual income $25,000) to join the "One World" family commune and work in its restaurant.

The four speak in a similar vein of the reasons that led to their changed lives. All talk of disenchantment with the Vietnam war and what they call America's racism. They believe that American society as it now is constituted has little place for them, at least in conventional careers. They express no concern about financial security, unlike their parents, who grew up in the Depression.

No one knows how many educated young people are shunning the jobs and professions for which they were trained. Undoubtedly the number is small, but some sociologists think it is growing. Philip Slater, a professor of sociology at Brandeis University, says dropping out is more widespread than ever before. "The universities are churning out vast numbers of people who don't want to join the system," he asserts.

Lament From a Coach

Some critics of the dropouts argue that their choice is immoral, amounting to an abandonment of the world and its problems. Mr. Oliver's line coach at USC, Marv Goux, laments, "I hate to see a fine young man like this who does have the ability to be a leader in our society go this way."

Whatever the ethics of their choice, the educated dropouts are clearly a new phenomenon in some ways. Mr. Slater, author of a critique of American society called "The Pursuit of Loneliness," says, "What's happening now is very different than those people who decided to join the utopian communities of Oneida and Brook Farm in the 1840s." The utopians, he contends, often had clear religious or political ideologies. "Now, people without a definitive alternative, without a specific ideology, are simply making a self-conscious rejection of the existing culture," Mr. Slater says.

The dropouts among today's youth share an enthusiasm for do-it-yourself projects. The bearded Mr. Spitzer, whose father is an executive of a Crown Zellerbach Corp. division, has taught himself auto repair "so that I don't have to depend on the people at the Volkswagen shop." He lives simply in a large, old house in the inexpensive but sunny section of San Francisco called Bernal Heights. He shares the house with an unmarried couple, bakes his own bread and has started making clothes.

Similarly self-reliant, Miss Perkinson says that being able to perform chores for herself is one of the main reasons she really likes her letter-carrier job. "I've discovered a new sense of my physical strength from lifting mail sacks," she says. "It's nice to know you're physically capable. And it's great to be able to spend half your working hours out-of-doors, particularly in California." Miss Perkinson is an attractive 125-pound brunette.

Still in Shape

Unlike many athletes who get flabby when they stop competing, Chip Oliver is trim and still has the muscular appearance of the outstanding linebacker he was. He has lost weight—50 pounds from his playing weight of 230—and he attributes this to a natural foods diet that excludes meat and any fruits or vegetables not grown with organic fertilizers.

Mr. Oliver rises early every morning to meditate and do yoga exercises. Then he "goes on schedule" with the 30 other members of his commune in Larkspur, which is a few miles from their restaurant. Everyone joins in cleaning the old Victorian house, cooking, taking care of the "family's" children and working in the restaurant. The former athlete's blond hair is longer than it was in his playing days. He says he has never felt more "together."

John Simmons, who with his wife, Charlotte, lives in a flat near the Berkeley campus with another couple, appears relieved to be out of the intense atmosphere they encountered at UC and Harvard. Although he concedes that life still has some of the same ups and downs it did while he was a student, there has been one marked change for the better. A rigorous diet over the past six months has trimmed him down to 190 pounds from a high of 276—his lowest weight since starting high school.

Mr. Simmons left Harvard law school after finishing one year in June 1968. He then worked for a while as a clothing salesman, a job he quit because he didn't like the "hype" (fraud) involved in selling. A short stint followed as an assistant in an OEO legal services project. Then he and Charlotte traveled around the country and through Canada in a Volkswagen camper. They say they "really loved" Canada and may return someday. This wouldn't be to avoid the draft. A knee injury suffered in high school football eliminated that problem for Mr. Simmons.

After the trip, John remained unemployed until his money ran out. Then he took his letter-sorter job, which he describes as "very alienating—you're constantly reminded of your relationship to a machine." Charlotte does part-time work as a Kelly Girl. "We're not sure about what we're doing now," she says, "but we don't want the other thing," referring to a more conventional life.

John has been a rock and roll devotee for many years, and he has periodic thoughts about seeking a job as a disc jockey. But at present both he and Charlotte express a desire to learn some sort of craft so that they can move to the country and "won't be chained to the city for sustenance."

A long-time activist, John compares the growth of his alienation with the different periods in the career of folk-rock singer Bob Dylan, a spokesman for America's disaffected youths. "When I was a senior, Dylan's 'Subterranean Homesick Blues' came out," says John as he pulls off his cowboy boots and runs a hand through his shoulder-length hair. "Remember, that's the one where he says 'twenty years in school and then they put you on the day shift.' That touched so many nerves for so many people; that said it all."

Off the Treadmill

Disenchantment with her Smith College experience was a factor in Clara Perkinson's decision to "get off the treadmill" after graduation in 1968, she says. College involved a lot of meaningless busywork, she says, not "the intellectual and emotional challenge I expected." She still reads "voraciously" and does a lot of hiking and camping in the mountainous areas near Berkeley.

Chip Oliver feels he has solved the problem of a treadmill life. "We're putting on a demonstration here," he says of the One World family. "We're showing people a new way of life. We're showing people that as soon as you start loving and relating to people, you'll find those people loving and relating to you."

While waiting for Mr. Oliver to return from his nightly post-dinner running and yoga stint, a reporter is greeted warmly by several of the young women who also live at the commune. The walls of the family's living room are dotted with quotes from the Scriptures, and a mix of classical and rock music emanates from a stereo.

Mr. Oliver expresses a lack of concern about economic security and financial advancement. When he joined the family, he donated $5,000 to help the group open another chapter in a defunct University of California fraternity house. All the possessions of the family are "held in common" says Mr. Oliver, and all incomes are pooled. He was a sociology student when he was at USC. Now he has become a fan of Buckminster Fuller. He also says he's "getting into painting, photography and acting," the last a hobby he began to pursue in the off-season while still playing football.

Although he still enjoys athletics, Mr. Oliver predicts the dawning of a "new age" where pro football will be no more. "People won't be doing things for money," he asserts. "People will be doing things for themselves rather than watching things being done."

Working as an Equal

Clara Perkinson says the letter-carrier job "doesn't satisfy all my intellectual desires, but it's very challenging compared to being a secretary." Her way of life also has been affected by the feminist ideal movement. "I enjoy working with men on an equal basis, not as a subordinate, which is the case in almost every job," she says.

Prof. Slater asserts there simply aren't enough paths for today's college graduates to follow. "A lot of young people would like to get into things that involve their sophistication and creativity," he says. "But they see activities like teaching and social work perpetuating what they don't want perpetuated."

That's how John Spitzer felt about his short stint as a high school teacher. "High schools are prisons," he says. "The kids don't want to be there, and after teaching for a summer at Berkeley High I concluded that kids should be out in the streets."

Although he has left the lucrative confines of pro football, Chip Oliver still has some friends in the pro ranks who are sympathetic to his choice. Tim Rossovich, All-Pro defensive end for the Philadelphia Eagles and a former teammate at USC, says of Mr. Oliver: "He doesn't care about driving a Cadillac or wearing custom-made suits. Let the man live his life." He adds, "If the world situation keeps going on like it is, you'll see a lot of people dropping out, and not just in athletics."

Some parents of the disaffected young people also are sympathetic. John G. Simmons, an activist Lutheran minister and a hospital administrator in North Hollywood, Calif., says his son is "too damn bright to be caught up in the system and he refuses to do it." Then he adds, somewhat wistfully, "But I hope he finds his niche soon, lest he lose his cutting edge."

There is a touch of uncertainty in some of the dropouts that suggests their rejection of society may not be permanent. Miss Perkinson admits her mail job "doesn't offer enough creative responsibility" and she is thinking about going to law school. Mr. Simmons and his wife hope to save enough money from their jobs to go to Europe.

John Spitzer finds relief from his taxi-driving by playing the piano and working on a play. He also likes bartending at Andre's, where a steady, friendly clientele dance, shoot pool and devour Irish coffee and "red lions," the house special.

But the future remains unresolved. When asked, "Where do you see yourself going?," Mr. Spitzer replies simply, "Nowhere in particular."

Henry Elliot Weinstein is a staff reporter for *The Wall Street Journal*.

Vocabulary Study

In the excerpts below, select the word or phrase in the parenthesis closest in meaning to the preceding italicized word:

A. the *pervasiveness* of youthful revolt in the U.S. (seriousness, vitality, strangeness, extensiveness, uniqueness)

B. to join the 'One World' family *commune* (small, self-governing social unit; church; Communist cell; front organization; revival group)

C. *disenchantment* with the Vietnam war (disillusionment, disinterestedness, disengagement, misinformation)

D. chained to the city for *sustenance* (treason, protection, livelihood, civil disobedience, overindulgence)

E. America's *disaffected* youths (discontented, unhealthy, hateful, uninvolved)

F. She still reads *'voraciously'* (with difficulty, hungrily, interminably, carelessly)

G. music *emanates* from a stereo (blares, dissipates, flows)

H. left the *lucrative* confines of pro football (ridiculous, profitable, inhuman, exciting, secure)

I. Then he adds, somewhat *wistfully*, 'But I hope . . .' (sentimentally, hopefully, faithfully, longingly)

J. young, white and *affluent* college graduates (wealthy, proficient in foreign languages, versatile, mobile)

Questions on Form and Content

A. Would you describe Mr. Weinstein's attitude toward the dropouts as sympathetic, antagonistic, or balanced? Why?

B. Clara Perkinson characterized present society as a "treadmill" How does the story of each of the dropouts illustrate a desire to "get off the treadmill"?

C. The author (or the newspaper copyeditor) uses the common journalistic device of subtitles to structure the essay. How closely does the writing stay with the subject implied by the subtitles?

D. Briefly characterize the political position common to the four dropouts.

E. What role does personal health play in the outlook of the dropouts?

F. Philip Slater, sociologist at Brandeis University, compares the philosophy of the dropouts to those of utopian movements of the past. What is his point?

G. What personal quality is most valued by each of the dropouts? Is the emphasis on this quality is a natural reaction to traits fostered by our society? If so, in what particulars?

Suggestions for Writing

A. "Some critics of the dropouts argue that their choice is immoral, amounting to an abandonment of the world and its problems," says Mr. Weinstein. Comment.

B. When this article was written, Chip Oliver lived in a commune in Larkspur, where everyone joined in cleaning house, cooking, taking care of the children and working in a restaurant. Describe a commune as it has been depicted in a recent movie—"Easy Rider," for example—or in a television show.

C. How have communes figured in recent court trials, the Charles Matson case, for example?

D. John Simmons characterizes his letter-sorter job as "very alienating—you're constantly reminded of your relationship to a machine." Comment.

E. John Simmons compared the growth of his alienation with that of the career of Bob Dylan. What other popular singers have been influential in the disaffection of today's youth? How?

F. Professor Slater says that today's college graduates "see activities like teaching and social work perpetuating what they don't want perpetuated." Do you agree? If so, what, specifically, would you wish discontinued?

G. After a short stint as a high school teacher, John Spitzer said: "High schools are prisons. The kids don't want to be there, and after teaching for a summer at Berkeley High I concluded that kids should be out in the streets." Comment on what Mr. Spitzer's statements reveal about the schools and about himself.

H. It could be argued that the young people, by dropping out, avoided the benefits as well as the shortcomings of the present system. Write a paper exploring this argument.

I. Do you consider that your college addresses itself to the vital issues of our time? Why or why not?

J. The post office is one of the key institutions in the present system, yet two of the dropouts from the system hold jobs there. Discuss this apparent inconsistency.

K. Why do you think that mostly "young, white and affluent" college graduates drop out?

L. A certain pattern of values seems to be common to all four of the dropouts. Write a paper describing this pattern and its implications for our present society.

M. Mr. Weinstein makes it clear in his article that the dropouts are not uniformly satisfied with their rejection of society. Write a paper in which you use this fact to explore the relationship between the values of change and those of reaction in our society. Your investigation might lead you to consider the question of the stability of value systems in general.

Thoreau

Ralph Waldo Emerson

Henry David Thoreau was the last male descendant of a French ancestor who came to this country from the Isle of Guernsey. His character exhibited occasional traits drawn from this blood, in singular combination with a very strong Saxon genius.

He was born in Concord, Massachusetts, on the 12th of July, 1817. He was graduated at Harvard College in 1837, but without any literary distinction. An iconoclast in literature, he seldom thanked colleges for their service to him, holding them in small esteem, whilst yet his debt to them was important. After leaving the University, he joined his brother in teaching a private school, which he soon renounced. His father was a manufacturer of lead-pencils, and Henry applied himself for a time to this craft, believing he could make a better pencil than was then in use. After completing his experiments, he exhibited his work to chemists and artists in Boston, and having obtained their certificates to its excel-

□ Ralph Waldo Emerson, "Biographical Sketch of Thoreau," in Henry David Thoreau, *Walden Or, Life in the Woods* (New York and Boston, 1893), pp. vii-xxxvii.

lence and to its equality with the best London manufacture, he returned home contented. His friends congratulated him that he had now opened his way to fortune. But he replied that he should never make another pencil. "Why should I? I would not do again what I have done once." He resumed his endless walks and miscellaneous studies, making every day some new acquaintance with Nature, though as yet never speaking of zoölogy or botany, since, though very studious of natural facts, he was incurious of technical and textual science.

At this time, a strong, healthy youth, fresh from college, whilst all his companions were choosing their professions, or eager to begin some lucrative employment, it was inevitable that his thoughts should be exercised on the same question, and it required rare decision to refuse all the accustomed paths and keep his solitary freedom at the cost of disappointing the natural expectations of his family and friends: all the more difficult that he had a perfect probity, was exact in securing his own independence, and in holding every man to the like duty. But Thoreau never faltered. He was a born protestant. He declined to give up his large ambition of knowledge and action for any narrow craft or profession, aiming at a much more comprehensive calling, the art of living well. If he slighted and defied the opinions of others, it was only that he was more intent to reconcile his practice with his own belief. Never idle or self-indulgent, he preferred, when he wanted money, earning it by some piece of manual labor agreeable to him, as building a boat or a fence, planting, grafting, surveying, or other short work, to any long engagements. With his hardy habits and few wants, his skill in woodcraft, and his powerful arithmetic, he was very competent to live in any part of the world. It would cost him less time to supply his wants than another. He was therefore secure of his leisure.

A natural skill for mensuration, growing out of his mathematical knowledge and his habit of ascertaining the measures and distances of objects which interested him, the size of trees, the depth and extent of ponds and rivers, the height of mountains, and the air-line distance of his favorite summits,—this, and his intimate knowledge of the territory about Concord, made him drift into the profession of land-surveyor. It had the advantage for him that it led him continually into new and secluded grounds, and helped his studies of Nature. His accuracy and skill in this work were readily appreciated, and he found all the employment he wanted.

He could easily solve the problems of the surveyor, but he was daily beset with graver questions, which he manfully confronted. He interrogated every custom, and wished to settle all his practice on an ideal foundation. He was a protestant *à outrance,* and few lives contain so many renunciations. He was bred to no profession; he never married; he lived alone; he never went to church; he never voted; he refused to pay a tax to the State; he ate no flesh; he drank no wine, he never knew the use of tobacco; and though a naturalist, he used neither trap nor gun. He chose, wisely no doubt for himself, to be the bachelor of thought and Nature. He had no talent for wealth, and knew how to be poor without the least hint of squalor or inelegance. Perhaps he fell into his way of living without forecasting it much, but approved it with later wisdom. "I am often reminded," he wrote in his journal, "that if I had bestowed on me the wealth of Crœsus, my aims must be still the same, and my means essentially the same." He had no temptations to fight against,—no appetites, no passions, no taste for elegant trifles. A fine house, dress, the manners and talk of highly cultivated people, were all thrown away on him. He much preferred a good Indian, and considered these refinements as impediments to conversation, wishing to meet his companion on the simplest terms. He declined invitations to dinner-parties, because there each was in every one's way, and he could not meet the individuals to any purpose. "They make their pride," he said, "in making their dinner cost much; I make my pride in making my dinner cost little." When asked at table what dish he preferred, he answered, "The nearest." He did not like the taste of wine, and never had a vice in his life. He said, "I have a faint recollection of pleasure derived from smoking dried lily-stems, before I was a man. I had commonly a supply of these. I have never smoked anything more noxious."

He chose to be rich by making his wants few, and supplying them himself. In his travels, he used the railroad only to get over so much country as was unimportant to the present purpose, walking hundreds of miles, avoiding taverns, buying a lodging in farmers' and fishermen's houses, as cheaper, and more agreeable to him, and because there he could better find the men and the information he wanted.

There was somewhat military in his nature, not to be subdued, always manly and able, but rarely tender, as if he did not feel himself except in opposition. He wanted a fallacy to expose, a blunder to pillory, I may say required a little sense of victory, a roll of the drum, to call his powers into full exercise. It cost him nothing to say No; indeed he found it much easier than to say Yes. It seemed as if his first instinct on hearing a proposition was to controvert it, so impatient was he of the limitations of our daily thought. This habit, of course, is a little chilling to the social affections; and though the companion would in the end acquit him of any malice or untruth, yet it mars conversation. Hence, no equal companion stood in affectionate relations with one so pure and guileless. "I love Henry," said one of his friends, "but I cannot like him; and as for taking his arm, I should as soon think of taking the arm of an elm-tree."

Yet, hermit and stoic as he was, he was really fond of sympathy, and threw himself heartily and childlike into the company of young people whom he loved, and whom he delighted to entertain, as he only could, with the varied and endless anecdotes of his experiences by field and river; and he was always ready to lead a huckleberry-party or a search for chestnuts or grapes. Talking, one day, of a public discourse, Henry remarked that whatever succeeded with the audience was bad. I said, "Who would not like to write something which all can read, like Robinson Crusoe? and who does not see with regret that his page is not solid with a right materialistic treatment, which delights everybody?" Henry objected, of course, and vaunted the better lectures which reached only a few persons. But, at supper, a young girl, understanding that he was to lecture at the Lyceum, sharply asked him "whether his lecture would be a nice, interesting story, such as she wished to hear, or whether it was one of those old philosophical things that she did not care about." Henry turned to her, and bethought himself, and, I saw, was trying to believe that he had matter that might fit her and her brother, who were to sit up and go to the lecture, if it was a good one for them.

He was a speaker and actor of the truth, born such, and was ever running into dramatic situations from this cause. In any circumstance it interested all bystanders to know what part Henry would take, and what he would say; and he did not disappoint expectation, but used an original judgment on each emergency. In 1845 he built himself a small framed house on the shores of Walden Pond, and lived there two years alone, a life of labor and study. This action was quite native and fit for him. No one who knew him would tax him with affectation. He was more unlike his neighbors in his thought than in his action. As soon as he had exhausted the advantages of that solitude, he abandoned it. In 1847, not approving some uses to which the public expenditure was applied, he refused to pay his town tax, and was put in jail. A friend paid the tax for him, and he was released. The like annoyance was threatened the next year. But, as his friends paid the tax, notwithstanding his protest, I believe he ceased to resist. No opposition or ridicule had any weight with him. He coldly and fully stated his opinion without affecting to believe that it was the opinion of the company. It was of no consequence if every one present held the opposite opinion. On one occasion he went to the University Library to procure some books. The librarian refused to lend them. Mr. Thoreau repaired to the President, who stated to him the rules and usages, which permitted the loan of books to resident graduates, to clergymen who were alumni, and to some others resident within a circle of ten miles' radius from the College. Mr. Thoreau explained to the President that the railroad had destroyed the old scale of distances,—that the library was useless, yes, and President and College useless, on the terms of his rules,—that the one benefit he owed to the College was its library,—that, at this moment, not only his want of books was imperative but he wanted a large number of books, and assured him that he, Thoreau, and not the librarian, was the proper custodian of these. In short, the President found the petitioner so formidable, and the rules getting to look so ridiculous, that he ended by giving him a privilege which in his hands proved unlimited thereafter.

No truer American existed than Thoreau. His preference of his country and condition was genuine and his aversation from English and European manners and tastes almost reached contempt. He listened impatiently to news or *bon-mots* gleaned from London circles; and though he tried to be civil, these anecdotes fatigued him. The men were all imitating each other, and on a small mould. Why can they not live as far apart as possible, and each be a man by himself? What he sought was the most energetic nature; and he wished to go to Oregon, not to London. "In every part of Great Britain," he wrote in his diary, "are discovered traces of the Romans, their funereal urns, their camps, their roads, their dwellings. But New England, at least, is not based on any Roman ruins. We have not to lay the foundations of our houses on the ashes of a former civilization."

But, idealist as he was, standing for abolition of slavery, abolition of tariffs, almost for abolition of government, it is needless to say he found himself not only unrepresented in actual politics, but almost equally opposed to every class of reformers. Yet he paid the tribute of his uniform respect to the Antislavery party. One man, whose personal acquaintance he had formed, he honored with exceptional regard. Before the first friendly word had been spoken for Captain John Brown, he sent notices to most houses in Concord that he would speak in a public hall on the condition and character of John Brown, on Sunday evening, and invited all people to come. The Republican Committee, the Abolitionist Committee, sent him word that it was premature and not advisable. He replied,—"I did not send to you for advice, but to announce that I am to speak." The hall was filled at an early hour by people of all parties, and his earnest eulogy of the hero was heard by all respectfully, by many with a sympathy that surprised themselves.

It was said of Plotinus that he was ashamed of his body, and 't is very likely he had good reason for it,—that his body was a bad servant, and he had not skill in dealing with the material world, as happens often to men of abstract intellect. But Mr. Thoreau was equipped with a most adapted and serviceable body. He was of short stature, firmly built, of light complexion, with strong, serious blue eyes, and a grave aspect,—his face covered in the late years with a becoming beard. His senses were acute, his frame well-knit and hardy, his hands strong and skillful in the use of tools. And there was a wonderful fitness of body and mind. He could pace sixteen rods more accurately than another man could measure them with rod and chain. He could find his path in the woods at night, he said, better by his feet than his eyes. He could estimate the measure of a tree very well by his eye; he could estimate the weight of a calf or a pig, like a dealer. From a box containing a bushel or more of loose pencils, he could take up with his hands fast enough just a dozen pencils at every grasp. He was a good swimmer, runner, skater, boatman, and would probably outwalk most countrymen in a day's journey. And the relation of body to mind was still finer than we have indicated. He said he wanted every stride his legs made. The length of his walk uniformly made the length of his writing. If shut up in the house he did not write at all.

* * * * * * * *

He lived for the day, not cumbered and mortified by his memory. If he brought you yesterday a new proposition, he would bring you to-day another not less revolutionary. A very industrious man, and setting, like all highly organized men, a high value on his time, he seemed the only man of leisure in town, always ready for any excursion that promised well, or for conversation prolonged into late hours. His trenchant sense was never stopped by his rules of daily prudence, but was always up to the new occasion. He liked and used the simplest food, yet, when some one urged a vegetable diet, Thoreau thought all diets a very small matter, saying that "the man who shoots the buffalo lives better than the man who boards at the Graham House." He said, "You can sleep near the railroad, and never be disturbed: Nature knows very well what sounds are worth attending to, and has made up her mind not to hear the railroad-whistle. But things respect the devout mind, and a mental ecstasy was never interrupted." He noted what repeatedly befell him, that, after receiving from a distance a rare plant, he would presently find the same in his own haunts. And those pieces of luck which happen only to good players happened to him. One day, walking with a stranger, who inquired where Indian arrow-heads could be found, he replied, "Everywhere," and, stooping forward, picked one on the instant from the ground. At Mount Washington, in Tuckerman's Ravine, Thoreau had a bad fall, and sprained his foot. As he was in the act of getting up from his fall, he saw for the first time the leaves of the *Arnica mollis.*

His robust common sense, armed with stout hands, keen perceptions, and strong will, cannot yet account for the superiority which shone in his simple and hidden life. I must add the cardinal fact, that there was an excellent wisdom in him, proper to a rare class of men, which showed him the material world as a means and symbol. This discovery, which sometimes yields to poets a certain casual and interrupted light, serving for the ornament of their writing, was in him an unsleeping insight; and whatever faults or obstructions of temperament might cloud it, he was not disobedient to the heavenly vision. In his youth, he said, one day, "The other world is all my art; my pencils will draw no other; my jack-knife will cut nothing else; I do not use it as a means." This was the muse and genius that ruled his opinions, conversation, studies, work, and course of life. This made him a searching judge of men. At first glance he measured his companion, and, though insensible to some fine traits of culture, could very well report his weight and calibre. And this made the impression of genius which his conversation sometimes gave.

He understood the matter in hand at a glance, and saw the limitations and poverty of those he talked with, so that nothing seemed concealed from such terrible eyes. I have repeatedly known young men of sensibility converted in a moment to the belief that this was the man they were in search of, the man of men, who could tell them all they should do. His own dealing with them was never affectionate, but superior, didactic, scorning their petty ways,—very slowly conceding, or not conceding at all, the promise of his society at their houses, or even at his own. "Would he not walk with them?" "He did not know. There was nothing so important to him as his walk; he had no walks to throw away on company." Visits were offered him from respectful parties, but he declined them. Admiring friends offered to carry him at their own cost to the Yellowstone River,—to the West Indies,—to South America. But though nothing could be more grave or considered than his refusals, they remind one, in quite new relations, of that fop Brummel's reply to the gentleman who offered him his carriage in a shower, "But where will *you* ride, then?"—and what accusing silences, and what searching and irresistible speeches, battering down all defenses, his companions can remember!

Mr. Thoreau dedicated his genius with such entire love to the fields, hills, and waters of his native town, that he made them known and interesting to all reading Americans, and to people over the sea. The river on whose banks he was born and died he knew from its springs to its confluence with the Merrimack. He had made summer and winter observations on it for many years, and at every hour of the day and night.

* * * * * * * *

It was a pleasure and a privilege to walk with him. He knew the country like a fox or a bird, and passed through it as freely by paths of his own. He knew every track in the snow or on the ground, and what creature had taken this path before him. One must submit abjectly to such a guide, and the reward was great. Under his arm he carried an old music-book to press plants; in his pocket, his diary and pencil, a spy-glass for birds, microscope, jack-knife, and twine. He wore a straw hat, stout shoes, strong gray trousers, to brave scrub-oaks and smilax, and to climb a tree for a hawk's or a squirrel's nest. He waded into the pool for the water-plants, and his strong legs were no insignificant part of his armor.

* * * * * * * *

No college ever offered him a diploma, or a professor's chair; no academy made him its corresponding secretary, its discoverer, or even its member. Perhaps these learned bodies feared the satire of his presence. Yet so much knowledge of Nature's secret and genius few others possessed; none in a more large and religious synthesis. For not a particle of respect had he to the opinions of any man or body of men, but homage solely to the truth itself; and as he discovered everywhere among doctors some leaning of courtesy, it discredited them. He grew to be revered and admired by his townsmen, who had at first known him only as an oddity. The farmers who employed him as a surveyor soon discovered his rare accuracy and skill, his knowledge of their lands, of trees, of birds, of Indian remains and the like, which enabled him to tell every farmer more than he knew before of his own farm; so that he began to feel a little as if Mr. Thoreau had better rights in his land than he. They felt, too, the superiority of character which addressed all men with a native authority.

Indian relics abound in Concord,—arrowheads, stone chisels, pestles, and fragments of pottery; and on the river-bank, large heaps of clam-shells and ashes mark spots which the savages frequented. These, and every circumstance touching the Indian, were important in his eyes. His visits to Maine were chiefly for love of the Indian. He had the satisfaction of seeing the manufacture of the bark-canoe, as well as of trying his hand in its management on the rapids. He was inquisitve about the making of the stone arrow-head, and in his last days charged a youth setting out for the Rocky Mountains to find an Indian who could tell him that: "It was well worth a visit to California to learn it." Occasionally, a small party of Penobscot Indians would visit Concord, and pitch their tents for a few weeks in summer on the river-bank. He failed not to make acquaintance with the best of them; though he well knew that asking questions of Indians is like catechising beavers and rabbits. In his last visit to Maine he had great satisfaction from Joseph Polis, an intelligent Indian of Oldtown, who was his guide for some weeks.

He was equally interested in every natural fact. The depth of his perception found likeness of law throughout Nature, and I know not any genius who so swiftly inferred universal law from the single fact. He was no pedant of a department. His eye was open to beauty, and his ear to music. He found these, not in rare conditions, but wheresoever he went. He thought the best of music was in single strains; and he found poetic suggestion in the humming of the telegraph-wire.

* * * * * * * *

Whilst he used in his writings a certain petulance of remark in reference to churches or churchmen, he was a person of a rare, tender, and absolute religion, a person incapable of any profanation, by act or by thought. Of course, the same isolation which belonged to his original thinking and living detached him from the social religious forms. This is neither to be censured nor regretted. Aristotle long ago explained it, when he said, "One who surpasses his fellow-citizens in virtue is no longer a part of the city. Their law is not for him, since he is a law to himself."

Thoreau was sincerity itself, and might fortify the convictions of prophets in the ethical laws by his holy living. It was an affirmative experience which refused to be set aside. A truth-speaker he, capable of the most deep and strict conversation; a physician to the wounds of any soul; a friend, knowing not only the secret of friendship, but almost worshiped by those few persons who resorted to him as their confessor and prophet, and knew the deep value of his mind and great heart. He thought that without religion or devotion of some kind nothing great was ever accomplished; and he thought that the bigoted sectarian had better bear this in mind.

His virtues, of course, sometimes ran into extremes. It was easy to trace to the inexorable demand on all for exact truth that austerity which made this willing hermit more solitary even than he wished. Himself of a perfect probity, he required not less of others. He had a disgust at crime, and no worldly success would cover it. He detected paltering as readily in dignified and prosperous persons as in beggars, and with equal scorn. Such dangerous frankness was in his dealing that his admirers called him "that terrible Thoreau," as if he spoke when silent, and was still present when he had departed. I think the severity of his ideal interfered to deprive him of a healthy sufficiency of human society.

* * * * * * * *

Had his genius been only contemplative, he had been fitted to his life, but with his energy and practical ability he seemed born for great enterprise and for command; and I so much regret the loss of his rare powers of action, that I cannot help counting it a fault in him that he had no ambition. Wanting this, instead of engineering for all America, he was the captain of a huckleberry-party. Pounding beans is good to the end of pounding empires one of these days; but if, at the end of years, it is still only beans!

But these foibles, real or apparent, were fast vanishing in the incessant growth of a spirit so robust and wise, and which effaced its defeats with new triumphs. His study of Nature was a perpetual ornament to him, and inspired his friends with curiosity to see the world through his eyes, and to hear his adventures. They possessed every kind of interest.

* * * * * * * *

There is a flower known to botanists, one of the same genus with our summer plant called "Life-Everlasting," a *Gnaphalium* like that, which grows on the most inaccessible cliffs of the Tyrolese mountains, where the chamois dare hardly venture, and which the hunter, tempted by its beauty, and by his love (for it is immensely valued by the Swiss maidens), climbs the cliffs to gather, and is sometimes found dead at the foot, with the flower in his hand. It is called by botanists the *Gnaphalium leontopodium*, but by the Swiss *Edelweisse*, which signifies *Noble Purity*. Thoreau seemed to me living in the hope to gather this plant, which belonged to him of right. The scale on which his studies proceeded was so large as to require longevity, and we were the less prepared for his sudden disappearance. The country knows not yet, or in the least part, how great a son it has lost. It seems an injury that he should leave in the midst his broken task which none else can finish, a kind of indignity to so noble a soul that he should depart out of Nature before yet he has been really shown to his peers for what he is. But he, at least, is content. His soul was made for the noblest society; he had in a short life exhausted the capabilities of this world; wherever there is knowledge, wherever there is virtue, wherever there is beauty, he will find a home.

Ralph Waldo Emerson (1803-1882), was born in Boston, where he attended Boston Latin School and enrolled at Harvard College, from which he was graduated in 1821. He helped to support himself in college, working as a messenger, waiter, and tutor. He later taught school for four years before enrolling in Harvard Divinity School to prepare for the ministry. Some years later he broke with the ministry and traveled abroad before beginning a career as a lecturer. He spent his later years writing, walking, and enjoying the company of friends, among whom was Henry David Thoreau, who though fourteen years younger was Emerson's friend during most of his mature years. Thoreau built his hut at Walden Pond on Emerson's land. When Thoreau died from tuberculosis in 1862, Emerson delivered the funeral address, which the *Atlantic Monthly* published shortly afterwards. The version here given appeared as an introduction to an 1893 edition of *Walden.*

Vocabulary Study

From the list below, select the word or phrase closest in meaning to the italicized word in the following excerpts from Emerson's "Thoreau." The list contains extra words.

A. An *iconoclast* in literature, he seldom thanked colleges for their service to him

B. he had a perfect *probity*

C. and few lives contain so many *renunciations.*

D. his habit of *ascertaining* the measures and distances of objects which interested him

E. the varied and endless *anecdotes* of his experiences by field and river

F. Henry . . . *vaunted* the better lectures which reach only a few persons.

G. No one who knew him would tax him with *affectation.*

H. his want of books was *imperative*

I. the President found the petitioner so *formidable*

J. He listened impatiently to news or *bon-mots*

K. But idealist as he was, standing for *abolition* of slavery

L. his earnest *eulogy* of the hero was heard by all respectfully

M. He lived for the day, not *cumbered* . . . by his memory.

N. His *trenchant* sense was never stopped by his rules of daily *prudence*

O. The river on whose banks he was born and died he knew from its springs to its *confluence* with the Merrimack

P. He was no *pedant* of a department.

Q. He was a person of a rare, tender, and absolute religion, a person incapable of any *profanation*

R. It was an *affirmative* experience

S. It was easy to trace to the *inexorable* demand on all for exact truth that austerity

T. the *incessant* growth of a spirit so robust and wise

U. which *effaced* its defeats with new triumphs

clergyman
great art works
a critic of cherished beliefs
ceaseless
vows

disease
short, interesting narratives
positive
clever sayings

important; urgent	lofty sentiments
pretense	praised boastfully
burdened	to be dreaded
a flowing together	unyielding
accuracy	sharp *or* cutting
things given up or abandoned	a speech in praise
full professor	wisdom
debasement *or* sacrilege	growing wildly
remedies	indignantly
legal extinction	scholar bound narrowly to his own discipline
determining exactly	integrity
erased	

Questions on Form and Content

A. One of the hallmarks of Mr. Emerson's style is his tendency to arrange the segments of his often long and involved sentences so that his most important points come at the beginning. Find an example of this strategy in the third paragraph.

B. To begin his fourth paragraph, Mr. Emerson uses what is called a *periodic* sentence, in which the main thought ("made him drift into the profession of land-surveyor") is suspended until the end. What are the merits of this strategy as compared with the one discussed in the question above?

C. Why, possibly, did no college or university ever make overtures to Mr. Thoreau?

D. The farmers for whom Mr. Thoreau worked sometimes felt that he had better rights to their land than they did. Why?

E. What deprived Mr. Thoreau of a "healthy sufficiency of human society"?

F. Show how Mr. Thoreau was "more unlike his neighbors in his thought than in his action."

G. How does Mr. Emerson show that "the length of his [Mr. Thoreau's] walk uniformly made the length of his writing?"

H. Mr. Thoreau said, "You can sleep near the railroad, and never be disturbed." Why?

I. What major fault did Mr. Emerson find with Mr. Thoreau? Why did he consider this fault so serious?

J. Mr. Emerson compares Mr. Thoreau to the Swiss mountaineer who seeks the *Edelweiss* flower. How are the two alike?

Suggestions for Writing

A. Though an early dropout from conventional employment, Mr. Thoreau tried several jobs. What were they? Why, from what you now know of his character, do you suppose he found each unsatisfactory?

B. Comment on Mr. Thoreau's reasons for refusing to make more pencils: "Why should I? I would not do again what I have done once." Apply that reasoning to a successful surgeon, lawyer, secretary, cook, or one in some other occupation.

C. Do you think Mr. Thoreau would have been happy in a commune? Would he have been popular? Why or why not?

D. What did Mr. Thoreau do well? What did he refuse to do? What were his strengths? His weaknesses?

E. If Mr. Thoreau were to be your dinner guest tonight, what would you serve? What topics would you initiate—or avoid—at the dinner table? Why? Whom else, assuming all dead or alive were available, would you invite?

F. Write a paper on one of the following sentences taken from Thoreau. Consider them not only as records of his thought and feeling but also for their descriptive power and literary excellence.

> "The youth gets together his materials to build a bridge to the moon, or, perchance, a palace or temple on the earth, and, at length the middle-aged man concludes to build a wood-shed with them."

> "The bluebird carries the sky on his back."

> "The tanager flies through the green foliage as if it would ignite the leaves."

> "Fire is the most tolerable third party."

> "Nothing is so much to be feared as fear. Atheism may comparatively be popular with God himself."

> "How can we expect a harvest of thought who have not had a seed-time of character?"

G. Mr. Emerson calls Mr. Thoreau "a born protestant." Write a paper explaining what he meant, paying particular attention to the use of the word "protestant."

H. According to Mr. Emerson, Mr. Thoreau's calling or profession was "the art of living well." Explain what "living well" meant to Mr. Thoreau, and then discuss the possibility of applying his terms to twentieth-century society in the United States.

I. Mr. Emerson uses the word "Nature" several times in his essay, always capitalizing it. Read the essay again carefully and then explain, as completely as you can, what the word meant to Mr. Emerson and Mr. Thoreau.

J. Mr. Thoreau "chose to be rich by making his wants few, and supplying them himself." Evidently, his concept of prosperity was far different from ours. Write a paper explaining his value system and comparing it with ours.

K. Mr. Emerson refers to an instinctive contrariness in Mr. Thoreau: "It seemed as if his first instinct on hearing a proposition was to controvert it." How effective in the realm of human affairs is such an attitude? In writing your essay, you might wish to refer to some modern "gadflies," such as Senator Fulbright, singer Joan Baez, and writer Eldridge Cleaver.

L. One of Mr. Thoreau's friends claimed that he loved Henry Thoreau, but could not like him. Explain this seeming paradox in terms of what Mr. Emerson reveals of Mr. Thoreau's personality.

M. In discussing the contemporary practice of public lecturing, Mr. Thoreau said that "whatever succeeded with the audience was bad." If Mr. Thoreau is using the term "succeeded" ironically here, what is the people's idea of a successful lecture? What is Mr. Thoreau's?

N. In his well-known essay entitled "Civil Disobedience," Mr. Thoreau says, "How does it become a man to behave toward this American government today? I answer, that he cannot without disgrace be associated with it." And yet in "Thoreau," Emerson says, "No truer American existed than Thoreau." What is Mr. Emerson's idea of a "true American?" What is a "true American" today?

O. In comparing England with New England, Mr. Thoreau says, "In every part of Great Britain are discovered traces of the Romans. . . . But New England, at least, is not based on any Roman ruins. We have not to lay the foundations of our houses on the ashes of a former civilization." What does this statement tell us about Mr. Thoreau's attitude toward history, human knowledge, and the authority of tradition?

P. Mr. Emerson makes the point that Mr. Thoreau was not only unaffiliated with any existing political party, but "opposed to every class of reformers." Yet Mr. Thoreau deeply respected the radical abolitionist,

John Brown. After learning all you can about John Brown, write a paper in which you explain Mr. Thoreau's attraction to the abolitionist in spite of his aversion to politics in general.

Q. In his essay entitled "Self-Reliance," Mr. Emerson says, "A foolish consistency is the hobgoblin of little minds." How would you describe Mr. Thoreau's "consistency?" Would he feel that consistency is a necessary attribute for a person who wishes to discover truth or contribute to real human progress?

R. Mr. Emerson refers to Mr. Thoreau's "genius" more than once in the essay. Locate these references and, with other facts from the essay, specifically describe the qualities of Mr. Thoreau's genius.

S. Mr. Emerson claims in the essay that Mr. Thoreau was a person of "rare, tender, and absolute religion." What was Mr. Thoreau's "religion?"

T. In describing Mr. Thoreau's character, Mr. Emerson uses the Aristotelian quotation: "One who surpasses his fellow-citizens in virtue is no longer a part of the city. Their law is not for him, since he is a law to himself." Discuss the ethical, social, and political implications of such a doctrine for a modern, democratic society.

U. The Emerson-Thoreau friendship deteriorated as the years passed until in 1856, six years before his death, Mr. Thoreau wrote that it had been "one long tragedy." Are there intimations of their disaffection in the funeral address?

Selections from Walden

Henry David Thoreau

I went to the woods because I wished to live deliberately, to front only the essential facts of life, and see if I could not learn what it had to teach, and not, when I came to die, discover that I had not lived. I did not wish to live what was not life, living is so dear; nor did I wish to practise resignation, unless it was quite necessary. I wanted to live deep and suck out all the marrow of life, to live so sturdily and Spartan-like as to put to rout all that was not life, to cut a broad swath and shave close, to drive life into a corner, and reduce it to its lowest terms, and, if it proved to be mean, why then to get the whole and genuine meanness of it, and publish its meanness to the world; or if it were sublime, to know it by experience, and be able to give a true account of it in my next excursion. For most men, it appears to me, are in a strange uncertainty about it, whether it is of the devil or of God, and have *somewhat hastily* concluded that it is the chief end of man here to "glorify God and enjoy him forever."

(*From* "Where I Lived, and What I Lived for")

□Henry David Thoreau, *Walden Or, Life in the Woods* (Boston and New York, 1893), pp. 143, 498-499, 502-503, 505-507.

* * * * * * * *

I left the woods for as good a reason as I went there. Perhaps it seemed to me that I had several more lives to live, and could not spare any more time for that one. It is remarkable how easily and insensibly we fall into a particular route, and make a beaten track for ourselves. I had not lived there a week before my feet wore a path from my door to the pond-side; and though it is five or six years since I trod it, it is still quite distinct. It is true, I fear that others may have fallen into it, and so helped to keep it open. The surface of the earth is soft and impressible by the feet of men; and so with the paths which the mind travels. How worn and dusty, then, must be the highways of the world, how deep the ruts of tradition and conformity! I did not wish to take a cabin passage, but rather to go before the mast and on the deck of the world, for there I could best see the moonlight amid the mountains. I do not wish to go below now.

I learned this, at least, by my experiment; that if one advances confidently in the direction of his dreams, and endeavors to live the life which he has imagined, he will meet with a success unexpected in common hours. He will put some things behind, will pass an invisible boundary; new, universal, and more liberal laws will begin to establish themselves around and within him; or the old laws be expanded, and interpreted in his favor in a more liberal sense, and he will live with the license of a higher order of beings. In proportion as he simplifies his life, the laws of the universe will appear less complex, and solitude will not be solitude, nor poverty poverty, nor weakness weakness. If you have built castles in the air, your work need not be lost; that is where they should be. Now put the foundations under them.

* * * * * * * *

Why should we be in such desperate haste to succeed and in such desperate enterprises? If a man does not keep pace with his companions, perhaps it is because he hears a different drummer. Let him step to the music which he hears, however measured or far away. It is not important that he should mature as soon as an apple-tree or an oak. Shall he turn his spring into summer? If the condition of things which we were made for is not yet, what were any reality which we can substitute? We will not be shipwrecked on a vain reality. Shall we with pains erect a heaven of blue glass over ourselves, though when it is done we shall be sure to gaze still at the true ethereal heaven far above, as if the former were not?

* * * * * * * *

However mean your life is, meet it and live it; do not shun it and call it hard names. It is not so bad as you are. It looks poorest when you are richest. The fault-finder will find faults even in paradise. Love your life, poor as it is. You may perhaps have some pleasant, thrilling, glorious hours, even in a poor-house. The setting sun is reflected from the windows of the alms-house as brightly as from the rich man's abode; the snow melts before its door as early in the spring. I do not see but a quiet mind may live as contentedly there, and have as cheering thoughts, as in a palace. The town's poor seem to me often to live the most independent lives of any. May be they are simply great enough to receive without misgiving. Most think that they are above being supported by the town; but it oftener happens that they are not above supporting themselves by dishonest means, which should be more disreputable. Cultivate poverty like a garden herb, like sage. Do not trouble yourself much to get new things, whether clothes or friends. Turn the old; return to them. Things do not change; we change. Sell your clothes and keep your thoughts. God will see that you do not want society. If I were confined to a corner of a garret all my days, like a spider, the world would be just as large to me while I had my thoughts about me. The philosopher said: "From an army of three divisions one can take away its general, and put it in disorder; from the man the most abject and vulgar one cannot take away his thought." Do not seek so anxiously to be developed, to subject yourself to many influences to be played on; it is all dissipation. Humility like darkness reveals the heavenly lights. The shadows of poverty and meanness gather around us, "and lo! creation widens to our view."[1] We are often reminded that if there were bestowed on us the wealth of Crœsus, our aims must still be the same, and our means essentially the same. Moreover, if you are restricted in your range by poverty, if you cannot buy books and newspapers, for instance, you are but confined to the most significant and vital experiences; you are compelled to deal with the material which yields the most sugar and the most starch. It is life near the bone where it is sweetest. You are defended from being a trifler. No man loses ever on a lower level by magnanimity on a higher. Superfluous wealth can buy superfluities only. Money is not required to buy one necessary of the soul.

(*From* "Conclusion")

Henry David Thoreau (1817-1862), essayist, poet, and transcendentalist, was born, lived most of his life, and died in Concord, Massachusetts. He loved hunting, fishing, and walking and took a passionate interest in nature throughout his life. An early nonconformist, he wore a green coat to chapel at Harvard because the rules said that he must wear a black one. After graduation he taught school and helped his father in the family business of pencil making. Between July 4, 1845, and September 6, 1846, he lived in a small house

[1]"And lo, creation widened in man's view."—From "Night and Death," Joseph Blanco White (1775-1841).

on the northwest shore of Walden Pond, Concord; during that period of retreat, his simple life gave him time to meditate and create. From the experience came his greatest achievement, *Walden,* in which he criticized the superficialities of society. Thoreau kept a journal from 1834, when he was a sophomore at Harvard, until the end of his life. Among his other works are *Excursions, The Maine Woods,* and *Cape Cod.*

Vocabulary Study

From the list below, select the word or phrase nearest in meaning to the italicized word in the following excerpts from *Walden.*

A. I wished to live *deliberately*
B. nor did I wish to practise *resignation*
C. to live so sturdily and *Spartan-like*
D. *to put to rout* all that was not life
E. live with the *license* of a higher order of beings
F. do not *shun* it and call it hard names
G. from the windows of the *alms-house*
H. the rich man's *abode*
I. by dishonest means, which should be more *disreputable*
J. confined to a corner of a *garret*
K. buy *superfluities* only
L. buy one *necessary* of the soul.

essential	necessitate
poorhouse	rigorously
avoid	unresisting acquiescence
absurdity	reflectively
freedom	avoid
abuse	attic
luxuries	dishonorable
to disperse in disorderly flight	dwelling

Questions on Form and Content

A. How do the sentences in the first paragraph reprinted here differ from those in the last paragraph? How do you account for the difference?

B. Evaluate Mr. Thoreau's reasons for going into the woods and for leaving them. Which, to you, seem more convincing? Why?

C. What did Mr. Thoreau learn from his experiment?

D. Mr. Thoreau says that life "looks poorest when you are richest." Do you agree? Why or why not?

E. Mr. Thoreau built the cabin in which he lived for two years and two months on land owned by his friend, Mr. Emerson. He later lived in the Emerson home for long periods as a member of the family. He lived much of the rest of his life under his parents' roof and died, at the age of forty-five, in his mother's house. With these facts in mind, evaluate his advice on poverty and wealth.

Suggestions for Writing

A. Stanley Edgar Hyman says that Mr. Thoreau's experiment was one in human ecology (though he preceded the term), "an attempt to work out a satisfactory relationship between man and his environment." From the excerpts reprinted here and from Mr. Emerson's account, how successfully do you think he did so?

B. At the age of twenty-six, Henry Thoreau wrote to his mother: "methinks I should be content to sit at the back-door in Concord, under the poplar-tree, henceforth forever." Comment.

C. Mr. Thoreau deliberately lived a life of paradox, exemplified, perhaps, in the statement: "In proportion as he simplifies his life, the laws of the universe will appear less complex, and solitude will not be solitude, nor poverty poverty, nor weakness weakness." What is solitude? Poverty? Weakness? What does Thoreau mean? How could a simplified life produce society in solitude, strength in weakness, wealth in poverty?

D. According to Mr. Thoreau: "The cost of a thing is the amount of what I will call life which is required to be exchanged for it, immediately or in the long run." Using that exchange criterion, what is the cost of a college education or the preparation for any career? Or for a job one dislikes? Or likes? Or for idleness?

E. If money saved is life saved, what does Mr. Thoreau mean by life? For what is life saved? What is of sufficient importance to spend one's life for it?

F. Mr. Thoreau writes: "If you have built castles in the air, your work need not be lost; that is where they should be. Now put foundations under them." How does one build foundations?

G. How would you answer Mr. Thoreau's question: "Why should we be in such desperate haste to succeed, and in such desperate enterprises?"

H. "Most think that they are above being supported by the town; but it oftener happens that they are not above supporting themselves by dishonest means, which should be more disreputable," Mr. Thoreau writes. Comment.

I. "Money is not required to buy one necessary of the soul," says Mr. Thoreau. For what is money required?

J. What superfluities would you like to buy if you had some superfluous wealth?

K. How are educated dropouts today like Mr. Thoreau? How do they differ from him?

L. If you agree with Mr. Thoreau's philosophy, write a paper supporting your—and his—belief. If you disagree, write a refutation.

Each paragraph within an essay should contribute to the development of the author's one central idea. And each paragraph should have its own topic idea or thought. This main thought is usually expressed in a topic sentence which is frequently either the first or last sentence of the paragraph, although it may occupy any other position. Sometimes the topic idea will be stated first, developed within the paragraph, then restated or summarized at the end of the paragraph. Occasionally the topic idea is not directly presented, but only implied. In any well-written paragraph, however, the reader either can find the topic sentence clearly stated or else can easily make a sentence himself that will embody the main thought developed within the paragraph.

As you write, you should ask yourself what you want to say in each paragraph and make certain that every sentence contributes to your statement of that central paragraph idea. Only in this way will you make the paragraph's sentences fit together and the paragraph achieve *unity.* You should also make sure that this topic idea is sufficiently developed—that is, that you say all you want or need to say about it, all the reader needs to know. Thus your paragraph achieves *com-*

pleteness. If you have trouble in attaining either unity or completeness in your papers, it would be helpful to start each paragraph with a topic sentence. Then keep your eye on that sentence to be sure you write nothing in the paragraph that does not develop the one central idea or theme.

William S. Burroughs's "Kicking Drugs: A Very Personal Story," the final essay in this chapter, is an excellent article for studying the effective use of topic sentences. In nearly every paragraph the topic sentence stands first, and in several instances the topic sentence is restated or summarized at the conclusion of the paragraph. In all paragraphs that have topic sentences, the other sentences relate directly to the topic sentence and develop it. No extraneous or irrelevant material is included.

Students are often puzzled as to how long to make their paragraphs and when to start new ones. Paragraphs differ greatly in length. Newspaper paragraphs are typically quite short, frequently containing only one sentence. Paragraphs in complex and serious works, on the other hand, are usually much longer—as many as three hundred words is not uncommon.

You should be guided by common sense in deciding your own paragraph length and in determining at what point to begin another paragraph. Remember that paragraphing is an aid to the reader as well as to the writer and that short paragraphs are easier to read than long ones. Usually your material will lend itself to logical paragraph division. You may need, for example, one paragraph for an introduction; one for each major point, division, or part of your paper; and one for your conclusion. Examples, illustrations, or anecdotes that require several sentences are often placed in separate paragraphs immediately following the material they illustrate. In recording conversation, you start a new paragraph to indicate a change of speaker. Note William Burroughs's paragraphing when he records the conversation of Lexington old-timers in the second section of his essay.

Paragraphs are developed in a number of ways. You may want to use *chronological* development, in which you relate your material in time sequence. You may find a *spatial* organization effective; in this you would describe something from top to bottom, or from side to side, or use any system that would serve for showing relationship through space. More often, you will desire to develop a paragraph through what might be called *logical* organization—from specific statements to a general statement, from a general statement to specific statements, from effect to cause or from cause to effect, from question to answer or from problem to solution. These methods of development will be treated more fully in Chapters 6-9 of this text as the patterns of organization for your complete paper. The same patterns and methods also apply to paragraphs.

Remember that if a topic sentence is important enough to include in your paper, it deserves adequate development. You may develop your topic sentence by clarifying, explaining, or analyzing it to make it clear to the reader; by the use of examples, illustrations, anecdotes, comparisons, or contrasts to support it and make it interesting to the reader; or by a combination of these methods. If you have developed your topic sentence adequately, your paragraph will be complete; if you have included no extraneous material, it will have unity.

Drugs That Shape Men's Minds

Aldous Huxley

In the course of history many more people have died for their drink and their dope than have died for their religion or their country. The craving for ethyl alcohol and the opiates has been stronger, in these millions,than the love of God, of home, of children; even of life. Their cry was not for liberty or death; it was for death preceded by enslavement. There is a paradox here, and a mystery. Why should such multitudes of men and women be so ready to sacrifice themselves for a cause so utterly hopeless and in ways so painful and so profoundly humiliating?

To this riddle there is, of course, no simple or single answer. Human beings are immensely complicated creatures, living simultaneously in a half dozen different worlds. Each individual is unique and, in a number of respects, unlike all the other members of the species. None of our motives is unmixed, none of our actions can be traced back to a single source and, in any group we care to study, behavior

□ Aldous Huxley, "Drugs That Shape Men's Minds," in *Collected Essays* (New York, 1959), pp. 336-346.

patterns that are observably similar may be the result of many constellations of dissimilar causes.

Thus, there are some alcoholics who seem to have been biochemically predestined to alcoholism. (Among rats, as Professor Roger Williams, of the University of Texas, has shown, some are born drunkards; some are born teetotalers and will never touch the stuff.) Other alcoholics have been foredoomed not by some inherited defect in their biochemical make-up, but by their neurotic reactions to distressing events in their childhood or adolescence. Again, others embark upon their course of slow suicide as a result of mere imitation and good fellowship because they have made such an "excellent adjustment to their group"—a process which, if the group happens to be criminal, idiotic or merely ignorant, can bring only disaster to the well-adjusted individual. Nor must we forget that large class of addicts who have taken to drugs or drink in order to escape from physical pain. Aspirin, let us remember, is a very recent invention. Until late in the Victorian era, "poppy and mandragora," along with henbane and ethyl alcohol, were the only pain relievers available to civilized man. Toothache, arthritis and neuralgia could, and frequently did, drive men and women to become opium addicts.

De Quincey, for example, first resorted to opium in order to relieve "excruciating rheumatic pains of the head." He swallowed his poppy and, an hour later, "What a resurrection from the lowest depths of the inner spirit! What an apocalypse!" And it was not merely that he felt no more pain. "This negative effect was swallowed up in the immensity of those positive effects which had opened up before me, in the abyss of divine enjoyment thus suddenly revealed. . . . Here was the secret of happiness, about which the philosophers had disputed for so many ages, at once discovered."

"Resurrection, apocalypse, divine enjoyment, happiness. . . ." De Quincey's words lead us to the very heart of our paradoxical mystery. The problem of drug addiction and excessive drinking is not merely a matter of chemistry and psychopathology, of relief from pain and conformity with a bad society. It is also a problem in metaphysics—a problem, one might almost say, in theology. In *The Varieties of Religious Experience,* William James has touched on these metaphysical aspects of addiction:

> The sway of alcohol over mankind is unquestionably due to its power to stimulate the mystical faculties in human nature, usually crushed to earth by the cold facts and dry criticisms of the sober hour. Sobriety diminishes, discriminates and says no. Drunkenness expands, unites and says yes. It is in fact the great exciter of the *Yes* function in man. It brings its votary from the chill periphery of things into the radiant core. It makes him for the moment one with truth. Not through mere perversity do

> men run after it. To the poor and the unlettered it stands in the place of symphony concerts and literature; and it is part of the deeper mystery and tragedy of life that whiffs and gleams of something that we immediately recognize as excellent should be vouchsafed to so many of us only through the fleeting earlier phases of what, in its totality, is so degrading a poison. The drunken consciousness is one bit of the mystic consciousness, and our total opinion of it must find its place in our opinion of that larger whole.

William James was not the first to detect a likeness between drunkenness and the mystical and premystical states. On the day of Pentecost there were people who explained the strange behavior of the disciples by saying, "These men are full of new wine."

Peter soon undeceived them: "These are not drunken, as ye suppose, seeing it is but the third hour of the day. But this is that which was spoken by the prophet Joel. And it shall come to pass in the last days, saith God, I will pour out of my Spirit upon all flesh."

And it is not only by "the dry critics of the sober hour" that the state of God-intoxication has been likened to drunkenness. In their efforts to express the inexpressible, the great mystics themselves have done the same. Thus, St. Theresa of Avila tells us that she "regards the center of our soul as a cellar, into which God admits us as and when it pleases Him, so as to intoxicate us with the delicious wine of His grace."

Every fully developed religion exists simultaneously on several different levels. It exists as a set of abstract concepts about the world and its governance. It exists as a set of rites and sacraments, as a traditional method for manipulating the symbols, by means of which beliefs about the cosmic order are expressed. It exists as the feelings of love, fear and devotion evoked by this manipulation of symbols.

And finally it exists as a special kind of feeling or intuition—a sense of the oneness of all things in their divine principle, a realization (to use the language of Hindu theology) that "thou art That," a mystical experience of what seems self-evidently to be union with God.

The ordinary waking consciousness is a very useful and, on most occasions, an indispensable state of mind; but it is by no means the only form of consciousness, nor in all circumstances the best. Insofar as he transcends his ordinary self and his ordinary mode of awareness, the mystic is able to enlarge his vision, to look more deeply into the unfathomable miracle of existence.

The mystical experience is doubly valuable; it is valuable because it gives the experiencer a better understanding of himself and the world and because it may help him to lead a less self-centered and more creative life.

In hell, a great religious poet has written, the punishment of the lost is to be "their sweating selves, but worse." On earth we are not worse than we are; we are merely our sweating selves, period.

Alas, that is quite bad enough. We love ourselves to the point of idolatry; but we also intensely dislike ourselves—we find ourselves unutterably boring. Correlated with this distaste for the idolatrously worshiped self, there is in all of us a desire, sometimes latent, sometimes conscious and passionately expressed, to escape from the prison of our individuality, an urge to self-transcendence. It is to this urge that we owe mystical theology, spiritual exercises and yoga—to this, too, that we owe alcoholism and drug addiction.

Modern pharmacology has given us a host of new synthetics, but in the field of the naturally occurring mind changers it has made no radical discoveries. All the botanical sedatives, stimulants, vision revealers, happiness promoters and cosmic-consciousness arousers were found out thousands of years ago, before the dawn of history.

In many societies at many levels of civilization attempts have been made to fuse drug intoxication with God-intoxication. In ancient Greece, for example, ethyl alcohol had its place in the established religion. Dionysus, or Bacchus, as he was often called, was a true divinity. His worshipers addressed him as *Lusios,* "Liberator," or as *Theoinos,* "Godwine." The latter name telescopes fermented grape juice and the supernatural into a single pentecostal experience. "Born a god," writes Euripides, "Bacchus is poured out as a libation to the gods, and through him men receive good." Unfortunately they also receive harm. The blissful experience of self-transcendence which alcohol makes possible has to be paid for, and the price is exorbitantly high.

Complete prohibition of all chemical mind changers can be decreed, but cannot be enforced, and tends to create more evils than it cures. Even more unsatisfactory has been the policy of complete toleration and unrestricted availability. In England, during the first years of the eighteenth century, cheap untaxed gin—"drunk for a penny, dead drunk for two-pence"—threatened society with complete demoralization. A century later, opium, in the form of laudanum, was reconciling the victims of the Industrial Revolution to their lot—but at an appalling cost in terms of addiction, illness and early death. Today most civilized societies follow a course between the two extremes of total prohibition and total toleration. Certain mind-changing drugs, such as alcohol, are permitted and made available to the public on payment of a very high tax, which tends to restrict their consumption. Other mind changers are unobtainable except under doctors' orders—or illegally from a dope pusher. In this way the problem is kept within manageable bounds. It is most certainly not solved. In their ceaseless search for self-transcendence, millions of would-be mystics become addicts, commit scores of thousands of crimes and are involved in hundreds of thousands of avoidable accidents.

Do we have to go on in this dismal way indefinitely? Up until a few years ago, the answer to such a question would have been a rueful "Yes, we do." Today, thanks to recent developments in biochemistry and pharmacology, we are offered a workable alternative. We see that it may soon be possible for us to do something better in the way of chemical self-transcendence than what we have been doing so ineptly for the last seventy or eighty centuries.

Is it possible for a powerful drug to be completely harmless? Perhaps not. But the physiological cost can certainly be reduced to the point where it becomes negligible. There are powerful mind changers which do their work without damaging the taker's psychophysical organism and without inciting him to behave like a criminal or a lunatic. Biochemistry and pharmacology are just getting into their stride. Within a few years there will probably be dozens of powerful but—physiologically and socially speaking—very inexpensive mind changers on the market.

In view of what we already have in the way of powerful but nearly harmless drugs; in view, above all, of what unquestionably we are very soon going to have—we ought to start immediately to give some serious thought to the problem of the new mind changers. How ought they to be used? How can they be abused? Will human beings be better and happier for their discovery? Or worse and more miserable?

The matter requires to be examined from many points of view. It is simultaneously a question for biochemists and physicians, for psychologists and social anthropologists, for legislators and law-enforcement officers. And finally it is an ethical question and a religious question. Sooner or later—and the sooner, the better—the various specialists concerned will have to meet, discuss and then decide, in the light of the best available evidence and the most imaginative kind of foresight, what should be done. Meanwhile let us take a preliminary look at this many-faceted problem.

Last year [1956] American physicians wrote 48,000,000 prescriptions for tranquilizing drugs, many of which have been refilled, probably more than once. The tranquilizers are the best known of the new, nearly harmless mind changers. They can be used by most people, not indeed with complete impunity, but at a reasonably low physiological cost. Their enormous popularity bears witness to the fact that a great many people dislike both their environment and "their sweating selves." Under tranquilizers the degree of their self-transcendence is not very great; but it is enough to make all the difference, in many cases, between misery and contentment.

In theory, tranquilizers should be given only to persons suffering from rather severe forms of neurosis or psychosis. In practice, unfortunately, many physicians have been carried away by the current pharmacological fashion and are prescribing tranquilizers to all and sundry. The history of medical fashions, it may be remarked, is at least as grotesque as the history of fashions in women's hats—at least as grotesque and, since human lives are at stake, considerably more tragic. In the present case, millions of patients who had no real need of the tranquilizers have been given the pills by their doctors and have learned to resort to them in every predicament, however triflingly uncomfortable. This is very bad medicine and, from the pill taker's point of view, dubious morality and poor sense.

There are circumstances in which even the healthy are justified in resorting to the chemical control of negative emotions. If you really can't keep your temper, let a tranquilizer keep it for you. But for healthy people to resort to a chemical mind changer every time they feel annoyed or anxious or tense is neither sensible nor right. Too much tension and anxiety can reduce a man's efficiency—but so can too little. There are many occasions when it is entirely proper for us to feel concerned, when an excess of placidity might reduce our chances of dealing effectively with a ticklish situation. On these occasions, tension mitigated and directed from within by the psychological methods of self-control is preferable from every point of view to complacency imposed from without by the methods of chemical control.

And now let us consider the case—not, alas, a hypothetical case—of two societies competing with each other. In Society A, tranquilizers are available by prescription and at a rather stiff price—which means, in practice, that their use is confined to that rich and influential minority which provides the society with its leadership. This minority of leading citizens consumes several billions of the complacency-producing pills every year. In Society B, on the other hand, the tranquilizers are not so freely available, and the members of the influential minority do not resort, on the slightest provocation, to the chemical control of what may be necessary and productive tension. Which of these two competing societies is likely to win the race? A society whose leaders make an excessive use of soothing syrups is in danger of falling behind a society whose leaders are not overtranquilized.

Now let us consider another kind of drug—still undiscovered, but probably just around the corner—a drug capable of making people feel happy in situations where they would normally feel miserable. Such a drug would be a blessing, but a blessing fraught with grave political dangers. By making harmless chemical euphoria freely available, a dictator could reconcile an entire population to a state of affairs to which self-respecting human beings ought not to be reconciled.

Despots have always found it necessary to supplement force by political or religious propaganda. In this sense the pen is mightier than the sword. But mightier than either the pen or the sword is the pill. In mental hospitals it has been found that chemical restraint is far more effective than strait jackets or psychiatry. The dictatorships of tomorrow will deprive men of their freedom, but will give them in exchange a happiness none the less real, as a subjective experience, for being chemically induced. The pursuit of happiness is one of the traditional rights of man; unfortunately, the achievement of happiness may turn out to be incompatible with another of man's rights—namely, liberty.

It is quite possible, however, that pharmacology will restore with one hand what it takes away with the other. Chemically induced euphoria could easily become a threat to individual liberty; but chemically induced vigor and chemically heightened intelligence could easily be liberty's strongest bulwark. Most of us function at about 15 per cent of capacity. How can we step up our lamentably low efficiency?

Two methods are available—the educational and the biochemical. We can take adults and children as they are and give them a much better training than we are giving them now. Or, by appropriate biochemical methods, we can transform them into superior individuals. If these superior individuals are given a superior education, the results will be revolutionary. They will be startling even if we continue to subject them to the rather poor educational methods at present in vogue.

Will it in fact be possible to produce superior individuals by biochemical means? The Russians certainly believe it. They are now halfway through a Five Year Plan to produce "pharmacological substances that normalize higher nervous activity and heighten human capacity for work." Precursors of these future mind improvers are already being experimented with. It has been found, for example, that when given in massive doses some of the vitamins—nicotinic acid and ascorbic acid for example—sometimes produce a certain heightening of psychic energy. A combination of two enzymes—ethylene disulphonate and adenosine triphosphate, which, when injected together, improve carbohydrate metabolism in nervous tissue—may also turn out to be effective.

Meanwhile good results are being claimed for various new synthetic, nearly harmless stimulants. There is iproniazid, which, according to some authorities, "appears to increase the total amount of psychic energy." Unfortunately, iproniazid in large doses has side effects which in some cases may be extremely serious! Another psychic energizer is an amino alcohol which is thought to increase the body's production of acetylcholine, a substance of prime importance in the functioning of the nervous system. In view of what has already been achieved, it seems quite possible that, within a few years, we may be able to lift ourselves up by our own biochemical bootstraps.

In the meantime let us all fervently wish the Russians every success in their current pharmacological venture. The discovery of a drug capable of increasing the average individual's psychic energy, and its wide distribution throughout the U.S.S.R., would probably mean the end of Russia's present form of government. Generalized intelligence and mental alertness are the most powerful enemies of dictatorship and at the same time the basic conditions of effective democracy. Even in the democratic West we could do with a bit of psychic energizing. Between them, education and pharmacology may do something to offset the effects of that deterioration of our biological material to which geneticists have frequently called attention.

From these political and ethical considerations let us now pass to the strictly religious problems that will be posed by some of the new mind changers. We can foresee the nature of these future problems by studying the effects of a natural mind changer, which has been used for centuries past in religious worship; I refer to the peyote cactus of Northern Mexico and the Southwestern United States. Peyote contains mescaline—which can now be produced synthetically—and mescaline, in William James' phrase, "stimulates the mystical faculties in human nature" far more powerfully and in a far more enlightening way than alcohol and, what is more, it does so at a physiological and social cost that is negligibly low. Peyote produces self-transcendence in two ways—it introduces the taker into the Other World of visionary experience, and it gives him a sense of solidarity with his fellow worshipers, with human beings at large and with the divine nature of things.

The effects of peyote can be duplicated by synthetic mescaline and by LSD (lysergic acid diethylamide), a derivative of ergot. Effective in incredibly small doses, LSD is now being used experimentally by psychotherapists in Europe, in South America, in Canada and the United States. It lowers the barrier between conscious and subconscious and permits the patient to look more deeply and understandingly into the recesses of his own mind. The deepening of self-knowledge takes place against a background of visionary and even mystical experience.

When administered in the right kind of psychological environment, these chemical mind changers make possible a genuine religious experience. Thus a person who takes LSD or mescaline may suddenly understand—not only intellectually but organically, experientially—the meaning of such tremendous religious affirmations as "God is love," or "Though He slay me, yet will I trust in Him."

It goes without saying that this kind of temporary self-transcendence is no guarantee of permanent enlightenment or a lasting improvement of conduct. It is a "gratuitous grace." which is neither necessary nor sufficient for salvation, but which if properly used, can be enormously helpful to those who have received it. And this is true of all such experiences, whether occurring spontaneously, or as the result of swallowing the right kind of chemical mind changer, or after undertaking a course of "spirtual exercises" or bodily mortification.

Those who are offended by the idea that the swallowing of a pill may contribute to a genuinely religious experience should remember that all the standard mortifications—fasting, voluntary sleeplessness and self-torture—inflicted upon themselves by the ascetics of every religion for the purpose of acquiring merit, are also, like the mind-changing drugs, powerful devices for altering the chemistry of the body in general and the nervous system in particular. Or consider the procedures generally known as spiritual exercises. The breathing techniques taught by the yogi of India result in prolonged suspensions of respiration. These in turn result in an increased concentration of carbon dioxide in the blood; and the psychological consequence of this is a change in the quality of consciousness. Again, meditations involving long, intense concentration upon a single idea or image may also result—for neurological reasons which I do not profess to understand—in a slowing down of respiration and even in prolonged suspensions of breathing.

Many ascetics and mystics have practiced their chemistry-changing mortifications and spiritual exercises while living, for longer or shorter periods, as hermits. Now, the life of a hermit, such as Saint Anthony, is a life in which there are very few external stimuli. But as Hebb, John Lilly and other experimental psychologists have recently shown in the laboratory, a person in a limited environment, which provides very few external stimuli, soon undergoes a change in the quality of his consciousness and may transcend his normal self to the point of hearing voices or seeing visions, often extremely unpleasant, like so many of Saint Anthony's visions, but sometimes beatific.

That men and women can, by physical and chemical means, transcend themselves in a genuinely spiritual way is something which, to the squeamish idealist, seems rather shocking. But, after all, the drug or the physical exercise is not the cause of the spiritual experience, it is only its occasion.

Writing of William James' experiments with nitrous oxide, Bergson has summed up the whole matter in a few lucid sentences. "The psychic disposition was there, potentially, only waiting a signal to express itself in action. It might have been evoked spiritually by an effort made on its own spiritual level. But it could just as well be brought about materially, by an inhibition of what inhibited it, by the removing of an obstacle; and this effect was the wholly negative one produced by the drug." Where, for any reason, physical or moral, the psychological dispositions are unsatisfactory, the removal of obstacles by a drug or by ascetic practices will result in a negative rather than a positive spiritual experience. Such an infernal experience is extremely distressing, but may also be extremely salutary. There are plenty of people to whom a few hours in hell—the hell that they themselves have done so much to create—could do a world of good.

Physiologically costless, or nearly costless, stimulators of the mystical faculties are now making their appearance, and many kinds of them will soon be on the market. We can be quite sure that, as and when they become available, they will be extensively used. The urge to self-transcendence is so strong and so general that it cannot be otherwise. In the past, very few people have had spontaneous experiences of a premystical or fully mystical nature; still fewer have been willing to undergo the psychophysical disciplines which prepare an insulated individual for this kind of self-transcendence. The powerful but nearly costless mind changers of the future will change all this completely. Instead of being rare, premystical and mystical experiences will become common. What was once the spiritual privilege of the few will be made available to the many. For the ministers of the world's organized religions, this will raise a number of unprecedented problems. For most people, religion has always been a matter of traditional symbols and of their own emotional, intellectual and ethical response to those symbols. To men and women who have had direct experience of self-transcendence into the mind's Other World of vision and union with the nature of things, a religion of mere symbols is not likely to be very satisfying. The perusal of a page from even the most beautifully written cookbook is no substitute for the eating of dinner. We are exhorted to "*taste* and see that the Lord is good."

In one way or another, the world's ecclesiastical authorities will have to come to terms with the new mind changers. They may come to terms with them negatively, by refusing to have anything to do with them. In that case, a psychological phenomenon, potentially of great spiritual value, will manifest itself outside the pale of organized religion. On the other hand, they may choose to come to terms with the mind changers in some positive way—exactly how, I am not prepared to guess.

My own belief is that, though they may start by being something of an embarrassment, these new mind changers will tend in the long run to deepen the spiritual life of the communities in which they are available. That famous "revival of religion," about which so many people have been talking for so long, will not come about as the result of evangelistic mass meetings or the television appearances of photogenic clergymen. It will come about as the result of biochemical discoveries that will make it possible for large numbers of men and women to achieve a radical self-transcendence and a deeper understanding of the nature of things. And this revival of religion will be at the same time a revolution. From being an activity mainly concerned with symbols, religion will be transformed into an activity concerned mainly with experience and intuition—an everyday mysticism underlying and giving significance to everyday rationality, everyday tasks and duties, everyday human relationships.

ALDOUS HUXLEY (1894-1963), English novelist and essayist, was born in Godalming in Surrey County, England. The grandson of the biologist T. H. Huxley and grandnephew of the poet Matthew Arnold, he wished to become a doctor. Shortly after he began to study biology, he contracted keratitis and in a few months became almost completely blind. Learning to read both music and books in Braille and to use a typewriter, he continued his education with a tutor. When one eye recovered sufficiently to allow him to read with a magnifying glass, he went to Oxford, where he read English literature and philology, his impaired vision making a scientific course impossible. During his last years he adopted a personal mysticism, saying, "It is with the problem of personal, psychological freedom that I now find myself predominately concerned." Recipient of the Award of Merit for the Novel and of the Gold Medal from the American Academy of Arts and Letters, Huxley wrote his first novel at eighteen on a typewriter, but the manuscript was lost before he regained sufficient eyesight to read it. Among his best-known books are *Crome Yellow, Antic Hay, Point Counter Point, Brave New World, Eyeless in Gaza, The Doors of Perception,* and *Literature and Science.*

Vocabulary Study

From the list below, select the word or phrase nearest in meaning to the italicized word in the following excerpts.

A. biochemically *predestined* to alcoholism
B. *excruciating* rheumatic pains
C. What an *apocalypse!*
D. the *unfathomable* miracle of existence
E. the price is *exorbitantly* high
F. Chemically induced *euphoria*
G. *Precursors* of these future mind improvers
H. not only intellectually, but organically, *experientially*
I. often extremely unpleasant, like so many of Saint Anthony's visions, but sometimes *beatific*
J. the removal of obstacles by a drug or by *ascetic* practices

blissful	revelation
macabre	exonerating
well-being	incomprehensible
empirically	forerunners
foreordained	self-denying
agonizing	excessively
bedeviled	predictors

Questions on Form and Content

A. What is the topic sentence of the first two paragraphs?

B. What is the pattern of development in the first four paragraphs? How are they connected with one another?

C. With what drugs is Mr. Huxley concerned in this essay?

D. How is the entire essay an answer to Mr. Huxley's initial question: "Why should multitudes of men and women be so ready to sacrifice themselves for a cause so utterly hopeless and in ways so painful and so profoundly humiliating?" In your reply, consider what Mr. Huxley says about the use of alcohol, opium, tranquilizers, peyote, mescaline, and LSD.

E. Mr. Huxley says that complete prohibition of all chemical mind changers can be decreed, but not enforced. What policy has been, according to Mr. Huxley, even more unsatisfactory than complete prohibition?

F. What course for drug control do most civilized societies follow today?

G. What political dangers might the unlimited use of drugs entail?

H. How does Mr. Huxley envision drugs as a possible method to make us more productive?

I. What change does Mr. Huxley think the new drugs may make in religion?

J. This essay was first published in 1957. What events have transpired since in respect to drug use and abuse, control, or treatment that might have caused Mr. Huxley to modify any of his ideas?

Suggestions for Writing

A. In California, alcololism is the sixth leading cause of death for people aged 35-54. An estimated eight out of every one hundred residents of California (men and women) are alcoholics. In the nation, there are thirty known alcoholics for every known drug abuser. "The blissful of self-transcendence which alcohol makes possible has to be paid for, and the price is exorbitantly high," says Mr. Huxley. Comment.

B. How high is the price for the user of heroin, or LSD, or marijuana, or tranquilizers?

C. "Complete prohibition of all chemical mind changers can be decreed, but cannot be enforced, and tends to create more evils than it cures. Even more unsatisfactory has been the policy of complete toleration and unrestricted availability," says Mr. Huxley. Should all alcohol and all drugs be completely prohibited? If not, should they be unrestrictedly available? If neither, what control would you suggest?

D. Charles McCabe, *San Francisco Chronicle* columnist, recently characterized California drug laws as "inhumane, unenforceable, and splendidly silly." He said that the present marijuana law under which possession or use is a felony is completely unenforceable. "A felony under old English common law was an offense serious enough to warrant the loss of the land or the goods or the life of the offender, such as homicide, rape, larceny, burglary, or arson. How drug use ever got tied up with such offenses in this country is one of the anomalies of the Puritan conscience which passes belief," says Mr. McCabe. Comment.

E. Recent legislation has decreed that it is no longer a felony to be found in the presence of one who is smoking marijuana unless he is in your home or automobile or in a similar location, where, presumably, you have responsibility for if not control of actions that occur. Comment on the justice of this decision. Would you advocate further changes in the laws governing the use of marijuana?

F. It was 1957 when Mr. Huxley wrote in this essay: "Within a few years there will probably be dozens of powerful but—physiologically and socially speaking—very inexpensive mind changers on the market." Was he right? If so, what are they? How inexpensive are they? On what market are they available?

G. Mr. Huxley says that we should begin immediately to consider seriously the problem of the new mind changers. How would you answer one or more of the questions he asks: "How ought they to be used? How can they be abused? Will human beings be better and happier for their discovery? Or worse and more miserable?"

H. Mr. Huxley says that "for healthy people to resort to a chemical mind changer every time they feel annoyed or anxious or tense is neither sensible nor right. Too much tension and anxiety can reduce a man's efficiency—but so can too little." Do you agree? Why or why not?

I. Are you "offended by the idea that the swallowing of a pill may contribute to a genuinely religious experience"? If so, why? If not, why not?

J. Through appropriate chemical methods, we can transform both adults and children into superior individuals, according to Mr. Huxley. Recently the nation's attention was drawn to reports that thousands of school children in Omaha, Nebraska, are taking drugs designed to improve their classroom behavior and increase their learning potential. A Federal agency and a congressional committee chairman ordered separate investigations of reports that five to ten per cent of Omaha's school children are involved in the experiment. "The rationale, or excuse, given for this frightening project is that the students involved are hyperactive. I seem to recall that many of western civilization's greatest minds and most brilliant achievers were similarly characterized during their school days," said Representative Cornelius E. Gallagher. He then asked: "Should drugs have been administered to Albert Einstein? What have we come to when we employ our own youngsters as guinea pigs in a grotesque game of psychological chance? How can we expect our national war against drug abuse to succeed when those in authority abuse drugs themselves?" Comment.

What Are Hallucinogens?

Hallucinogens (also called psychedelics) are drugs capable of provoking changes of sensation, thinking, self-awareness and emotion. Alterations of time and space perception, illusions, hallucinations and delusions may be either minimal or overwhelming depending on the dose. The results are very variable; a "high" or a "bad trip" ("freakout" or "bummer") may occur in the same person on different occasions.

LSD is the most potent and best-studied hallucinogen. Besides LSD, a large number of synthetic and natural hallucinogens are known. Mescaline from the peyote cactus, psilocybin from the Mexican mushroom, morning glory seeds, DMT, STP, MDA and dozens of others are known and abused. Along with its active component THC, marihuana is medically classified as an hallucinogen.

☐National Clearinghouse for Drug Abuse Information, *A Federal Source Book: Answers to the most frequently asked questions about drug abuse* (Washington, D.C., 1970), pp. 13-16.

Is It True that Any Drug Will Make You Hallucinate if Taken in Sufficient Amounts?

Many drugs will cause a delirium, accompanied by hallucinations and delusions, when taken by people who are hypersensitive to them. Extraordinarily large amounts of certain drugs may also produce hallucinations. However, the mind-altering drugs are much more likely to induce hallucinations because of their direct action on the brain-cells.

What Is LSD?

Lysergic acid comes from ergot, the fungus that spoils rye grain. It was first converted in 1938 to lysergic acid diethylamide (LSD) by the Swiss chemist, Albert Hoffman, who accidentally discovered its mind-altering properties in 1943.

What Are the Immediate Physical Effects of LSD?

A person who has consumed LSD will have dilated pupils, a flushed face, perhaps a rise in temperature and heartbeat, a slight increase in blood pressure, and a feeling of being chilly. A rare convulsion has been noted. These effects disappear as the action of the drug subsides.

What Is the LSD State Like?

The LSD state varies greatly according to the dosage, the personality of the user and the conditions under which the drug is taken. Basically, it causes changes in sensation. Vision is most markedly altered. Changes in depth perception and the meaning of the perceived object are most frequently described. Illusions and hallucinations can occur. Thinking may become pictorial and reverie states are common. Delusions are expressed. The sense of time and of self are strangely altered. Strong emotions may range from bliss to horror, sometimes within a single experience. Sensations may "crossover," that is, music may be seen or color heard. The individual is suggestible and, especially under high doses, loses his ability to discriminate and evaluate his experience.

What Is a "Good Trip"? a "Bad Trip"?

In the parlance of the LSD user, the "good trip" consists of pleasant imagery and emotional feelings. The "bad trip" or "bummer" is the opposite. Perceived images are terrifying and the emotional state is one of dread and horror.

What Are Some of the More Harmful Effects of LSD?

During the LSD state, the loss of control can cause panic reactions or feelings of grandeur. Both have led to injury or death when the panic or the paranoia was acted upon.

The prolonged reactions consist of anxiety and depressive states, or psychotic breaks with reality which may last from a few days to years.

What Is a "Flashback"?

A "flashback" is a recurrence of some of the features of the LSD state days or months after the last dose. It can be invoked by physical or psychological stress, or by medications such as antihistamines, or by marihuana.

Those individuals who have used LSD infrequently rarely report flashbacks; intensive use seems to produce them more frequently. Often a flashback occurring without apparent cause can induce anxiety and concern that one is going mad. This can result in considerable fear and depression and has been known to culminate in suicide.

Can LSD Damage Chromosomes?

A number of reputable scientists have reported chromosomal fragmentation in connection with LSD exposure in the test tube, in animals, and in man. A similar number of equally capable scientists have been unable to confirm these findings. The question whether LSD itself can induce congenital abnormalities remains unresolved. Further work is continuing and will clarify this question.

Is There Any Evidence that Heavy LSD Use Causes Brain Cell Changes?

In experiments designed to answer this question, some changes in mental functions have been detected in heavy users, but they are not present in all cases.

Heavy users of LSD sometimes develop impaired memory and attention span, mental confusion, and difficulty with abstract thinking. These signs of organic brain changes may be subtle or pronounced. It is not known whether these alterations persist or whether they are reversible if the use of LSD is discontinued.

Are People More Creative Under or After LSD?

People who have taken LSD feel more creative. Whether they actually are or not is difficult to determine. In studies done to compare individuals' creative capabilities before and after LSD experiences, it was found that no significant changes had occurred. Creativity might conceivably be enhanced in a few instances, but it is diminished in others because LSD may reduce the motivation to work and execute creative ideas.

Is the LSD State Like the Mystical State?

The transcendental or mystical state includes feelings of wonder or ecstasy, a sense of perceiving beauty, the absence of rational thought, a sense of discovering great meaning. Many of these phenomena can be mimicked by the LSD state, which is why it has been called a "religious" drug. The LSD-induced mystical state differs as significantly from the natural one as an artificial pearl from the real thing.

Do You Really Get to Know Yourself after LSD?

The *illusion* that one obtains insights about one's personality and behavior while under LSD may occur. From an analysis of these "insights" and of subsequent behavior, it is doubtful that true insights happen with any regularity.

Why Would Anybody Try a Drug like LSD?

People give many reasons for trying LSD, ranging from curiosity to a desire to "know oneself." The overwhelming majority of people take the drug for the "high"—to feel better. This may be because they are unable to deal with life's frustrations, or feel alienated. If the LSD state were not accompanied by a "high," it would never have become popular.

What Percentage of Students Have Tried LSD?

Most surveys indicate that about 4 percent of college students have tried LSD at least once. This figure has remained relatively stable for the past three years. However, numbers of high school and junior high school students are known to have tried this drug recently.

Is the Use of LSD Increasing?

The use of LSD has levelled off and may be decreasing. Although some very young people are turning to LSD, a number of the older users are discontinuing its use. This shift is probably due to the growing knowledge of the side effects, the "flashbacks," the possibility of chromosomal changes, or simply because the users finally have come to recognize the illusory nature of the LSD experience.

What Have We Learned from LSD?

LSD is the most potent of all hallucinogenic substances used by man. A minute amount reaching the brain produces striking effects on mental functioning.

From research with LSD we have gained much basic information about the nature of brain cell transmission, and how distortion of the chemical mediators of transmission can result in disruptive mental functioning. Experiments that have sought to find a use for this unusual chemical have been inconclusive. It has been tried for the severe alcoholic, in certain character disorders, in childhood autism and as an aid to psychotherapy. At present no medical usefulness has been found.

Is Much Research Going on Using LSD?

More than 300 investigators have been given supplies of this drug through the National Institute of Mental Health to carry out research in the past three years. Considerable important work is continuing.

What Is the Source of Illicit LSD?

Almost invariably, illicit LSD comes from clandestine laboratories or is smuggled in from abroad. The precursors, lysergic acid and lysergic acid amide, can be converted into lysergic acid diethylamide (LSD) by a proficient chemist who has a reasonably well-equipped laboratory.

When obtained from illicit sources, the quality of LSD varies. Some LSD is fairly pure; other samples contain impurities and adulterants. The amount contained in each capsule or tablet usually differs greatly from the amount claimed by the "pusher." The user has no way of knowing the quality or the quantity of his LSD.

The preceding and following selections are from *A Federal Source Book: Answers to the most frequently asked questions about drug abuse,* produced jointly by the Department of Defense; Department of Health, Education, and Welfare; Department of Justice; Department of Labor; and Office of Economic Opportunity.

Drug Glossary

National Clearinghouse for Drug Abuse Information

Acid	LSD, LSD-25 (lysergic acid diethylamide)
Acidhead	Frequent user of LSD
Bag	Packet of drugs
Ball	Absorption of stimulants and cocaine via genitalia
Bang	Injection of drugs
Barbs	Barbiturates
Bennies	Benzedrine, an amphetamine
Bindle	Packet of narcotics
Blank	Extremely low-grade narcotics
Blast	Strong effect from a drug
Blue angels	Amytal, a barbiturate
Blue velvet	Paregoric (camphorated tincture of opium) and Pyribenzamine (an antihistamine) mixed and injected

□ National Clearinghouse for Drug Abuse Information, *A Federal Source Book: Answers to the most frequently asked questions about drug abuse* (Washington, D.C., 1970), pp. 27-29.

Bombita	Amphetamine injection, sometimes taken with heroin
Bread	Money
Bum trip	Bad experience with psychedelics
Bummer	Bad experience with psychedelics
Busted	Arrested
Buttons	The sections of the peyote cactus
Cap	Capsule
Chipping	Taking narcotics occasionally
Coasting	Under the influence of drugs
Cokie	Cocaine addict
Cold turkey	Sudden withdrawal of narcotics (from the gooseflesh, which resembles the skin of a cold plucked turkey)
Coming down	Recovering from a trip
Connection	Drug supplier
Cop	To obtain heroin
Cop out	Quit, take off, confess, defect, inform
Crash	The effects of stopping the use of amphetamines
Crash pad	Place where the user withdraws from amphetamines
Crystal	Methedrine, an amphetamine
Cubehead	Frequent user of LSD
Cut	Dilute drugs by adding milk sugar or another inert substance
Dealer	Drug supplier
Deck	Packet of narcotics
Dexies	Dexedrine, an amphetamine
Dime bag	$10 package of narcotics
Dirty	Possessing drugs, liable to arrest if searched
Dollies	Dolophine (also known as methadone), a synthetic narcotic
Doper	Person who uses drugs regularly
Downers	Sedatives, alcohol, tranquilizers, and narcotics
Drop	Swallow a drug
Dummy	Purchase which did not contain narcotics
Dynamite	High-grade heroin
Fix	Injection of narcotics
Flash	The initial feeling after injecting
Flip	Become psychotic

Floating	Under the influence of drugs
Freakout	Bad experience with psychedelics; also a chemical high
Fuzz	The police
Gage	Marihuana
Good trip	Happy experience with psychedelics
Goofballs	Sleeping pills
Grass	Marihuana
H	Heroin
Hard narcotics	Opiates, such as heroin and morphine
Hard stuff	Heroin
Hash	Hashish, the resin of *Cannabis*
Hay	Marihuana
Head	Person dependent on drugs
Hearts	Dexedrine tablets (from the shape)
Heat	The police
High	Under the influence of drugs
Holding	Having drugs in one's possession
Hooked	Addicted
Hophead	Narcotics addict
Horse	Heroin
Hustle	Activities involved in obtaining money to buy heroin
Hustler	Prostitute
Hype	Narcotics addict
Joint	Marihuana cigarette
Jolly beans	Pep pills
Joy-pop	Inject narcotics irregularly
Junkie	Narcotics addict
Kick the habit	Stop using narcotics (from the withdrawal leg muscle twitches)
Layout	Equipment for injecting drug
Lemonade	Poor heroin
M	Morphine
Mainline	Inject drugs into a vein

Maintaining	Keeping at a certain level of drug effect
(The) Man	The police
Manicure	Remove the dirt, seeds, and stems from marihuana
Mesc	Mescaline, the alkaloid in peyote
Meth	Methamphetamine (also known as Methedrine, Desoxyn)
Methhead	Habitual user of methamphetamine
Mikes	Micrograms (millionths of a gram)
Narco	Narcotics detective
Nickel bag	$5 packet of drugs
O. D.	Overdose of narcotics
On the nod	Sleepy from narcotics
Panic	Shortage of narcotics on the market
Pillhead	Heavy user of pills, barbiturates or amphetamines or both
Pop	Inject drugs
Pot	Marihuana
Pothead	Heavy marihuana user
Purple hearts	Dexamyl, a combination of Dexedrine and Amytal (from the shape and color)
Pusher	Drug peddler
Quill	A matchbook cover for sniffing Methedrine, cocaine, or heroin
Rainbows	Tuinal (Amytal and Seconal), a barbiturate combination in a blue and red capsule
Red devils	Seconal, a barbiturate
Reefer	Marihuana cigarette
Reentry	Return from a trip
Roach	Marihuana butt
Roach holder	Device for holding the butt of a marihuana cigarette
Run	An amphetamine binge
Satch cotton	Cotton used to strain drugs before injection; may be used again if supplies are gone
Scag	Heroin
Score	Make a purchase of drugs

Shooting gallery — Place where addicts inject
Skin popping — Injecting drugs under the skin
Smack — Heroin
Smoke — Wood alcohol
Snorting — Inhaling drugs
Snow — Cocaine
Speed — Methedrine, an amphetamine
Speedball — An injection of a stimulant and a depressant, orginally heroin and cocaine
Speedfreak — Habitual user of speed
Stash — Supply of drugs in a secure place
Stick — Marihuana cigarette
Stoolie — Informer
Strung out — Addicted

Tracks — Scars along veins after many injections
Tripping out — High on psychedelics
Turned on — Under the influence of drugs
Turps — Elixir of Terpin Hydrate with Codeine, a cough syrup
25 — LSD (from its original designation, LSD-25)

Uppers — Stimulants, cocaine, and psychedelics

Weed — Marihuana
Works — Equipment for injecting drugs

Yellow jacket — Nembutal, a barbiturate
Yen sleep — A drowsy, restless state during the withdrawal period

Vocabulary Study

Since most drug use has been illicit, its vocabulary has evolved mostly from an underground culture. For obvious reasons, its purpose is often to obfuscate or conceal rather than to elucidate or reveal. In spite of—or perhaps because of—that fact, the vocabulary is often colorful and figurative. What words in the Drug Glossary seem particularly so to you? Are you familiar with most of the terms in this list, which was prepared for the Federal Resource Book? Are there others you have read or heard which are not included here? Are there definitions here which seem inaccurate to you?

Questions on Form and Content

A. What is the value of the question-and-answer format in which this section of the *Federal Source Book* is written?

B. If written in a more conventional essay pattern, the material in "Questions about Hallucinogens" is sufficient to support a fairly common pattern of development, namely, the introduction and definition of the subject—in this case hallucinogens or, more specifically, LSD—followed by an analysis (including a discussion of the effects of the drug—both its purported advantages and disadvantages, the reason for and scope of its use, research into its medical potential, and its source and supply). What, in comparison, are the stylistic limitations of the question-and-answer format?

C. What harmful effects of LSD are listed?

D. Can LSD damage chromosomes or cause brain cell damages?

E. Compare the view expressed here on LSD as a "religious drug" with that expressed by Mr. Huxley. How effective is the comparison employed here: "The LSD-induced mystical state differs as significantly from the natural one as an artificial pearl from the real thing"? Can you always differentiate between the two pearls?

F. Does the material in the *Source Book* seem objective and fair-minded, or do you consider it propaganda? Why, in either case?

Suggestions for Writing

A. How would you answer the question: "Why would anybody try LSD?"

B. From your observation and reading, how would you answer the question: "Is the use of LSD declining?"

C. Panic reactions during the LSD state have led to injury or death. Some victims of the drug have been highly publicized. Do you know of others?

D. Linda Kasabian, a member of Charles Manson's hippie family, was a prosecution witness in the Sharon Tate murder trials. She testified that she had taken LSD approximately fifty times in the past five years and gone on "trips" of varying character in which she experienced hallucinations. When asked why she took LSD and peyote, she replied: "The sole purpose was for God realization." And, later, she added, "I realized you don't have to take peyote or LSD to discover God." Comment on her experience in the light of the Huxley essay and the material in "Questions about Hallucinogens."

E. The Health Insurance Institute said in July, 1970, that at least one out of every forty Americans has smoked marijuana. At the same time a report from the California State Attorney General's Office said "dangerous drug arrests now make up a greater proportion of the total number of drug and narcotic arrests than do those for marijuana." Drug arrest figures reveal that between 1960 and 1969 juvenile arrests for offenses involving methamphetamines, hallucinogens, and synthetic drugs rose a staggering 3316.5 per cent. Similar arrests for adults rose 1067 per cent. Should LSD and the other hallucinogens be legalized? Why or why not?

F. Write a paper discussing some of the colorful or figurative language in the "Drug Glossary."

Kicking Drugs: A Very Personal Story

William S. Burroughs

There is a general feeling in America that the official narcotics agencies must be doing the right thing, a feeling that the officials in question take great pains to foster. Why they should be listened to when what they say adds up neither to good sense nor good intentions is difficult to understand. The official agencies have failed to solve the narcotics problem or to state it honestly. And the nonofficial agencies have done little better. Recently centers of treatment have sprung up where the addicts receive no other medication than prayer. This inspirational and quasi-religious approach to a metabolic illness is ill-advised. It would be equally logical to prescribe prayer for malaria.

In New York many doctors currently prescribe methadone for heroin addicts. They say addicts lose the desire for heroin in the course of this treatment. Over a period of five years they hope to reduce the dosage of methadone, which is an opiate stronger than morphine and quite as addictive. To say that addicts have

□ William S. Burroughs, "Kicking Drugs: A Very Personal Story," *Harper's Magazine,* January, 1967, pp. 39-42.

been cured of heroin by the use of methadone is like saying an alcoholic has been cured of whiskey by the use of gin. If the addicts lose their desire for heroin it is because the methadone dosage is stronger than the diluted heroin they receive from pushers.

Junk is a generic term for all habit-forming preparations and derivatives of opium including the synthetics; any form of junk can cause addiction. Nor does it make much difference whether it is injected, sniffed, or taken orally. The result is always the same—addiction. The addict depends on his junk, just as a diver depends on his air line. When his junk is cut off he suffers agonizing withdrawal symptoms: watering, burning eyes, light fever, hot and cold flashes, leg and stomach cramps, diarrhea, insomnia, prostration—in some cases death from circulatory collapse and shock. Withdrawal symptoms differ from any syndrome of comparable severity in that they are immediately relieved by administering a sufficient quantity of opiates. The withdrawal symptoms reach their peak on the fourth day then gradually disappear over a period of three to six weeks. The later stages of withdrawal are marked by profound depression.

Addiction is an illness of exposure. By and large those who have access to junk become addicts. In Iran, when opium was sold openly in shops there were three million addicts. But there is no pre-addict personality any more than there is a pre-malarial personality, all the hogwash of psychiatry to the contary. (Parenthetically it is my opinion that nine out of ten psychiatrists should be broken down to veterinarians and their books called in for pulping.) To say it country-simple, most folks enjoy junk. Having once experienced this pleasure the human organism will tend to repeat it and repeat it and repeat it. The addict's illness *is* junk.

Knock on any door. Whatever answers, give it four half-grain shots of God's Own Medicine every day for six months and the so-called "addict personality" is there . . . an old junky selling Christmas seals on North Clark Street—the "Priest" they called him, seedy and with furtive, cold fish eyes that seem to be looking at something other folks can't see. That something he is looking at is junk. The whole addict personality can be summed up in one sentence: *The addict needs junk.* He will do a lot to get junk just as you would do a lot for water if you were thirsty enough.

You see junk *is* a personality—a seedy gray man; a rooming house; a shabby street; a room on the top floor; stairs; cough; the "Priest" pulling himself up along the banister; bathroom with yellow wood panels, dripping toilet, works stashed under the wash basin; back in his room now cooking up. A gray shadow on a distant wall—that used to be me, mister.

I was on junk for almost fifteen years. In that time I took ten cures. I have been to Lexington and have taken the reduction treatment. I have taken abrupt withdrawal treatments and prolonged withdrawal treatments; cortisone, tranquilizers, antihistamines and the prolonged sleep cure. In every case I relapsed at the first opportunity.

Why do addicts voluntarily take a cure and then relapse? I think on a deep biological level most addicts want to be cured. Junk *is* death and your body knows it. I relapsed because I was never physiologically cured until 1957. Then I took the apomorphine treatment under the care of a British physician, the late Dr. John Yerbury Dent. Apomorphine is the only agent I know that evicts the "addict personality," an old friend who used to inhabit my body. I called him Opium Jones. We were mighty close in Tangier in 1957, shooting 15 grains of methadone every hour, which equals 30 grains of morphine and that's a lot of junk. I never changed my clothes. Jones likes his clothes to season in stale rooming-house flesh until you can tell by a hat on the table, a coat hung over a chair, that Jones lives there. I never took a bath. Old Jones don't like the feel of water on his skin. I spent whole days looking at the end of my shoe just communing with Jones.

Then one day I saw that Jones was not a real friend, that our interests were in fact divergent. So I took a plane to London and found Dr. Dent, with a charcoal fire in the grate, Scottish terrier, cup of tea. He told me about the treatment and I entered the nursing home the following day. It was one of those four-story buildings on Cromwell Road; my room with rose wallpaper was on the third floor. I had a day nurse and a night nurse and received an injection of apomorphine—one twentieth grain—every two hours.

One's Own Special Symptom

Now every addict has his special symptom, the one that hits him hardest when his junk is cut off. Listen to the old-timers in Lexington talking:

"Now with me it's puking is the worst."

"I never puke. It's this cold burn on my skin drives me up the wall."

"My trouble is sneezing."

With me it's feeling the slow painful death of Mr. Jones. I feel myself encased in his old gray corpse. Not another person in this world I want to see. Not a thing I want to do except revive Mr. Jones.

The third day with my cup of tea at dawn the calm miracle of apomorphine began. I was learning to live without Jones, reading newspapers, writing letters (usually I can't write a letter for a month), and looking forward to a talk with Dr. Dent who isn't Jones at all.

Apomorphine had taken care of my special symptom. After ten days I left the hospital. During the entire cure I had received only two grains of morphine, that is, less than I had been using in one shot. I went back to Tangier, where junk was readily available at that time. I didn't have to use will power, whatever that is. I just didn't want any junk. The apomorphine treatment had given me a long calm look at all the gray junk yesterdays, a long calm look at Mr. Jones standing there in his shabby black suit and gray felt hat with his stale rooming-house flesh and cold undersea eyes.

It Does Its Work and Goes

Apomorphine is made from morphine by boiling with hydrochloric acid but its physiological action is quite different. Morphine sedates the front brain. Apomorphine stimulates the back brain and the vomiting centers. For many years the drug was used only as an emetic in cases of poisoning.

When Dr. Dent started using the apomorphine treatment forty years ago all his patients were alcoholics. He would put a bottle of whiskey by the bed and invite the patient to drink all he wanted. But with each drink the patient received an injection of apomorphine. After a few days the patient conceived such a distaste for alcohol that he would ask to have the bottle removed from the room. Dr. Dent thought at first that this was due to a conditioned aversion since the liquor was associated with a dose of apomorphine that often produced vomiting. However he found that some of his patients were not in the least nauseated by the apomorphine. (There is considerable individual variation.) Nonetheless they experienced the same distaste for alcohol and voluntarily stopped drinking after a few days of treatment. He concluded that his patients conceived a distaste for alcohol because they *no longer needed it* and that apomorphine acts on the back brain to regulate metabolism so that the body no longer needs a sedative to which it has become accustomed. From that time he stressed the fact that apomorphine *is not an aversion treatment.* Apomorphine is a *metabolic regulator* and is the only drug known that acts in this way. Once it has done its work of regulating the metabolism its use can be discontinued. There is no kick to apomorphine and no one would take it for pleasure. Like a good policeman apomorphine does its work and goes. The fact that apomorphine *is not* an addictive substitute drug is crucial. In any reduction cure the addict knows that he is still receiving narcotics and he dreads the time when the last dose is withdrawn. In the apomorphine treatment the addict knows he is getting better *without* morphine.

I feel that any form of so-called psychotherapy is strongly contra-indicated for addicts. Addicts should not be led to dwell on or relive the addict experience since this conduces to relapse. The question, "Why did you start using narcotics in the first place?" should never be asked. It is quite as irrelevant to treatment as it would be to ask a malarial patient why he went to a malarial area.

Dr. Xavier Coore of Paris told me that he finds apomorphine an extremely useful drug in general practice. He has prescribed it for anxiety, grief, nervousness, insomnia, and in short for all the conditions where tranquilizers and barbituates are usually given. Certainly it is a much safer drug since there is no danger of addiction or even dependence. When you take apomorphine for a severe emotional state you have faced the problem, not avoided it. The apomorphine has normalized your metabolism, always disturbed in any emotional upset, so that you can face the problem with calmness and sanity. Apomorphine is the *antianxiety* drug. I have witnessed on others and experienced myself dramatic relief from anxiety caused by mescaline after a dose of apomorphine where tranquilizers were quite ineffective.

A number of addicts have taken the apomorphine treatment at my suggestion. All agree that it is the only treatment that works and also the least painful form of treatment. Yet most American doctors are completely ignorant of its use in treating addictions. Apomorphine is listed as a narcotic in the United States and subject to the same regulations as morphine and heroin. In both France and England apomorphine is not on the dangerous drug list. A doctor's prescription is required but the prescription can be refilled any number of times. It is difficult to avoid the conclusion that a deliberate attempt has been made in the United States to mislead medical opinion and minimize the value of the apomorphine treatment.

WILLIAM SEWARD BURROUGHS was born in St. Louis in 1914. He received the A.B. degree from Harvard in 1936, where he subsequently pursued graduate studies in ethnology and archeology. Later he studied medicine at the University of Vienna. He served with AUS in World War II and has been a newspaper reporter, a private detective, and an exterminator. His books include *Junkie: Confessions of an Unredeemed Drug Addict; Naked Lunch; The Exterminator; Minutes to Go; The Soft Machine; The Ticket that Exploded; Dead Fingers Talk; Nova Express;* and *The Yage Letters* (with Allen Ginsberg).

Vocabulary Study

From the list below, select the word or phrase nearest in meaning to the word italicized in the following excerpts.

A. a feeling that the officials in question take great pains to *foster.*
B. any *syndrome* of comparable severity
C. relieved by *administering* a sufficient quantity of opiates
D. seedy and with *furtive,* cold fish eyes
E. works *stashed* under the wash basin
F. the *prolonged* sleep cure
G. *relapsed* at the first opportunity
H. a conditioned *aversion*
I. prescribed it for anxiety, grief, nervousness, *insomnia*
J. to mislead medical opinion and *minimize* the value of

damaged	encourage
belittle	patterns of symptoms
fell back	extended
sleeplessness	shifty
giving	exaggerate
deviate	abhorrence
stowed	belittle

Questions on Form and Content

A. Where do the topic sentences occur throughout Mr. Burroughs' account?

B. What pattern of development does Mr. Burroughs use in paragraph 7 ("I was on junk . . ."), paragraph 8 ("Why do addicts . . ."), paragraph 10 ("Now every addict . . ."). Study the material following paragraph 10 to see correct paragraph form for conversation. How many different speakers are quoted there?

C. How does Mr. Burroughs regard official narcotics agencies?

D. How effective does he consider methadone as a treatment for heroin?

E. Who, according to Mr. Burroughs, become addicts? Why?

F. Mr. Burroughs says that he took ten cures and, in every case, relapsed at the first opportunity. Why?

G. On what grounds does Mr. Burroughs disapprove of "so-called psychotherapy" for adults?

H. To what does Mr. Burroughs attribute the fact that most American doctors were ignorant of the use of apomorphine in treating addiction?

Suggestions for Writing

A. "This inspirational and quasi-religious approach to a metabolic illness is ill advised," says Mr. Burroughs. Recently a number of such groups have been formed for the purpose of helping drug addicts. The best known, perhaps, is Synanon, which was founded in 1958 by Charles E. Dederich with a $33 unemployment check. By 1963, the organization was a million-dollar enterprise with establishments in Santa Monica; San Francisco; San Diego; Westport, Connecticut; and Reno, Nevada. Synanon members have spoken to college, university, church, high-school, civic, and other community groups throughout the nation. One of the speakers said recently that college groups were the most difficult and hostile of all groups before which she had appeared. What might explain this fact?

B. Write a paper on a community of former drug addicts. If you would like to read more about their organization, the story of Synanon is related in a book entitled *The Tunnel Back*, by Lewis Yablonsky.

C. In the preface to his book, Mr. Yablonsky says: "Not everyone has supported Synanon. Many segments of society have balked at the spectacle of criminals and addicts living in 'respectable' communities and trying to solve their problems in their own way. Cries of fear and outrage have been followed up by a variety of legal maneuvers. The enemies of Synanon have attempted to drive Synanon people and their families (children included) from their newfound homes and their foothold on a constructive way of life." Discuss some of the reasons, whether you consider them just or unjust, for a Synanon's having been unwelcome.

D. Mr. Yablonsky writes: "The word 'Synanon' originated with a newly arrived addict in the early days of the organization. In his attempt to say two 'foreign' words, 'symposium' and 'seminar,' in the same breath, he blurted out 'synanon': 'I want to get into one of those—symp . . . sen—synanons.' In this way, a new word was introduced into the language to describe a new social phenomenon." What are some other words or expressions that have been introduced into our language—and have now become well known—through the drug culture?

E. Nelson Algren's novel *The Man with the Golden Arm* was one of the first fictional treatments in the United States of drug addiction. Mr. Algren, through this book, added the phrase "monkey on his back" to the English language. Comment on the symbolism and significance of the phrase.

F. If you have read *The Man with the Golden Arm* or seen the movie made from the book, discuss the reasons for Frankie Machine's addiction.

G. "Synanon is more than symposiums and seminars," according to Mr. Yablonsky. "It is a new kind of group therapy; an effective approach to racial integration; a humane solution to some facets of bureaucratic organization; a different way of being religious; a new method of attack therapy; an unusual kind of communication; an exciting, fresh approach to the cultural arts and philosophy." Discuss his remarks in relation to Mr. Huxley's and to Mr. Burroughs's articles.

H. A group similar to Synanon lives in the Swift mansion in Chicago. At open houses, curiously similar to sorority or fraternity rush parties, the ex-addicts explain to their guests the lives they now lead and the experiences they previously had "on the street." Some men and boys have shaved heads; others, exceedingly short hair. They say that their heads have been shorn as punishment for infraction of rules. When asked why no women are similarly identifiable, they explain that, though no more docile or tractable, women suffer more psychological damage from shaved heads and, consequently, wear stocking caps instead when they have broken regulations, caps they are permitted to remove for open houses. Comment on the symbolic meaning of hair. How and why has hair become of particular significance during the past few years?

I. Synanon methods are sometimes used by people who have never been addicts or had serious emotional problems. The "Synanon game," a verbal-emotional encounter, has become famous. Some participants feel it has given them a greater sense of self-awareness and identity. If you have either observed or participated in such a game, evaluate its effect.

J. In their book entitled *The Varieties of Psychedelic Experience,* R. E. L. Masters and Jean Houston say: "There are at least a million users of pot in the country. More important than the number is the fact that it pervades all social classes. Why? Because we are a drug-ridden society. The average adult consumes 3 to 5 drugs a day, starting with coffee and cigarettes in the morning, cokes, booze, aspirin, stimulants, tranquilizers, and a sleeping pill or medication at night. Television is a perfect reflection of this: every time there's a pain or a problem, turn to a drug." How average are you in this regard? How many drugs—that you would care to discuss—have you used today? Are you addicted to any of them?

K. In the fiction of Carson McCullers, Flannery O'Connor, and other Southern writers, a Coca-Cola is called a "dope." What other relatively innocent substances are sometimes so identified? Why?

L. Does it seem consistent that the use of marijuana should be considered a crime while the decision to use alcohol is regarded as a personal moral decision?

M. "Addiction is an illness of exposure. By and large those who have access to junk become addicts," says Mr. Burroughs. The heroin trade amounts to about $2.8 billion a year in this country. By conservative estimate there are about 200,000 addicts in the United States and the number is growing rapidly. Police attribute the great increase in the number of robberies of private homes to heroin addicts who steal in order to support their habit, an expensive one often costing from $50 to $100 a day. The heroin trade is a highly profitable industry. It was recently estimated that about twenty-two pounds of the raw material costs $350 but, processed and packaged, sells for $280,000 to $500,000, yielding profits of perhaps 15 to 1000 per cent to each tradesman involved. What attempts are made to control—or eliminate—the heroin trade?

N. Mr. Burroughs has little faith in methadone, which is widely prescribed in the United States for heroin addicts. Methadone was created by German chemists during World War II as a cheap pain killer to substitute for morphine. Doctors claim that it is a harmless substitute for heroin since it satisfies the physical craving without giving addicts a sublime sense of well-being. By conservative estimate the average heroin addict spends $20,000 a year; $10 worth of methadone would relieve his destructive pressures. But, like heroin, methadone is an addictive drug. It is a pain killer and by strict ethical definition therapeutic for nothing else. Medical ethics says any treatment is unethical which is not therapeutic—which does not cure the disease or eliminate its symptoms. Is it moral to substitute one addiction for another? Is it expedient to do so?

O. Mr. Burroughs concludes: "It is difficult to avoid the conclusion that a deliberate attempt has been made in the United States to mislead medical opinion and minimize the value of the apomorphine treatment." Evaluate this view. Who might make such an attempt? Why? Have you heard of the use of apomorphine recently for drug addition? If so, with what results?

The purpose of most writing is, as we have seen, the development of a central idea. Students usually realize this fact, but they are frequently at a loss for a way to proceed and, as a result, write only masses of unsubstantiated and unillustrated judgments and assertions. One of the easiest and most effective ways to support and clarify an idea is through examples and illustrations. But remember that an example must be clear and that it must be relevant or it will confuse rather than clarify.

In your papers you must decide whether to use one sustained, carefully worked-out example to illustrate your thesis, as Clifton Fadiman does in the final article in this chapter, "More on Emancipated Woman," or whether to use several short ones. In general, if you are trying to show a tendency, trend, or need, several examples are more convincing than a single one, which the reader might consider only an exception and not typical. Sometimes a writer profitably combines both methods by using one or more extended examples developed in considerable detail and several very short ones. Such is the case in "The Oppressed Emancipated Woman," the second selection in this chapter. The author, Eric Goldman, relates early in his essay an extended anecdote which illustrates his main idea: Emancipated woman is really enslaved. As he develops the essay, he uses other anecdotes and many short examples to support this main or theme idea. As you read the selection, notice both methods of illustration.

The Natural Superiority of Women

Ashley Montagu

Oh, no!, I can hear it said, *not* superior. Equal, partners, complementary, different, but *not* superior. I can even foresee that men will mostly smile, while women, alarmed, will rise to the defense of men—women always have, and always will. I hope that what I shall have to say in this article will make them even more willing to do so, for men need their help more than they as yet, mostly, consciously realize.

Women superior to men? This is a new idea. There have been people who have cogently, but apparently not convincingly, argued that women were as good as men, but I do not recall anyone who has publicly provided the evidence or even argued that women were better than or superior to men. How, indeed, could one argue such a case in the face of all the evidence to the contrary? Is it not a fact that by far the largest number of geniuses, great painters, poets, philosophers, scientists, etc., etc., have been men, and that women have made, by comparison,

☐ Ashley Montagu, "The Natural Superiority of Women," *Saturday Review* (March 1, 1952), 8-9+.

a very poor showing? Clearly the superiority is with men. Where are the Leonardos, the Michelangelos, the Shakespeares, the Donnes, the Galileos, the Whiteheads, the Kants, the Bachs, *et. al.*, of the feminine sex? In fields in which women have excelled, in poetry and the novel, how many poets and novelists of the really first rank have there been? Haven't well-bred young women been educated for centuries in music? And how many among them have been great composers or instrumentalists? Composers—none of the first rank. Instrumentalists—well, in the recent period there have been such accomplished artists as Myra Hess and Wanda Landowska. Possibly there is a clue here to the answer to the question asked. May it not be that women are just about to emerge from the period of subjection during which they were the "niggers" of the masculine world?

The Royal Society of London has at last opened its doors and admitted women to the highest honor which it is in the power of the English scientific world to bestow—the Fellowship of the Royal Society. I well remember that when I was a youth—less than a quarter of a century ago—it was considered inconceivable that any woman would ever have brains enough to attain great distinction in science. Mme. Curie was an exception. But the half dozen women Fellows of the Royal Society in England are not. Nor is Lisa Meitner. And Mme. Curie no longer remains the only woman to share in the Nobel Prize award for science. There is Marie Curie's daughter, Irene Joliot-Curie, and there is Gerty Cory (1947) for physiology and medicine. Nobel prizes in literature have gone to Selma Lagerlof, Grazia Deledda, Sigrid Undset, Pearl Buck, and Gabriela Mistral. As an artist Mary Cassatt (1845-1926) was every bit as good as her great French friends Degas and Manet considered her to be, but it has taken the rest of the world another fifty years grudgingly to admit it. Among contemporaries Georgia O'Keeffe can hold her own with the best.

It is not, however, going to be any part of this article to show that women are about to emerge as superior scientists, musicians, painters, or the like. I believe that in these fields they may emerge as equally good, and possibly not in as large numbers as men, largely because the motivations and aspirations of most women will continue to be directed elsewhere. But what must be pointed out is that women are, in fact, just beginning to emerge from the period of subjection when they were treated in a manner not unlike that which is still meted out to the Negro in the Western world. The women of the nineteenth century were the "niggers" of the male-dominated world. All the traits that are mythically attributed to the Negro at the present time were for many generations saddled upon women. Women had smaller brains than men and less intelligence, they were more emotional and unstable, in a crisis you could always rely upon them to swoon or become otherwise helpless, they were weak and sickly creatures, they had little judgment and less sense, could not be relied upon to handle money, and as for the world outside, there they could be employed only at the most menial and routine tasks.

The biggest dent in this series of myths was made by World War I, when women were for the first time called upon to replace men in occupations which were formerly the exclusive preserve of men. They became bus drivers, conductors, factory workers, farm workers, laborers, supervisors, executive officers, and a great many other things at which many had believed they could never work. At first it was said that they didn't do as well as men, then it was grudgingly admitted that they weren't so bad, and by the time the war was over many employers were reluctant to exchange their women employees for men. But the truth was out—women could do as well as men in most of the fields which had been considered forever closed to them because of their alleged natural incapacities, and in many fields, particularly where delicate precision work was involved, they had proved themselves superior to men. From 1918 to 1939 the period for women was one essentially of consolidation of gains, so that by the time that World War II broke out there was no hesitation on the part of anyone in calling upon women to serve in the civilian roles of men and in many cases also in the armed services.

But women have a long way to go before they reach full emancipation—emancipation from the myths from which they themselves suffer. It is, of course, untrue that women have smaller brains than men. The fact is that in proportion to body weight they have larger brains than men; but this fact is in itself of no importance because within the limits of normal variation of brain size and weight there exists no relation between these factors and intelligence. Women have been conditioned to believe that they are inferior to men, and they have assumed that what everyone believes is a fact of nature; and as men occupy the superior positions in almost all societies, this superiority is taken to be a natural one. "Woman's place is in the home" and man's place is in the counting house and on the board of directors. "Women should not meddle in men's affairs." And yet the world does move. Some women have become Members of Parliament and even attained Cabinet rank. In the United States they have even gotten as far as the Senate. They have participated in peace conferences, but it is still inconceivable to most persons that there should ever be a woman Prime Minister or President. And yet that day, too, will come. *Eppur, si muove!*

Woman has successfully passed through the abolition period, the abolition of her thraldom to man; she has now to pass successfully through the period of emancipation, the freeing of herself from the myth of inferiority, and the realization of her potentialities to the fullest.

And now for the evidence which proves the superiority of woman to man. But first, one word in explanation of the use of the word "superiority." The word is used in its common sense as being of better quality than, or of higher nature or character. Let us begin at the very beginning. What about the structure of the sexes? Does one show any superiority over the other? The answer is a resounding "Yes!" And I should like this "Yes" to resound all over the world, for no one has made anything of this key fact which lies at the base of all the differences between the sexes and the superiority of the female to the male. I refer to the chromosomal structure of the sexes. The chromosomes, those small cellular bodies which contain the hereditary particles, the genes, which so substantially influence one's development and fate as an organism, provide us with our basic facts.

In the sex cells there are twenty-four chromosomes, but only one of these is a sex chromosome. There are two kinds of sex chromosomes, X and Y. Half the sperm cells carry X and half carry Y chromosomes. All the female ova are made up of X-chromosomes. When an X-bearing sperm fertilizes an ovum the offspring is always female. When a Y-bearing chromosome fertilizes an ovum the offspring is always male. And this is what makes the difference between the sexes. So what? Well, the sad fact is that the Y-chromosome is but an iota, the merest bit of a remnant of an X-chromosome; it is a crippled X-chromosome. The X-chromosomes are fully developed structures; the Y-chromosome is the merest comma. It is as if in the evolution of sex a particle one day broke away from an X-chromosome, and thereafter in relation to X-chromosomes could produce only an incomplete female—the creature we now call the male! It is to this original chromosomal deficiency that all the various troubles to which the male falls heir can be traced.

In the first place the chromosomal deficiency of the male determines his incapacity to have babies. This has always been a sore point with men, though consciously they would be the last to admit it, although in some primitive societies, as among the Australian aborigines, it is the male who conceives a child by dreaming it, and then telling his wife. In this way a child is eventually born to them, the wife being merely the incubator who hatches the egg placed there through the grace of her husband.

The fact that men cannot have babies and suckle them nor remain in association with their children as closely as the wife has an enormous effect upon their subsequent psychological development. Omitting altogether from consideration the psychologic influences exercised by the differences in the hormonal secretions of the sexes, one can safely say that the mother-child relationship confers enormous benefits upon the mother which are not nearly so substantively operative in the necessary absence of such a relationship between father and child. The maternalizing influences of being a mother in addition to the fact of being a woman has from the very beginning of the human species—about a million years ago—made the female the more humane of the sexes. The love of a mother for her child is the basic patent and the model for *all* human relationships. Indeed, to the extent to which men approximate in their relationships with their fellow men to the love of the mother for her child, to that extent do they move more closely to the attainment of perfect human relations. The mother-child relationship is a dependent-interdependent one. The interstimulation between mother and child is something which the father misses, and to that extent suffers from the want of. In short, the female in the mother-child relationship has the advantage of having to be more considerate, more self-sacrificing, more cooperative, and more altruistic than usually falls to the lot of the male.

The female thus acquires, in addition to whatever natural biological advantages she starts with, a competence in social understanding which is usually denied the male. This, I take it, is one of the reasons why women are usually so much more able to perceive the nuances and pick up the subliminal signs in human behavior which almost invariably pass men by. It was, I believe, George Jean Nathan who called woman's intuition merely man's transparency. With all due deference to Mr. Nathan and sympathy for his lot as a mere male, I would suggest that man's opacity would be nearer the mark. It is because women have had to be so unselfish and forbearing and self-sacrificing and maternal that they possess a deeper understanding than men of what it is to be human. What is so frequently termed feminine indecision, the inability of women to make up their minds, is in fact an inverse reflection of the trigger-thinking of men. Every salesgirl prefers the male customer because women take time to think about what they are buying, and the male usually hasn't the sense enough to do so. Women don't think in terms of "Yes" or "No." Life isn't as simple as all that—except to males. Men tend to think in terms of the all-or-none principle, in terms of black and white. Women are more ready to make adjustments, to consider the alternative possibilities, and see the other colors and gradations in the range between black and white.

By comparison with the deep involvement of women in living, men appear to be only superficially so. Compare the love of a male for a female with the love of the female for the male. It is the difference between a rivulet and a great deep ocean. Women love the human race; men are, on the whole, hostile to it. Men act as if they haven't been adequately loved, as if they had been frustrated and rendered hostile, and becoming aggressive they say that aggressiveness is natural and women are inferior in this respect because they tend to be gentle and unaggressive! But it is precisely in this capacity to love and unaggressiveness that the superiority of women to men is demonstrated, for whether it be natural to be loving and cooperative or not, so far as the human species is concerned, its evolutionary destiny, its very survival is more closely tied to this capacity for love and cooperation than with any other. So that unless men learn from women how to be more loving and cooperative they will go on making the kind of mess of the world which they have so effectively achieved thus far.

And this is, of course, where women can realize their power for good in the world, and make their greatest gains. *It is the function of women to teach men how to be human.* Women must not permit themselves to be deviated from this function by those who tell them that their place is in the home in subservient relation to man. It is, indeed, in the home that the foundations of the kind of world in which we live are laid, and in this sense it will always remain true that the hand that rocks the cradle is the hand that rules the world. And it is in this sense that women must assume the job of making men who will know how to make a world fit for human beings to live in. The greatest single step forward in this direction will be made when women consciously assume this task—the task of teaching their children to be like themselves, loving and cooperative.

As for geniuses, I think that almost everyone will agree that there have been more geniuses for being human among women than there have among men. This, after all, is the true genius of women, and it is because we have not valued the qualities for being human anywhere nearly as highly as we have valued those for accomplishment in the arts and sciences that we have out-of-focusedly almost forgotten them. Surely, the most valuable quality in any human being is his capacity for being loving and cooperative. We have been placing our emphases on the wrong values—it is time we recognized what every man and every woman at the very least subconsciously knows—the value of being loving, and the value of those who can teach this better than anyone else.

Physically and psychically women are by far the superiors of men. The old chestnut about women being more emotional than men has been forever destroyed by the facts of two great wars. Women under blockade, heavy bombardment, concentration camp confinement, and similar rigors withstand them vastly more successfully than men. The psychiatric casualties of civilian populations under such conditions are mostly masculine, and there are more men in our mental hospitals than there are women. The steady hand at the helm is the hand that has had the practice at rocking the cradle. Because of their greater size and weight men are physically more powerful than women—which is not the same thing as saying that they are stronger. A man of the same size and weight as a woman of comparable background and occupational status would probably not be any more powerful than a woman. As far as constitutional strength is concerned women are stronger than men. Many diseases from which men suffer can be shown to be largely influenced by their relation to the male Y-chromosome. From fertilization on, more males die than females. Deaths from almost all causes are more frequent in males at all ages. Though women are more frequently ill than men, they recover from illness more easily and more frequently than men.

Women, in short, are fundamentally more resistant than men. With the exception of the organ systems subserving the functions of reproduction women suffer much less frequently than men from the serious disorders which affect mankind. With the exception of India women everywhere live longer than men. For example, the expectation of life of the female child of white parentage in the United States at the present time is over seventy-one years, whereas for the male it is only sixty-five and a half years. Women are both biologically stronger and emotionally better shock absorbers than men. The myth of masculine superiority once played such havoc with the facts that in the nineteenth century it was frequently denied by psychiatrists that the superior male could ever suffer from hysteria. Today it is fairly well known that males suffer from hysteria and hysteriform conditions with a preponderance over the female of seven to one! Epilepsy is much more frequent in males, and stuttering has an incidence of eight males to one female.

At least four disorders are now definitely known to be due to genes carried in the Y-chromosomes, and hence are disorders which can appear only in males. These are barklike skin (ichthyosis hystrix gravior), dense hairy growth on the ears (hypertrichosis), nonpainful hard lesions of the hands and feet (keratoma dissipatum), and a form of webbing of the toes. It is, however, probable that the disadvantages accruing to the male are not so much due to what is in the Y-chromosome as to what is wanting in it. This is well shown in such serious disorders as hemophilia or bleeder's disease. Hemophilia is inherited as a single sex-linked recessive gene. The gene, or hereditary particle, determining hemophilia is linked to the X-chromosome. When, then, an X-chromosome which carries the hemophilia gene is transmitted to a female it is highly improbable that it will encounter another X-chromosome carrying such a gene; hence, while not impossible, hemophilia has never been described in a female. Females are the most usual transmitters of the hemophilia gene, but it is only the males who are affected, and they are affected because they don't have any properties in their Y-chromosome capable of suppressing the action of the hemophilia gene. The mechanism of and the explanation for (red-green) color blindness is the same. About 8 per cent of all white males are color blind, but only half of one per cent of females are so affected.

Need one go on? Here, in fact, we have the explanation of the greater constitutional strength of the female as compared with the male, namely, in the possession of two complete sex chromosomes by the female and only one by the male. This may not be, and probably is not, the complete explanation of the physical inferiorities of the male as compared with the female, but it is certainly physiologically the most demonstrable and least questionable one. To the unbiased student of the facts there can no longer remain any doubt of the constitutional superiority of the female. I hope that I have removed any remaining doubts about her psychological superiority where psychological superiority most counts, namely, in a human being's capacity for loving other human beings.

I think we have overemphasized the value of intellectual qualities and grossly underemphasized the value of the qualities of humanity which women possess to such a high degree. I hope I shall not be taken for an anti-intellectual when I say that intellect without humanity is not good enough, and that what the world is suffering from at the present time is not so much an overabundance of intellect as an insufficiency of humanity. Consider men like Lenin, Stalin, and Hitler. These are the extreme cases. What these men lacked was the capacity to love. What they possessed in so eminent a degree was the capacity to hate. It is not for nothing that the Bolsheviks attempted to abolish the family and masculinize women, while the Nazis made informers of children against their parents and put the state so much before the family that it became a behemoth which has well-nigh destroyed everyone who was victimized by it.

What the world stands so much in need of at the present time, and what it will continue to need if it is to endure and increase in happiness, is more of the maternal spirit and less of the masculine. We need more persons who will love and less who will hate, and we need to understand how we can produce them; for if we don't try to understand how we may do so we shall continue to flounder in the morass of misunderstanding which frustrated love creates. For frustrated love, the frustration of the tendencies to love with which the infant is born, constitutes hostility. Hatred is love frustrated. This is what too many men suffer from and an insufficient number of women recognize, or at least too many women behave as if they didn't recognize it. What most women have learned to recognize is that the the much-bruited superiority of the male isn't all that it's cracked up to be. The male doesn't seem to be as wise and as steady as they were taught to believe. But there appears to be a conspiracy of silence on this subject. Perhaps women feel that men ought to be maintained in the illusion of their superiority because it might not be good for them or the world to learn the truth. In this sense this article, perhaps, should have been entitled "What Every Woman Knows." But I'm not sure that every woman knows it. What I am sure of is that many women don't appear to know it, and that there are even many women who are horrified at the thought that anyone can entertain the idea that women are anything but inferior to men. This sort of childishness does no one any good. The world is in a mess. Men, without any assistance from women, have created it, and they have created it not because they have been failed by women, but because men have never really given women a chance to serve them as they are best equipped to do—by teaching men how to love their fellow men.

Women must cease supporting men for the wrong reasons in the wrong sort of way, and thus cease causing men to marry them for the wrong reasons, too. "That's what a man wants in a wife, mostly," says Mrs. Poyser (in *Adam Bede*), "he wants to make sure o' one fool as 'ull tell him he's wise." Well, it's time that men learned the truth, and perhaps they are likely to take it more gracefully from another male than from their unacknowledged betters. It is equally important that women learn the truth, too, for it is to them that the most important part, the more fundamental part, of the task of remaking the world will fall, for the world will be remade only by remaking, or rather helping, human beings to realize themselves more fully in terms of what their mothers have to give them. Without adequate mothers life becomes inadequate, nasty, and unsatisfactory, and Mother Earth becomes a battlefield on which fathers slay their young and are themselves slain.

Men have had a long run for their money in running the affairs of the world. It is time that women realized that men will continue to run the world for some time yet, and that they can best assist them to run it more humanely by teaching them, when young, what humanity means. Men will thus not feel that they are being demoted, but rather that their potentialities for good are so much more increased, and what is more important, instead of feeling hostile towards women they will for the first time learn to appreciate them at their proper worth. There is an old Spanish proverb which has it that a good wife is the workmanship of a good husband. Maybe. But of one thing we can be certain: a good husband is the workmanship of a good mother. The best of all ways in which men can help themselves is to help women realize themselves. This way both sexes will come for the first time fully into their own, and the world of mankind may then look forward to a happier history than it has thus far enjoyed.

Ashley Montagu, anthropologist and social biologist, was born in London, studied at the Universities of London, Florence, and Columbia, from which he received his Ph.D. in 1937. He has served as research associate at the British Museum of Natural History, Associate Professor of Anatomy at New York University and at Hahnemann Medical College and Hospital, as Chairman of the Anthropology Department at Rutgers University, as Regents Professor at the University of California at Santa Barbara, as lecturer at Harvard, and, since 1930, as an expert witness on legal and scientific problems relating to race.

Among his books are *The Natural Superiority of Women; Man: His First Two Million Years; The Humanization of Man; The Idea of Race; Up the Ivy; The American Way of Life;* and *Sex, Man, and Society.*

Vocabulary Study

A. In an attempt to insure that the reader interprets certain words Mr. Montagu uses in the way he intends them or, simply, that the reader knows the meaning of other words he employs, Mr. Montagu defines or explains them. What meaning does he give for each of the following?

1. superiority (paragraph 8: "And now . . .")
2. chromosomes and genes (also paragraph 8)
3. hemophilia (paragraph 18: "At least . . .")
4. hatred (paragraph 21: "What the world. . . ")

B. Discuss the meanings of *transparency* and *opacity* as Mr. Montagu uses them in these sentences: "It was, I believe, George Jean Nathan who called woman's intiution merely man's transparency. With all due deference to Mr. Nathan and sympathy for his lot as a mere male, I would suggest that man's opacity would be nearer the mark."

Questions on Form and Content

A. How would you describe Mr. Montagu's introduction?

B. What tone does the author set in his introduction? How? Notice the diction, the direct questions to the reader, and the use of incomplete sentences. Is his style more typical of oral or written communication? How does the punctuation itself lend to the effect?

C. What specific examples does Mr. Montagu use in the second paragraph? In the third? In each case, for what purpose?

D. Mr. Montagu begins his argument by using the familiar debater's technique of yielding a point. What point is it?

E. After making the concession mentioned in D, the author gives a possible explanation for it. What is it?

F. What mythical traits, according to Mr. Montagu, are or have been attributed to both Negroes and women?

G. Mr. Montague attempts to refute these myths. Do his arguments convince you? Why or why not?

H. What does the author use as his chief argument for the superiority of women?

I. What reasons does the author give for considering the female more humane than the male?

J. Criticize Mr. Montagu's conclusion. Where does it begin? What is it? What is its purpose? How effective is it?

Suggestions for Writing

A. Write a rejoinder to Mr. Montagu's arguments. At least one has been published. If you would like to read it, look in *Bluebook*, March, 1954, for Lester David's "The Natural Inferiority of Women."

B. In the article mentioned in A, Mr. David says: "The facts are that women are less intelligent than men, more suspicious, more obstinate, more susceptible to illusions and hallucinations, less judicious, less critical, less able to make long-range plans and almost completely lacking in the ethics that have permitted the growth of the United States." Comment on one or more of these "facts."

C. Mr. Montagu says: "Women have been conditioned to believe that they are inferior to men." If a woman, do you feel inferior to men? Why or why not? In what way does your "conditioning" determine your answer?

D. According to the author, "women, alarmed, will rise to the defense of men—women always have, and always will." Comment.

E. Discuss a woman you consider a "really first rank" poet and explain why you so consider her. Or substitute *novelist, dramatist, painter, philosopher, scientist, composer,* or *instrumentalist* for the word *poet* in the sentence.

F. Mr. Montagu says: "The women of the nineteenth century were the 'niggers' of the male-dominated world." Compare the positions of the two in the world as you know it.

G. Do you believe that a woman's place is in the home? Why or why not?

H. Mr. Montagu says that "it is still inconceivable to most persons that there should ever be a woman Prime Minister or President." Is it quite as inconceivable now as when he wrote the article? Why or why not?

I. Discuss the role of a woman or women in politics today. Consider your local, state, or the national government. If you choose the federal level, are there any women in the President's Cabinet at present? Any United States Senators who are women?

J. Man's incapacity to have babies has always been a sore point with him, contends Montagu. Comment.

K. In relation to J, Lester David wrote: "Women wear all the men's clothes they possibly can, don't they? They don slacks, put on men's shirts, dungarees, polo shirts, other wearables which are strictly masculine. On the other hand, have you ever known a normal male to put on a single item of feminine attire at any time—except for a gag? Wouldn't this show that women subconsciously envy men, want to be men? In any event it proves no more nor less than Professor Montagu's astonishing suggestion that men are jealous of women because they can't have babies." Comment.

L. Mr. Montagu says: "Every salesgirl prefers the male customer." Discuss the buying habits of men and women.

M. The author asks you to "compare the love of a male for a female with the love of the female for the male." He adds: "It is the difference between a rivulet and a great deep ocean." Make the comparison yourself and see if you come to the same conclusion.

N. If you are a woman and dislike the word *female* so much that you try to avoid using it, see if you can give your reasons for doing so. With what do you associate the word? What words do you substitute for it? Why?

O. Discuss the author's views: "The world is in a mess. Men, without any assistance from women, have created it, and they have created it not because they have been failed by women, but because men have never really given women a chance to serve them as they are best equipped to do—by teaching men how to love their fellow men."

P. Mr. Montagu says that women must "cease causing men to marry them for the wrong reasons." For what reasons would you marry a woman? Or for what reasons would you want a man to marry you?

Q. Discuss the logic of Mr. Montagu's argument. Does it sometimes seem questionable to you? Perhaps inconsistent? If so, where and why? Are all of his generalizations substantiated?

R. Discuss the author's style. Do you find lapses or unconventional usage in both grammar and sentence structure? If so, give examples.

S. Discuss Mr. Montagu's statement: "But of one thing we can be certain: a good husband is the workmanship of a good mother." If you are not familiar with Philip Wylie's chapter called "Common Women" from his book *A Generation of Vipers,* you might consult it for a far different view of some kinds of women. It was this chapter, Mr. Wylie says, that put the word "momism" indelibly in our language.

The Oppressed Emancipated Woman

Eric F. Goldman

Every so often, being a historian, I get to brooding about just what History really is. Sometimes History seems to me Fate, graven-faced and ineluctable, marching everything down some long-prescribed path. At other times History appears to be Justice, firm but compassionate and flexible, patiently working out a program that in the long run will give each people about what it deserves. Here of late, more times than not, History has seemed to me a kind of Cosmic Imp, shrewd and puckish and infinitely ironical, delighting in nothing so much as turning upside down the best-laid plans of statesmen and nations, not to speak of you and me.

I get this feeling when I contemplate Nikita Khrushchev or the august leaders of the Western nations endlessly tripping over their endless stratagems. I get it watching the Democratic and Republican Parties, roaring and gasconading their unique virtues and ending up exchanging programs. But less earth-shaking mat-

□ Eric F. Goldman, "The Oppressed Emancipated Woman," *Holiday* (May, 1961), 11-15. Originally titled "Party of One."

ters also call up to me the Cosmic Imp, and never more so than when a social function at Princeton, some business to conduct in New York City, or a chance conversation on a plane brings me face-to-face with that American phenomenon, the emancipated woman. For there she stands, surely one of the Imp's most perfect creations, cocktail deftly poised, well fed, well dressed, well housed, painstakingly educated, wielder of the nation's biggest vote and owner of much of its property, infinitely emancipated, and trapped.

If there is a Harriet Beecher Stowe in the Republic these days, I have just the oppressed Uncle Tom for the new manifesto. She's a young woman, thirty-or-so, with whom I do business in a New York publishing house. She's a Mt. Holyoke graduate, bright, attractive, married to an up-and-coming lawyer, the mother of two children. One afternoon, wondering vaguely about the emancipated woman, I asked her if she would itemize for me just what her day had been like. Her answer was that she got up at seven, made breakfast for the family, drove her husband to the train station, came back to arrange the day with the maid only to find that the maid had not shown up, drove the older child to school, finally found a baby-sitter for the younger child, got a train herself. She had a twenty-minute lunch at the nearby drugstore—she had to make a hair appointment. During afternoon coffee break, she shopped for a present for her husband's nephew, who was getting married. "Jim was busy at the office."

As she went on, some wisp of humanitarianism in me got the better of my sociological interest. "If you've had that kind of day," I blurted out, "for heaven's sake let's get out of here and have a drink."

She replied, "I'd love to," and then the phone rang once again. She put down the phone and told me: "That was Jim. Give me a rain check on the drink, will you? Jim's having cocktails later with a client. He thinks that things go better when I'm there and Jim gets cross if I'm late."

"Jim gets cross if I'm late." In the five thousand years of recorded history, we males never had it so good. It's such a delicious situation for us I have sometimes wondered whether our grandfathers didn't plan it this way. But they didn't; they weren't that smart. Nobody forged the shackles on the feet of the emancipated American women. Nobody marched them into Babylon. They did it all themselves: they heaved, proclaimed, picketed, emancipated themselves right smack into serfdom.

That Cosmic Imp must be holding his sides as he contemplates the women's-rights movement in the United States. No crusade has ever been more certain that it marched with Truth and Right. I can still hear the strident voice of a feminist, which I first heard in some long-forgotten document, opening a suffragette meeting with: "Let us pray to God. *She* understands." No movement has ever been more certain that its victory would bring only good to its rank and file. "Today," declared the redoubtable Carrie Chapman Catt, "we are in the hell of man-created slavery. With women's rights, we will move into God's green acres." The ladies won the rights, all right. They won the right to stand up on buses and trains; the right to add to the care and feeding of babies the care and promotion of the Organization Man; the right to work at a job eight hours a day in addition to running the house.

The feminist crusaders managed a further irony. History's browbeaten groups have generally been at the bottom of society—poor people or black people or people who belonged to the low-status church. But the oppressed emancipated woman falls into none of these categories. Today's Harriet Beecher Stowe could have no Uncle Tom in burlap rags; the figure of affliction would have to be in a trim wool suit, if not a mink stole. Uncle Tom's cabin must be a split-level or perhaps a thirty-acre estate.

As for poor Eliza struggling across the ice floes with her child in her arms, the scene has to be centered on poor Mrs. Crowinshed, Jr., struggling from cocktail party to cocktail party with an Organization Man on her back.

In fairness to the ladies who crusaded their sex into such a fix, it ought to be said that it was not easy to foresee just where the women's-rights movement would end up putting the women. For one thing, there has always been a whirling inner dynamic, a frenetic imperialism in the feminist attitude that sweeps it on and on past every barrier of good sense. Give an emancipated woman half a loaf and she promptly wants the whole loaf, especially when the half loaf is already choking her. For another thing, women's rights came along at a time when the United States was in a state of rapid change. The results of a rampant feminism were the more rococo because of the vogue of psychology, shifting male habits, lavish prosperity, the rise of suburbia and a dozen other facts of the country's crazy-quilt 20th Century. Almost everything that has happened in America in recent decades has conspired to turn feminism into a blueprint for stripping the middle- and upper-middle-class woman of the usufructs and pleasures of being a woman.

The process goes on from womb to tomb, or, perhaps more accurately, from womb to womb. The daughter is born. Mother, filled with decades of talk by emancipators and child psychologists, is not going to let *her* daughter turn into any clinging vine. Almost before the child can walk, she is being tossed into the community pool. The little girl may be a little girl, shy and soft and very, very feminine, in short, one of God's most endearing creations. The pool experience may mangle her soul. Nonsense—she is going to be sports-minded and outgoing, able to meet any man on his own terms, able to stand on her own two feet.

A few more years and mother has installed a phone in the girl's bedroom. None of this blushing-violet stuff. She has to get used to dealing with people, especially the opposite sex. By fifteen, daughter is an old pro at dating. She knows which boys she has to neck with, and just how far she has to go. She knows how to maneuver Tom into a prom invitation, how to get the prestige of going steady with Dick while having the sadistic pleasure of luring Harry to break it up, how to make a sound, ten-second estimate of the social status of any male possibility at the dance. All she has lost is woman's most precious heritage—the right to grow up slowly, being fuzzily and fumblingly and wonderfully feminine. And mother, there she stands at 2:00 A.M., peeking furtively out the window for daughter's return from the date—no emancipated mother could possibly admit that she worries—worrying and worrying whether some day daughter is going to announce that she is pregnant.

College—especially the good girls' college to which mother has been steering daughter since infancy—adds new dimensions to the entrapment. You can take it as a law of life, at least as sound as Einstein's Law of Relativity, that the more esteemed a girls' college, the more sure it is to have a faculty studded with superannuated suffragettes, who war with infinite persistence and skill against the happiness of womankind. Somehow or another they stumbled into the improbable business of being a woman professor. They know that everybody else thinks they are a little peculiar and, as a matter of fact, they feel more than a little peculiar themselves. They hate women who live a life that feels natural to the sex and, out of their bile, they are determined to make every other woman as miserable as they are. With an instinctive sense of strategy worthy of a Napoleon, they have hit upon just the doctrine to do it.

The doctrine is simple—and lethal. Don't be a "mere woman." Avoid any situation where you will be subordinate to a man. Be "creative." Reach "self-fulfillment." Whether you are going to get married or not, prepare for a "career." And in having a career, don't, under any circumstances, be a secretary. Never mind that secretaries get better salaries than most other female employees; never mind that society urgently needs them; never mind that many a secretary is so important to her boss and fulfills so many genuine responsibilities that he has for her a respect akin to awe. Never mind any of this—being a secretary is an "uncreative" job, merely a "lackey" to a man.

The girls listen—most girls' colleges are situated in such outlandish villages that there is little to do except listen to the professors—and they come away from commencement just so many sitting ducks for the system. Go off to paint the fishermen of Brittany or marry some fellow and let him worry about supporting the home? If you must work, take a job as a secretary, earn a good salary, enjoy a sense of solid usefulness? Heavens no! By the tens of thousands the girl graduates descend on the "creative" jobs—taking two-thirds of the salary of a secretary to do something or other known as "research," "publicity liaison," or "executive planning." The girl graduates do not march to the sacrificial altar entirely in vain. Today employers with "creative" jobs to offer—publishers, radio and TV stations, educational institutions—have the greatest supply of cheap labor since industrialists used to herd the peasants off the steppes of Europe.

The changing mores of 20th Century America add further to the caricature of the emancipated woman. Twenty or thirty years ago, most men, if they went to college, graduated and proceeded forthwith to go to work and make a living. Today an increasing percentage continue going to school—business administration, law, veterinary school, or what have you. At the same time, more and more men are marrying young. Put these two facts together and you have the latest link in the entrapment of the emancipated woman. She is graduated from college, marries, and proceeds to support the husband while he goes to graduate school —thus promptly breaking herself in to the thralldom of the two-check family income.

So, in a flourish of freedom, the emancipated career woman puts on the yoke of being wife, mother, house manager and wage earner. She joins with the non-working emancipated woman in a dogged determination to be the "creative" wife, which means playing eighteen-hours-a-day nursemaid to the Organization Man who sits fretfully at the head of the table. She must, at all times, be dressed with the proper careful casualness; be ready, amid the yawps of her children, for the bridge game, the golf, the cocktail party which "we can't afford not to show up at"; maintain the family's reputation for interest in the right things (and make some contacts that might come in handy for her husband's career) by dutifully attending the PTA meeting; learn how to denounce conformity, with just the right conformity to the sophisticated air, on all conspicuous occasions. And all of this, unless she is quite wealthy, with a rickety succession of maids or that reluctant and easily evanescent character, the cleaning woman.

The maids and the cleaning woman are not only disappearing from somebody else's kitchen; they are inheriting the earth. Far down the hierarchy of American society are the women who, never having heard of emancipation, are free to be themselves. The Irish maid's daughter, the truck driver's wife, the Carpatho-Ruthenian immigrant who is still an unabashed Carpatho-Ruthenian—they move serenely ahead, full panoplied with all the immemorial powers and pleasures of being a woman.

They are hardly Woman the Entrancing, but they are also not Woman the Overwhelmed. The truck driver's wife has no problem about her "role in society."

She's there, she cooks dinner and runs the house, sleeps with the old man, raises the children, and, when she gets a little weary of it all, plops down in front of the TV. She has no need of a creative career. Her creations are all around her, scratching up the furniture, clouting her eardrums, making her feel the most important person in the world. If she goes to work, it is for a plain, untraumatic, easily terminable reason: the household needs some money. She doesn't have to squeeze out time to have cocktails with her husband's superiors. Her husband's superiors don't give a damn about her, or she about them. She doesn't even have to be chic or up on the latest thinking of Arthur Schlesinger, Jr. She just gets up, performs her tasks, manipulates in her own amused way the inanities of a world that men have created, and ambles off to a magnificently purposeless coffee *klatsch.*

As I write on, I feel a crusade coming on me. I want to found a National Association for the Emancipation of Emancipated Women. But then, a little sense takes hold.

For the most wondrous feature of this wondrous women's emancipation movement is that it has built into it the most automatic, most sure-fire, most self-satisfying answer-to-everything since Karl Marx taught the Russians how to enslave themselves while preening their liberties. So you wonder about the oppressed emancipated woman? So you think somebody should do something about her? Generations of suffragettes glare down at you and speak through their daughters the all-crunching doctrine: "*Cherchez l'homme.* Beware—he's trying to trick you back into the kitchen."

I caught the full flavor of this a year or so ago when I participated on a TV program with a group of graduating seniors from various colleges. Before the program, I fell to talking with a Smith girl about the mood at Northampton. Most of the girls, she said, had their minds on their forthcoming marriages. As she talked on, the young woman piqued my interest; I thought I sniffed a revolt. She mentioned with a trace of acridness how "we have to carry them along these days." She repeated a favorite wisecrack at Smith: "The husband lives by the sweat of his *frau.*" She even got off the opening lines of what she called the "collegeman's theme song":

> The girl that I marry will have to be
> Independent financially.

At one point, she raised her hand and there, on finger number three, was a ring.

"You're engaged too?" I said.

"Oh, yes."

"But, after all, weren't you just saying——"

I had done it. The generations of feminists reared back. Archly, each word chilled, the Smith girl said: "I'm getting married the day after graduation—to a graduate student in physics. And I am going to work in a challenging job." The cool voice was now pure ice. "*He* understands that a woman is a whole human being." Politely, she edged away from me.

Well, I guess it was ever thus, when that Cosmic Imp takes over.

ERIC F. GOLDMAN, historian, writer, and lecturer, was educated at Johns Hopkins University, where he received his Ph.D. at the age of twenty-two and subsequently taught history from 1938 to 1941. After writing for *Time* magazine from 1941 to 1943, he joined the faculty at Princeton, where he is now a history professor. In addition he has lectured for the State Department in Europe and in India, served since 1959 as moderator for the NBC television panel "The Open Mind" (recipient of an Emmy Award in 1962), contributed to popular and scholarly magazines, and written, among other books, *The Crucial Decade* and *Rendezvous with Destiny.* He was a special consultant to the White House from 1964 to 1966.

Vocabulary Study

A. Much of Mr. Goldman's article is built upon paradox, that is, upon the use of statements apparently contradictory, but which yet express truths. The title itself is an example. What do the words *oppressed* and *emancipated* mean? And how can a woman be both?

B. Glance through the article again and list the words and phrases which, as Mr. Goldman uses them, are clearly indicative of oppression.

C. Mr. Goldman uses several learned words with which you may not be familiar. What do the following italicized words mean in the context in which the author uses them?

1. Sometimes History seems to me Fate, graven-faced and *ineluctable,* marching everything down some long-prescribed path.
2. History has seemed to me a kind of *Cosmic* Imp.
3. I get it watching the Democratic and Republican Parties, roaring and *gasconading* their unique virtues.
4. declared the *redoubtable* Carrie Chapman Catt
5. a blueprint for stripping the middle- and upper-middle-class woman of the *usufructs* and pleasures of being a woman
6. that reluctant and easily *evanescent* character, the cleaning woman

Questions on Form and Content

A. Mr. Goldman uses references to History as the Cosmic Imp both to introduce and conclude his essay. For what purpose?

B. Filled with numerous specific examples, this article also contains two fairly lengthy anecdotes, one near the beginning concerning the young Mt. Holyoke graduate and one at the end relating his conversation with a Smith undergraduate. What does each illustrate?

C. Mr. Goldman uses two characters from Harriet Beecher Stowe's *Uncle Tom's Cabin* to make a forceful analogy. Who are they and to whom does Mr. Goldman compare them?

D. The Jews were exiled by Nebuchadnezzar to Babylonia in 597 B.C. Babylon, an ancient city on the Euphrates River, was famous for wealth, luxury, and vice. "Nobody marched them [the emancipated American women] into Babylon," Mr. Goldman declares. What does he mean?

E. What rights, according to Mr. Goldman, have the ladies won?

F. How do today's emancipated women differ from History's brow-beaten groups, according to the author?

G. What does Mr. Goldman consider woman's most precious heritage —now lost?

H. Discuss the process that "goes on from womb to tomb, or, perhaps more accurately, from womb to womb" as Mr. Goldman describes it. From your experience, would you say his description is accurate? If not, why not?

Suggestions for Writing

A. Eric Goldman, an eminent historian, says: "Sometimes history seems to me Fate, graven-faced and ineluctable, marching everything down some long-prescribed path." What historical event or events would seem to you to have been prescribed by Fate? You could discuss war or wars, famine, flood, plagues, or earthquakes in your paper.

B. "At other times History appears to be Justice, firm but compassionate and flexible, patiently working out a program that in the long run will give each people about what it deserves," continues Mr. Goldman. What events seem to you to show History in this aspect? You might consider the history of the Irish, the Jews, the American Indians, the Negroes, or the Chinese in your answer.

C. Discuss times or events, other than those Mr. Goldman mentions, when History appears in the guise of a "Cosmic Imp, shrewd and puckish and infinitely ironical, delighting in nothing so much as turning upside down the best-laid plans of statesmen and nations, not to speak of you and me."

D. Itemize just what your day has been like. You may wish to use the young woman's answer to Mr. Goldman's same request as a guide.

E. If you have read *Uncle Tom's Cabin,* write a paper concerning the book, paying particular attention to the use Mr. Goldman makes of it in his article. He points up likenesses and differences between Mrs. Stowe's characters and modern American women. What additional ones can you mention?

F. Do a little research, if necessary, then write a paper on the Babylonian Captivity. An encyclopedia will furnish sufficient material for a short paper.

G. Write a paper on "The Organization Man." Who is he; what made him what he is; how does he function?

H. If, in your experience, the process "from womb to tomb, or, perhaps more accurately, from womb to womb" differs from that which Mr. Goldman describes, write a paper describing the process as you have either experienced or observed it.

I. Will your chosen profession be a "creative" one? In both your eyes and Mr. Goldman's? Why or why not?

J. If you take Mr. Goldman's discussions of careers at face value, what would you infer that he considers the best fields of work for a woman to enter? Why?

K. Compare Mr. Goldman's picture of the life of the truck driver's wife with the life of the Mt. Holyoke graduate. Which life would you prefer to lead? Why?

L. Would you be willing to support your husband while he goes to graduate school? Why or why not? Or would you want your wife to work while you attend college? Again, give your reasons.

M. Would you volunteer to crusade for the "National Association for the Emancipation of Emancipated Women"? If so, what plans would you suggest to effect the emancipation?

N. Mr. Goldmann, a Princeton University professor, writes of "the improbable business of being a woman professor." Do you think he is fair to the women in his profession? Why or why not?

More on Emancipated Woman

Clifton Fadiman

Last month these columns were graced by my guest, Prof. Eric Goldman of Princeton University, who entered a plea, as I understand it, for what he called "the oppressed emancipated woman." He believes that the career woman has, by flinging off her chains, also hurled herself "right back into serfdom." That the feminist revolution has stripped "the middle- and upper-middle-class woman of the usufructs and pleasures of being a woman." That lady college professors have successfully maligned the "life that feels natural to the sex." That most of the "creative jobs" held down by women are piddling. That it is not the sweet (and brainy) girl graduate but the truck driver's wife who "moves serenely ahead, full panoplied with all the immemorial powers and pleasures of being a woman."

Doctor Goldman is not only one of our most brilliant historians. He is also intrepid. Apparently he does not mind playing Pentheus to the Bacchae of our

□ Clifton Fadiman, "More on Emancipated Woman," *Holiday* (June, 1961), 11, 14, 16, 17, 19. Originally titled "Party of One."

female readers. I doubt not that one of these days a triumphant cleaning woman will, with a shrill *"Evoe!"*, salute his dismembered corpse on the floor of a lecture room in Nassau Hall. In the interim, while he remains in one piece, I should like to enter a few reflections on his Proclamation of Disemancipation.

I am that curious animal, a married male who works at home. Thus I have for many years been in a good position to observe closely those female powers and pleasures and usufructs which Doctor Goldman lauds but does not enumerate. The conclusion I have come to is a bit different from Doctor Goldman's. It seems to me that the intelligent middle-class woman who is the subject of Doctor Goldman's remarks is half slave and half free. Insofar as she is a citizen, a voter, a property owner and an immortal rational soul, she is free. Insofar as she is a home-maker, enjoying those glorious powers and pleasures and usufructs, she is a slave. And anything she can do to mitigate that slavery I am for, even if it involves what Doctor Goldman calls "the thralldom of the two-check family income,"[1] even if it involves such mildly dubious jobs as "research," "publicity liaison" and "executive planning," if I may borrow the Doctor's inverted commas.

The blunt fact, particularly in suburban and exurban households, is that today the "life that feels natural to the sex" is largely concerned with the unredeemably dreary, toilsome and complex business of household and child-rearing drudgery; and that the situation, instead of improving, is getting worse. The philosophers of the ladies' magazines call this business "nest building," ignoring the fact that a bird spends a couple of hours building a nest and the rest of her time just flying around jauntily and eating food she doesn't have to lug home from the supermarket, clean, cook and serve.

I have learned so much from Doctor Goldman's distinguished studies in American history that I feel I ought to discharge a little of my heavy debt by teaching him something about American households. Let me tell you, Doctor, about our little nest.

In common with many other homes in our happy neighborhood, all dedicated to gracious living, we are at this writing maidless. That is, we have been maidless for four months, with every prospect of continued maidlessness. After all, we have nothing to offer a maid beyond a private four-room apartment, a beginning salary of seventy dollars a week, one and a half days off a week, three or four meals a day, clean linen, TV and radio sets, a two-week paid vacation and unremitting servile homage. As no self-respecting maid would work under these conditions, my wife has, for the last four months, cooked an average of twenty meals a week for four people, plus lunches for a weekly cleaning woman, plus lunches for a weekly sitter. She has made four beds daily, picked up dozens of objects and put them somewhere else, washed piles of clothes, done minimum daily light house-cleaning, dreamed up menus for two grownups as well as for two children who like nothing but ravioli, ordered or shopped for groceries and disposed them properly, left notes for milkmen, polished shoes, chauffeured the children at times to and from school and to lessons in hockey, riding, French and skiing, as well as to the endless succession of birthday parties without which no child can become a decent American citizen.

In addition of course she entertains the children, looks over homework, buys their clothes, sews on their buttons and name tapes, dresses the younger one, puts on them and takes off them (it was a hard winter) a gross total of several hundred boots, overshoes, snowpants, mittens, coats and hats, hangs them up. . . . Need I go on?

Yes, I think I will go on.

My wife has just spent a typical hour enjoying the powers and pleasures and usufructs of being a woman. This is how the hour was passed. She transferred dirty lunch dishes, silverware, paper napkins, glasses and table mats from dining room to kitchen. Cleaned mats in pantry and hung up to dry. Scraped lunch remains onto waxed paper, folded, deposited in garbage can. Ditto paper napkins. Noted on kitchen table seven glasses, each filled with water at different levels, and eight root-beer bottles ditto. About to empty these, rinse, and transfer glasses to dishwasher when struck by sudden thought: maybe precious to children? Conferred with children: told objects represent two sets of musical glasses, not to be touched on pain of matricide. Set musical instruments carefully on shelf. Warned by nine-year-old son not to attempt cleaning of pantry, as full-scale chemical experiment now in process, involving muriatic acid, salt, ammonia, borax, and complete kitchen battery of pots, pans, spoons, funnels. Retreated from pantry taking note of future necessary cleanup. Rinsed glasses, dishes, silverware in hot water, rubbed briefly with soaped brush, racked same in dishwasher. Cleaned kitchen sink, transferring remains neatly to square of waxed paper, thence to garbage can. Washed counter tops. Washed sink tops. Washed sink. Baited dishwasher with detergent, pushed button. Transferred contents of garbage can to outside bigger garbage can. Transferred contents of kitchen waste basket to outside bigger waste can. Found clean garbage bag, folded same to proper size, inserted in kitchen garbage can. Ditto for waste-paper bag. Discovered aluminum foil exhausted. Descended to cellar, brought up three rolls, fixed one in holder, shelved other two in pantry. Remembered bottle of wine needed for dinner. Re-descended. Unpacked and shelved large case of toilet paper. Ascending with wine, passed freezer in pantry, remembered must thaw orange juice. Transferred can of orange juice from freezer to kitchen refrigerator. Emptied large tray of water from defrosting refrigerator. Refilled ice-cube trays. Mopped shelves and bottom of refrigerator. Quietly murmured three or four short words that are today, as a result of her emancipation, no longer exclusively reserved for the male sex.

Multiply this hour by eight or ten, many of them devoted to tasks even more onerous and stupid. Multiply these eight or ten hours by as many household working days as there are in about a score of years. You will then have some notion of why wives eye wistfully the serfdom against which Doctor Goldman warns them, why they fall for that "challenging job," why, in fact, the whole idea of being "a woman" seems to them open to question. Repetitious, mindless, perspectiveless activities of the sort I have described may be the right thing for specialized low-I.Q. females (or males for that matter) incapable of boredom or curiosity. They are certainly the right thing for termites.

Among the satisfactions that are supposed to accrue to the female is the enjoyment of her children and her husband. These are genuine goods, and it is a pity that the modern wife and mother has so little time to experience them. If she is to feed, clothe, clean and transport her family in the style to which they are accustomed, she will have little time or energy for companionship or guidance, and must be content to get good marks as a serf. Much as she may love her husband, she is usually so worn out from exercising Doctor Goldman's powers and pleasures that there's mighty little time left for usufructing.

Doctor Goldman is convinced that the outside world has little to offer the intelligent woman. I am equally convinced that housekeeping has *nothing whatsoever* to offer the intelligent woman. Perhaps on a 19th Century farm, when the family was genuinely integrated (instead of a child-dominated chaos) and when no alternative to "home-making" appeared on the horizon, housekeeping may have been something resembling a way of life. Today it is nothing but a dreary succession of ever-repeated, mentally and emotionally stultifying and degrading chores, most of them filthy, none of them adequately appreciated by husband, children or historians. The modern world has freed the specialized slave class that previously performed this slave labor. That noble step forward is, under the aspect of eternity, doubtless a good thing. At the same time the modern world has substituted for the specialized slave class a generalized slave class. This class is known as wives and mothers.

It is not the purpose of these comments to suggest that anything can be done about all this. It *is* the purpose of these remarks merely to get women a little sorer than they already are. If they cannot escape from the house of bondage, let them at least enjoy the grim satisfaction of knowing that that is where they are living. If they cannot love their fate, let them at least react to it with the only suitable emotion: absolute, unmitigated, icy hatred.

Of course—except for an unbluffable minority that refuses to have the dishrag pulled over its eyes—they do not so react. I would suggest at least four reasons for this blindness.

The first is the perhaps incurable human tendency to rationalization. One could doubtless produce from our pre-Civil War history ample evidence that a great many slaves were quite "content" with their lot. It is not that they were *truly* content. It is that they had a genius for inventing protective walls of self-delusion.

The second reason is corollary to the first. The Southern apologists for slavery produced a remarkable persuasive literature. (Indeed it was almost always better written than the creeds of the Abolitionists.) The apologists for the home, that contemporary Old Plantation, are often males with overwhelming rhetorical powers; and women, who are carefully taught that men write and reason better than they do, submit to brainwashing.

The third reason is connected with the second: it is the *mystique* of the ladies' magazines, generally owned and brilliantly run by males who have never cleaned a sink in their lives. The ladies' magazines, on the "home-making" side, are simply a vast and wonderful smoke screen of words designed to make the average woman feel that she is the boss of a paradise of togetherness, that she is, in Doctor Goldman's phrase, "the most important person in the world." The fiction in these magazines is often quite skillful; but it pales before the creative inventiveness demonstrated in the nonfiction.

The fourth reason has to do with what may be called the furniture of this paradise: labor-saving gadgets. To say that technology has freed the modern woman from the curse of the kitchen is nonsense. I do not say that the machine has made things worse, though anyone who has had any experience with those triumphs of inefficiency, certain automatic can openers, may well entertain doubts. I do say that mechanized household appliances are simply part of a disguised treadmill on which the poor housewife wearily trots. The more gadgets, the more attractive a higher standard of living becomes; we have replaced our foremothers' rude simplicity with frenzied elegance plus repair bills.

Everybody wants to live better electrically; we succeed in living more complicatedly. I am prepared to admit that the vacuum cleaner is more efficient than the broom; but the advent of the vacuum cleaner is exactly contemporary with the advent of filthy, dust-smothered, gasoline-fume-drenched city living, the kind of living that in fifty years will be found along the entire east coast, from Washington to Boston. The telephone is of course quicker than the one-horse shay, but it leaves the poor housewife open to a hundred interruptions her grandmother never knew. The most you can say for household gadgetry is that it enables the housewife to just about hold her own in an increasingly tense and difficult environment. But only the most rigid time analysis would convince her of this; and she hasn't the time for time analysis. And so she accepts, with a wistful hope that it's really so, the assurances of the TV barkers that the new dishwasher will leave her free to lead the life of a Hollywood star.

Doctor Goldman speaks with warmth of "the pleasures of being a woman." But the fact is that modern "comfortable" living has altered these traditional pleasures to the point where women have largely become men. The fantastic effort involved in running a modern household and rearing the multiple spawn most of us seem to insist on having has made the female a creature more and more "masculine." It is she who undertakes business negotiations with a swarm of tradesmen, repairmen, tree surgeons and door-to-door salesmen. It is she who must become an expert chauffeur and minor mechanic. It is she who has to transfer heavy parcels and bundles from the store to the car, the car to the house, and from one part of the house to another. Indeed, I know mothers who can handle a baseball or football better than their husbands, because their ten-year-old sons demand it, and they're around and the husbands aren't. The husband gets flabby from lack of hard male labor. The wife gets muscular—and dead, dead tired—from too much of it. I'm all for those female usufructs of which Doctor Goldman speaks, but I fail to see how the female can get many of them when modern life forces her to spend so much of her time acting like a male.

Doctor Goldman's bill of indictment is factually correct. It *is* true that "in a flourish of freedom, the emancipated career woman puts on the yoke of being wife, mother, house manager . . . wage earner . . . and 'creative' wife." But the point is that, paradoxically, a fivefold yoke is more welcome than a single one. The part-time job (or even full-time job), the cocktail party, the P.T.A. meeting—such activities at least have some connection with dynamic living, they open out to *some*thing, they are not infinitely and heartsickeningly repetitious. And so an energetic woman will, thank God, skimp her household tasks and let a little dust accumulate in the corners in order that she may make at least a minimum contact with the world of real human beings that is supposed to be her birthright. She will wear herself out doing this, as Doctor Goldman rightly suggests; and she will probably die a little sooner; and of course she will "get" nowhere in the end. But anything is better than permanent house arrest. Anything is better than being a zombie, even though she is partly conditioned by the airwaves, the magazines and persuasive male philosophers to believe that she is not a zombie at all but a kind of queen bee living "a life that feels natural to her sex."

The crux of the matter is one that Doctor Goldman touches on without carrying it through to a conclusion. The basic fact is that two social movements have occurred at the same time, and that one is canceling the effect of the other.

Women won their right to be "whole human beings" at about the same time that the opportunities offered by industry and the seductions of the big city destroyed the servant class. The servant class discovered that there's no future in housework; and it's hard to blame them, even though most of them will discover that there's no future in anything else either. Their disappearance has forced the modern middle-class woman into a situation where, in order to obtain any of the fruits of the emancipation she has technically gained, she must be about five times as smart and energetic as her husband. And in every suburbia and exurbia I have observed, she is becoming so.

In the meantime she remains half slave and half free. Lincoln predicted that no government could permanently endure under such conditions, and he proved right. So far the middle-class female has shown herself tougher than any government. We privileged males may well praise her for her toughness. But let us at least not deny her the bitter consolation of knowing exactly what she is up against. And, if, some bright day, surrounded by a hundred gleaming gadgets, she suddenly lunges at us with a carving knife, let us not commit the error of arguing with her. For we have no argument. Let's just run.

Clifton Fadiman has appeared frequently on radio and television and written for numerous magazines. He received his A.B. from Columbia University in 1925, served as editor for Simon and Schuster book publications from 1929 to 1935 and as master of ceremonies on the radio program "Information Please" from 1938 to 1948. He has also written a number of books; among them are *Any Number Can Play* and *The Lifetime Reading Plan.*

Vocabulary Study

Supply an antonym, a word with an opposite meaning, for each of the italicized words below as it is used in this article.

A. That lady college professors have successfully *maligned* the "life that feels natural to the sex."
B. He is also *intrepid.*
C. which Doctor Goldman *lauds* but does not enumerate
D. And anything she can do to *mitigate* that slavery I am for
E. tasks even more *onerous* and stupid
F. mentally and emotionally *stultifying* and degrading chores

Questions on Form and Content

A. Mr. Fadiman bases his argument primarily on one extended example. Why do you think he does so? Do you find the one example more convincing than several treated in less detail would have been? Why or why not? Does Mrs. Fadiman's lot sound like that of a typical housewife and mother to you?

B. How, according to Mr. Fadiman, should housewives react to their fate? He lists four reasons why most women fail to do so. What are they?

C. What, according to the author, is the most you can say for household gadgetry?

D. Why does Mr. Fadiman consider woman's fivefold yoke superior to a single one?

E. Does Mr. Fadiman offer a solution to woman's half-slave, half-free condition? If so, what? On what does he blame her plight?

F. Mr. Fadiman alludes to a classic myth about Pentheus and the Bacchae. Pentheus was a Theban king who tried to abolish the orgies of Bacchus. The angry god drove the King mad in retaliation. Pentheus climbed into a tree to watch the rites he had tried unsuccessfully to stop. When discovered, he was torn to pieces by the Bacchantes. In Mr. Fadiman's allusion (paragraph 2), who is in the role of Pentheus? Who of the Bacchae?

Suggestions for Writing

A. Write an answer to "More on Emancipated Woman." You might follow Mr. Fadiman's pattern in writing his rebuttal to Mr. Goldman. First summarize Mr. Fadiman's case, then develop the point or points on which you disagree by supporting your argument with an extended example worked out in detail.

B. Write a paper developing the thesis that man, too, is half slave, half free.

C. Mr. Fadiman writes that "a bird spends a couple of hours building a nest and the rest of her time just flying around jauntily and eating food she doesn't have to lug home from the supermarket, clean, cook and serve." Write a paper on the activities of a female bird as you have observed or read about them, or both.

D. Relate in detail how you spent the hour that has just passed, using as a guide Mr. Fadiman's description of the way his wife spent a typical hour.

E. Mr. Fadiman asserts that his wife's activities as a housewife would be the right thing for termites. Do some research, if necessary, and then write a paper on the way of life of a termite.

F. Mr. Fadiman is "convinced that housekeeping has *nothing whatsoever* to offer the intelligent woman." Comment.

G. "The ladies' magazines, on the 'home-making' side, are simply a vast and wonderful smoke screen of words designed to make the average woman feel that she is the boss of a paradise of togetherness, that she is, in Doctor Goldman's phrase 'the most important person in the world,' " writes Mr. Fadiman. Look through an issue of *McCall's, Ladies' Home Journal,* or *Good Housekeeping,* and write a paper discussing its contents.

H. Discuss Mr. Fadiman's remark: "Everybody wants to live better electrically; we succeed in living more complicatedly." Use a number of examples in your paper.

I. Write a paper on labor-saving gadgets you consider worthwhile.

J. Discuss the telephone as a menace.

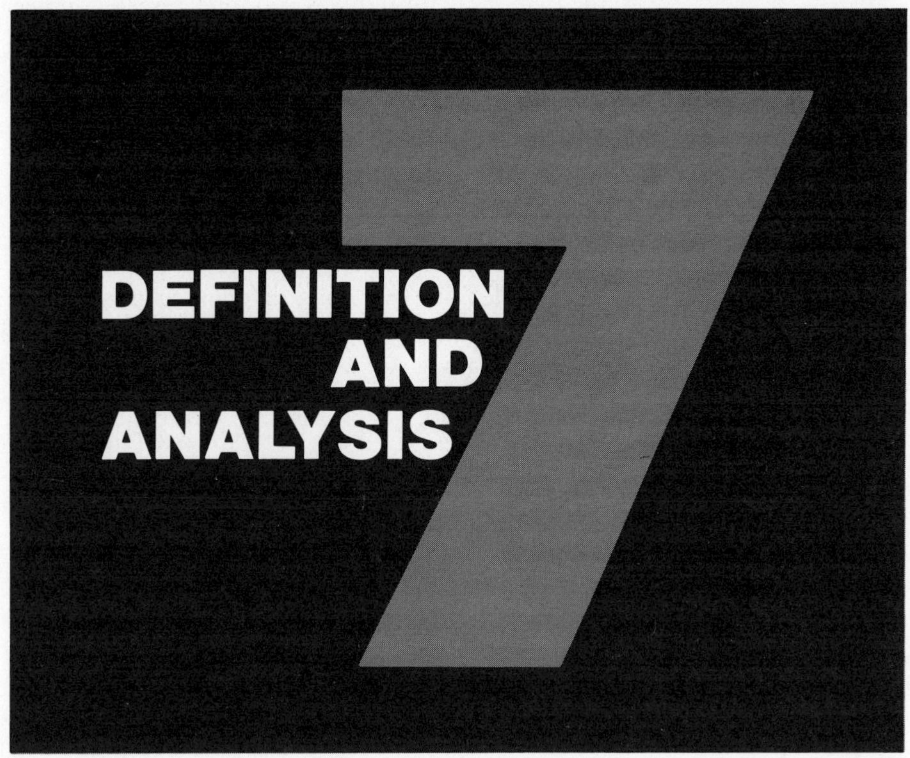

7 DEFINITION AND ANALYSIS

Definition can often be useful and is sometimes essential as a device for the development of an idea. You should always make every effort to insure that your reader understands what you mean by the words you use in the context in which you are using them. If you feel there is a chance that he might be confused by your terms, define them. Sometimes a simple dictionary definition will suffice; sometimes an extended definition is necessary. Cardinal Newman wrote a complete book on *The Idea of a University.*

A simple definition nearly always places the term in a general class and then points out how it differs from other members of that general class. Longer definitions go from these two basic steps of classifying and differentiating to discussing the meaning of a word so that the reader understands what it means in the special sense in which it is intended. You need to use this method of extended definition when you are using terms that people may interpret in different ways, when you are limiting your subject more than is customary, or when you are writing on a complex subject or one with which your readers may be unfamiliar.

Such extended definitions may be formed in one or more of several ways: by analyzing or dividing a subject into its parts and discussing each part; by exclusion, showing what the term does not mean; by repeating or restating the essence of the definition in different words; by treating the history or development of the subject; or by using examples, comparisons, or contrasts.

Russell Lynes exemplifies all of these methods in "Is There a Gentleman in the House?" He uses simple definition at the beginning, then divides his definition into two parts: "I have come to the conclusion that a woman's idea of a gentleman and a man's idea are two quite different fellows." Then he defines and analyzes both concepts of a gentleman. In his conclusion he gives his own definition: "In America, we pay a male no higher compliment than to say he is a 'real man.' " To be "a real man," he tells us, means that a man is thoughtful, courteous, and generous. "It means that he is a gentleman at heart."

Mr. Lynes' essay is actually, therefore, an extended definition. He treats the history and development of the gentleman. He tells what the term does and does not include. He uses H. L. Mencken, William Lyon Phelps, George Washington, and others as examples. He compares and contrasts varying ideas as to what constitutes a gentleman.

Analysis is in itself a major method of development for the explanation of anything complex. Analysis, or organization by division, is the process of breaking a subject into its parts and studying the parts individually, in relation to each other, and in relation to the whole. The analytical method of development can be applied to an object, to an organization, to a plan, to a process, to an event, or to anything that can be discussed by division into parts. Thus we can analyze the structures of an object, the functions of an organization, the reasons for a plan, the chronological development of a process, the causes or results of an event.

In "The Case for the American Woman," Diana Trilling analyzes the persistent attack which has been made upon the American woman in relation to her husband (she has robbed him of his spark of manhood), in her position as a mother (she dominates home and family, especially male children), and in her position outside her home, as a competitor in the economic world. Next Mrs. Trilling outlines for us some of the reasons why, in our complex society, these attacks have been made. She explains further how the modern American woman herself feels about her predicament. While reading this essay, look for these and other examples of analysis.

The New Feminism

Lucy Komisar

A dozen women are variously seated in straight-backed chairs, settled on a couch, or sprawled on the floor of a comfortable apartment on Manhattan's West Side. They range in age from twenty-five to thirty-five, and include a magazine researcher, a lawyer, a housewife, an architect, a teacher, a secretary, and a graduate student in sociology.

They are white, middle-class, attractive. All but one have college degrees; several are married; a few are active in social causes. At first, they are hesitant. They don't really know what to talk about, and so they begin with why they came.

"I wanted to explore my feelings as a woman and find out what others think about the things that bother me." Slowly, they open up, trust growing. "I always felt so negative about being a woman; now I'm beginning to feel good about it."

They become more personal and revealing. "My mother never asked me what I was going to be when I grew up." "I never used to like to talk to girls. I always

☐ Lucy Komisar, "The New Feminism," *Saturday Review,* February 21, 1970, pp. 27-30, 35.

thought women were inferior—I never *liked* women." "I've been a secretary for three years; after that, you begin to think that's all you're good for." "I felt so trapped when my baby was born. I wanted to leave my husband and the child."

Repeated a hundred times in as many different rooms, these are the voices of women's liberation, a movement that encompasses high school students and grandmothers, and that is destined to eclipse the black civil rights struggle in the force of its resentment and the consequence of its demands.

Some of us have become feminists out of anger and frustration over job discrimination. When we left college, male students got aptitude tests, we got typing tests. In spite of federal law, most women still are trapped in low-paying, dead-end jobs and commonly earn less than men for the same work—sometimes on the theory that we are only "helping out," though 42 per cent of us support ourselves or families.

Others have discovered that the humanistic precepts of the radical movement do not always apply to women. At a peace rally in Washington last year, feminists were hooted and jeered off the speakers' platform, and white women working in civil rights or antipoverty programs are expected to defer to the black male ego. Many of us got out to salvage our own buffeted egos. However, most of the new feminists express only a general malaise they were never able to identify.

Nanette Rainone is twenty-seven, the wife of a newspaperman, the mother of a seven-month-old child, and a graduate of Queens College, where she studied English literature. She married while in graduate school, then quit before the year was out to become an office clerk at *Life* magazine. "I could have known the first day that I wasn't going to be promoted, but it took me eight months to find it out."

She spent the next five months idly at home, began doing volunteer public affairs interviews for WBAI radio, and now produces *Womankind*, a weekly program on the feminist movement.

"I always felt as though I was on a treadmill, an emotional treadmill. I thought it was neurotic, but it always focused on being a woman. Then I met another woman, who had two children. We talked about my pregnancy—my confusion about my pregnancy—and the problems she was having in caring for her children now that she was separated from her husband and wanted to work."

One evening Nanette Rainone's friend took her to a feminist meeting, and immediately she became part of the movement. "The child had been an escape. I was seeking a role I couldn't find on the outside," she says. "Then I became afraid my life would be overwhelmed, that I would never get out from under and do the things I had hoped to do.

"You struggle for several years after getting out of college. You know—what are you going to do with yourself? There's always the external discrimination, but somehow you feel you are talented and you should be able to project yourself. But you don't get a good job, you get a terrible job.

"I think I was typical of the average woman who is in the movement now, because the contradictions in the system existed in my life. My parents were interested in my education. I had more room to develop my potential than was required for the role I eventually was to assume.

"I don't put down the care of children. I just put down the fixated relationship that the mother has, the never-ending association, her urge that the child be something so that *she* can be something. People need objective projects. We all feel the need to actively participate in society, in something outside ourselves where we can learn and develop.

"The closest I've been able to come to what's wrong is that men have a greater sense of self than women have. Marriage is an aspect of men's lives, whereas it is the very center of most women's lives, the whole of their lives. It seemed to me that women felt they couldn't exist except in the eyes of men—that if a man wasn't looking at them or attending to them, then they just weren't there."

If women need more evidence, history books stand ready to assure us that we have seldom existed except as shadows of men. We have rarely been leaders of nations or industry or the great contributors to art and science, yet very few sociologists, political leaders, historians, and moral critics have ever stopped to ask why. Now, all around the country, women are meeting in apartments and conference rooms and coffee shops to search out the answers.

The sessions begin with accounts of personal problems and incidents. For years, we women have believed that our anger and frustration and unhappiness were "our problems." Suddenly, we discover that we are telling *the same story!* Our complaints are not only common, they are practically universal.

It is an exhilarating experience. Women's doubts begin to disappear and are replaced by new strength and self-respect. We stop focusing on men, and begin to identify with other women and to analyze the roots of our oppression. The conclusions that are drawn challenge the legitimacy of the sex role system upon which our civilization is based.

At the center of the feminist critique is the recognition that women have been forced to accept an inferior role in society, and that we have come to believe in our own inferiority. Women are taught to be passive, dependent, submissive, not to pursue careers but to be taken care of and protected. Even those who seek outside work lack confidence and self-esteem. Most of us are forced into menial and unsatisfying jobs: More than three-quarters of us are clerks, sales personnel, or factory and service workers, and a fifth of the women with B.A. degrees are secretaries.

Self-hatred is endemic. Women—especially those who have "made it"—

BRIDE

Moulin Studios, S.F.

MOTHER AND CHILD

David Wolfgang, San Francisco

WIFE

Helen Ansell—Photophile, S.F.

WOMEN

Michelle Vignes, San Francisco

identify with men and mirror their contempt for women. The approval of women does not mean very much. We don't want to work for women or vote for them. We laugh, although with vague uneasiness, at jokes about women drivers, mothers-in-law, and dumb blondes.

We depend on our relationships with men for our very identities. Our husbands win us social status and determine how we will be regarded by the world. Failure for a woman is not being selected by a man.

We are trained in the interests of men to defer to them and serve them and entertain them. If we are educated and gracious, it is so we can please men and educate their children. That is the thread that runs through the life of the geisha, the party girl, the business executive's wife, and the First Lady of the United States.

Men define women, and until now most of us have accepted their definition without question. If we challenge men in the world outside the home, we are all too frequently derided as "aggressive" and "unfeminine"—by women as readily as by men.

A woman is expected to subordinate her job to the interests of her husband's work. She'll move to another city so he can take a promotion—but it rarely works the other way around. Men don't take women's work very seriously, and, as a result, neither do most women. We spend a lot of time worrying about men, while they devote most of theirs to worrying about their careers.

We arc taught that getting and keeping a man is a woman's most important job; marriage, therefore, becomes our most important achievement. One suburban housewife says her father started giving her bridal pictures cut from newspapers when she was six. "He said that was what I would be when I grew up."

Most feminists do not object to marriage per se, but to the corollary that it is creative and fulfilling for an adult human being to spend her life doing housework, caring for children, and using her husband as a vicarious link to the outside world.

Most people would prefer just about any kind of work to that of a domestic servant; yet the mindless, endless, repetitious drudgery of housekeeping is the central occupation of more than fifty million women. People who would oppose institutions that portion out menial work on the basis of race see nothing wrong in a system that does the same thing on the basis of sex. (Should black and white roommates automatically assume the Negro best suited for housekeeping chores?) Even when they work at full-time jobs, wives must come home to "their" dusting and "their" laundry.

Some insist that housework is not much worse than the meaningless jobs most people have today, but there is a difference. Housewives are not paid for their work, and money is the mark of value in this society. It is also the key to independence and to the feeling of self-reliance that marks a free human being.

The justification for being a housewife is having children, and the justification for children is—well, a woman has a uterus, what else would it be for? Perhaps not all feminists agree that the uterus is a vestigial organ, but we are adamant and passionate in our denial of the old canard that biology is destiny.

Men have never been bound by their animal natures. They think and dream and create—and fly, clearly something nature had not intended, or it would have given men wings. However, we women are told that our chief function is to reproduce the species, prepare food, and sweep out the cave—er, house.

Psychologist Bruno Bettelheim states woman's functions succinctly: "We must start with the realization that, as much as women want to be good scientists or engineers, they want first and foremost to be womanly companions of men and to be mothers."

He gets no argument from Dr. Spock: "Biologically and temperamentally, I believe women were made to be concerned first and foremost with child care, husband care, and home care." Spock says some women have been "confused" by their education. (Freud was equally reactionary on the woman question, but he at least had the excuse of his Central European background.)

The species must reproduce, but this need not be the sole purpose of a woman's life. Men want children, too, yet no one expects them to choose between families and work. Children are in no way a substitute for personal development and creativity. If a talented man is forced into a senseless, menial job, it is deplored as a waste and a personal misfortune; yet, a woman's special skills, education, and interests are all too often deemed incidental and irrelevant, simply a focus for hobbies or volunteer work.

Women who say that raising a family is a fulfilling experience are rather like the peasant who never leaves his village. They have never had the opportunity to do anything else.

As a result, women are forced to live through their children and husbands, and they feel cheated and resentful when they realize that is not enough. When a woman says she gave her children everything, she is telling the truth—and that is the tragedy. Often when she reaches her late thirties, her children have grown up, gone to work or college, and left her in a bleak and premature old age. Middle-aged women who feel empty and useless are the mainstay of America's psychiatrists—who generally respond by telling them to "accept their role."

The freedom to choose whether or not to have children has always been illusory. A wife who is deliberately "barren"—a word that reinforces the worn-out metaphor of woman as Mother Earth—is considered neurotic or unnatural. Not only is motherhood not central to a woman's life, it may not be necessary or desirable. For the first time, some of us are admitting openly and without guilt that we do not want children. And the population crisis is making it even clearer that as a symbol for Americans motherhood ought to defer to apple pie.

The other half of the reproduction question is sex. The sexual revolution didn't liberate women at all; it only created a bear market for men. One of the most talked-about tracts in the movement is a pamphlet by Ann Koedt called "The Myth of the Vaginal Orgasm," which says most women don't have orgasms because most men won't accept the fact that the female orgasm is clitoral.

We are so used to putting men's needs first that we don't know how to ask for what *we* want, or else we share the common ignorance about our own physiology and think there is something wrong with us when we don't have orgasms "the right way." Freudian analysts contribute to the problem. The realization that past guilt and frustration have been unnecessary is not the least of the sentiments that draws women to women's liberation.

Feminists also protest the general male proclivity to regard us as decorative, amusing sex objects even in the world outside bed. We resent the sexual sell in advertising, the catcalls we get on the street, girlie magazines and pornography, bars that refuse to serve unescorted women on the assumption they are prostitutes, the not very subtle brainwashing by cosmetic companies, and the attitude of men who praise our knees in miniskirts, but refuse to act as if we had brains.

Even the supposedly humanistic worlds of rock music and radical politics are not very different. Young girls who join "the scene" or "the movement" are labeled "groupies" and are sexually exploited; the flashy porno-sheets such as *Screw* and *Kiss* are published by the self-appointed advocates of the new "free," anti-Establishment life-style. *"Plus ça change . . . ."*

We are angry about the powers men wield over us. The physical power—women who study karate do so as a defense against muggers, not lovers. And the social power—we resent the fact that men take the initiative with women, that women cannot ask for dates but must sit home waiting for the phone to ring.

That social conditioning began in childhood when fathers went out to work and mothers stayed home, images perpetuated in schoolbooks and games and on television. If we were bright students, we were told, "You're smart—for a girl," and then warned not to appear *too* smart in front of boys—"Or you won't have dates."

Those of us who persisted in reaching for a career were encouraged to be teachers or nurses so we would have "something to fall back on." My mother told me: "You're so bright, it's a pity you're not a boy. You could become president of a bank—or anything you wanted."

Ironically, and to our dismay, we discovered that playing the assigned role is precisely what elicits masculine contempt for our inferiority and narrow interests. *Tooth and Nail,* a newsletter published by women's liberation groups in the San Francisco area, acidly points out a few of the contradictions: "A smart woman never shows her brains; she allows the man to think himself clever. . . . Women's talk is all chatter; they don't understand things men are interested in."

Or: "Don't worry your pretty little head about such matters. . . . A woman's brain is between her legs. . . . Women like to be protected and treated like little girls. . . . Women can't make decisions."

The feminist answer is to throw out the whole simplistic division of human characteristics into masculine and feminine, and to insist that there are no real differences between men and women other than those enforced by culture.

Men say women are not inferior, we are just different; yet somehow they have appropriated most of the qualities that society admires and have left us with the same distinctive features that were attributed to black people before the civil rights revolution.

Men, for example, are said to be strong, assertive, courageous, logical, constructive, creative, and independent. Women are weak, passive, irrational, overemotional, empty-headed, and lacking in strong superegos. (Thank Freud for the last.) Both blacks and women are contented, have their place, and know how to use wiles—flattery, and wide-eyed, open-mouthed ignorance—to get around "the man." It is obviously natural that men should be dominant and women submissive. Shuffle, baby, shuffle.

Our "sexist" system has hurt men as well as women, forcing them into molds that deny the value of sensitivity, tenderness, and sentiment. Men who are not aggressive worry about their virility just as strong women are frightened by talk about their being castrating females. The elimination of rigid sex-role definitions would liberate everyone. And that is the goal of the women's liberation movement.

Women's liberation groups, which which have sprung up everywhere across the country, are taking names like Radical Women or the Women's Liberation Front or the Feminists. Most start as groups of ten or twelve; many, when they get too large for discussion, split in a form of mitosis. Sometimes they are tied to central organizations set up for action, or they maintain communications with each other or cosponsor newsletters with similar groups in their area.

Some are concerned with efforts to abolish abortion laws, a few have set up cooperative day-care centers, others challenge the stereotypes of woman's image, and many are organized for "consciousness-raising"—a kind of group therapy or encounter session that starts with the premise that there is something wrong with the system, not the women in the group.

The amorphousness and lack of central communication in the movement make it virtually impossible to catalogue the established groups, let alone the new ones that regularly appear; many of the "leaders" who have been quoted in newspapers or interviewed on television have been anointed only by the press.

The one organization with a constitution, board members, and chapters (some thirty-five) throughout the country is the National Organization for Women. Its founding in 1966 was precipitated by the ridicule that greeted the inclusion of sex in the prohibitions against job discrimination in the 1964 Civil Rights Act. (A staff member in the federal Equal Employment Opportunity Commission, which enforces the act, said it took pressure from NOW to get the EEOC to take that part of the law seriously.)

NOW members are not very different from women in other feminist groups, though they tend to include more professionals and older women. In general, they eschew "consciousness-raising" in favor of political action, and they are more likely to demonstrate for job equality and child-care centers than for the abolition of marriage or the traditional family unit.

NOW's president is Betty Friedan, who in 1963 published *The Feminine Mystique,* a challenge to the myth that a woman's place is either in a boudoir in a pink, frilly nightgown, on her hands and knees scrubbing the kitchen floor, or in a late model station wagon taking the kids to music lessons and Cub Scout meetings. (An article that previewed the theme of the book was turned down by every major women's magazinc. "Onc was horrified and said I was obviously talking to and for a few neurotic women." When the book came out, two of these magazines published excerpts and several now have commissioned articles about the movement.)

Today, Betty Friedan says, the movement must gain political power by mobilizing the 51 per cent of the electorate who are women, as well as seeking elected offices for themselves. "We have to break down the actual barriers that prevent women from being full people in society, and not only end explicit discrimination but build new institutions. Most women will continue to bear children, and unless we create child-care centers on a mass basis, it's all talk."

Women are beginning to read a good deal about their own place in history, about the determined struggles of the suffragettes, the isolation of Virginia Woolf, and the heroism of Rosa Luxemburg. The Congress to Unite Women, which drew some 500 participants from cities in the Northeast, called for women's studies in high schools and colleges.

Present are all the accouterments of any social movement—feminist magazines such as *No More Fun and Games* in Boston, *Up from Under* in New York, and *Aphra,* a literary magazine published in Baltimore. (Anne Sexton wrote in the dedication, "As long as it can be said about a woman writer, 'She writes like a man' and that woman takes it as a compliment, we are in trouble.")

There are feminist theaters in at least New York and Boston, buttons that read "Uppity Women Unite," feminist poems and songs, a feminist symbol (the biological sign for woman with an equal sign in the center), and, to denounce specific advertisements, gum stickers that state, "This ad insults women."

With a rising feminist consciousness, everything takes on new significance—films, advertisements, offhand comments, little things that never seemed important before. A few women conclude that chivalry and flirting reduce women to mere sex objects for men. We stop feeling guilty about opening doors, and some of us experiment with paying our own way on dates.

Personal acts are matched by political ones. The National Organization for Women went to court to get a federal ruling barring segregated help-wanted ads in newspapers, and it regularly helps women file complaints before the EEOC and local human rights commissions.

A women's rights platform was adopted last year by the State Committee of the California Democratic Party, and the Women's Rights Committee of the New Democratic Coalition plans to make feminist demands an issue in New York politics. A women's caucus exists in the Democratic Policy Council, headed by Senator Fred Harris.

At Grinnell College in Iowa, students protested the appearance of a representative from *Playboy* magazine, and women from sixteen cities converged on Atlantic City to make it clear what they think of the Miss America Pageant. In New York, a group protested advertisements by toymakers that said "Boys were born to build and learn" and "girls were born to be dancers."

Women's caucuses have been organized in the American Political Science, Psychological, and Sociological associations. At New York University, a group of law students won their fight to make women eligible for a series of coveted $10,000 scholarships.

Pro-abortion groups have organized around the country to repeal anti-abortion laws, challenge them in the courts, or openly defy them. In Bloomington, Indiana, New York City, and elsewhere, women's liberation groups have set up cooperative day-care centers, which are illegal under strict state rules that regulate child care facilities.

Free child care is likely to become the most significant demand made by the movement, and one calculated to draw the support of millions of women who may not be interested in other feminist issues. About four million working mothers have children under six years of age, and only 2 per cent of these are in day-care centers.

Even Establishment institutions appear to reflect the new attitudes. Princeton, Williams, and Yale have begun to admit women students, though on an unequal quota basis—and not to the hallowed pine-paneled halls of their alumni clubhouses.

Nevertheless, most people have only a vague idea of the significance of the new movement. News commentators on year-end analysis shows ignored the question or sloughed it off uncomfortably. One said the whole idea frightened him.

Yet, the women's movement promises to affect radically the life of virtually everyone in America. Only a small part of the population suffers because it is black, and most people have little contact with minorities. Women are 51 per cent of the population, and chances are that every adult American either is one, is married to one, or has close social or business relations with many.

The feminist revolution will overturn the basic premises upon which these relations are built—stereotyped notions about the family and the roles of men and women, fallacies concerning masculinity and femininity, and the economic division of labor into paid work and homemaking.

If the 1960s belonged to the blacks, the next ten years are ours.

Lucy Komisar, free-lance writer, is a dedicated leader of the struggle for women's rights. She is vice president of the National Organization for Women and is currently writing a book on feminism.

Vocabulary Study

From the list below, select the word or phrase nearest in meaning to the italicized word in the following excerpts. The list contains extra words.

A. voices of women's *liberation*

B. a movement that *encompasses* high school students and grandmothers

C. destined to *eclipse* the black civil rights struggle

D. *salvage* our own *buffeted egos*

E. we are *adamant* and passionate in our denial

F. the old *canard* that biology is destiny

G. Bruno Bettelheim states woman's functions *succinctly*

H. a senseless *menial* job

I. The freedom to choose whether or not to have children has always been *illusory.*

J. the general male *proclivity* to regard us as decorative

K. playing the assigned role is precisely what *elicits* masculine contempt

L. *amorphousness* and lack of central communication

M. frequently *derided* as "aggressive"

N. they *eschew* "consciousness-raising"

O. the *accouterments* of any social movement

trappings	release	embattled
evokes	concisely	propensity
save	endemic	formlessness
hoax	corollary	surpass
mocked	abstain from	vicarious
selves	contains	perpetuated
stereotypes	firm	
deceptive	servile	

Questions on Form and Content

A. Miss Komisar's essay is an extended definition of the new feminism. What is the movement? Why does it exist? Of whom is it composed?

B. What difference does Miss Komisar point out between housework and other meaningless jobs most people have today?

C. What are some of the trappings that have accompanied the feminist movement?

D. What advertisements on television or elsewhere seem to you objectionable in their portrayal of women?

E. In her concluding paragraphs, what contrasts does Miss Komisar draw between the feminist revolution and other movements?

Suggestions for Writing

A. "Men define women, and until now most of us have accepted their definition without question," says Miss Komisar. What is a woman?

B. Freud once asked: "What does woman want? Dear God! What does she want?" How would you answer his question?

C. When Nanette Rainone said at a feminist meeting, "Marriage is an aspect of men's lives, whereas it is the very center of most women's lives, the whole of their lives," she was perhaps inadvertently paraphrasing Byron, who wrote: "Man's love is of man's life a thing apart, / 'Tis woman's whole existence." Comment.

D. "We don't want to work for women or vote for them," says Miss Komisar. Do you? Why or why not?

E. Miss Komisar says that "we [women] resent the fact that men take the initiative with women, that women cannot ask for dates but must sit home waiting for the phone to ring." Are such patterns changing? If so, why? If not, should they? Why, in either case?

F. The Congress to Unite Women recently called for women's studies in high schools and colleges. Would you be inclined to support their call? If so, of what should the studies consist and why should they exist?

G. Discuss the stereotype of woman in some of America's songs.

H. According to a child's poem, what are little girls made of? Little boys? How do such lyrics influence the behavior of children?

I. Marya Mannes says: "Advertisers will have to stop selling products by showing women only as teenage playgirls whose sole function is sex, or as saw-voiced matrons whose only purpose is housekeeping." Discuss the portrayal of women in television advertising.

J. Feminists have objected to the Miss America and other beauty pageants. Do you? Why or why not?

K. Do you think women are discriminated against in college? If so, how?

L. Miss Komisar concludes her essay: "If the 1960s belonged to the blacks, the next ten years are ours." Comment.

M. Men's Liberation Movements have recently arisen all over Europe. Handcuffed husbands paraded recently with signs reading: "Wives no longer need our protection. Let them pay their own bills," "Women can be free if they grant male independence, too," and "Men, watch your freedom as carefully as your wives watch you." Comment.

O. Comment on one of the following remarks:

> One thing that bothers me about WLU—which I'm for in so many respects—is that it's so man-hating. Surely, it can't be *all* their fault that we're the way they are.—*Helen Gurley Brown*
>
> And don't get me started on alimony and how women exploit *men!—Helen Gurley Brown*
>
> If a feminist revolution is to come into its long-delayed own in

this new decade, a lot has to happen. Mothers will have to stop grooming daughters from childhood for marriage and motherhood. Men will have to accept and work with women as full partners in decision-making in all areas that affect human society. . . . And women themselves will have to forgo the luxury of dependence by assuming the burdens of a separate and equal identity. It could take more than ten years to emerge from centuries of brain-washing.—*Marya Mannes*

We have been given ample warning that the next ten or fifteen years will decide whether the human race can survive. Our survival is threatened by almost certain war, by famine, by contamination, by climatic change due to pollution. Perhaps the sex war could be postponed until more urgent issues are settled?—*Doris Lessing*

Woman is the lesser man.—*Alfred, Lord Tennyson*

It is not good that the man should be alone; I will make him an help meet for him.—*The Lord God, in the Book of Genesis*

Cocksure Women and Hensure Men

D. H. Lawrence

It seems to me there are two aspects to women. There is the demure and the dauntless. Men have loved to dwell, in fiction at least, on the demure maiden whose inevitable reply is: Oh, yes, if you please, kind sir! The demure maiden, the demure spouse, the demure mother—this is still the ideal. A few maidens, mistresses and mothers *are* demure. A few pretend to be. But the vast majority are not. And they don't pretend to be. We don't expect a girl skilfully driving her car to be demure, we expect her to be dauntless. What good would demure and maidenly Members of Parliament be, inevitably responding: Oh, yes, if you please, kind sir!—Though of course there are masculine members of that kidney.—And a demure telephone girl? Or even a demure stenographer? Demureness, to be sure, is outwardly becoming, it is an outward mark of femininity, like bobbed hair. But it goes with inward dauntlessness. The girl who has got to make her way in life has got to be dauntless, and if she has a pretty,

□ D. H. Lawrence, "Cocksure Women and Hensure Men," from D. H. Lawrence, *Assorted Articles* (London, 1930), pp. 71-76.

demure manner with it, then lucky girl. She kills two birds with two stones.

With the two kinds of femininity go two kinds of confidence: there are the women who are cocksure, and the women who are hensure. A really up-to-date woman is a cocksure woman. She doesn't have a doubt nor a qualm. She is the modern type. Whereas the old-fashioned demure woman was sure as a hen is sure, that is, without knowing anything about it. She went quietly and busily clucking around, laying the eggs and mothering the chickens in a kind of anxious dream that still was full of sureness. But not mental sureness. Her sureness was a physical condition, very soothing, but a condition out of which she could easily be startled or frightened.

It is quite amusing to see the two kinds of sureness in chickens. The cockerel is, naturally, cocksure. He crows because he is *certain* it is day. Then the hen peeps out from under her wing. He marches to the door of the hen-house and pokes out his head assertively: *Ah ha! daylight, of course, just as I said!*—and he majestically steps down the chicken ladder towards *terra firma,* knowing that the hens will step cautiously after him, drawn by his confidence. So after him, cautiously, step the hens. He crows again: *Ha-ha! here we are!*—It is indisputable, and the hens accept it entirely. He marches towards the house. From the house a person ought to appear, scattering corn. Why does the person not appear? The cock will see to it. He is cocksure. He gives a loud crow in the doorway, and the person appears. The hens are suitably impressed, but immediately devote all their henny consciousness to the scattered corn, pecking absorbedly, while the cock runs and fusses, cocksure that he is responsible for it all.

So the day goes on. The cock finds a tit-bit, and loudly calls the hens. They scuffle up in henny surety, and gobble the tit-bit. But when they find a juicy morsel for themselves, they devour it in silence, hensure. Unless, of course, there are little chicks, when they most anxiously call the brood. But in her own dim surety, the hen is really much surer than the cock, in a different way. She marches off to lay her egg, she secures obstinately the nest she wants, she lays her egg at last, then steps forth again with prancing confidence, and gives that most assured of all sounds, the hensure cackle of a bird who has laid her egg. The cock, who is never so sure about anything as the hen is about the egg she has laid, immediately starts to cackle like the female of his species. He is pining to be hensure, for hensure is so much surer than cocksure.

Nevertheless, cocksure is boss. When the chicken-hawk appears in the sky, loud are the cockerel's calls of alarm. Then the hens scuffle under the verandah, the cock ruffles his feathers on guard. The hens are numb with fear, they say: Alas, there is no health in us! How wonderful to be a cock so bold!—And they huddle, numbed. But their very numbness is hensurety.

Just as the cock can cackle, however, as if he had laid the egg, so can the hen bird crow. She can more or less assume his cocksureness. And yet she is never so easy, cocksure, as she used to be when she was hensure. Cocksure, she is cocksure, but uneasy. Hensure, she trembles, but is easy.

It seems to me just the same in the vast human farmyard. Only nowadays all the cocks are cackling and pretending to lay eggs, and all the hens are crowing and pretending to call the sun out of bed. If women to-day are cocksure, men are hensure. Men are timid, tremulous, rather soft and submissive, easy in their very henlike tremulousness. They only want to be spoken to gently. So the women step forth with a good loud *cock-a-doodle-do!*

The tragedy about cocksure women is that they are more cocky, in their assurance, than the cock himself. They never realise that when the cock gives his loud crow in the morning, he listens acutely afterwards, to hear if some other wretch of a cock dare crow defiance, challenge. To the cock, there is always defiance, challenge, danger and death on the clear air; or the possibility thereof.

But alas, when the hen crows, she listens for no defiance or challenge. When she says *cock-a-doodle-do!* then it is unanswerable. The cock listens for an answer, alert. But the hen knows she is unanswerable. *Cock-a-doodle-do!* and there it is, take it or leave it!

And it is this that makes the cocksureness of women so dangerous, so devastating. It is really out of scheme, it is not in relation to the rest of things. So we have the tragedy of cocksure women. They find, so often, that instead of having laid an egg, they have laid a vote, or an empty ink-bottle, or some other absolutely unhatchable object, which means nothing to them.

It is the tragedy of the modern woman. She becomes cocksure, she puts all her passion and energy and years of her life into some effort or assertion, without ever listening for the denial which she ought to take into count. She is cocksure, but she is a hen all the time. Frightened of her own henny self, she rushes to mad lengths about votes, or welfare, or sports, or business: she is marvellous, outmanning the man. But alas, it is all fundamentally disconnected. It is all an attitude, and one day the attitude will become a weird cramp, a pain, and then it will collapse. And when it has collapsed, and she looks at the eggs she has laid, votes, or miles of typewriting, years of business efficiency—suddenly, because she is a hen and not a cock, all she has done will turn into pure nothingness to her. Suddenly it all falls out of relation to her basic henny self, and she realises she has lost her life. The lovely henny surety, the hensureness which is the real bliss of every female, has been denied her: she has never had it. Having lived her life with such utmost strenuousness and cocksureness, she has missed her life altogether. Nothingness!

David Herbert Lawrence (1885-1930), English novelist, poet, playwright, and critic, was born in Eastwood, a small village near Nottingham, England, the son of a coal miner. He attended the University of Nottingham and taught school for a short time, before quitting his school with an excellent reputation in order to live by literature. Always living frugally, in a constant search for a cure for his tuberculosis and for a place where he could put his ideas about primitive religions and his other controversial philosophies into practice, he traveled and lived in Italy, Australia, New Zealand, Tahiti, the French Riviera, Mexico, and the southwestern part of the United States. His best known novels are *Sons and Lovers, The Rainbow,* and *Women in Love.* Among his short-story collections are *The Prussian Officer* and *The Lovely Lady.* Essays and criticism are represented in *Studies in Classical American Literature, Pornography and Obscenity,* and *Phoenix: The Posthumous Papers of D. H. Lawrence.*

Vocabulary Study

From the list below, select the word or phrase nearest in meaning to the word italicized in the following excerpts:

A. the *demure* and the *dauntless*
B. masculine members of that *kidney*
C. a doubt nor a *qualm*
D. steps down the chicken ladder towards *terra firma*
E. gobble the *tit-bit*
F. she secures *obstinately* the nest
G. *pining* to be hensure
H. Men are timid, *tremulous*
I. he listens *acutely* afterwards
J. so dangerous, so *devastating*
K. a *weird* cramp, a pain
L. such utmost *strenuousness*

fearful
unavoidably
misgiving
decorous
stubbornly
vigor
solid earth
uncanny
intensely
intrepid
kind
ravaging
painfully longing
stricture
choice morsel
strident

Questions on Form and Content

A. Into what two initial categories or aspects does Mr. Lawrence divide women?

B. When the two aspects coexist, what is the result?

C. What two kinds of confidence are the basis for the next section of Lawrence's analysis?

D. Which quality or confidence is natural to women? Why? Which quality is more certain?

E. Who is boss of the farmyard? What are his duties?

F. What does the hen do?

G. What happens in the vast human farmyard when, as nowadays, roles become confused?

H. What is the tragedy of cocksure women?

Suggestions for Writing

A. Do you consider the demure maiden, the demure spouse, the demure mother, the ideal? Why or why not?

B. "A really up-to-date woman is a cocksure woman," says Mr. Lawrence. Comment.

C. Using Mr. Lawrence's essay as a model, illustrate some other traits observable in the vast human farmyard by describing the actions of their animal counterparts.

D. Cocksure women, Mr. Lawrence says, "find, so often, that instead of having laid an egg, they have laid a vote, or an empty ink-bottle, or some other absolutely unhatchable object, which means nothing to them." Are results sometimes worse when the egg—or vote—does hatch? If so, develop and illustrate.

E. The tragedy of modern woman, Mr. Lawrence declares, is that "the lovely henny surety, the hensureness which is the real bliss of every female, has been denied her: she has never had it." How attractive does he make the life of the hensure hen, "busily clucking around, laying the eggs and mothering the chickens in a kind of anxious dream that still was full of sureness"? How do you think a new feminist would reply to Mr. Lawrence's argument?

F. If the cocksure woman loses her life when it ends in nothingness, what does the hensure woman have left when the eggs are all laid and hatched, the brood gone, and the nest empty?

G. "Nevertheless, cocksure is boss," says Mr. Lawrence. Define bossdom.

H. If you have read one of D. H. Lawrence's novels or short stories, or seen a film based on his work—*Sons and Lovers, The Fox*, or *Women in Love*—comment on the fiction or film in the light of this brief essay.

Is There a Gentleman in the House?

Russell Lynes

"A gentleman," said H. L. Mencken some years ago, "is one who never strikes a woman without provocation." I note this because a little less than a year ago I was accused of not being a gentleman.

The accusation came when I wrote an article [*Look*, July 22, 1958] in which I tried to define the modern lady. A good many women thought I had struck them without provocation. Some of them wrote and suggested that I take a look at the modern gentleman, if, indeed, there were any gentlemen left.

Are there any left?

Well, I have been looking about me and asking some questions. I have come to the conclusion that a woman's idea of a gentleman and a man's idea are two quite different fellows. Women want all men to be gentlemen, but are surprised when they are. Men expect other men to be gentlemen, and are disappointed when they are not. If you put the female idea together with the male idea, you run the risk of finding that the American gentleman is obsolete.

□Russell Lynes, "Is There a Gentleman in the House?" *Look* (June 9, 1959), 19-21.

Whether there are any gentlemen in America today depends on your attitude, your definition.

Let's take the male point of view first. Mr. Mencken's observation is obviously a prime example of the male attitude, and Mr. Mencken, who was known as the "Sage of Baltimore," was obviously a gentleman himself. He did not go on to say that a gentleman is expected to strike a woman just because she provokes him. This is probably just as well, for there is a wife-beating tradition in America. The law once provided a husband with the right to beat his wife, so long as he used a cane no thicker than his thumb. If Mr. Mencken's definition were carried to its logical conclusion, the pink-and-white sex (which we often sentimentally call the "weaker sex") might soon become the black-and-blue sex. It takes little imagination to recognize that Mr. Mencken was under the impression that American men take a good deal of unnecessary guff from women.

But to most men, the quality of being a gentleman, in America at least, includes accepting and making the best of this situation. It seems to be generally taken for granted that wife-beaters are not gentlemen in twentieth-century terms and that self-control is expected of a gentleman, under even the most trying circumstances. A gentleman does not lose his temper so thoroughly that he commits violence, even on a golf course. Profanity may be permissible, even to the clergy, under such circumstances, but no gentleman wraps his number-four iron around his caddy's neck or throws his spoon into the water hazard. Indeed, Nicholas Murray Butler, the late president of Columbia University, said, "One of the embarrassments of being a gentleman is that you are not permitted to be violent in asserting your rights."

In general, this is true, and most men who regard themselves as gentlemen today will let their patience be sorely tried before they make a scene. Our nineteenth-century ancestors, however, were perhaps stricter in this regard than we are now. In a book of etiquette called *The Illustrated Manners Book*, published about a century ago, men were cautioned thus: "Preserve your calmness and presence of mind under all circumstances. If you are so heedless as to scald your mouth; if a careless waiter pours a plate of soup in your lap, smile serenely. The gentleman who remarked, when his servant dropped a boiled tongue on the dining room floor, ' 'Tis a mere *lapsus linguae* [slip of the tongue], gentlemen,' set a good example."

But the male definition of the gentleman, I have found, almost never mentions the question of how a man behaves toward women. I have found this to be true not only by talking with friends, but also in searching through dictionaries, books of quotations and even books of etiquette for definitions of a gentleman. A gentleman makes no distinctions in his behavior toward men and women; he regards both sexes equally as human beings. He thinks of himself as one who is as good as his word, respects other people's privacy and their idiosyncrasies, doesn't push himself forward at the expense of others or make himself conspicuous. He is not a snob, toadies to nobody and expects nobody to toady to him. The late William Lyon Phelps, perhaps more of a gentleman than a scholar, put it this way: "This is the final test of a gentleman: his respect for those who can be of no possible service to him."

Female definitions of a gentleman (if you don't believe me, ask the first woman you meet) almost invariably have something to do with how a man behaves toward women and whether, as one of them said to me, "he has the capacity for making any female feel like a lady."

Now, all women want to be made to feel like ladies whether they are actually ladies or not. It is too bad that so many of them aren't quite sure they are unless some gentleman makes them feel like one, but that is aside from my point. To women, the first quality of a gentleman is his manners. If his manners are courtly, so much the better. If to courtliness he adds flattery, she thinks him a "perfect" gentleman. But "perfect" though he may be, he must also be well-dressed, well-groomed and completely at ease. He must, too, be respectful of her wishes, indulgent of her whims and subject to her wiles. If he so charms her that she stoops to folly, he is a gentleman because, however far she may have strayed as a woman, he does not let her feel for a moment that she has been anything but a lady.

I have discovered that when men and women disagree on so fundamental a definition as what a gentleman is, there are two sensible ways to find out what the truth is. The first is to look at history, which gives you a running start, and the second, and more important one, is to ask the young what they think.

Historically, the word "gentleman" goes back to the eleventh century, the time of the early Crusades, when it meant a freeman, as opposed to a serf or slave. A gentleman had the right to bear arms and he was of "gentle" birth, as opposed to "noble" birth. It was, incidentally, in the days when men wore armor that the custom of tipping one's hat to a lady originated. They didn't tip their helmets, of course, but they raised their visors as a gesture of respect to ladies, a practice that lasted about a thousand years.

Lawyers and scholars were called gentlemen long before physicians were. (Surgery, one is likely to forget, was a side line for barbers.) And merchants, even those who ran large and prosperous establishments, were not considered gentlemen even so recently as a few decades ago. To "be in trade" or to be an actor, an artist or a writer was to indulge in a not quite respectable way of making a living, and there are still some men who call themselves gentlemen who look down on those engaged in such pursuits.

Some time back, the word "gentleman" became associated with wealth and with the leisure that not having to make a living provided. A gentleman had time to study in universities, to cultivate the arts and sciences and to indulge in the niceties of courtly manners. But he seems not to have tried too hard at anything; he was never a "grind." The qualifications for a fellow at All Souls College in Oxford in 1440 were: "Well-born, well-dressed and moderately learned." It was a definition that would fit the undergraduate gentleman of today to a T—or so, anyway, he would like to think.

But for many centuries, it has been not just breeding and wealth that made a gentleman; it has been an attitude toward life and one's fellow men that distinguished the gentleman from the well-born boor. "Virtue" was a quality of gentlemen; so were "honesty" and "liberality" and "generosity." Being a gentleman was the very opposite of being a snob or social climber. Shakespeare said it more neatly, as usual, than anyone else:

We are gentlemen,
That neither in our hearts nor outward eyes
Envy the great, nor do the low despise.

The gentleman in America has gone through a number of stages in the last few hundred years. When George Washington was a boy, he copied rules of behavior from a book called *Youth's Behavior, or Decency in Conversation Amongst Men.* It was a translation of a French manual that was first published nearly a century before Washington was born. He learned such rules as these:

In Speaking to men of Quality do not lean nor Look them full in the Face.
Cleanse not your teeth with the Table Cloth, Napkin, Fork or Knife.
Spit not in the Fire.
Kill no Vermin as Fleas, lice, ticks &c in the Sight of Others.
Put not another bit into your mouth til the former be Swallowed.

And there were moral rules as well as rules of etiquette, such as:

Labor to keep alive in your Breast that Little Spark of Celestial fire Called Conscience.

A favorite maxim of authors of books of etiquette in America for a long time has been that "manners are minor morals," and many generations of American gentlemen have been brought up on this principle. The manners of the nineteenth-century gentleman were much more elaborate than those of today. There was a good deal more bowing from the waist and tipping of the hat. He did not smoke in the presence of ladies. He was punctilious in opening the doors of carriages and paid many formal calls. There was more concern for "a lady's reputation" then than now, and a man went to great lengths to preserve at least the appearance of decorum, whatever his darker motives may have been.

While these niceties are disappearing, the hardiest thing about the tradition of the gentleman in America is that we judge him not on the basis of his forebears, but on himself. That is not to say that we haven't our lineage snobs; we have. Consider the *Mayflower* descendants and the Daughters of the American Revolution. But generally, we agree with Charles A. Munn, who defined a gentleman as "a man who for three generations has pronounced 'to-may-to' 'to-mah-to.' "

When you turn from history, once over lightly, to my other source of information about a gentleman, the young, you find a somewhat different frame of mind. In the first place, it is not a word that they think much about one way or another. To the very young male, another young male who is a gentleman is likely also to be a "sissy." To a teen-age boy, his contemporary who is a gentleman is likely to be a snob; he puts on airs. When you get to college age, the definition changes, and a gentleman is likely to belong to the "right" clubs or fraternities; his dress is "tweedy" ("Ivy League" seems to be old hat by now); he works but does not "grind," plays but does not go out for the varsity (he often refers to those who do as "animals"). In other words, he is likely to keep himself uncommitted, "loose" and slightly, but not energetically, aloof from what in my day was called "being collegiate." When I went to college 25-odd years ago, there was a scholastic grade called a "gentleman's 'C.' " This seems to have gone up a notch today, because college grades have a direct effect on how good a job a man can get when he graduates. The grade now seems to be "gentleman's 'B.' " "A's" are for "grinds," "brains" and "eggheads." The undergraduate gentleman is none of these.

The attitude of girls is somewhat different. A junior at Bryn Mawr rather wistfully told me, "Gentlemen are a dying race, but those who have survived are much appreciated." Another girl at the same college said, "I'd like to think a gentleman is a person who can stand on his own two feet without treading on other people's toes," which, you'll admit, is a pretty nice definition.

But most young women, like their mothers, seem to think of gentlemen in terms of their manners toward ladies. "A gentleman can wear blue jeans and still open car doors," one says. Another says, "A gentleman is more than ordinarily sensitive to the nature of the ingredients of a lady."

Several years ago, a prominent English poet, who had spent some time teaching in an American college, said in the presence of a friend of mine in London, "There are no gentlemen in America." My friend was infuriated by this piece of insolence, and so was I when I first heard it. Now, I'm not so sure. After all, the English definition of what makes a gentleman starts with the old-school-tie and gentleman-by-birth concept. Ours does not.

It is, therefore, easier to say what the gentleman is not than what he is. In America, a gentleman is not a well-bred boor; good will means more than good breeding. He is not a man whose graceful manners conceal his ambition to get the better of other people; or, to put it another way, a gentleman's manners do not camouflage his character, but reflect it. A gentleman is not uneasy in any social situation, but neither is he aggressive. (One college man said to me, "A gentleman is someone who can zip up his fly in public and not be embarrassed.") Nobody in America is a gentleman by birth (which is scarcely true anywhere else) or by right of wealth or of talent. A gentleman does not try to be one.

In America, we pay a male no higher compliment than to say he is a "real man." It means that we trust, admire and respect him. It means that he is thoughtful, courteous and generous. It means that he is a gentleman at heart. And where else does it matter?

(Joseph) Russell Lynes, Jr., formerly managing editor and now contributing editor of *Harper's Magazine,* has been concerned with matters of taste and manners and customs in America for some time. In 1954 his book, *The Tastemakers,* was a best seller; in 1957 *A Surfeit of Honey,* an exploration of our manners, also appeared on the best-seller list. A Yale man, he is the chairman of the publications committee for the Yale University Council and a member of the humanities committee of the John Hay Whitney Foundation. His other books include *Highbrow, Lowbrow, Middlebrow; The Domesticated Americans;* and *Confessions of a Dilettante.*

Vocabulary Study

A. If a gentleman hits a lady only with *provocation,* how does the assault come about (paragraph 1)?

B. A high golf score may make profanity *permissible,* even to the clergy. Discuss the word *permissible* (paragraph 7: "But to most . . .").

C. What are *idiosyncrasies* (paragraph 9: "But the male . . .")?

D. A gentleman *"toadies* to nobody." What is the connotation of the word *toady* (also paragraph 9)?

E. *Punctilious* is a word that refers to "small points" or "fine points." What does it mean in paragraph 19 ("A favorite . . .")?

F. *Decorum* is (a) the observance of the proprieties; (b) good behavior; (c) the code of good form (also paragraph 19)?

G. *Lineage* snobs are (a) proud of their good looks; (b) proud of their horses' blood lines; (c) proud of their own blood lines (paragraph 20: "While these . . .")?

H. *Camouflage,* from the French *camoufler,* is an interesting word. It is often found in a military context. How is it used in the next to the last paragraph?

Questions on Form and Content

A. What is the historical meaning of the word *gentleman,* according to Mr. Lynes?

B. What details does Mr. Lynes cite to show how the concept of a gentleman has undergone many changes in America?

C. What was H. L. Mencken's definition of a gentleman? How does Mr. Lynes explain this definition?

D. What does Mr. Lynes consider a gentleman's grade to be in college today? What was it formerly, in his time? Have you ever felt a little embarrassed at receiving an "A" in any subject?

E. What is a "lineage snob"? How does the subject of lineage snobs arise in connection with a discussion of gentlemen?

F. Mr. Lynes says that if you put the female idea of a gentleman together with the male idea, you run the risk of discovering that the American gentleman is obsolete. On what does he base this opinion? Do you agree?

G. Mr. Lynes has a very fitting conclusion to his essay in that it sums up what the word *gentleman* means to most men. What is the term he uses in summation, and how does he define it?

H. This essay makes excellent use of simple and extended definition. How?

I. "It is hard to live by a personal code any more, just as it is hard to live by a religion. Life today demands too many compromises. A man can't be a gentleman any more," lamented one East Coast columnist, not long ago. Discuss.

Suggestions for Writing

A. "But to most men, the quality of being a gentleman, in America at least, includes accepting and making the best of this situation," Mr. Lynes says early in his article. Explain what this statement means to you, giving examples to support your points.

B. Write a paper on the different definitions men and women have for the word *gentleman.* Conclude with your own attitude toward these two concepts. Which seems more realistic? More just?

C. "Being a gentleman was the very opposite of being a snob or social climber." Discuss.

D. Mr. Lynes says that a visiting English poet said: "There are no gentlemen in America." Do you agree? Develop, explaining and defining your point of view.

E. The late William Lyon Phelps said: "This is the final test of a gentleman: his respect for those who can be of no possible service to him." What did he mean? Do you think this is a fair appraisal? Develop.

F. Mr. Lynes seems to feel that when women discuss a gentleman their definition almost invariably has to do with how a man behaves toward women. Defend or attack this point of view.

G. Discuss the difference between historical concepts of a gentleman and today's concept.

H. One of the girls Mr. Lynes talked to at Bryn Mawr said, "I'd like to think a gentleman is a person who can stand on his own two feet without treading on other people's toes." Discuss the meaning of her definition and compare it to your own.

I. Do you think that college helps to form a gentleman? Or does it make him a snob and a boor? Discuss.

J. As you are a gentleman, discuss your gentleman's code in a paper.

K. As you are a lady, discuss what you think should be a gentleman's code.

L. One writer once said, "A woman's best asset is a man's imagination." Discuss.

The Case for the American Woman

Diana Trilling

For some years now, the American woman has been under persistent attack as the cause of the major ills of modern American life. She is blamed for the marked decline in masculine self-esteem and for the nervous tension that seems to characterize both men and women. The instability of the modern home, the rise in juvenile delinquency and male homosexuality, even the alarming incidence of heart disease among American men—all of these are blamed on the American woman's distortion of her traditional female role.

Specifically, the American wife is accused of displacing her husband as head of the family and of reversing the established order of male sexual dominance and female passivity. She is said to have subdued the old American spirit of self-reliance and to have set the patterns of conformity which are so strangling to free enterprise. And she is pictured as so greedy for social status that she drives her husband to death to provide the mink coat or new refrigerator or whatever it is

□ Diana Trilling, "The Case for the American Woman," *Look* (March 3, 1959), 50-54.

that bestows prestige within her particular social group.

As for the American mother, she is alternately accused of seducing her sons and tyrannizing them out of all semblance of masculinity. In her rearing of boys, she is charged with substituting possessiveness for pride in their young manliness. In her rearing of girls, she is accused of teaching them to feel superior to boys and to believe that male sexuality is theirs to permit or forbid, entirely at their own will.

And outside the home, the American woman is similarly charged with undermining men—by challenging their economic ascendancy and invading territories once thought to be the province of males only. But she is also accused of winning success in business and the professions by unfair sexual advantage, using the office for a parade of charms once reserved for the home!

It is a heavy indictment, and if the American woman is not crushed by the weight, she must indeed be hard—or innocent. Or perhaps she has a more complicated view of her situation than she has yet communicated to her critics.

For actually no thoughtful woman can fail to agree that her sex has lost its way and that the modern woman no longer knows how to behave as a woman. But she also realizes that her confusions are not her fault. While she may join in the chorus of accusations against her own sex, in her heart she knows that men are just as lost as women and that if either sex is to blame—which is highly questionable—the male sex is as guilty as the female.

This is, in fact, the secret knowledge shared by most intelligent women today—the modern version of the "secret" revealed by Sir James Barrie many years ago in his play, *What Every Woman Knows.* Barrie's heroine was a clever woman who helped her husband to professional success by subtly feeding him ideas which were much better than his own while convincing him he was the brilliant partner in the marriage. As the title indicates, not only the wife in the play but all the women in the audience were supposed to understand that men live by their male pride and that it is a woman's duty to preserve her husband's self-confidence at whatever sacrifice of her own claims to equal esteem.

But what was important about Barrie's story was that the wife's self-effacement brought its own reward. If the wife flattered her husband's male vanity, the husband flattered her femininity no less. Certain of his natural male superiority, he never thought that his wife might be cleverer than he or be manipulating him, and he could even make his wife feel the more womanly for tenderly outwitting him for his own good.

Today, such a play would have to be quite differently conceived. The husband in *What Every Woman Knows* is surely no hero, but the wife is a heroine. Today, however, the play would have no heroine either, just a pair of bewildered, hopeless creatures struggling to overcome their "inner resentments." If the wife tried to preserve her husband's pride, her overanxious, oversensitive husband would be convinced this was because he was "inadequate." And the wife would be tied in knots with fear that she was being "competitive." Instead of putting her wits at her husband's service, Barrie's heroine would have one baby after another, to demonstrate his manliness and her femaleness!

One wonders what accounts for this deterioration in male self-regard—whether, as many writers suggest, it is due to feminism that men suffer such a paralyzing sense of being less than they should be. But the fact is, of course, that long before feminism was anything but a gleam in the eye of a few social visionaries, there had been planted the seeds of self-doubt which now bear fruit in the extreme conflicts and frustrations which we blame on female emancipation.

To explain today's sexual dilemma, we have to return to an earlier century and to the beginnings of the slow and irreversible process, involving every phase of life—religious, economic and political as well as sexual—which robbed modern man of his self-confidence. Only history is to blame for our present-day loss of faith in ourselves. The decline of the modern male is but a single aspect of the large fundamental change which has taken place in man's relation to society over the last hundred and fifty years.

It is as meaningless to seek the cause of our sexual disequilibrium in the presumed impulse of women to steal male authority as it would be to hold the scientists responsible for disasters which can result from scientific discovery.

Nevertheless we live as persons, not as incidents in history. And where there is as much anxiety and doubt as now exists in the relations of men and women, it is only natural that blame should be parceled out. Men blame women for robbing them of their manhood? Well, women blame men for depriving them of their womanhood. The chief difference is that women would rather join in the public attack against their own sex than further jeopardize the good opinion of men by countercharges.

If one tries to sum up the substance of the modern woman's self-defense, it seems to me her "case" runs somewhat as follows:

No woman—no resasonably normal woman—wants to assert superiority over men, let alone dominate them. On the contrary, women want to be cherished and protected by men and dependent on men's superior strength. It is by this that they are made to feel most feminine.

But the modern man seems incapable of the traditional assertions of masculinity. He cannot give a woman the emotional support she desires because he has come to believe that it is he who needs the supporting, from a woman. Instead of exercising the authority which was once thought to define a mature man, he tries to impose himself by demands for deference and attention which are essentially childish. He often retreats into passivity, forcing women into attitudes alien to their sexual disposition—and then he resents them for being more active and positive than he.

In short, if the modern woman is defeminized, she believes she has the right to say that it is not of her own free choice. It is because she has inevitably responded to the demasculinization of the modern man.

The American woman is accused of displacing her husband as head of the family. In her mind, she meets this familiar charge with the countercharge that she knows scarcely a household in which the mother doesn't struggle—in vain—to have the father make the important decisions in the children's lives, exercise the discipline, be a model of manliness to his sons. But the father, it always seems, is too tired, or too unsure of his maleness, to behave in the traditional ways of fatherhood. The wife is perfectly aware that this father of her children may comply more sweetly or docilely than her own father would have dreamed of doing to her demands for his participation in all kinds of family activity. But this fools no one, least of all himself, that he is head of the family. By his own choice, and in the face of his wife's protests, he leaves the vital decisions in his children's lives—their schooling, their sexual instruction, their religious and moral training—to their mother. He says that she "knows more about these things" than he does, but even as he says this, he is entirely convinced than his wife robs him of authority in the home.

Then it is said of the American woman that, in order to satisfy her ambition, she urges men to killing extremes of competition. Undoubtedly, there are greedy women in America, just as there are lazy men. But they are the exception, not the rule. The economic rat race, as men like to call it, far from being a female creation, terrifies the American woman, who by and large would make almost any sacrifice to reduce the work pressure on her husband and keep him healthy. But the American man is certain he is loved for his money, not for himself—he brings this idea into marriage and nothing his wife can do will disabuse him of it. It is he, far more than his wife, who is the victim of the materialism he deplores in her. The American man, unlike the American woman, doesn't have to be conspicuously shallow, he has only to be average in his society, to measure his personal worth by the kind of house he lives in, the car he drives, the show his family makes in the community.

Or, outside the domestic sphere, there is the famous phenomenon of the "office wife." What honest man can deny that what he looks for in his secretary is precisely the sort of attention—without obligation—that he ideally would ask of a wife? An employer talks about his secretary as someone he can really depend upon and he means more than her technical proficiency, he means just what he says—dependence. He means someone he can count on to choose his neckties, see that he takes his tranquilizer, and in general continue the mothering, the "momism," for which the modern woman is so widely condemned.

In other words, wherever the sexes meet, the American male would seem to repeat his pattern of self-contrived defeat. And it is the American woman's awareness of this pattern that lies at the heart of her defense: If she seems to act aggressively or too assertively or in other ways unattractively, she acts as she must act. She acts as men force her to act by their own unmanly behavior.

And of course her situation is full of paradoxes. Not least of them is the fact that at the same time that she bends so much effort to persuading men that she is really a female and not in competition with men, she has more and more demands made on her for a competence that never used to be asked of women. A couple of decades ago, a noted psychoanalyst named, and lamented, the many roles the modern women is called upon to play—wife, mistress, mother, sports companion, intellectual companion, etc. Today, the list would be twice as long. To these roles, we have added engineer, mechanic, carpenter, chauffeur, psychologist, economist, local politician, even bartender! Although these new demands aren't actually roles but only skills, they represent enough of a departure from the traditional notion of what should engage a woman to create a quite new self-image for her, which works a fundamental change both in her response to men and in her expectations from men.

The change shows itself most openly in the middle class, where the disappearance of servants and of other household services—plumbers, painters, repairmen—is most keenly felt. The myriad new skills required of the middle-class housewife inevitably increase her sense of power—no matter what is asked of her, she seems able to meet the challenge. And this sense of power festers within her because it is not acknowledged by the men in her society nor met by some parallel show of male power.

To undertake a defense of the modern woman and yet speak sympathetically of her awareness of power is obviously a risky business. Not only in our personal relations but even in our public affairs we Americans dislike the idea of power; we prefer the ideas of helpfulness and co-operation. Progressive education favors the helpful co-operative child over the forceful child. So-called enlightened politics prefers to coexist with communism rather than throw our whole moral weight against it. Power is a dirty word in our society.

Yet the impulse to power is entirely human. We repress it at great cost to our well-being, as individuals and as a society. It is not only understandable, it is unavoidable that the modern woman who cooks, cleans, bears and raises children, golfs, swims, sails, drives her car, gardens, repairs the family radio, paints the spare bedroom, fulfills her community obligations, engages in local politics and still has the energy to give and attend dinner parties should feel proud of her resourcefulness and that she should seek male approval of her accomplishments. But this approval is exactly what is withheld from her—this and a show of male strength equal to her own.

Instead of the admiration and respect accorded to her pioneer ancestress for the sturdiness with which she coped with her environment, the modern woman is told she is destroying men. Instead of being given the emotional support which the pioneer woman got from a sex which didn't feel itself threatened by the competence of its women, the modern woman is made to fend for herself emotionally and is even required to sustain her mate.

In such circumstances it should be no surprise that female pride has become tinged with self-pity and bitterness. What else except acerbity is ever the response of a group or individual that feels unloved? For, in addition to the overt criticisms leveled against her, the modern woman is made aware of her reduced position by dozens of small outward signs—the refusal of men to rise for her in crowded buses and subways, the way in which even well-bred men have taken to ordering food in restaurants without attention to the woman's needs, her rude exclusion from conversation even at functions supposedly designed for and by herself.

These tokens of unconcern and contempt are not cheering. Women notice them, though they may not often speak of them. Yet actually they play no larger part in a woman's self-assessment than certain automatic tributes which are also regularly directed to her—the gifts on Mother's Day, the flattery of her sex in advertising and in the women's magazines. In the last analysis, it is not public but private confirmation that a woman seeks. She wants private reassurance that despite her new "masculine" skills, she has not lost her womanly grace and charm.

No public attack would reach the modern woman were it not that this private reassurance is so sadly lacking, and where it hurts most—in her closest sexual relationships. It is in the privacy of her bedroom that the modern woman learns that men really mean what they say when they complain of her sex, and here we have no statistics—even Dr. Kinsey couldn't supply us with the figures on the results of the American male's poor opinion of women and the sexual sullenness which must be its consequence. But we have sufficient hints that all is not as it should be in the sexual life of the American woman—in her lack of repose, in the nervous compulsiveness so common in her approach to men, in the overintellectualization and timidity with which she confronts the sexuality of her children. That these clues could also be interpreted as evidence of her own sexual shortcomings rather than those of her male partner, there is, of course, no denying. But this still leaves us with the question: Why have female grace and responsiveness deteriorated rather than improved in a society which boasts such a large conquest of female sexual inhibition and ignorance?

It is not a matter one wants to press beyond conjecture, however. A defense of the American woman implies no wish to draw up a final reckoning on who is at fault where. What it does require is simple recognition that the modern woman is begging for reassurance that she has not lost her femininity by her forced advance along new lines of masculine competence—and equally simple recognition that the American male is apparently unable to give her this reassurance.

And there are many reasons he cannot. In their statement lies the "case" of the American man. Chief among them, of course, is the fact that while a whole new world of possibility has opened up for female enterprise and skill in modern life, man's world has consistently closed in on him. At the same time that the modern woman widens the scope of her individual capacities, the individual man becomes mass man—a smaller and smaller cog in an always vaster machine, denied the kind of test and confirmation of his masculinity which enabled his grandfather to take the competence of *his* women all in his manly stride.

It would be a poor sort of argument which, in trying to redress the wrongs done the modern woman by her critics, perpetrated an even greater wrong against the modern man by ignoring the desperate deal he is being given by history. A male sex every day more grievously deprived of means to assert its masculinity is not to be harshly judged because it denies women their femaleness. This the thoughtful woman appreciates, at least intuitively.

Perhaps this is why women are so ready to join the critics of their own sex. Or perhaps they have a more subtle and cogent reason, however unconscious.

What I mean is this:

No matter how strong our belief in sexual equality, we all of us operate on the premise that men are the more important sex, whose condition determines the fate of society. While we grant that women exert a variety of subsidiary influences in the world, we have only to consult the record of Western civilization to see that it is men who steer the main course. The way women behave or are treated in a society may be a sound index to its health. But social survival depends neither on the virtue nor the achievements of women. It depends upon the force and vision of men.

All around us today we see a male sex which, if not yet defeated in its ability to control our human destiny, is certainly frightened by the gigantic tasks it faces. Since women are themselves unprepared to take over the national life, let alone the fate of Western civilization, in reason they must try to eliminate those mistakes in behavior which could possibly contribute to the general male feeling of powerlessness. Perhaps the self-criticism in which modern women indulge so freely nowadays can therefore be understood as more than an expression of their own personal confusion. It may also be understood as an attempt to restore to men the strength of which women are said to have robbed them, in the hope that this will enable men to save society.

What *really* makes the misery of the modern woman, in other words, is not the fear that her own sex is lost. Were this her sole problem, she would soon enough find her female way again—and not symbolically, with fluffy petticoats and elaborate hairdos, but actually. What really torments her is the fear that life itself may be lost, without possibility of salvation by this or that gesture or alteration of attitude on the part of mere women. This is the tragic awareness which hides behind—which is indeed masked by—her readiness to accept any case which may be made against her. What difference if the case is unjust? She will assume it is just because she could wish it were true. She could wish she had only to learn once more how to behave as a woman for civilization to be assured its survival.

DIANA TRILLING in private life is Mrs. Lionel Trilling. She was born in New York City, where she still lives. A graduate of Radcliffe College, she was for eight years the fiction critic of *The Nation.* She has written literary criticism and political essays for *The New York Times, The New York Herald Tribune, Partisan Review, Harper's Magazine,* and many other periodicals. She edited and wrote a long critical introduction to *The Portable D. H. Lawrence* and to *The Selected Letters of D. H. Lawrence.* Chairman of the board of directors of the American Committee for Cultural Freedom from 1955 to 1957, she is still a member of its executive board.

Vocabulary Study

A. The American wife is accused of "reversing the established order of male sexual dominance and female passivity" (paragraph 2). Define *passivity.*

B. The charges Mrs. Trilling presents are "a heavy *indictment*" (paragraph 5). Define *indictment.*

C. *Subtle* comes from a Latin word, a weaver's term meaning "under the cloth." Can you then guess the meaning of *subtly* in paragraph 7 ("This is, in fact . . .")?

D. In paragraph 8 ("But what . . ."), what does *self-effacement* mean? How does the wife make herself appear through *self-effacement?*

E. By sexual *disequilibrium*, Mrs. Trilling again refers in paragraph 12 ("It is as . . .") to the situation mentioned in A, above. What is it?

F. When a game or contest ended in a draw, the old Romans called it *jocus partitus*, divided game, and split the wagers evenly. Later the expression was applied to contests between adversaries evenly matched, when the outcome was in doubt or there was a certain risk of life. English *jeopardy* thus comes to us. Can you determine the meaning of *jeopardize* (paragraph 13: "Nevertheless we live . . .")?

G. Our word *doctor* comes from the Latin *docere*, "to teach." The word *docile* belongs to the same family, but refers to someone else in the teaching relationship. Can you determine the meaning of *docilely* in paragraph 18 ("The American woman is accused . . .")?

H. Originally, the word *myriad* had a definite limit in its meaning. Now it has not. What does it mean (paragraph 23: "The change . . .")?

I. An unripe grapefruit tastes *acerb*. Some groups or individuals feel *acerbity* over their outcast state. What does *acerbity* mean (paragraph 27: "In such . . .")?

J. Appreciating something *intuitively* is better than appreciating it only when it is pointed out to you. In what way? (See paragraph 32: "It would be . . .")

K. When you *redress* a wrong do you (a) aggravate it; (b) apologize for it; (c) set it right (also paragraph 32)?

Questions on Form and Content

A. State in your own words the three areas in society in which the modern woman is attacked.

B. The analytical method of development is a process of breaking a subject down into its parts and studying them in relation to each other and the whole. Can you explain how this method is used in Mrs. Trilling's article?

C. How would James Barrie's play, *What Every Woman Knows*, be changed to explain the relationship of the modern woman and man?

D. Mrs. Trilling says: "No woman—no reasonably normal woman—wants to assert superiority over men." On what basis does she make this assertion? Do you agree?

E. What, according to Mrs. Trilling, is the famous phenomenon of the "office wife"?

F. In her conclusion, Mrs. Trilling says that modern woman's fear is not that her own sex is lost, but that life itself may be lost. Explain.

G. What are some of the many new responsibilities of the modern woman which her ancestors did not have to assume?

Suggestions for Writing

A. Mrs. Trilling says that a large part of woman's misery today is rooted in the fear that men have lost their power. Do you agree that they have? Are her fears justified, then? Develop.

B. "Not only in our personal relations but even in our public affairs we Americans dislike the idea of power; we prefer the ideas of helpfulness and co-operation." Develop this proposition in the light of the male-female relationship that Mrs. Trilling discusses.

C. Mrs. Trilling says that woman today wants "private reassurance that despite her new 'masculine' skills, she has not lost her womanly grace and charm." Do you think what she says is true? If so, how can the assurance be achieved? Comment.

D. The author, in her opening statements, says that the modern American woman is blamed for the marked decline of masculine self-esteem. To what does she ascribe this blame? Do you believe the blame is properly placed? Take one side of this argument, and give your point of view.

E. "Only history," Mrs. Trilling says, "is to blame for our present-day loss of faith in ourselves. The decline of the modern male is but a single aspect of the large fundamental change" taking place with regard to man's relation to society. From your knowledge of recent world events, discuss whether or not you consider her opinion is sound.

F. "Don't make a hero of your husband, because you're sure to find him out. Make a comrade of him. It's far safer, and lasts longer." Develop this quotation from Philip Gibbs in the light of Mrs. Trilling's article.

G. What, in your opinion, is the present position of the modern woman—or the modern man?

H. Write a summary of Mrs. Trilling's main points, in which you show effectively how she incorporates the three main points in her introduction.

I. According to the author, "Power is a dirty word in our society." Write an extended definition of *power.*

J. Compare and contrast Mrs. Trilling's views with those expressed by Lucy Komisar in "The New Feminism."

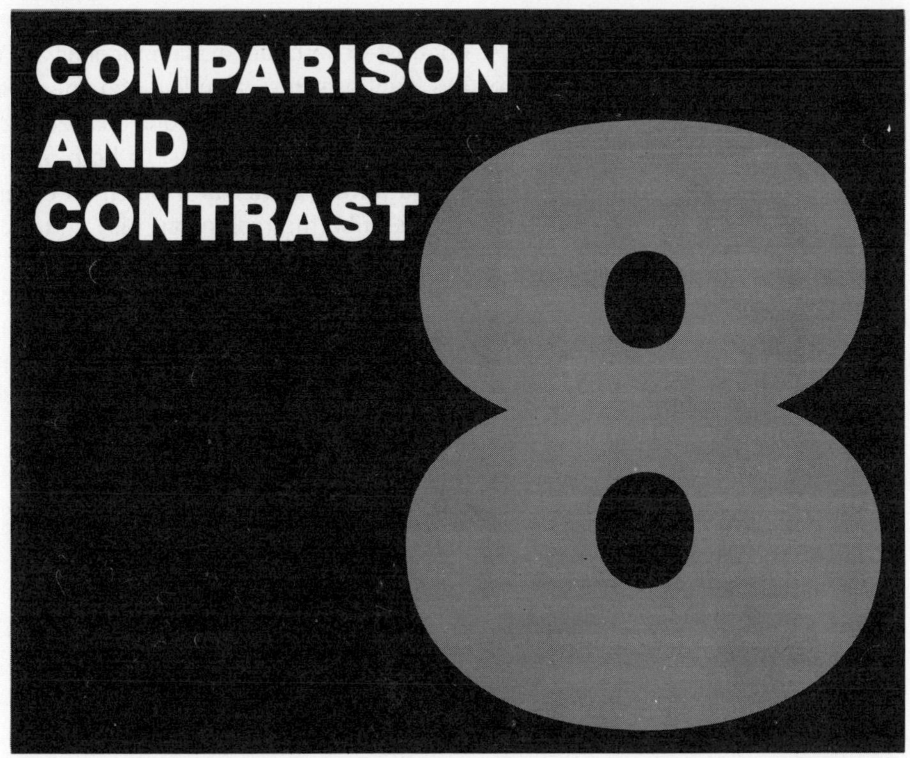

When you want to point up similarities, you compare; when you want to stress differences, you contrast.

Comparisons are often used to emphasize a basic fact. In a preceding chapter, Eric Goldman compares the social life of the emancipated woman with that of man in order to support and strengthen his theme idea. Comparisons are helpful, too, when one is attempting to explain something complex or unfamiliar to a reader by showing how it is like something familiar and known. Richard Vasquez uses comparison in this way in the final selection in this chapter: "Wetbacks—A Life of Fear."

The most frequent use of contrast is to show the superiority of one object, plan, candidate, or the like over another. Ashley Montagu contrasts women and men in order to show the natural superiority of the former. Martin Luther King contrasts the relative positions, both past and present, of the white and Negro races in America to show why he feels that his race can wait no longer for improvement in their status.

Even if you are not interested in showing that one thing is superior to another, however, you can use contrast to describe, explain, or analyze. Vine Deloria, Jr., in the essay which follows, contrasts the real Indian, the one who exists, with the unreal, the figment of fantasy, in order to explain and analyze the Indian "plight."

When you apply either comparison or contrast or both methods of development in extended form, you have a particular problem in organization. Should Mr. Deloria, for example, describe the real Indian fully and then the imaginary one, or should he describe one facet of one and then one facet of another until he discusses all the elements he wishes to compare or contrast?

The latter method is generally preferable when a great many details are involved. You can combine the two methods by presenting the first description in full. Then, while presenting the second, you can call the readers' attention, point by point, to the first description.

Notice how the authors of the following essays use comparison and contrast.

Indians Today, the Real and the Unreal

Vine Deloria, Jr.

INDIANS ARE LIKE the weather. Everyone knows all about the weather, but none can change it. When storms are predicted, the sun shines. When picnic weather is announced, the rain begins. Likewise, if you count on the unpredictability of Indian people, you will never be sorry.

One of the finest things about being an Indian is that people are always interested in you and your "plight." Other groups have difficulties, predicaments, quandaries, problems, or troubles. Traditionally we Indians have had a "plight."

Our foremost plight is our transparency. People can tell just by looking at us what we want, what should be done to help us, how we feel, and what a "real" Indian is really like. Indian life, as it relates to the real world, is a continuous attempt not to disappoint people who know us. Unfulfilled expectations cause grief and we have already had our share.

Because people can see right through us, it becomes impossible to tell truth

□ Vine Deloria, Jr., "Indians Today, the Real and the Unreal," in Vine Deloria, Jr., *Custer Died for Your Sins: An Indian Manifesto* (New York, 1969), pp. 1-13.

from fiction or fact from mythology. Experts paint us as they would like us to be. Often we paint ourselves as we wish we were or as we might have been.

The more we try to be ourselves the more we are forced to defend what we have never been. The American public feels most comfortable with the mythical Indians of stereotype-land who were always THERE. These Indians are fierce, they wear feathers and grunt. Most of us don't fit this idealized figure since we grunt only when overeating, which is seldom.

To be an Indian in modern American society is in a very real sense to be unreal and ahistorical. In this book we will discuss the other side—the unrealities that face *us* as Indian people. It is this unreal feeling that has been welling up inside us and threatens to make this decade the most decisive in history for Indian people. In so many ways, Indian people are re-examining themselves in an effort to redefine a new social structure for their people. Tribes are reordering their priorities to account for the obvious discrepancies between their goals and the goals whites have defined for them.

Indian reactions are sudden and surprising. One day at a conference we were singing "My Country 'Tis of Thee" and we came across the part that goes:

> *Land where our fathers died*
> *Land of the Pilgrims' pride . . .*

Some of us broke out laughing when we realized that our fathers undoubtedly died trying to keep those Pilgrims from stealing our land. In fact, many of our fathers died because the Pilgrims killed them as witches. We didn't feel much kinship with those Pilgrims, regardless of who they did in.

We often hear "give it back to the Indians" when a gadget fails to work. It's a terrible thing for a people to realize that society has set aside all non-working gadgets for their exclusive use.

During my three years as Executive Director of the National Congress of American Indians it was a rare day when some white didn't visit my office and proudly proclaim that he or she was of Indian descent.

Cherokee was the most popular tribe of their choice and many people placed the Cherokees anywhere from Maine to Washington State. Mohawk, Sioux, and Chippewa were next in popularity. Occasionally I would be told about some mythical tribe from lower Pennsylvania, Virginia, or Massachusetts which had spawned the white standing before me.

At times I became quite defensive about being a Sioux when these white people had a pedigree that was so much more respectable than mine. But eventually I came to understand their need to identify as partially Indian and did not resent

INDIAN, REAL

Beth Bagby—Photophile, S.F.

INDIAN, UNREAL

Moulin Studios, S.F.

them. I would confirm their wildest stories about their Indian ancestry and would add a few tales of my own hoping that they would be able to accept themselves someday and leave us alone.

Whites claiming Indian blood generally tend to reinforce mythical beliefs about Indians. All but one person I met who claimed Indian blood claimed it on their grandmother's side. I once did a projection backward and discovered that evidently most tribes were entirely female for the first three hundred years of white occupation. No one, it seemed, wanted to claim a male Indian as a forebear.

It doesn't take much insight into racial attitudes to understand the real meaning of the Indian-grandmother complex that plagues certain whites. A male ancestor has too much of the aura of the savage warrior, the unknown primitive, the instinctive animal, to make him a respectable member of the family tree. But a young Indian princess? Ah, there was royalty for the taking. Somehow the white was linked with a noble house of gentility and culture if his grandmother was an Indian princess who ran away with an intrepid pioneer. And royalty has always been an unconscious but all-consuming goal of the European immigrant.

The early colonists, accustomed to life under benevolent despots, projected their understanding of the European political structure onto the Indian tribe in trying to explain its political and social structure. European royal houses were closed to ex-convicts and indentured servants, so the colonists made all Indian maidens princesses, then proceeded to climb a social ladder of their own creation. Within the next generation, if the trend continues, a large portion of the American population will eventually be related to Powhattan.

While a real Indian grandmother is probably the nicest thing that could happen to a child, why is a remote Indian princess grandmother so necessary for many whites? Is it because they are afraid of being classed as foreigners? Do they need some blood tie with the frontier and its dangers in order to experience what it means to be an American? Or is it an attempt to avoid facing the guilt they bear for the treatment of the Indian?

The phenomenon seems to be universal. Only among the Jewish community, which has a long tribal-religious tradition of its own, does the mysterious Indian grandmother, the primeval princess, fail to dominate the family tree. Otherwise, there's not much to be gained by claiming Indian blood or publicly identifying as an Indian. The white believes that there is a great danger the lazy Indian will eventually corrupt God's hard-working people. He is still suspicious that the Indian way of life is dreadfully wrong. There is, in fact, something *un-American* about Indians for most whites.

I ran across a classic statement of this attitude one day in a history book which was published shortly after the turn of the century. Often have I wondered how many Senators, Congressmen, and clergymen of the day accepted the attitudes of that book as a basic fact of life in America. In no uncertain terms did the book praise God that the Indian had not yet been able to corrupt North America as he had South America:

> It was perhaps fortunate for the future of America that the Indians of the North rejected civilization. Had they accepted it the whites and Indians might have intermarried to some extent as they did in Mexico. That would have given us a population made up in a measure of shiftless half-breeds.

I never dared to show this passage to my white friends who had claimed Indian blood, but I often wondered why they were so energetic if they did have some of the bad seed in them.

Those whites who dare not claim Indian blood have an asset of their own. They *understand* Indians.

Understanding Indians is not an esoteric art. All it takes is a trip through Arizona or New Mexico, watching a documentary on TV, having known *one* in the service, or having read a popular book on *them.*

There appears to be some secret osmosis about Indian people by which they can magically and instantaneously communicate complete knowledge about themselves to these interested whites. Rarely is physical contact required. Anyone and everyone who knows an Indian or who is *interested,* immediately and thoroughly understands them.

You can verify this great truth at your next party. Mention Indians and you will find a person who saw some in a gas station in Utah, or who attended the Gallup ceremonial celebration, or whose Uncle Jim hired one to cut logs in Oregon, or whose church had a missionary come to speak last Sunday on the plight of Indians and the mission of the church.

There is no subject on earth so easily understood as that of the American Indian. Each summer, work camps disgorge teen-agers on various reservations. Within one month's time the youngsters acquire a knowledge of Indians that would astound a college professor.

Easy knowledge about Indians is historical tradition. After Columbus "discovered" America he brought back news of a great new world which he assumed to be India and, therefore, filled with Indians. Almost at once European folklore devised a complete explanation of the new land and its inhabitants which featured the Fountain of Youth, the Seven Cities of Gold, and other exotic attractions. The absence of elephants apparently did not tip off the explorers that they weren't in

India. By the time they realized their mistake, instant knowledge of Indians was a cherished tradition.

Missionaries, after learning some of the religious myths of tribes they encountered, solemnly declared that the inhabitants of the new continent were the Ten Lost Tribes of Israel. Indians thus received a religious-historical identity far greater than they wanted or deserved. But it was an impossible identity. Their failure to measure up to Old Testament standards doomed them to a fall from grace and they were soon relegated to the status of a picturesque species of wildlife.

Like the deer and the antelope, Indians seemed to play rather than get down to the serious business of piling up treasures upon the earth where thieves break through and steal. Scalping, introduced prior to the French and Indian War by the English,[1] confirmed the suspicion that Indians were wild animals to be hunted and skinned. Bounties were set and an Indian scalp became more valuable than beaver, otter, marten, and other animal pelts.

American blacks had become recognized as a species of human being by amendments to the Constitution shortly after the Civil War. Prior to emancipation they had been counted as three-fifths of a person in determining population for representation in the House of Representatives. Early Civil Rights bills nebulously state that other people shall have the same rights as "white people," indicating there *were* "other people." But Civil Rights bills passed during and after the Civil War systematically excluded Indian people. For a long time an Indian was not presumed capable of initiating an action in a court of law, of owning property, or of giving testimony against whites in court. Nor could an Indian vote or leave his reservation. Indians were America's captive people without any defined rights whatsoever.

[1]Notice, for example the following proclamation:

"Given at the Council Chamber in Boston this third day of November 1755 in the twenty-ninth year of the Reign of our Sovereign Lord George the Second by the Grace of God of Great Britain, France, and Ireland, King Defender of the Faith.—By His Honour's command / J. Willard, Secry. / God Save the King

"Whereas the tribe of Penobscot Indians have repeatedly in a perfidious manner acted contrary to their solemn submission unto his Majesty long since made and frequently renewed.

"I have, therefore, at the desire of the House of Representatives . . . thought fit to issue this Proclamation and to declare the Penobscot Tribe of Indians to be enemies, rebels and traitors to his Majesty. . . . And I do hereby require his Majesty's subjects of the Province to embrace all opportunities of pursuing, captivating, killing and destroying all and every of the aforesaid Indians.

"And whereas the General Court of this Province have voted that a bounty . . . be granted and allowed to be paid out of the Province Treasury . . . the premiums of bounty following viz:

"For every scalp of a male Indian brought in as evidence of their being killed as aforesaid, forty pounds.

"For every scalp of such female Indian or male Indian under the age of twelve years that shall be killed and brought in as evidence of their being killed as aforesaid, twenty pounds."

Then one day the white man discovered that the Indian tribes still owned some 135 million acres of land. To his horror he learned that much of it was very valuable. Some was good grazing land, some was farm land, some mining land, and some covered with timber.

Animals could be herded together on a piece of land, but they could not sell it. Therefore it took no time at all to discover that Indians were really people and should have the right to sell their lands. Land was the means of recognizing the Indian as a human being. It was the method whereby land could be stolen legally and not blatantly.

Once the Indian was thus acknowledged, it was fairly simple to determine what his goals were. If, thinking went, the Indian was just like the white, he must have the same outlook as the white. So the future was planned for the Indian people in public and private life. First in order was allotting them reservations so that they could sell their lands. God's foreordained plan to repopulate the continent fit exactly with the goals of the tribes as they were defined by their white friends.

It is fortunate that we were never slaves. We gave up land instead of life and labor. Because the Negro labored, he was considered a draft animal. Because the Indian occupied large areas of land, he was considered a wild animal. Had we given up anything else, or had anything else to give up, it is certain that we would have been considered some other thing.

Whites have had different attitudes toward the Indians and the blacks since the Republic was founded. Whites have always refused to give non-whites the respect which they have been found to legally possess. Instead there has always been a contemptuous attitude that although the law says one thing, "we all know better."

Thus whites steadfastly refused to allow blacks to enjoy the fruits of full citizenship. They systematically closed schools, churches, stores, restaurants, and public places to blacks or made insulting provisions for them. For one hundred years every program of public and private white America was devoted to the exclusion of the black. It was, perhaps, embarrassing to be rubbing shoulders with one who had not so long before been defined as a field animal.

The Indian suffered the reverse treatment. Law after law was passed requiring him to conform to white institutions. Indian children were kidnapped and forced into boarding schools thousands of miles from their homes to learn the white man's ways. Reservations were turned over to different Christian denominations for governing. Reservations were for a long time church operated. Everything possible was done to ensure that Indians were forced into American life. The wild animal was made into a household pet whether or not he wanted to be one.

Policies for both black and Indian failed completely. Blacks eventually began the Civil Rights movement. In doing so they assured themselves some rights in white society. Indians continued to withdraw from the overtures of white society and tried to maintain their own communities and activities.

Actually both groups had little choice. Blacks, trapped in a world of white symbols, retreated into themselves. And people thought comparable Indian withdrawal unnatural because they expected Indians to behave like whites.

The white world of abstract symbols became a nightmare for Indian people. The words of the treaties, clearly stating that Indians should have "free and undisturbed" use of their lands under the protection of the federal government, were cast aside by the whites as if they didn't exist. The Sioux once had a treaty plainly stating that it would take the signatures or marks of three-fourths of the adult males to amend it. Yet through force the government obtained only 10 percent of the required signatures and declared the new agreement valid.

Indian solutions to problems which had been defined by the white society were rejected out of hand and obvious solutions discarded when they called for courses of action that were not proper in white society. When Crow Dog assassinated Spotted Tail the matter was solved under traditional Sioux customs. Yet an outraged public, furious because Crow Dog had not been executed, pressured for the Seven Major Crimes Act for the federal government to assume nearly total criminal jurisdiction over the reservations. Thus foreign laws and customs using the basic concepts of justice came to dominate Indian life. If, Indians reasoned, justice is for society's benefit, why isn't our justice accepted? Indians became convinced they were the world's stupidest people.

Words and situations never seemed to fit together. Always, it seemed, the white man chose a course of action that did not work. The white man preached that it was good to help the poor, yet he did nothing to assist the poor in his society. Instead he put constant pressure on the Indian people to hoard their worldly goods, and when they failed to accumulate capital but freely gave to the poor, the white man reacted violently.

The failure of communication created a void into which poured the white do-gooder, the missionary, the promoter, the scholar, and every conceivable type of person who believed he could help. White society failed to understand the situation because this conglomerate of assistance blurred the real issues beyond recognition.

The legend of the Indian was embellished or tarnished according to the need of the intermediates to gain leverage in their struggle to solve problems that never existed outside of their own minds. The classic example, of course, is the old-time missionary box. People were horrified that Indians continued to dress in their traditional garb. Since whites did not wear buckskin and beads, they equated such dress with savagery. So do-gooders in the East held fantastic clothing drives to supply the Indians with civilized clothes. Soon boxes of discarded evening gowns, tuxedos, tennis shoes, and uniforms flooded the reservations. Indians were made to dress in these remnants so they could be civilized. Then, realizing the ridiculous picture presented by the reservation people, neighboring whites made fun of the Indian people for having the presumption to dress like whites.

But in the East, whites were making great reputations as "Indian experts," as people who devoted their lives to helping the savages. Whenever Indian land was needed, the whites pictured the tribes as wasteful people who refused to develop their natural resources. Because the Indians did not "use" their lands, argued many land promoters, the lands should be taken away and given to people who knew what to do with them.

White society concentrated on the individual Indian to the exclusion of his group, forgetting that any society is merely a composite of individuals. Generalizations by experts universalized "Indianness" to the detriment of unique Indian values. Indians with a common cultural base shared behavior patterns. But they were expected to behave like a similar group of whites and rarely did. Whites, on the other hand, generally came from a multitude of backgrounds and shared only the need for economic subsistence. There was no way, therefore, to combine white values and Indian behavior into a workable program or intelligible subject of discussion.

One of the foremost differences separating white and Indian was simply one of origin. Whites derived predominantly from western Europe. The earliest settlers on the Atlantic seaboard came from England and the low countries. For the most part they shared the common experiences of their peoples and dwelt within the world view which had dominated western Europe for over a millenium.

Conversely Indians had always been in the western hemisphere. Life on this continent and views concerning it were not shaped in a post-Roman atmosphere. The entire outlook of the people was one of simplicity and mystery, not scientific or abstract. The western hemisphere produced wisdom, western Europe produced knowledge.

Perhaps this distinction seems too simple to mention. It is not. Many is the time I have sat in Congressional hearings and heard the chairman of the committee crow about "our" great Anglo-Saxon heritage of law and order. Looking about the hearing room I saw row after row of full-blood Indians with blank expressions on their faces. As far as they were concerned, Sir Walter Raleigh was a brand of pipe tobacco that you got at the trading post.

When we talk about European background, we are talking about feudalism, kings, queens, their divine right to rule their subjects, the Reformation, Christianity, the Magna Charta and all of the events that went to make up European history.

American Indians do not share that heritage. They do not look wistfully back across the seas to the old country. The Apache were not at Runnymede to make King John sign the Magna Charta. The Cherokee did not create English common law. The Pima had no experience with the rise of capitalism and industrialism. The Blackfeet had no monasteries. No tribe has an emotional, historical, or political relationship to events of another continent and age.

Indians have had their own political history which has shaped the outlook of the tribes. There were great confederacies throughout the country before the time of the white invader. The eastern Iroquois formed a strong league because as single tribes they had been weak and powerless against larger tribes. The Deep South was controlled by three confederacies: the Creeks with their town system, the Natchez, and the Powhattan confederation which extended into tidelands Virginia. The Pequots and their cousins the Mohicans controlled the area of Connecticut, Massachusetts, Rhode Island, and Long Island.

True democracy was more prevalent among Indian tribes in pre-Columbian days than it has been since. Despotic power was abhorred by tribes that were loose combinations of hunting parties rather than political entities.

Conforming their absolute freedom to fit rigid European political forms has been very difficult for most tribes, but on the whole they have managed extremely well. Under the Indian Reorganization Act Indian people have generally created a modern version of the old tribal political structure and yet have been able to develop comprehensive reservation programs which compare favorably with governmental structures anywhere.

The deep impression made upon American minds by the Indian struggle against the white man in the last century has made the contemporary Indian somewhat invisible compared with his ancestors. Today Indians are not conspicuous by their absence from view. Yet they should be.

In *The Other America,* the classic study of poverty by Michael Harrington, the thesis is developed that the poor are conspicuous by their invisibility. There is no mention of Indians in the book. A century ago, Indians would have dominated such a work.

Indians are probably invisible because of the tremendous amount of misinformation about them. Most books about Indians cover some abstract and esoteric topic of the last century. Contemporary books are predominantly by whites trying to solve the "Indian problem." Between the two extremes lives a dynamic people in a social structure of their own, asking only to be freed from cultural oppression.

The future does not look bright for the attainment of such freedom because the white does not understand the Indian and the Indian does not wish to understand the white.

Vine Deloria, Jr., was thirty-five and a law student at the University of Colorado when *Custer Died for Your Sins* was published. He had been executive director of the National Congress of American Indians (1964-1967) after receiving in 1963 the degree of Bachelor of Divinity from Augustana Lutheran Seminary, where he enrolled after serving an enlistment in the United States Marine Corps. He is a Sioux, son and grandson of Indian Episcopal missionaries. Although in early life he considered the ministry as a career, he decided that church life was irrelevant to Indian needs.

Vocabulary Study

Mr. Deloria plays upon words in order to make a satiric comment. Note his use of "plight" in paragraph two; his use of "transparency" and "real" in paragraph three. Find other examples of words used satirically in the essay.

A. Mr. Deloria's entire essay is based upon a series of comparisons and contrasts. Beginning with those mentioned in the title, how many can you name?

B. What functions does an Indian grandmother serve for a non-Indian, according to the author?

C. What reason does Mr. Deloria offer for Jews not claiming an Indian grandmother?

D. Indians are historically notorious for scalping whites. What new slant on that practice does the proclamation, provided in the footnote, present?

E. According to Mr. Deloria, how did the "missionary box" tend to do more harm than good?

F. What, according to Mr. Deloria, do the Indian people today want? How does he assess their chances of success?

Questions on Form and Content

A. The title of Mr. Deloria's book, from which this section is taken, is *Custer Died for Your Sins.* Do some research on Custer, if necessary; then discuss the effectiveness of the title.

B. In 1967 the American Broadcasting Company began a television series on Custer, whom the National Congress of American Indians called the "Adolph Eichmann" of the nineteenth century. Indians were able to get the series banned only after a tribal lawyer devised the tactic of getting every tribe to file for equal time against ABC's local affiliate. The series was canceled after nine episodes had been shown. Comment on other television shows or films the Indians might find objectionable.

C. How do both Indians and non-Indians make use of "Indian myths"?

D. How is the Indian learning to use white man's values and techniques for his own purposes? Consider Indian-financed movies, tourist attractions, and other business enterprises.

E. In what ways are white and Indian problems similar? How do they differ?

F. Discuss some of the basic differences in political and legal attitudes toward blacks and Indians in the history of the United States.

G. Indians have recently occupied Alcatraz Island and certain lands in California now owned by the Pacific Gas and Electric Company. Discuss their right to either.

H. Could you defend an Indian's claim to perpetual hunting and fishing rights on any land in America?

I. What recent legislation has been designed to help solve the Indian "plight" and compensate for past wrongs?

J. Mr. Deloria refers to the evils of boarding schools established by the government for Indians. For many years the Bureau of Indian Affairs has maintained boarding schools on the reservations, many of which have been located a considerable distance from the pupils' homes. Attempts have been made on some reservations (the Navajo, for example) to provide mobile schools. Recently the emphasis has been upon giving local control of schools to Indians themselves. Such a program has proved beneficial, but it is often not feasible when "settlements" or "communities" as such do not exist. Write a paper in which you either justify the present boarding-school system or suggest a reasonable alternative.

K. Winthrop Jordan, in his book *White over Black*, claims: "The Indian became for Americans a symbol of their American experience. . . . Confronting the Indian was a testing experience, common to all the colonies. Conquering the Indian symbolized and personified the conquest of the American difficulties, the surmounting of the wilderness. To push back the Indian was to prove the worth of one's own mission, to make straight in the desert a highway for civilization." Use this quotation as a basis for an essay on Indian reservations, schools, or any other attempts of whites to Christianize or civilize the Indians.

L. As Daniel Boorstin points out in his book *The Americans*, various federal officials repeatedly suggested, up to the time of the Civil War, the possibility of setting aside several states for the Indians. Similar proposals were made for the blacks. Such proposals generate several questions: What differences in development for each race and for the nation as a whole might have resulted? How do these proposals relate to the demands of present-day black groups (the Black Muslims, in particular) and Indians? Comment.

M. Discuss the achievement of an Indian in recent times. How does this individual bear out Mr. Deloria's point that it is essential for an Indian to realize that he is caught in a myth before he can succeed?

N. Apply the idea of a myth which ensnares to blacks, Chicanos, Orientals, or some other minority group—Southerners, for example—or to that majority group, women.

Selections from *Why We Can't Wait*

Martin Luther King, Jr.

It is the beginning of the year of our Lord 1963. I see a young Negro boy. He is sitting on a stoop in front of a vermin-infested apartment house in Harlem. The stench of garbage is in the halls. The drunks, the jobless, the junkies are shadow figures of his everyday world. The boy goes to a school attended mostly by Negro students with a scattering of Puerto Ricans. His father is one of the jobless. His mother is a sleep-in domestic, working for a family on Long Island.

I see a young Negro girl. She is sitting on the stoop of a rickety wooden one-family house in Birmingham. Some visitors would call it a shack. It needs paint badly and the patched-up roof appears in danger of caving in. Half a dozen small children, in various stages of undress, are scampering about the house. The girl is forced to play the role of their mother. She can no longer attend the all-Negro school in her neighborhood because her mother died only recently after

☐ Martin Luther King, Jr., "Introduction" and "The Negro Revolution—Why 1963?" from *Why We Can't Wait* (New York, 1964).

AMERICAN

Declan Haun—Black Star, N.Y.

a car accident. Neighbors say if the ambulance hadn't come so late to take her to the all-Negro hospital the mother might still be alive. The girl's father is a porter in a downtown department store. He will always be a porter, for there are no promotions for the Negro in this store, where every counter serves him except the one that sells hot dogs and orange juice.

This boy and this girl, separated by stretching miles, are wondering: Why does misery constantly haunt the Negro? In some distant past, had their forebears done some tragic injury to the nation, and was the curse of punishment upon the black race? Had they shirked in their duty as patriots, betrayed their country, denied their national birthright? Had they refused to defend their land against a foreign foe?

Not all of history is recorded in the books supplied to school children in Harlem or Birmingham. Yet this boy and this girl know something of the part of history which has been censored by the white writers and purchasers of board-of-education books. They know that Negroes were with George Washington at Valley Forge. They know that the first American to shed blood in the revolution which freed his country from British oppression was a black seaman named Crispus Attucks. The boy's Sunday-school teacher has told him that one of the team who designed the capital of their nation, Washington, D. C., was a Negro, Benjamin Banneker. Once the girl had heard a speaker, invited to her school during Negro History Week. This speaker told how, for two hundred years, without wages, black people, brought to this land in slave ships and in chains, had drained the swamps, built the homes, made cotton king and helped, on whip-lashed backs, to lift this nation from colonial obscurity to commanding influence in domestic commerce and world trade.

Wherever there was hard work, dirty work, dangerous work—in the mines, on the docks, in the blistering foundries—Negroes had done more than their share.

The pale history books in Harlem and Birmingham told how the nation had fought a war over slavery. Abraham Lincoln had signed a document that would come to be known as the Emancipation Proclamation. The war had been won but not a just peace. Equality had never arrived. Equality was a hundred years late.

The boy and the girl knew more than history. They knew something about current events. They knew that African nations had burst the bonds of colonialism. They knew that a great-great-grandson of Crispus Attucks might be ruled out of some restricted, all-white restaurant in some restricted, all-white section of a southern town, his United States Marines uniform notwithstanding. They knew that Negroes living in the capital of their own nation were confined to ghettos and could not always get a job for which they were qualified. They knew that white supremacists had defied the Supreme Court and that southern governors had attempted to interpose themselves between the people and the highest law of the land. They knew that, for years, their own lawyers had won great victories in the courts which were not being translated into reality.

They were seeing on television, hearing from the radio, reading in the newspapers that this was the one-hundredth birthday of their freedom.

But freedom had a dull ring, a mocking emptiness when, in their time—in the short life span of this boy and girl—buses had stopped rolling in Montgomery; sit-inners were jailed and beaten; freedom riders were brutalized and mobbed; dogs' fangs were bared in Birmingham; and in Brooklyn, New York, there were certain kinds of construction jobs for whites only.

It was the summer of 1963. Was emancipation a fact? Was freedom a force?

The boy in Harlem stood up. The girl in Birmingham arose. Separated by stretching miles, both of them squared their shoulders and lifted their eyes toward heaven. Across the miles they joined hands, and took a firm, forward step. It was a step that rocked the richest, most powerful nation to its foundations.

The bitterly cold winter of 1962 lingered throughout the opening months of 1963, touching the land with chill and frost, and then was replaced by a placid spring. Americans awaited a quiet summer. That it would be pleasant they had no doubt. The worst of it would be the nightmare created by sixty million cars, all apparently trying to reach the same destination at the same time. Fifty million families looked forward to the pleasure of two hundred million vacations in the American tradition of the frenetic hunt for relaxation.

It would be a pleasant summer because, in the mind of the average man, there was little cause for concern. The blithe outlook about the state of the nation was reflected from as high up as the White House. The administration confidently readied a tax-reduction bill. Business and employment were at comfortable levels. Money was—for many Americans—plentiful.

Summer came, and the weather was beautiful. But the climate, the social climate of American life, erupted into lightning flashes, trembled with thunder and vibrated to the relentless, growing rain of protest come to life through the land. Explosively, America's third revolution—the Negro Revolution—had begun.

For the first time in the long and turbulent history of the nation, almost one thousand cities were engulfed in civil turmoil, with violence trembling just below the surface. Reminiscent of the French Revolution of 1789, the streets had become a battleground, just as they had become the battleground, in the 1830's, of England's tumultuous Chartist movement. As in these two revolutions, a submerged social group, propelled by a burning need for justice, lifting itself with sudden swiftness, moving with determination and a majestic scorn for risk and danger, created an uprising so powerful that it shook a huge society from its comfortable base.

Never in American history had a group seized the streets, the squares, the sacrosanct business thoroughfares and the marbled halls of government to protest and proclaim the unendurability of their oppression. Had room-size machines turned human, burst from the plants that housed them and stalked the land in revolt, the nation could not have been more amazed. Undeniably, the Negro had been an object of sympathy and wore the scars of deep grievances, but the nation had come to count on him as a creature who could quietly endure, silently suffer and patiently wait. He was well trained in service and, whatever the provocation, he neither pushed back nor spoke back.

Just as lightning makes no sound until it strikes, the Negro Revolution generated quietly. But when it struck, the revealing flash of its power and the impact of its sincerity and fervor displayed a force of a frightening intensity. Three hundred years of humiliation, abuse and deprivation cannot be expected to find voice in a whisper. The storm clouds did not release a "gentle rain from heaven," but a whirlwind, which has not yet spent its force or attained its full momentum.

Because there is more to come; because American society is bewildered by the spectacle of the Negro in revolt; because the dimensions are vast and the implications deep in a nation with twenty million Negroes, it is important to understand the history that is being made today.

Some years ago, I sat in a Harlem department store, surrounded by hundreds of people. I was autographing copies of *Stride Toward Freedom*, my book about the Montgomery bus boycott of 1955-56. As I signed my name to a page, I felt something sharp plunge forcefully into my chest. I had been stabbed with a letter opener, struck home by a woman who would later be judged insane. Rushed by ambulance to Harlem Hospital, I lay in a bed for hours while preparations were made to remove the keen-edged knife from my body. Days later, when I was well enough to talk with Dr. Aubrey Maynard, the chief of the surgeons who performed the delicate, dangerous operation, I learned the reason for the long delay that preceded surgery. He told me that the razor tip of the instrument had been touching my aorta and that my whole chest had to be opened to extract it.

"If you had sneezed during all those hours of waiting," Dr. Maynard said, "your aorta would have been punctured and you would have drowned in your own blood."

In the summer of 1963 the knife of violence was just that close to the nation's aorta. Hundreds of cities might now be mourning countless dead but for the operation of certain forces which gave political surgeons an opportunity to cut boldly and safely to remove the deadly peril. What was it that gave us the second chance? To answer this we must answer another question. Why did this Revolution occur in 1963? Negroes had for decades endured evil. In the words of the poet, they had long asked: "Why must the blackness of nighttime collect in our mouth; why must we always taste grief in our blood?" Any time would seem to have been the right time. Why 1963?

Why did a thousand cities shudder almost simultaneously and why did the whole world—in gleaming capitals and mud-hut villages—hold its breath during those months? Why was it this year that the American Negro, so long ignored, so long written out of the pages of history books, tramped a declaration of freedom with his marching feet across the pages of newspapers, the television screens and the magazines? Sarah Turner closed the kitchen cupboard and went into the streets; John Wilkins shut down the elevator and enlisted in the nonviolent army; Bill Griggs slammed the brakes of his truck and slid to the sidewalk; the Reverend Arthur Jones led his flock into the streets and held church in jail. The words and actions of parliaments and statesmen, of kings and prime ministers, movie stars and athletes, were shifted from the front pages to make room for the history-making deeds of the servants, the drivers, the elevator operators and the ministers. Why in 1963, and what has this to do with why the dark threat of violence did not erupt in blood?

The Negro had been deeply disappointed over the slow pace of school desegregation. He knew that in 1954 the highest court in the land had handed down a decree calling for desegregation of schools "with all deliberate speed." He knew that this edict from the Supreme Court had been heeded with all deliberate delay. At the beginning of 1963, nine years after this historic decision, approximately 9 per cent of southern Negro students were attending integrated schools. If this pace were maintained, it would be the year 2054 before integration in southern schools would be a reality.

In its wording the Supreme Court decision had revealed an awareness that attempts would be made to evade its intent. The phrase "all deliberate speed" did not mean that another century should be allowed to unfold before we released Negro children from the narrow pigeonhole of the segregated schools; it meant that, giving some courtesy and consideration to the need for softening old attitudes and outdated customs, democracy must press ahead, out of the past of ignorance and intolerance, and into the present of educational opportunity and moral freedom.

Yet the statistics make it abundantly clear that the segregationists of the South remained undefeated by the decision. From every section of Dixie, the announcement of the high court had been met with declarations of defiance. Once recovered from their initial outrage, these defenders of the status quo had seized the offensive to impose their own schedule of change. The progress that was supposed to have been achieved with deliberate speed had created change for less than 2 per cent of Negro children in most areas of the South and not even one-tenth of 1 per cent in some parts of the deepest South. There was another factor in the slow pace of progress, a factor of which few are aware and even fewer understand. It is an unadvertised fact that soon after the 1954 decision the Supreme Court retreated from its own position by giving approval to the Pupil Placement Law. This law permitted the states themselves to determine where school children might be placed by virtue of family background, special ability and other subjective criteria. The Pupil Placement Law was almost as far-reaching in modifying and limiting the integration of schools as the original decision had been in attempting to eliminate segregation. Without technically reversing itself, the Court had granted legal sanction to tokenism and thereby guaranteed that segregation, in substance, would last for an indefinite period, though formally it was illegal.

In order, then, to understand the deep disillusion of the Negro in 1963, one must examine his contrasting emotions at the time of the decision, and during the nine years that followed. One must understand the pendulum swing between the elation that arose when the edict was handed down and the despair that followed the failure to bring it to life.

A second reason for the outburst in 1963 was rooted in disappointment with both political parties. From the city of Los Angeles in 1960, the Democratic party had written an historic and sweeping civil-rights pronouncement into its campaign platform. The Democratic standard bearer had repeated eloquently and often that the moral weight of the Presidency must be applied to this burning issue. From Chicago, the Republican party had been generous in its convention vows on civil rights, although its candidate had made no great effort in his campaign to convince the nation that he would redeem his party's promises.

Then 1961 and 1962 arrived, with both parties marking time in the cause of justice. In the Congress, reactionary Republicans were still doing business with the Dixiecrats. And the feeling was growing among Negroes that the administration had oversimplified and underestimated the civil-rights issue. President Kennedy, if not backing down, had backed away from a key pledge of his campaign—to wipe out housing discrimination immediately "with the stroke of a pen." When he had finally signed the housing order, two years after taking office, its terms, though praiseworthy, had revealed a serious weakness in its failure to attack the key problem of discrimination in financing by banks and other institutions.

While Negroes were being appointed to some significant jobs, and social hospitality was being extended at the White House to Negro leaders, the dreams of the masses remained in tatters. The Negro felt that he recognized the same old bone that had been tossed to him in the past—only now it was being handed to him on a platter, with courtesy.

The administration had fashioned its primary approach to discrimination in the South around a series of lawsuits chiefly designed to protect the right to vote. Opposition toward action on other fronts had begun to harden. With each new Negro protest, we were advised, sometimes privately and sometimes in public, to call off our efforts and channel all of our energies into registering voters. On each occasion we would agree with the importance of voting rights, but would patiently seek to explain that Negroes did not want to neglect all other rights while one was selected for concentrated attention.

It was necessary to conclude that our argument was not persuading the administration any more than the government's logic was prevailing with us. Negroes had manifested their faith by racking up a substantial majority of their votes for President Kennedy. They had expected more of him than of the previous administration. In no sense had President Kennedy betrayed his promises. Yet his administration appeared to believe it was doing as much as was politically possible and had, by its positive deeds, earned enough credit to coast on civil rights. Politically, perhaps, this was not a surprising conclusion. How many people understood, during the first two years of the Kennedy administration, that the Negroes' "Now" was becoming as militant as the segregationists' "Never?" Eventually the President would set political considerations aside and rise to the level of his own unswerving moral commitment. But this was still in the future.

No discussion of the influences that bore on the thinking of the Negro in 1963 would be complete without some attention to the relationship of this Revolution to international events. Throughout the upheavals of cold-war politics, Negroes had seen their government go to the brink of nuclear conflict more than once. The justification for risking the annihilation of the human race was always expressed in terms of America's willingness to go to any lengths to preserve freedom. To the Negro that readiness for heroic measures in the defense of liberty disappeared or became tragically weak when the threat was within our own borders and was concerned with the Negro's liberty. While the Negro is not so selfish as to stand isolated in concern for his own dilemma, ignoring the ebb and flow of events around the world, there is a certain bitter irony in the picture of his country championing freedom in foreign lands and failing to ensure that freedom to twenty million of its own.

From beyond the borders of his own land, the Negro had been inspired by another powerful force. He had watched the decolonization and liberation of nations in Africa and Asia since World War II. He knew that yellow, black and brown people had felt for years that the American Negro was too passive, unwilling to take strong measures to gain his freedom. He might have remembered the visit to this country of an African head of state, who was called upon by a delegation of prominent American Negroes. When they began reciting to him their long list of grievances, the visiting statesman had waved a weary hand and said:

"I am aware of current events. I know everything you are telling me about what the white man is doing to the Negro. Now tell me: What is the Negro doing for himself?"

The American Negro saw, in the land from which he had been snatched and thrown into slavery, a great pageant of political progress. He realized that just thirty years ago there were only three independent nations in the whole of Africa. He knew that by 1963 more than thirty-four African nations had risen from colonial bondage. The Negro saw black statesmen voting on vital issues in the United Nations—and knew that in many cities of his own land he was not permitted to take that significant walk to the ballot box. He saw black kings and potentates ruling from palaces—and knew he had been condemned to move from small ghettos to larger ones. Witnessing the drama of Negro progress elsewhere in the world, witnessing a level of conspicuous consumption at home exceeding anything in our history, it was natural that by 1963 Negroes would rise with resolution and demand a share of governing power, and living conditions measured by American standards rather than by the standards of colonial impoverishment.

An additional and decisive fact confronted the Negro and helped to bring him out of the houses, into the streets, out of the trenches and into the front lines. This was his recognition that one hundred years had passed since emancipation, with no profound effect on his plight. With the dawn of 1963, plans were afoot all over the land to celebrate the Emancipation Proclamation, the one-hundredth birthday of the Negro's liberation from bondage. In Washington, a federal commission had been established to mark the event. Governors of states and mayors of cities had utilized the date to enhance their political image by naming commissions, receiving committees, issuing statements, planning state pageants, sponsoring dinners, endorsing social activities. Champagne, this year, would bubble on countless tables. Appropriately attired, over thick cuts of roast beef, legions would listen as luminous phrases were spun to salute the great democratic landmark which 1963 represented.

But alas! All the talk and publicity accompanying the centennial only served to remind the Negro that he still wasn't free, that he still lived a form of slavery disguised by certain niceties of complexity. As the then Vice-President, Lyndon

B. Johnson, phrased it: "Emancipation was a Proclamation but not a fact." The pen of the Great Emancipator had moved the Negro into the sunlight of physical freedom, but actual conditions had left him behind in the shadow of political, psychological, social, economic and intellectual bondage. In the South, discrimination faced the Negro in its obvious and glaring forms. In the North, it confronted him in hidden and subtle disguise.

The Negro also had to recognize that one hundred years after emancipation he lived on a lonely island of economic insecurity in the midst of a vast ocean of material prosperity. Negroes are still at the bottom of the economic ladder. They live within two concentric circles of segregation. One imprisons them on the basis of color, while the other confines them within a separate culture of poverty. The average Negro is born into want and deprivation. His struggle to escape his circumstances is hindered by color discrimination. He is deprived of normal education and normal social and economic opportunities. When he seeks opportunity, he is told, in effect, to lift himself by his own bootstraps, advice which does not take into account the fact that he is barefoot.

By 1963, most of America's working population had forgotten the Great Depression or had never known it. The slow and steady growth of unemployment had touched some of the white working force but the proportion was still not more than one in twenty. This was not true for the Negro. There were two and one-half times as many jobless Negroes as whites in 1963, and their median income was half that of the white man. Many white Americans of good will have never connected bigotry with economic exploitation. They have deplored prejudice, but tolerated or ignored economic injustice. But the Negro knows that these two evils have a malignant kinship. He knows this because he has worked in shops that employ him exclusively because the pay is below a living standard. He knows it is not an accident of geography that wage rates in the South are significantly lower than those in the North. He knows that the spotlight recently focused on the growth in the number of women who work is not a phenomenon in Negro life. The average Negro woman has always had to work to help keep her family in food and clothes.

To the Negro, as 1963 approached, the economic structure of society appeared to be so ordered that a precise sifting of jobs took place. The lowest-paid employment and the most tentative jobs were reserved for him. If he sought to change his position, he was walled in by the tall barrier of discrimination. As summer came, more than ever the spread of unemployment had visible and tangible dimensions to the colored American. Equality meant dignity and dignity demanded a job that was secure and a pay check that lasted throughout the week.

The Negro's economic problem was compounded by the emergence and growth of automation. Since discrimination and lack of education confined him to unskilled and semi-skilled labor, the Negro was and remains the first to suffer in these days of great technological development. The Negro knew all too well that there was not in existence the kind of vigorous retraining program that could really help him to grapple with the magnitude of his problem.

The symbol of the job beyond the great wall was construction work. The Negro whose slave labor helped to build a nation was being told by employers on the one hand and unions on the other that there was no place for him in this industry. Billions were being spent on city, state and national building for which the Negro paid taxes but could draw no pay check. No one who saw the spanning bridges, the grand mansions, the sturdy docks and stout factories of the South could question the Negro's ability to build if he were given a chance for apprenticeship training. It was plain, hard, raw discrimination that shut him out of decent employment.

In 1963, the Negro, who had realized for many years that he was not truly free, awoke from a stupor of inaction with the cold dash of realization that 1963 meant one hundred years after Lincoln gave his autograph to the cause of freedom.

The milestone of the centennial of emancipation give the Negro a reason to act —a reason so simple and obvious that he almost had to step back to see it.

Simple logic made it painfully clear that if this centennial were to be meaningful, it must be observed not as a celebration, but rather as a commemoration of the one moment in the country's history when a bold, brave *start* had been made, and a rededication to the obvious fact that urgent business was at hand—the resumption of that noble journey toward the goals reflected in the Preamble to the Constitution, the Constitution itself, the Bill of Rights and the Thirteenth, Fourteenth and Fifteenth Amendments.

Yet not all of these forces conjoined could have brought about the massive and largely bloodless Revolution of 1963 if ther had not been at hand a philosophy and a method worthy of its goals. Nonviolent direct action did not originate in America, but it found its natural home in this land, where refusal to cooperate with injustice was an ancient and honorable tradition and where Christian forgiveness was written into the minds and hearts of good men. Tested in Montgomery during the winter of 1955-56, and toughened throughout the South in the eight ensuing years, nonviolent resistance had become, by 1963, the logical force in the greatest mass-action crusade for freedom that has ever occurred in American history.

Nonviolence is a powerful and just weapon. It is a weapon unique in history, which cuts without wounding and ennobles the man who wields it. It is a sword that heals. Both a practical and a moral answer to the Negro's cry for justice, nonviolent direct action proved that it could win victories without losing wars, and so become the triumphant tactic of the Negro Revolution of 1963.

Martin Luther King, Jr. (1929-1968), was born in Atlanta, received his A.B. from Morehouse College, his Ph.D. from Boston University, and his D.D. from Chicago Theological Seminary. Pastor of a Montgomery, Alabama, Baptist Church, he was also President of the Christian Leadership Conference and the Montgomery Improvement Association. A leader in the civil rights movement, he was selected as one of the ten outstanding personalities of 1956 by *Time,* and awarded the Nobel Peace Prize in 1964. He contributed numerous articles to popular and religious periodicals and was the author of *Stride Toward Freedom.* The material below is from his book *Why We Can't Wait,* published in 1964. Martin Luther King, Jr., was assassinated in Memphis, Tennessee, on April 4, 1968.

Vocabulary Study

Select a synonym from the list at the end of this exercise for each of the italicized words below. The words appear as they are used by Mr. King. The list contains extra words.

A. had their *forebears* done some tragic injury to the nation
B. had they *shirked* in their duty
C. in the American tradition of the *frenetic* hunt for relaxation
D. the *blithe* outlook about the state of the nation
E. But the climate, the social climate of American life, *erupted* into lightning flashes.
F. in the long and *turbulent* history
G. the *sacrosanct* business thoroughfares
H. Whatever the *provocation,* he neither pushed back nor spoke back.
I. The Court had granted legal *sanction* to tokenism
J. the justification for risking the *annihilation* of the human race
K. in hidden and *subtle* disguise

incitement	frantic	disturbed
destruction	burst forth	denied
ingenious	concentric	inviolable
unique	ancestors	authorization
neglected	bright	potentates

Questions on Form and Content

A. What major contrast is the basis for the thesis of Mr. King's entire article?

B. The author's introductory paragraphs are based upon what comparison?

C. Mr. King compares the Negro Revolution with two other revolts which have occurred in other countries. What are they? In what way does he say that all three are alike?

D. Mr. King contrasts the progress of the American Negro with that of the African Negro. How do they differ?

E. The author contrasts the economic position of the American Negro with that of the white man. What differences between the two does he note?

F. What, according to Mr. King, brought on the Negro Revolution of 1963?

G. What philosophy or method did the Negro have at hand which, according to Mr. King, he found worthy of his goals? What qualities does Mr. King claim for this weapon?

Suggestions for Writing

A. Write a paper either supporting or questioning the proposition: "All Men Are Created Equal."

B. If you can do so with conviction, write an answer to Mr. King entitled "Why You Must Wait."

C. Mr. King mentions that "part of history which has been censored by the white writers and purchasers of board-of-education books." Comment.

D. Write a paper on the life and work of a prominent Negro.

E. Discuss the most recent developments in school desegregation in your immediate section or across the nation.

F. Is there discrimination in housing in your city or state? If so, do you think anything should be done to eliminate it? If so, what? If not, why not?

G. "In the South, discrimination faced the Negro in its obvious and glaring forms. In the North, it confronted him in hidden and subtle disguise," writes the author. Comment.

H. Mr. King says: "The Negro's economic problem was compounded by the emergence and growth of automation." Discuss the implication of automation for all workers.

I. Mr. King notes that nonviolent direct action did not originate in America. Discuss its history.

J. Mr. King says: "Nonviolence is a powerful and just weapon. It is a weapon unique in history, which cuts without wounding and ennobles the man who wields it. It is a sword that heals." From what you know of nonviolent action as it has been practiced during the Negro Revolution, do you agree with Mr. King's assessment of it? Do you think that those against whom it has been used would agree that it does not wound, but heals?

K. Discuss developments that have occurred in the Negro Revolution since 1963.

L. Write a paper on the assassination of Martin Luther King, Jr.

Wetbacks—A Life of Fear

Richard Vasquez

Los Angeles—He sips his beer in a poorly lighted tavern. His eyes are quickly alert; he speaks practically no English, but his attitude reflects matter-of-factly the unspeakable poverty he has known.

"*Soy mojado,*" he said. "I am a wetback."

He is a swarthy, small, but powerfully built man—age about 30, he thinks. It would be incorrect to say he lives in terror day by day. It is more a nagging fear that makes him automatically choose a seat where he can face the door, scrutinizing those who enter, like a gunman of the old west.

He—and an estimated 100,000 to 200,000 like him in the Los Angeles area—came to the United States illegally from Mexico. He is subject to immediate deportation if he is discovered by immigration authorities.

"Why did you enter this country illegally?" he was asked.

He prefaced his answer with a bitter chuckle.

□ Richard Vasquez, "Wetbacks—A Life of Fear," *San Francisco Sunday Examiner and Chronicle*, July 5, 1970, from Times-Post Service (p. 4, *Chronicle Sunday Punch*).

WORKERS IN THE VINEYARDS

George Ballis in *Basta!*

"Here, I get two, sometimes three dollars an hour. In Mexico, that's more than I ever made in a day."

But why not apply for papers, enter legally?

Again the little laugh. "There's a waiting list of thousands. It takes years. I eat every day."

Rosario, the name he claims, worked his way north, walking, hanging onto the rear of trucks, and found a job in a city in the state of Sonora, which borders the United States.

One day he saw some passengers unloading from a bus. Inquiring, he learned they were aliens being transported at U.S. government expense from Los Angeles to their home towns in Sonora.

Rosario became friendly with two other young men and they agreed to take him to a border town and show him how to "enter."

At the border town he had little difficulty obtaining a *tarjeta local,* a local card, which allows the holder to enter the United States for 72 hours, provided he stays within 25 miles of the port of entry.

Once across the border, the real task began: Finding a way into the interior where an alien can lose himself in the population. His companions told him that a person could live in East Los Angeles all his life without speaking English and not be conspicuous.

The trio made contact with a man who, for a price, agreed to smuggle them through the various checkpoints the U.S. immigration service has set up between the border and Los Angeles.

In East Los Angeles, his friends steered him to a man who would give him food and lodging until he found work. Within a short time he was working in the dye room of a carpet factory.

In a few months immigration agents caught up with him. They got him and several other workers as they left the factory one evening. He was taken to a holding center for illegal aliens.

Rosario accepted voluntary deportation and the next day found himself back in Sonora.

"But this time it was different," he said. "I had money. I took a bus to Mexicali, got a *tarjeta local,* crossed over into Calexico, and paid the same man to bring me back to Los Angeles. I only missed a few days' work."

Since then, Rosario has been taken back to Mexico nine times. He now knows other routes of entry; he has learned the ropes.

Prying a little deeper into Rosario's personal life, one learns more. Rosario has a wife, also here illegally, whom he married between deportations. His wife works as a domestic in a large home in a residential section. And she is pregnant.

Rosario had heard on Spanish-language radio programs and had read in Spanish-language newspapers that certain people who call themselves "immigration consultants" could get him legal status if he had an American-born child.

He found one such consultant. The man told him that for $150 he would start papers that would automatically make Rosario a citizen when the baby arrived. Rosario paid and the man filled out some papers. Not long after the man called Rosario in and said there were legal snags. He would need another $150 to file more papers. Rosario paid again.

When nothing happened, Rosario demanded to know what was being done. Why couldn't he have a card, or some proof that legal papers were being processed, so he could walk the streets without fear?

The consultant said he'd have to be patient and then, in a veiled threat, said it would cost still more, and if Rosario didn't pay, that might draw the attention of the immigration people and he (the consultant) might be forced to tell the agents where Rosario and his wife were working.

Rosario is beaten and he knows it. Although the consultant is fleecing him—giving him misinformation, probably doing nothing—Rosario cannot go to the police or the immigration authorities. He is stuck, and so are thousands of other "wetbacks."

Immigration authorities feel frustrated and futile.

In the meantime, Rosario will pick a seat in a cafe where he can watch the door. When a stranger speaks to him he will smile and nod, pretending he understands, and wonder how much longer he can get away with it.

Richard Vasquez is a reporter for the Times-Post Service.

Vocabulary Study

A. One of the primary objectives of a newspaper article is to convey information rapidly and clearly. You will note that both language and style are simple and straightforward. However, Mr. Vasquez does use some words and terms unfamiliar to the general reader. How does he manage to clarify these words and terms within the context of his article?

1. *mojado*
2. *tarjeta local*

3. immigration consultant

B. What is the origin of the term "wetback"?

Questions on Form and Content

A. What techniques does Mr. Vasquez use to make his article interesting?

B. What actions does the author cite to indicate that Mr. Rosario has "learned the ropes"?

C. Why does Mr. Vasquez consider Mr. Rosario's plight hopeless?

D. Why did Mr. Rosario get involved with the immigration consultant?

E. Why did Mr. Rosario enter the United States in the first place? With nine deportations, why did he continue to return?

F. What is the attitude of immigration officials toward the plight and problems of the wetbacks?

G. What solution can you suggest to Mr. Rosario's problem?

Suggestions for Writing

A. Compare the immigration consultants with the immigration authorities in Mr. Vasquez's account.

B. There are an estimated 5.6 million Mexican-Americans in the United States. The Chicanos—the name is a shortened version of "Mexicano"—once lived mostly in the Southwest but are beginning to spread throughout the country, either as permanent residents in California and Texas or as summer migrant workers as far north as Minnesota and as far east as New Jersey and Florida. In the light of Mr. Vasquez's article, discuss the necessity of learning to speak English if one wishes to live in the United States.

C. A young Mexican-American said recently: "When I was ten, a teacher punished me for speaking Spanish on the school grounds. She kept me after school and made me write one hundred times: 'English is the proper language of the United States.' " Comment on the teacher's probable motivations and on her methods.

D. Write a paper in which you discuss the immigration-control system. Consider both its strengths and weaknesses.

E. Write a paper in which you explore the exploitation of members of a minority group by their fellow members. Mr. Rosario's "friends" are but one example. Some research into the Chinese-immigration situation in places like San Francisco will afford still another slant.

F. Mr. Rosario thinks his status will be legalized when his baby is born. Is he right? Do some research on this question; then write a simple, straightforward essay designed to explain the legal situation to Mr. Rosario and to others like him.

G. Write an essay in which you discuss another example of injustices suffered by minority groups. You may wish to base your essay on some popular protest song, such as "Deportee" by Woody Guthrie, or on some of Buffy St. Marie's work.

H. When the San Jose State College student newspaper carried an advertisement featuring "Tio Taco"—that stereotype of the motionless Mexican drowsing under his sombrero in the afternoon sun—the Chicano students threw all the papers they could find into the college fountain. Bill Dana, the comedian, has held a public interment for his "Jose Jiminez" television character, who offended many Chicanos. Do you know of other unfavorable Mexican-American images?

I. Discuss some Mexican-Americans, either real or fictional, in whom Chicanos can take great pride.

J. Spanish-language classes for some subjects in some schools have become a key Chicano demand. Discuss the justness of that demand, particularly in a town where Mexican-Americans make up half or more of the population.

The writer often develops his central idea through seeing facts in relationship to one another. He can show these relationships to the reader by the way he arranges the facts and supports them by evidence.

One common method of development through reasoning is the *inductive method,* building from specific statements to a general conclusion or hypothesis. The writer literally leads the reader to the main idea of the paragraph or entire paper, whichever the case may be. This method is reliable when enough typical instances are given to support the generalization. It is certainly one of the most useful patterns of development for the student to understand and practice, as it is one of the best correctives for unsubstantiated judgments and opinions.

Another popular order for expository development is just the reverse: the *deductive method,* in which the writer begins with a general statement and follows it with particulars—examples, facts, statistics, details—that support it. Ralph Nader's fourth paragraph in "The Safe Car You Can't Buy" ("Almost no feature . . .") is built deductively. He states a general premise, then presents specific examples to support it.

The *question-to-answer,* the *cause-to-effect* or *effect-to-cause* (Mr. Nader's second paragraph—"This experimental car . . .") and the *problem-to-solution* arrangements are also often used. These patterns are self-explanatory. You will find many examples of them in the essays in this book and you should have frequent use for them in your own writing. You must realize, of course, that often in a paper or even in a paragraph a writer will use a combination of methods. Thus Mr. Nader uses a variety of patterns of development in his individual paragraphs even though in his complete essay he sets up a problem and offers a solution.

No matter what pattern you choose for developing your ideas, evidence will support your reasoning. Hearsay, legend, mere opinion, or speculation cannot support a generalization. To be acceptable as evidence, a fact must either be verified or be attested by a reliable authority. To be reliable, an authority must be unprejudiced and competent.

The Nader essay is a good example of the use as evidence of both factual material and the appeal to authority. Mr. Nader does not ask the reader to rely on his word alone but also supplies statistics, uses particular incidents illustrating car safety or the lack thereof with specific reference to car manufacturers, gives results of surveys, and cites other authorities. We can be sure, too, that such authorities as those in the Cornell University and University of California research groups are competent and unprejudiced on this subject.

As you read the next three essays, notice how reasoning and evidence are used by the authors. Ask yourself if all of the evidence presented is acceptable and if all the authorities are reliable.

The Safe Car — You Can't Buy

Ralph Nader

The Cornell Aeronautical Laboratory has developed an exhibition automobile embodying over sixty new safety concepts which would enable an occupant to withstand a head-on collision at 50 mph with at most only minor scratches. In its design, six basic principles of crash protection were followed:

1. The car body was strengthened to prevent most external blows from distorting it against the passengers.
2. Doors were secured so that crash impacts could not open them, thereby saving passengers from ejection and maintaining the structural strength of the side of the car body.
3. Occupants were secured to prevent them from striking objects inside the car.
4. Interior knobs, projections, sharp edges and hard surfaces have been

□ Ralph Nader, "The Safe Car You Can't Buy," *The Nation* (April 11, 1959), 310-313.

removed and the ceiling shaped to produce only glancing blows to the head (the most vulnerable part of the body during a crash).

5. The driver's environment was improved to reduce accident risk by increasing visibility, simplifying controls and instruments, and lowering the carbon monoxide of his breathing atmosphere.

6. For pedestrian safety, dangerous objects like hood ornaments were removed from the exterior.

This experimental car, developed with funds representing only a tiny fraction of the annual advertising budget of, say, Buick, is packed with applications of simple yet effective safety factors. In the wrap-around bumper system, for instance, plastic foam material between the front and rear bumpers and the back-up plates absorbs some of the shock energy; the bumpers are smoothly shaped to convert an increased proportion of blows from direct to glancing ones; the side bumpers are firmly attached to the frame, which has been extended and reinforced to provide support. Another feature is the installment of two roll-over bars into the top of the car body as added support.

It is clear that Detroit today is designing automobiles for style, cost, performance and calculated obsolescence, but not—despite the 5,000,000 reported accidents, nearly 40,000 fatalities, 110,000 permanent disabilities and 1,500,000 injuries yearly—for safety.

Almost no feature of the interior design of our current cars provides safeguards against injury in the event of collision. Doors that fly open on impact, inadequately secured seats, the sharp-edged rear-view mirror, pointed knobs on instrument panel and doors, flying glass, the overhead structure—all illustrate the lethal potential of poor design. A sudden deceleration turns a collapsed steering wheel or a sharp-edged dashboard into a bone- and chest-crushing agent. Penetration of the shatterproof windshield can chisel one's head into fractions. A flying seat cushion can cause a fatal injury. The apparently harmless glove-compartment door has been known to unlatch under impact and guillotine a child. Roof-supporting structure has deteriorated to a point where it provides scarcely more protection to the occupants, in common roll-over accidents, than an open convertible. This is especially true of the so-called "hardtops." Nor is the automobile designed as an efficient force moderator. For example, the bumper does not contribute significantly to reduction of the crash deceleration forces that are transmitted to the motorist; its function has been more to reflect style than absorb shock.

These weaknesses of modern automobile construction have been established by the investigation of several groups, including the Automotive Crash Injury Research of the Cornell University Medical College, the Institute of Transportation and Traffic Engineering of the University of California and the Motor Vehicle Research of Lee, New Hampshire. Careful coverage of all available reports does not reveal a single dissent from these findings:

1. There are direct causal relationships between automotive design and the frequency, type and severity of injuries.
2. Studies of body tolerances to abrupt deceleration show that the forces in most accidents now fatal are well within the physiological limits of survival under proper conditions.
3. Engineering improvement in safety design and restraining devices would materially reduce the injury and fatality rate (estimates range from twenty to thirty thousand lives saved annually).
4. Redesign of injury-causing automotive components is well within the capabilities of present engineering technique and would require no radical changes in present styling.
5. Many design improvements have already been developed but are not in production.

The remarkable advances in crash-protection knowledge achieved by these research organizations at a cost of some $6 million stands in marked contrast to the glacier-like movements of car manufacturers, who spend that much to enrich the sound of a door slam. This is not due to any dearth of skill—the industry possesses many able, frustrated safety engineers whose suggestions over the years invariably have taken a back seat to those of the stylist. In 1938, an expert had this to say in *Safety Engineering:*

> The motor industry must face the fact that accidents occur. It is their duty, therefore, to so design the interiors of automobiles that when the passenger is tossed around, he will get an even break and not suffer a preventable injury in accidents that today are taking a heavy toll.

In 1954, nearly 600,000 fatalities later, a U.C.L.A. engineer could conclude that "There has been no significant automotive-engineering contribution to the safety of motorists since about the beginning of World War II. . . ." In its 1955 annual report, the Cornell crash-research group came to a similar conclusion, adding that "the newer model automobiles [1950-1954] are increasing the rate of fatalities in injury-producing accidents."

In 1956, Ford introduced the double-grip safety-door latch, the "dished" steering wheel, and instrument panel padding; the rest of the industry followed with something less than enthusiasm. Even in these changes, style remained the dominant consideration, and their effectiveness is in doubt. Tests have failed to establish, for example, an advantage for the "deep-dish" steering wheel compared with the conventional wheel; the motorist will still collapse the rim to the hub.

This year [1959], these small concessions to safety design have virtually been discontinued. "A square foot of chrome sells ten times more cars than the best safety-door latch," declared one industry representative. Dashboard padding remains one of a few safety accessories available as optional equipment. This is like saying to the consumer: "Here's a hot car. Now, if you wish to be safe in it, you'll have to pay more."

None of this should be construed as placing the increasingly popular mites from abroad in a more favorable light. Most foreign cars offer far less protection to the motorist than domestic ones.

Prevailing analyses of vehicular accidents circulated for popular consumption tend to impede constructive thinking by adherence to some monistic theory of causation. Take one of the more publicized ogres—speed. Cornell's findings, based on data covering 3,203 cars in injury-producing accidents, indicate that 74 per cent of the cars were going at a *traveling* speed under 60 mph and about 88 per cent involved *impact* speeds under 60 mph. The average impact speed on urban roads was 27 mph; on rural roads, 41 mph. Dangerous or fatal injuries observed in accidents when the traveling speed was less than 60 mph are influenced far more by the shape and structure of interior car components with which the body came into contact than by the speed at which the cars were moving. Many fatalities have been recorded which occurred in panic stops or collisions at a speed under 25 mph. Cornell's concluding statement:

> Statistical tests indicated that even if a top speed limit of 60 mph could be uniformly and absolutely maintained, 73 per cent of the dangerous and fatal injuries observed would still be expected to occur. . . . the control of speed alone would have only limited effect on the frequency of dangerous and fatal injuries.

In brief, automobiles are so designed as to be dangerous at any speed.

Our preoccupation has been almost entirely with the cause of accidents seen primarily in terms of the driver and not with the instruments that produce the injuries. Erratic driving will always be characteristic, to some degree, of the traffic scene; exhortation and stricter law enforcement have at best a limited effect. Much more significant for saving life is the application of engineering remedies to minimize the lethal effects of human error by designing the automobile so as to afford maximum protection to occupants in the event of a collision. In a word, the job, in part, is to make accidents safe.

The task of publicizing the relation between automotive design and highway casualties is fraught with difficulties. The press, radio and television are not likely to undertake this task in terms of industry responsibility when millions in advertising dollars are being poured into their coffers. Private researchers are reluctant to stray from their scholarly and experimental pursuits, especially when cordial relations with the industry are necessary for the continuation of their projects with the maximum of success. Car manufacturers have thought it best to cooperate with some of these programs and, in one case, when findings became embarrassing, have given financial support. The industry's policy is bearing fruit; most investigators discreetly keep their private disgust with the industry's immobility from seeping into the public limelight. They consider themselves fact-finders and leave the value judgments to others. This adherence to a rigid division of labor provides a convenient rationalization for the widespread amorality among our scholarly elite, who appear insensitive to the increased responsibility as citizens which their superior knowledge should require them to shoulder.

For the past three years [1956-] a Special Congressional House Sub-committee on Traffic Safety has been conducting extensive hearings on automobile design. The industry and research organizations have all submitted their testimony and reports. Some revealing facts came out of these hearings, but the press, by and large, has chosen to ignore them. In any case, the subcommittee is proceeding too cautiously for so urgent a matter. It has been too solicitous of recommendations for delay advanced by some academicians who see automotive design from the viewpoint of engineering perfection rather than as a national health emergency requiring immediate, even if not perfect, engineering remedy. Better techniques will be developed, but at least for the present, there will be added protection from remedying known design hazards. This has been the point that many safety engineers and physicians have vainly been urging.

Even if all the facts, laid before the public, did not increase consumer demand for safety design (which is unlikely), the manufacturers should not be relieved of their responsibility. Innumerable precedents show that the consumer must be protected at times from his own indiscretion and vanity. Dangerous drugs cannot be dispensed without a licensed physician's prescription; meat must pass federal inspection before distribution; railroads and other interstate carriers are required to meet safety standards regarding their equipment.

State motor-vehicle codes set minimum standards for certain vehicular equipment. This legislation has not compelled manufacturers to adopt known safety-design features (with the exception of safety glass), but has merely endorsed previous standards long employed by the car producers. Examples: brake requirements, headlight specifications, horns, mufflers, windshield wipers, rear-view mirrors. Thus the impact of these requirements falls primarily on the operator, who has to keep this equipment functioning. The legislative purpose is directed to *accident* prevention and only peripherally to implementing standards that might prevent *injuries.*

But state laws do not begin to cope with design defects of the postwar car which increase the *risk of collision.* Examples: the terrific visual distortion of the wrap-around windshield; leakage of carbon monoxide; rear-end fishtailing in hard turns; undue brake fade and the decreased braking area of the recent fourteen-inch wheel; the tinted windshield condemned as violative of all basic optical principles to the extent that visual loss at night ranges from 15 per cent to 45 per cent; and the fire hazard of the undercoating and some upholstery.

Motor vehicles have been found to be poorly designed with regard to human capacities and limitations both physical and psychological. For example, there are —especially in truck cabs—unnecessary difficulties in reaching and operating control levers, in reading half-hidden dials and gauges; there are seats that induce poor posture or discomfort, mirrors whose poor placement and size impair vision, visors inadequately shielding eyes from bright light, and uncomfortable temperature, humidity and noise levels. The cumulative effects lead to fatigue, deterioration of driving efficiency and reaction time, and frequently to an accident which cannot be attributed, in the light of such poor design, to the driver.

Recourse to the courts for judgment against a manufacturer by a plaintiff injured by the defective interior design of his car while involved in an accident stands a dim chance of success. While the courts have hung liability on manufacturers for injuries due to defectively designed products, the closest they have come in motor-vehicle cases has been to hold the producer liable for a design defect instrumental in causing the accident, e.g., the braking system. The question of automotive death-traps cannot be dealt with adequately by the limited authority and resources of the judiciary, although a few pertinent decisions would have a salutary effect.

By all relevant criteria, a problem so national in scope and technical in nature can best be handled by the legislative process, on the federal level, with delegation to an appropriate administrative body. It requires uniformity in treatment and central administration, for as an interstate matter, the job cannot be left to the states with their dissimilar laws setting low requirements that are not strictly enforced and that do not strike at the heart of the malady—the blueprint on the Detroit drawing board. The thirty-three-year record of the attempt to introduce state uniformity in establishing the most basic equipment standards for automobiles has been disappointing.

Perhaps the best summation of the whole issue lies in a physician's comment on the car manufacturer's design policy: "Translated into medicine," he writes, "it would be comparable to withholding known methods of life-saving value."

RALPH NADER, lawyer and author, was graduated from Princeton University, then took an LL.B. from Harvard Law School. He was selected as one of the ten outstanding young men of the year in 1967 by the United States Junior Chamber of Commerce. A member of the Connecticut Bar, he has made a prolonged study of the relation between automotive design and highway casualties. Mr. Nader's book on the designed-in dangers of the American automobile, *Unsafe at Any Speed,* was a best seller in 1965 and 1966.

Vocabulary Study

A. "The most *vulnerable* part of the body" refers to a part of the body that is (a) well protected; (b) open to injury; (c) in the line of impact?

B. Poor design has a *lethal* potential. As this word is central to Mr. Nader's case, define it.

C. Find *guillotine* in a dictionary and read something about how the machine operates. Does Mr. Nader use the word appropriately when he says that a glove-compartment door can *guillotine* a child in a wreck?

D. The lack of advancement in safety design is not due to a *dearth* of skill. Are there too few safety-design engineers?

E. If you have carefully *construed* his statements, you know that Mr. Nader does not mean that small foreign cars are safer than large domestic ones. Define the word.

F. The word *impede* comes from a Latin word meaning literally "to ensnare" or "entangle the feet." Explain how it is appropriately used here in the expression "to impede constructive thinking."

G. To say that *erratic* driving will always be with us is to reaffirm the old saying that to err is human. How would you describe the course of an *erratic* driver?

H. What sort of attitude characterizes a person who does something *discreetly?*

I. The automotive industry moves ahead rapidly in some aspects of design. But it is characterized by *immobility* in others. Define the word.

J. Certain persons of the scholarly elite could help us out of the problem Mr. Nader describes, but they suffer from a widespread *amorality.* Explain.

K. A *solicitous* person is (a) a door-to-door salesman; (b) a lawyer; (c) a person moved to seek after your desires?

L. *Precedents* show that the American consumer is often too gullible and vain. What are *precedents?*

Questions on Form and Content

A. Does Mr. Nader tell you much about the safe car? What is some of the evidence he presents that the car is safer than others? Is the *safe* car really the subject of the essay, or just the springboard into his real subject?

B. Throughout, Mr. Nader keeps a comparison close to the surface: automobile makers are just as much obliged to give you safety in car design as your doctor is to give you medicine that will cure you when you are sick. Is this a valid and effective comparison?

C. What effect does speed really have on the accident rate?

D. What does Mr. Nader say concerning the safety of the hardtop?

E. We are told how much a little money spent in the right way has accomplished. What does Mr. Nader say by implication about the advertising budgets for Detroit's autos?

F. Can you agree that there has been "no significant automotive-engineering contribution to the safety of motorists since about the beginning of World War II"?

G. How would a small foreign car fare in an accident?

H. On what level can the tragedy of highway accidents best be handled: the local, state, or federal?

I. What is the idea behind most legislative attempts to handle this problem: to prevent accidents, or to force standards that might prevent *injuries?*

Suggestions for Writing

A. The most woeful man in the world is he who is driving last year's "insolent chariot," a model that looks like a scuffed sneaker beside the latest Detroit creation. Discuss "calculated obsolescence," the ideas behind it, and what the author says it leads to.

B. If you have ever been in an accident, or if you have a first-hand account from one who has, discuss the safety features, or lack of them, of the cars involved. As Mort Sahl would have said, which part of the car "chickened out" first?

C. If you feel that Mr. Nader's indictment is unjust, and that Detroit is really doing something to make cars safer, answer him in rebuttal, listing whatever features you feel he omitted or overlooked.

D. Perhaps the most sober note of this article, aside from the array of staggering statistics, is the ethical one, summed up at the end by a physician. Discuss the automobile manufacturer's *ethical* obligation to give us safer cars.

E. What steps would you suggest be taken to eliminate our bone-shattering, life-taking highway accidents? Discuss.

F. Should there be a horsepower limit to passenger cars? Discuss.

G. If you have some facts about how other nations have handled this problem, write a paper wherein you offer a comparison of our system with theirs.

H. As Mr. Nader states it, car safety presents an ethical, almost a moral problem. An old bromide has it that you cannot legislate morals; this argument was used against prohibition. How do you think legislation might effectively proceed in this case? Discuss.

I. In September, 1964, Edward J. Speno, New York State Senator, said: "The automobile is murderously unsafe for the conditions under which it is used. It is the only component in the highway carnage complex that can easily be modified for safety purposes." Comment.

J. In 1966, Congress passed legislation establishing minimum safety regulations for automobiles. Discuss the provisions of the law.

K. What part has Mr. Nader played in the fight for safer cars since he wrote this article in 1959?

—And Sudden Death

J. C. Furnas

Publicizing the total of motoring injuries never succeeds in jarring the motorist into a realization of the appalling risks of motoring. He does not translate dry statistics into a reality of blood and agony.

Figures[1] exclude the pain and horror of savage mutilation—which means they leave out the point. They need to be brought closer home. A passing look at a bad smash or the news that a fellow you had lunch with last week is in a hospital with a broken back will make any driver but a born fool slow down at least temporarily. But what is needed is a vivid and *sustained* realization that every time you step on the throttle death gets in beside you, waiting for his chance. That horrible accident you may have witnessed is no isolated horror. That sort of thing happens every hour of the day, everywhere in the United States.

A judge now and again sentences reckless drivers to tour the accident end of a city morgue. But even a mangled body on a slab, waxily portraying the conse-

[1]In 1965 1,800,000 were injured, 49,000 were killed.

☐ J. C. Furnas, "—And Sudden Death," *The Reader's Digest* (October, 1966), 153-157. First printed in *The Reader's Digest* August, 1935.

quences of bad motoring judgment, isn't a patch on the scene of the accident itself. No safety-poster artist would dare depict that in full detail.

That picture would have to include motion-picture and sound effects, too—the flopping, pointless efforts of the injured to stand up; the queer, grunting noises; the steady, panting groaning of a human being with pain creeping up on him as the shock wears off. It should portray the slack expression on the face of a man, drugged with shock, staring at the Z-twist in his broken leg, the insane crumpled effect of a child's body after its bones are crushed inward, a realistic portrait of a hysterical woman with her screaming mouth opening a hole in the bloody drip that fills her eyes and runs off her chin. Minor details would include the raw ends of bones protruding through flesh in compound fractures, and the dark-red oozing surfaces where clothes and skin were flayed off at once.

Those are all standard, everyday sequels to the modern passion for going places in a hurry and taking a chance or two by the way. If ghosts could be put to a useful purpose, every bad stretch of road in the United States would greet the oncoming motorist with groans and screams and the educational spectacle of ten or a dozen corpses, all sizes, sexes and ages, lying horribly still on the bloody grass.

Last year a state trooper of my acquaintance stopped a big red car for speeding. Papa was obviously a responsible person, obviously set for a pleasant weekend with his family—so the officer cut into Papa's well-bred expostulations: "I'll let you off this time, but if you keep on this way you won't last long. Get going—but take it easier." Later a passing motorist hailed the trooper and asked if the red car had got a ticket. "No," said the trooper, "I hated to spoil their party." "Too bad you didn't," said the motorist. "I saw you stop them—and then I passed that car again 50 miles up the line. It still makes me feel sick at my stomach. The car was all folded up like an accordion. They were all dead but one of the kids—and he wasn't going to live to the hospital."

Maybe it will make you sick at your stomach, too. But unless you're a heavy-footed incurable, a firsthand acquaintance with the results of mixing gasoline with speed and bad judgment ought to be well worth your while. I can't help it if the facts are revolting. If you have the nerve to drive fast and take chances, you ought to have the nerve to take the appropriate cure. You can't ride an ambulance or watch the doctor working on the victim in the hospital, but you can read.

The automobile is treacherous. It is tragically hard to realize that it can become a deadly missile. As enthusiasts tell you, it makes 65 feel like nothing at all. But 65 miles an hour is 100 feet a second, a speed which puts a viciously unjustified responsibility on brakes and human reflexes, and can instantly turn this docile luxury into a mad bull elephant.

Collision, turnover or sideswipe, each type of accident produces either a shattering dead stop or a crashing change of direction, and, since the occupant—meaning you—continues in the old direction at the original speed, every surface and angle of the car's interior immediately becomes a battering, tearing projectile, aimed squarely at you—inescapable. There is no bracing yourself against these imperative laws of momentum.

Anything can happen in the split second of crash, even those lucky escapes you hear about. People have dived through windshields and come out with only superficial scratches. They have run cars together head on, reducing both to twisted junk, and been found unhurt and arguing bitterly two minutes afterward. But death was there just the same—he was only exercising his privilege of being erratic. This spring a wrecking crew pried the door off a car which had been overturned down an embankment, and out stepped the driver with only a scratch on his cheek. But his mother was still inside, a splinter driven four inches into her brain as a result of son's taking a greasy curve a little too fast. No blood—no horribly twisted bones—just a gray-haired corpse still clutching her pocketbook in her lap as she had clutched it when she felt the car leave the road.

On that same curve a month later, a light touring car crashed into a tree. In the middle of the front seat they found a nine-month-old baby surrounded by broken glass and yet absolutely unhurt. A fine practical joke on death—but spoiled by the baby's parents, still sitting on each side of him, instantly killed by shattering their skulls on the dashboard.

If you customarily pass without clear vision a long way ahead, make sure that every member of the party carries identification papers—it's difficult to identify a body with its whole face bashed in or torn off. The driver is death's favorite target. If the steering wheel holds together, it ruptures his liver or spleen so he bleeds to death internally. Or, if the steering wheel breaks off, the matter is settled instantly by the steering column's plunging through his abdomen.

By no means do all head-on collisions occur on curves. The modern death trap is likely to be a straight stretch with three lanes of traffic. This sudden vision of broad, straight road tempts many an ordinarily sensible driver into passing the man ahead. Simultaneously a driver coming the other way swings out at high speed. At the last moment each tries to get into line again, but the gaps are closed. As the cars in line are forced into the ditch to capsize or ram fences, the passers meet, almost head on, in a swirling, grinding smash that sends them caroming obliquely into the others.

A trooper described such an accident—five cars in one mess, seven killed on the spot, two dead on the way to the hospital, two more dead in the long run. He remembered it far more vividly than he wanted to—the quick way the doctor turned away from a dead man to check up on a woman with a broken back; the three bodies out of one car so soaked with oil from the crankcase that they looked like wet brown cigars and not human at all; a man, walking around and babbling to himself, oblivious of the dead and dying, even oblivious of the daggerlike sliver of steel that stuck out of his streaming wrist; a pretty girl with her forehead laid open, trying hopelessly to crawl out of a ditch in spite of her smashed hip. A first-class massacre of that sort is only a question of scale and numbers—seven corpses are no deader than one. Each shattered man, woman or child who went to make up the fatality statistics chalked up last year had to die a personal death.

A car careening and rolling down a bank, battering and smashing its occupants every inch of the way, can wrap itself so thoroughly around a tree that front and rear bumpers interlock, requiring an acetylene torch to cut them apart. In a recent case of that sort they found the old lady who had been sitting in back, lying across the lap of her daughter, who was in front, each soaked in her own and the other's blood indistinguishably, each so shattered and broken that there was no point whatever in an autopsy to determine whether it was broken neck or ruptured heart that caused death.

Overturning cars specialize in certain injuries. Cracked pelvis, for instance, guaranteeing agonizing months in bed, motionless, perhaps crippled for life—broken spine resulting from sheer sidewise twist—the minor details of smashed knees and splintered shoulder blades caused by crashing into the side of the car as she goes over with the swirl of an insane roller coaster—and the lethal consequences of broken ribs, which puncture hearts and lungs with their raw ends. The consequent internal hemorrhage is no less dangerous because it is the pleural instead of the abdominal cavity that is filling with blood.

Glass contributes its share to the spectacular side of accidents. Even safety glass may not be wholly safe when the car crashes into something at high speed. You hear picturesque tales of how a flying human body will make a neat hole in the stuff with its head—the shoulders stick—the glass holds—and the raw, keen edge decapitates the body as neatly as a guillotine.

Or, to continue with the decapitation motif, going off the road into a post-and-rail fence can put you beyond worrying about other injuries immediately when a rail pierces the windshield and tears off your head with its splintery end—not as neat a job but just as efficient. Bodies are often found with shoes off, and feet broken out of shape. The shoes are on the floor of the car, empty and with laces still neatly tied. That is the kind of impact produced by modern speeds.

But all that is routine in every American community. To be remembered individually by doctors and policemen, you have to do something as grotesque as the lady who burst the windshield with her head, splashing splinters all over the other occupants of the car, and then, as the car rolled over, rolled with it down the edge of the windshield frame and cut her throat from ear to ear. Or park on the pavement too near a curve at night and stand in front of the tail light as you take off the spare tire—which will immortalize you in somebody's memory as the fellow who was mashed three feet broad and two inches thick by the impact of a heavy-duty truck against the rear of his own car. Or be as original as the two youths who were thrown out of an open roadster—thrown clear—but each broke a windshield post with his head in passing and the whole top of each skull, down to the eyebrows, was missing. Or snap off a nine-inch tree and get impaled by a ragged branch.

None of all that is scare-fiction; it is just the horrible raw material of the year's statistics as seen in the ordinary course of duty by policemen and doctors, picked at random. The surprising thing is there is so little dissimilarity in their stories.

It's hard to find an accident victim who can bear to talk. After you come to, the gnawing, searing pain throughout your body is accounted for by learning that you have both collarbones smashed, both shoulder blades splintered, your right arm broken in three places and three ribs cracked, with every chance of bad internal ruptures. But the pain can't distract you, as the shock begins to wear off, from realizing that you are probably on your way out. You can't forget that, not even when they shift you from the ground to the stretcher and your broken ribs bite into your lungs and the sharp ends of your collarbones slide over to stab deep into each side of your screaming throat. When you've stopped screaming, it all comes back—you're dying and you hate yourself for it.

And every time you pass on a blind curve, every time you hit it up on a slippery road, every time you step on it harder than your reflexes will safely take, every time you drive with your reactions slowed down by a drink or two, every time you follow the man ahead too closely, you're gambling a few seconds against blood and agony and sudden death.

Take a look at yourself as the man in the white jacket shakes his head over you, tells the boys with the stretcher not to bother and turns away to somebody else who isn't quite dead yet. And then take it easy.

Joseph Chamberlain Furnas, born in Indianapolis, was a Phi Beta Kappa at Harvard, where he received an A.B. degree in 1927. He was awarded the Anisfield-Wolf nonfiction award for *Anatomy of Paradise* in 1948. Among his other works are *The Prophet's*

Chamber, Many People Prize It, So You're Going to Stop Smoking, Voyage to Windward: The Life of Robert Louis Stevenson, Sudden Death and How to Avoid It (with Ernest M. Smith), *Goodbye to Uncle Tom, The Road to Harper's Ferry, The Devil's Rainbow,* and *The Life and Times of the Late Demon Rum.* Jerome Beatty, Jr., in the November 5, 1966, *Saturday Review* calls "—And Sudden Death" "the most famous magazine article of all time," and says that when it first appeared in 1935, it shocked Americans with its gruesome, realistic descriptions of people maimed and killed in automobile accidents, but that in the violent sixties it seemed tame.

Vocabulary Study

From the list below, select the word or phrase most like the italicized word in the following excerpts. The list contains extra words.

A. the *appalling* risks of motoring

B. smash that sends them *caroming obliquely*

C. *oblivious* of the dead and dying

D. a first-class *massacre* of that sort

E. a car *careening* and rolling down a bank

F. an *autopsy* to determine whether it was broken neck or ruptured heart

G. and the *lethal* consequences of broken ribs, which puncture hearts

H. keen edge *decapitates* the body as neatly as a guillotine

I. you have to do something as *grotesque* as the lady who burst the windshield with her head

J. which will *immortalize* you in somebody's memory

K. by the *impact* of a heavy-duty truck against the rear of his own car

L. get *impaled* by a ragged branch

collision	giving lasting fame to
postmortem	enmeshes
slantingly	transfixed
unmindful	fatal
beheads	hitting and rebounding
horrifying	wholesale slaughter
impartial	lurching
impasse	fantastic

Questions on Form and Content

A. What does Mr. Furnas believe essential for the realization of the appalling risks of driving? Why is the publication of figures and statistics not enough?

B. What is Mr. Furnas's purpose? Is he successful?

C. Did you find the facts revolting? Do you think that the author is justified in presenting them as he does? Are Mr. Nader's figures and statistics as convincing? Which, if either, may influence your driving?

D. What specific driving hazards does Mr. Furnas exemplify?

E. In the conclusion, what particular practices does he caution against?

Suggestions for Writing

A. This article first appeared in the August 1935 issue of the *Reader's Digest* and was reprinted by special request in October 1966. How much progress do we seem to have made in creating safer highways? Or do you consider them more dangerous today? If so, how and why? (The author reported in the 1935 article that almost a million were injured, 36,000 killed in automobile accidents during the previous year; the 1966 version gives the figures for 1965 as 1,800,000 injured, 49,000 killed.)

B. Susan Langland, then a freshman at Tulane University, asked that *The Reader's Digest* reprint the article. She wrote:

> Like most American teen-agers, I have more or less grown up riding in automobiles. Perhaps this is why I often exceeded the speed limit without giving it a second thought. I drive fairly carefully, so the possibility of an accident seemed rather remote. Then I read an article which made the consequences of even the remotest possibility seem too horrible to risk. . . .
>
> No article has ever made so great an impression on me. Perhaps it would do the same to someone else—someone who might otherwise have become a freeway casualty. If you reprint this article, it might prevent one death or many. In any case I want to thank you for possibly saving my life.

Comment.

C. If you have been involved in an automobile accident, describe your experience.

D. What recommendations would you make for the prevention of automobile accidents?

E. What are the speed limits in your state? How realistic are they? How well observed?

F. What do you consider the greatest driving hazards? Why?

G. Write an assessment of your own driving habits.

H. Assess the driving tests required in your state. Are they lenient, adequate, or prohibitive in nature? Do they realistically test physical condition, ability to drive, and knowledge of rules and regulations? Are they administered honestly and fairly?

I. Discuss the role of policemen and highway patrolmen in controlling traffic and preventing accidents. Are traffic fines, as you have experienced them, educational as well as punitive?

J. Discuss the rules and regulations concerning driving in your state. Do you feel that some should be changed or eliminated? Others added? If so, which, and why in each case?

K. On July 25, 1967, Judson P. Branch, Allstate Insurance Companies Chairman, said: "Every other child born in the United States from now on is destined to be injured or killed in a traffic crash unless drastic action is taken soon." He announced that his company was launching a national traffic-safety advertising program, which would cost, in addition to their regular advertising program, nearly $1 million. The program would be concentrated on high school driver education. Have you had a course in driver education? If so, describe and evaluate it.

L. Mr. Branch said: "We concentrate on driver education because the under-twenty-four-year driver group, though only one-fifth of the drivers on the road, is involved in far more than one-fifth of the traffic crashes in each state. This is a group that needs special attention because of their special problems." What special problems do drivers under twenty-four have?

M. What role has television played in recent years in attempting to cut down highway accident tolls?

N. Do you think driving regulations should be uniform throughout the United States? Why or why not?

O. Mr. Furnas says: "A judge now and again sentences reckless drivers to tour the accident end of a city morgue." Comment on what you consider to be the justice and value of such a sentence.

P. "If ghosts could be put to a useful purpose, every bad stretch of road in the United States would greet the oncoming motorist with groans and screams and the educational spectacle of ten or a dozen corpses, all sizes, sexes and ages, lying horribly still on the bloody grass," writes Mr.

Furnas. Some states use small white crosses along the highway to mark places where fatalities have occurred. What effect do you think they have? Do you know of other similar practices designed to help prevent highway accidents?

Q. Read through Karl Shapiro's "Auto Wreck" once; then reread it carefully and answer the following questions:

1. What is the setting? Who are the characters? What happens? How are the policemen described? What are they doing? What metaphor is used for the wrecks? What similes for the onlookers? How does the speaker contrast death by automobile to death from war, suicide, stillbirth, and cancer? What is a dénouement? How are the stones both expedient and wicked?
2. Write a paraphrase of the poem.
3. How are the article "—And Sudden Death" and the poem "Auto Wreck" alike? How do they differ? Which do you consider more effective? Why?

Auto Wreck

Karl Shapiro

Its quick soft silver bell beating, beating,
And down the dark one ruby flare
Pulsing out red light like an artery,
The ambulance at top speed floating down
Past beacons and illuminated clocks
Wings in a heavy curve, dips down,
And brakes speed, entering the crowd.
The doors leap open, emptying light;
Stretchers are laid out, the mangled lifted
And stowed into the little hospital.
Then the bell, breaking the hush, tolls once,
And the ambulance with its terrible cargo
Rocking, slightly rocking, moves away,

□Karl Shapiro, "Auto Wreck," in *Poems 1940-1953* (New York, 1941), p. 483.

As the doors, an afterthought, are closed.

We are deranged, walking among the cops
Who sweep glass and are large and composed.
One is still making notes under the light.
One with a bucket douches ponds of blood
Into the street and gutter.
One hangs lanterns on the wrecks that cling,
Empty husks of locusts, to iron poles.

Our throats were tight as tourniquets,
Our feet were bound with splints, but now,
Like convalescents intimate and gauche,
We speak through sickly smiles and warn
With the stubborn saw of common sense,
The grim joke and the banal resolution.
The traffic moves around with care,
But we remain, touching a wound
That opens to our richest horror.
Already old, the question Who shall die?
Becomes unspoken Who is innocent?
For death in war is done by hands;
Suicide has cause and stillbirth, logic;
And cancer, simple as a flower, blooms.
But this invites the occult mind,
Cancels our physics with a sneer,
And spatters all we knew of denouement
Across the expedient and wicked stones.

AUTOMOBILE

Moulin Studios, S.F.

The Case for the Electric Automobile

Donald E. Carr

As an urban-suburban "subcompact" vehicle, the electric automobile is undeniably the only hope for stopping the otherwise inevitable asphyxiation of our cities. Yet only two years ago, when I brought out a book recommending the electric car as a solution to air pollution of the Los Angeles kind, both oil and automobile industries reacted as if I had recommended returning to the surrey with the fringe on top. An oil company spokesman said, "Pollution problems have become aggravated to the point where we cannot afford to spend money and waste time going up blind alleys."

The implication here is that the electric automobile is a blind alley. On the contrary, the darkest of blind alleys is the pathetic attempt to doctor up the internal-combustion engine so that it will stop emitting poisons. Since this attempt is going to be enforced by federal law beginning with all 1968 cars and pickup trucks, it is worthwhile to discuss the present emission-control program.

□ Donald E. Carr, "The Case for the Electric Automobile," *The Atlantic* (June 1967), 92-95.

Two systems now prevail: air-injection to the exhaust manifold to reduce the concentration of unburned fuel and carbon monoxide; and improved piston design to accomplish more complete primary combustion combined with carburetion tuning so that the fuel-air mixture never becomes excessively fuel-rich. The latter is the "Chrysler Clean Air Package" and seems to be gaining ground, since Ford and American and probably General Motors are switching to it, primarily because it is much less expensive (about $14 compared with about $40 extra for air injection, as factory installed). Both of these systems when correctly adjusted in brand-new cars will reduce hydrocarbons in the exhaust to the legal maximum of 275 parts per million and carbon monoxide to the 1.5 percent limit.

As shown by recent tests on 1966 cars in California, where emission control is now required by law, these systems falter, get out of kilter, and after as little as 2000 miles of city driving, no longer can do the job. Pollution control officials in Los Angeles County and elsewhere in the state agree with the car manufacturers that frequent mechanical checks, inspections, and revamps are going to be necessary, yet the checking process is so time-consuming that a car owner must sacrifice his vehicle for twelve hours or at least overnight just to find out whether he is obeying the law. Moreover, there are not enough trained mechanics to go around.

Far worse than the matter of inefficiency or inconvenience is the fact that the 1966 emission control systems, especially the now dominant Chrysler technique, would actually increase the nitrogen oxide content of the exhaust. This result, predicted by all combustion chemists, including myself, has been borne out by recent surveys which showed an average of 50 percent more nitrogen dioxide. This is the whiskey-brown poison gas that killed 125 people in 1929, when an explosion in a stack of nitrocellulose X-ray films released deadly NO_2 fumes throughout the wards of the Cleveland Clinic Hospital. In experiments it has been possible to convert the nitrogen oxide to inert nitrogen gas with a catalytic muffler. But because this requires a reducing rather than an oxidizing atmosphere,

OBSOLETE

David Wolfgang, San Francisco

where the present factory-installed systems emit to the exhaust manifold, one is faced with complication piled upon complication. It would be necessary, for example, to inject hydrogen or carbon monoxide into the muffler upstream of the catalyst bed. This would involve a snake pit of pipes, tubes, and control valves that would frighten even the most sophisticated mechanic.

With one rather fantastic but conceivable exception, the electric automobile gives off no pollutants at all. Mr. B. C. Lucas, a professional engineer, has claimed that a city full of electric automobiles would be badly polluted with ozone, because ozone, perhaps the most dangerous of all smog ingredients, is produced by the opening and closing of electric circuits. Ozone is in fact detectable in some generating plants and transformer stations, but in such cases the voltage and corresponding field intensity are high enough to result in ionization of the air and actual electric discharge. It is doubtful that atmospheric discharge would occur in the case of the battery voltage involved in automobiles. Nevertheless, this is a point that needs to be cleared up.

The power train of an electric vehicle consists fundamentally of a number of batteries (the number depending on the horsepower required), an electric motor or motors, and simple transmission connections with the drive wheels. The connection may actually consist merely of placing the motors on the wheels. Since the electricity is produced as direct current, the simplest system would involve a DC motor. Usually these are somewhat ponderous, with a low ratio of horsepower to weight, although Ford and its subsidiaries and others have experimentally designed much more efficient DC machines of one quarter the conventional weight. By the use of an inverter or rectifier to convert the electric flow from the batteries to alternating current, the more highly developed technology of small AC motors can be used—for example, the brushless induction, squirrel-cage motor, which has a very high ratio of horsepower to weight and size. In modern designs for electric cars a modulating voltage control system is included, which automatically prevents an excessive rate of discharge and delivers the current in pulses to the motor. The pulse rate or width is automatically adjusted to the required torque, the technical term for the "push" needed for the wheels. (One needs more torque to start a car from a dead stop than to cruise at high speed.)

The torque characteristics of an electric car are ideally suited for stop-and-go driving. Unlike the gas-turbine car, acceleration from standing still in traffic is strong and instantaneous. I know this from personal experience because I drove the Yardney Electric Company's electric Renault Dauphine in rush-hour traffic in the Wall Street district. After scores of years with a gasoline engine, which keeps up a little snorting even when idling, it is an uncanny and delicious sensation to wait at a red light with no noise at all, not even a gentle hum (because nothing whatever is happening in the power train), then suddenly to ease gracefully and instantly into motion at the change of the signal.

I believe it is safe to say that there are no really bristly problems connected with converting electricity into the horsepower of motion. There are many alternatives, and no serious obstacles. One of the interesting options is to design the motor-transmission hookup so that some electric power can be recovered by converting the energy of the wheel motion into reverse current to recharge the batteries when coasting. This can increase the range of the vehicle between charges by 25 percent. One can also arrange the motor-transmission train so that the equivalent of engine-braking is obtained—an important brake-saving function in hilly cities like San Francisco. Within a city as large as Los Angeles, for example, one would need a range of at least fifty miles before stopping to recharge. There are two solutions to this problem, one of them purely technical, the other involving primarily a marketing or dispensing innovation. Let us take the technical solution first.

The classic lead-acid battery used to start the ordinary car has been improved in efficiency by 75 percent since it drove competing starting systems such as Edison's nickel-iron battery out of the automotive market; but it still has a rather low ratio of energy to weight and size. The more recent nickel-cadmium cell, used in a special form for cordless service in electric toothbrushes and the like, is better than the lead-acid battery; but the so-called Jung-Berg nickel-cadmium battery, more suitable for motive uses and applied widely in Europe for many years, has for some mysterious reason not been available commercially in this country. (The Electric Automobile Club of America blames this on the worldwide cartelization of the battery industry.)

The silver-zinc battery, developed primarily by Yardney Electric Company for missile, space, and torpedo use, is very efficient on an energy-in-relation-to-weight basis, but it is intrinsically quite expensive, although, as we shall see later, this need not make the investment cost of the customer's car any higher. Other new concepts in high-energy cells that have recently come upon the scene include Ford's liquid-sodium—molten-sulfur system, the metal-air cell (especially the zinc-air combination developed primarily by General Dynamics), and three new experimental cells which all use lithium as anode but use different electrolytes and different cathodes (Gulton Industries, General Motors, and Electrochimica Corporation).

Although at the present stage of development, it is popular to compare the various systems on a theoretical energy per pound basis, this doesn't mean very much practically, since the *available* energy in a battery will always depend on the rate of discharge. On the basis of a hypothetical "commuter" passenger car somewhat smaller than a Volkswagen, but improved in tire-rolling resistance and aerodynamics, the range between charges in stop-and-go city driving would be 38 miles with the lead-acid battery, up to 100 miles with the zinc-air cell or with the lithium anode cells. This is about half the distance between refuelings for a heavy conventional gasoline-powered car, which can go about 180 miles in stop-and-go driving on a tankful of gasoline.

In my opinion the most practical developmental possibility is the zinc-air battery, which is also being studied by Yardney, Leesona, Gould-National, and Electric Storage Battery as well as General Dynamics, although one should by no means discount the already well demonstrated silver-zinc system. The Ford battery, although very ingenious, operates at high temperatures and presents some collision hazard. Hot liquid sodium is an uncomfortable commodity which will react explosively with water. The GM lithium battery also operates at elevated temperatures. From a certain standpoint, however, the hot batteries may have one advantage in that they may serve as a source of heat for the passengers in cold weather. But to divert any appreciable energy from a battery pack for this purpose would cut down on the precious miles between recharges.

Most exponents of the electric car make a big point out of the fact that one would recharge the batteries overnight in one's garage. Or that parking lots would be equipped for recharging during a day of business or shopping. Recharging is a rather slow affair for most available batteries, and I am not inclined to be optimistic about the car owner as a do-it-yourself recharging serviceman. The better, and it seems to me quite inevitable, answer for the electrified urban and suburban areas would be to convert service stations to battery-exchange stops. Exchanging a fully charged battery pack for a run-down pack in a simple low horsepower vehicle should take no more time than filling up a tank with gasoline and checking the oil. From a business standpoint there are alluring possibilities in this field for the ambitious entrepreneur, which are compatible with the major problem of financing a car inherently more costly than a gasoline-powered vehicle only because the batteries cost so much.

The obvious financial answer is the one that has put the electric forklift truck suddenly ahead of competition from internal-combustion trucks. Electric Storage Battery Company *leases* the batteries and charges only on the basis of energy consumed.

If the battery pack is leased and a system of battery exchange is set up, the two transactions being coupled by credit card accounting, then we approach the present forklift financing plan. One would, in effect, be paying for energy consumed, plus a service charge, just as one pays for electricity for the home or for energy in the form of gasoline. Under such circumstances, the electric car would not only cost less than the present car in primary investment, but even with a rather steep service charge for battery exchange, the operating cost would be much lower than that of the gasoline-engine car. Although much depends on the precise nature of the two different automobiles being compared—gasoline-powered versus electric—it has been conservatively estimated that the operating cost of the electric would run about one third that of the internal-combustion auto.

Professor Henri André's 2200-pound Dyna-Panhard car (somewhat smaller than present Corvair and Falcon compacts, which weigh 2600 and 2500 pounds, respectively), using silver-zinc batteries, has been running around Paris since 1954, gets a range of 150 miles on only one charge at a top speed of 50 miles per hour, and he claims, with vouchers to prove it, that the total operating cost has averaged one tenth that of a conventional car of the same weight. Of course, gasoline costs more in Europe because of the tax load, but the one-third ratio mentioned previously could obviously be improved both by technical advances and by the functioning of economic laws. For example, with more or less nationwide electrification of automobiles, the need for electric power would about double, since approximately one half of the energy consumed in the United States now goes into automotive use. Since the battery industry could do its recharging at off-peak hours, mainly at night, the cost of battery power should be reduced by as much as 20 percent. In this connection it is vitally important that additional power plants be so designed that the smog abolished by electrification of the automobile is not restored by burning more coal or higher-sulfur fuel. Indeed, the policy seems to be shaping up in southern California to require all new power plants to be nuclear, with incremental power to be obtained by long-distance transmission from the Northwest.

Perhaps the most important economic advantage would be an eventual reduction in automobile insurance rates. This stems from what could turn out in the long run to be the single greatest boon of the electric car—one that Warren Magnuson, senator from the state of Washington, has justifiably emphasized in his vigorous speeches—a reduction in the appalling mortality and injury rates from car accidents which at the present time far overshadow the smog problem. Senator Magnuson reasons that a new world of car safety could be attained if full advantage were taken of the degree of freedom allowed the designer in planning a new kind of vehicle in which the power package can be located in any convenient place, instead of wrapping a large glossy envelope around a fixed-position power plant as we do in the current automobiles. The present pusillanimous safety regulations consist, in effect, of adding things like belts (which only 20 percent of the drivers use, even when factory-installed) or substituting foam rubber for hard plastic or removing outside rear mirrors. But if we start from scratch, the inherent performance properties of the electric car (high low-speed torque, low maximum speed, low momentum because of light weight) could combine with clean, imaginative interior and exterior design to add a new dimension—systematic planning of the whole vehicle and its operating habits precisely and deliberately for safety. We might not have an idiot-proof car, but we would have one we could better entrust to teen-agers, old men, and the vast army of the absent-minded and accident-prone among us.

Hubert Humphrey has said, "You do not put in charge of transportation the man who runs the local livery stable." One might paraphrase this to read, "You do not put in charge of transportation, as it affects the nation's health and safety, the private companies which now make a hundred billion dollars from the gasoline-powered automobile." It is noteworthy, however, that both Ford and Chrysler are optimistic and that Ford is even working on a hybrid vehicle that would run on batteries in metropolitan areas and switch to gasoline power when out on the highways. The batteries would be recharged by the gasoline engine.

In addition to the enormous inertia of a vested energy industry (which includes the petroleum companies), we have public inertia and pride of car ownership to cope with. Frank Stead, chief of the Division of Environmental Sanitation, California State Department of Public Health, has demanded that state legislation be passed to serve legal notice that after 1980 no gasoline-powered motor vehicle shall be permitted to operate in California. Especially in the West, Mr. Stead points out, car ownership is a "deep-seated question of culture and self-image. . . . The West was won by men on horseback and the private motor is today's horse." His basic contention is that Western man will not go for mass transportation. But will he take a more modest horse?

To get the electric automobile on the streets before the Europeans take away the initiative (Great Britain has some 50,000 electric vehicles in continual operation and has ambitious plans), the best suggestion is probably that of Dr. M. L. Feldman of General Electric. His organization is in a strategic position since it has the only fuel cell development which eventually might make possible an electric car that could also run, without toxic emissions, on gasoline or kerosene and air.

Dr. Feldman believes that the first electric cars should be glorified golf carts, like the shopper-type electric vehicles used by old people in Long Beach, California, and that they should not be exposed to the dangerous abrasion of gasoline-powered traffic. They should be introduced in new cities, such as Irvine, California, where the community could be laid out with "transportation paths" to accommodate them. Eventually, when they graduate to the great smogged-in cities, separate streets and routes should be set aside for them.

As an indication that American enterprise is not going to wait for the turning of the ponderous wheels of Detroit, or even for a new kind of battery, Westinghouse Electric Corporation has announced an immediate program to make and sell electric cars. The model, several hundred of which will be offered for sale this year at "under $2000," is called the Markette, uses 12 six-volt conventional lead-acid batteries, reaches a top speed of 125 miles per hour in acceleration time of 12 seconds, and has a range of 50 miles between rechargings. It is recharged in 8 hours from an ordinary AC retractable-cord outlet.

In spite of the weight penalty of the antiquated battery system (800 pounds of battery for a total curb weight of 1630 pounds), Westinghouse is optimistic that the car will attract owners interested in two-passenger vehicles for short-range city driving. It is a noteworthy commercial experiment, and although it follows a series of failures by smaller concerns somewhat along the same line, one cannot afford to laugh it off. Westinghouse is a big company, and the Markette may prove to be the first salvo of a healthy cannonade which is bound to become more sophisticated as the battle goes on.

Donald Eaton Carr was born in Los Angeles and educated at Phillips Academy at Andover and at the University of California, where he was Phi Beta Kappa and graduated summa cum laude in 1930. He worked as a research chemist, supervisor, and manager from 1930 to 1947 for the Union Oil Company of California, then as director of research and as research consultant for the Phillips Petroleum Company. Since 1962 he has served as an independent research consultant in various fields. A contributor to numerous newspapers and periodicals, he is also the author of two books, *The Breath of Life: A Report on Air Pollution,* 1965, and *Death of the Sweet Waters,* 1966.

Vocabulary Study

From the list below, select the word or phrase nearest in meaning to the italicized word in the following excerpts. The list contains extra words.

A. the otherwise *inevitable* asphyxiation of our cities
B. problems have become *aggravated* to the point
C. the darkest of blind alleys is the *pathetic* attempt
D. it will stop *emitting* poisons
E. these are somewhat *ponderous*
F. it is an *uncanny* and delicious sensation

G. a marketing or dispensing *innovation*

H. with *incremental* power to be obtained by long-distance transmission

I. present *pusillanimous* safety regulations

J. Ford is even working on a *hybrid* vehicle

K. the enormous *inertia* of a *vested* energy industry

L. the dangerous *abrasion* of gasoline-powered traffic

fixed	inspiration	heavy
inactivity	heightened	pitiable
exuding	fainthearted	new method
unavoidable	wearing down	increased
thoughtful	one of mixed origin	preternaturally good

Questions on Form and Content

A. With what argument does the author begin his case?

B. With what does he compare the electric automobile throughout the article? On what grounds does he base his argument for the superiority of the electric automobile?

C. What does Mr. Carr predict to be the potential single greatest boon of the electric car? Why?

D. Who, according to the author, offer the most opposition to the development of the electric car?

E. What are some of the problems still to be solved in its development?

F. Do you find Mr. Carr's case convincing? Why or why not? In your reply, consider the evidence he uses to support his argument.

Suggestions for Writing

A. Write a paper refuting Mr. Carr's argument or present a case against the electric automobile.

B. Write a paper supporting Mr. Carr's case, supplying additional arguments for the electric automobile.

C. On February 13, 1968, John Newell, a reliability engineer on Lockheed's Poseidon missile program and an officer of the Santa Clara Valley Electric Automobile Association, said: "It's a cinch electric cars are coming. It's not a question of 'if' but 'when?' " He says his organization hopes to get younger people excited about electric cars. The engineers in his organization say that almost anyone can build his own electric car for a few hundred dollars, starting with a $30 military-surplus motor, and that the simplicity of the task lends itself to father-and-son garage programs. Members recently exhibited their experimental vehicles, including an "advanced vehicle design," a fiberglass-covered Volkswagen chassis, powered by a $30 nine-horsepower surplus electric engine. Concerning the feasibility of the electric automobile, Mr. Newell said: "We don't think it will replace the internal combustion engine, but it will complement it." How do you think it could best do so?

D. If you have seen an electric car, describe it. Would you like to own one? Why or why not?

E. Mr. Stead pointed out that car ownership, especially in the West, is a "deep-seated question of culture and self-image." Comment.

F. After quoting Mr. Stead's comment, "The West was won by men on horseback and the private motor is today's horse," Mr. Carr asks, "But will he [Western man] take a more modest horse?" How would you answer him? Why?

G. Would you like to drive a "glorified golf cart" like the electric vehicles used by the elderly in Long Beach, California? Why or why not?

H. In April, 1968, William S. Guttenberg, President of Bogue Electric Manufacturing Company, announced that the company is designing and developing an advanced propulsion system for a new prototype electric car which will upgrade the performance and range of existing experimental models. The new system for the "second-generation" electric car will include solid-state speed controls, regenerative electric braking, and a more efficient electric motor. Estimated maximum speed with the new propulsion system will be seventy miles per hour and its range will be extended by up to 25 percent on a charge, said Mr. Guttenberg. In the light of Mr. Carr's article, comment on this new or second-generation electric automobile.

I. In an interview in May, 1968, Henry Ford said: "There may be an electric car sometime for certain uses. Specifically, I'm not interested in really pushing hard on this project, but I don't want to discourage anyone else at Ford from doing what we are doing. [Ford won an electric-car sweepstakes in 1966 with the development of a long-life, lighter weight battery.] I don't see the electric car as a feasible method of transportation in my lifetime. . . . We have tremendous investment in facilities for engines, transmissions, and axles, and I can't see throwing these away just because the electric car doesn't emite fumes." He added that he preferred to work with major oil companies on research and development to prevent pollution. Discuss Mr. Ford's remarks in relation to Mr. Carr's article.

J. Is air pollution a problem in your state? If so, what is being done about it?

K. Mr. Carr says that Frank Stead, of the California State Department of Health, has demanded state legislation forbidding the operation of any gasoline-powered motor vehicle in California after 1980. Discuss the possible consequences of such a law. How would you assess its chances for enactment? for enforcement? Write a case for or against such legislation.

L. Mr. Carr says of electric automobiles: "Perhaps the most important economic advantage would be an eventual reduction in automobile insurance rates." Write a paper on present automobile insurance rates. Do you consider some plans discriminatory in regard to both age and sex? Why or why not? What is the best insurance plan you know? Use reasoning and evidence to support your answers.

M. In the search for an alternative to the internal-combustion machine, the steam car is being taken seriously again even though the Stanley brothers went bankrupt about forty-five years ago. A new steamer roadster, designed by Calvin and Charles Williams, can go 100 miles an hour and get 25 miles to a gallon of kerosene. Its proponents claim that far less development is required for its mass production than for the electric car. A study financed by the Ford Foundation revealed that modern steamers not only produce less pollution and noise than gasoline cars but are "smoother, simpler, peppier, and more economical." The Senate Commerce Committee scheduled hearings for May, 1968, to decide whether the government should finance further research. If you know of subsequent developments in the production of modern steamers, discuss them.

N. Write a case for another mode of transportation that is considered controversial, perhaps the motorcycle or a projected airplane that embodies extensive innovations.

O. In 1970, newspapers reported that a freon-vapor engine for automobiles would shortly go into production in Japan for the United States market. (Freon is a gas of the type used in refrigerators, freezers, air conditioners, and aerosol dispensers.) Ascertain the status of this project and explore the advantages and disadvantages of such power plants in respect to pollution, safety, efficiency, and other pertinent considerations.

P. Although the electric automobile promises to be less generative of pollutants than the internal-combustion gasoline automobile, it presents some problems. What about the battery material—lead, mercury, or other? Can these be kept out of the environment? Will our natural resources provide these materials in sufficient quantity? Can these materials be kept from polluting the environment after use? What may be the impact of need for additional electricity to charge batteries—additional powerplants? additional transmission facilities? peak demand and timing? What other problems occur to you or have been mentioned to you?

The writer must obtain coherence both within and between his paragraphs. In other words, his sentences and paragraphs must relate to each other in such a way that one sentence leads logically to another and one paragraph to the next. A basic arrangement of material which is naturally logical and clear is the first necessity. Most incoherent writing is a result of thinking in isolated sentences, for coherence naturally follows continuity of thought.

In this chapter, James Thurber's "Recollections of the Gas Buggy" is a good example of material which gains coherence primarily through a chronological ordering of events. After his introduction, Mr. Thurber uses a time sequence to reveal the fundamental incompatibility between him and the automobile.

An additional method of gaining coherence is the use of transitional words or phrases. These connectives are often used to introduce an example or illustration *(namely, for instance, for example, that is)*; to introduce a contrast or alternative *(but, on the other hand, on the contrary, or, nor, still, however, nevertheless);* to note an addition or conclusion *(and, again, next, in addition, moreover, finally, therefore, for, then, consequently, as a result, in conclusion).* Note the transitional words in Mr. White's first paragraph: *but, yet,* and *and.*

Transitions between sentences are established by the repetition of key words and ideas and by the use of pronouns to refer to words and ideas in the preceding sentence. Related sentence patterns are aids to continuity, too, as parallel thoughts are placed in parallel constructions and subordination is used to indicate the relation of less important ideas to main ideas.

Look at the second paragraph of "Farewell, My Lovely," and note how effectively the pronoun *it* is used repeatedly throughout the paragraph. Mr. White also uses the word *And* to begin sentence two, thereby gaining coherence through addition to his ideas. He also uses similar sentence patterns throughout the paragraph, usually giving his subject, the Model T, primary importance and position.

Transitional devices commonly used between paragraphs include starting a paragraph with a reference to the topic idea or last sentence of the preceding paragraph, ending a paragraph with a sentence which introduces the following paragraph, and using a transitional word (such as *furthermore, therefore,* or *on the contrary*) in the first sentence of a paragraph.

In "Recollections of the Gas Buggy," Mr. Thurber often achieves transition between paragraphs by reference to time. Note such introductory expressions as "Now that," "Years ago," "When I got," "Once when," and "After I had got back" with which he begins his paragraphs.

As you read these essays, pay particular attention to the methods used to obtain coherence within sentences, between sentences, and between paragraphs.

Farewell, My Lovely!

Lee Strout White
(E. B. White)

An Aging Male Kisses an Old Flame Goodbye, circa 1936

I see by the new Sears Roebuck catalogue that it is still possible to buy an axle for a 1909 Model T Ford, but I am not deceived. The great days have faded, the end is in sight. Only one page in the current catalogue is devoted to parts and accessories for the Model T; yet everyone remembers springtimes

☐ Lee Strout White (E. B. White), "Farewell, My Lovely!" in *The Second Tree from the Corner* (New York, 1954), pp. 32-40. This essay originally appeared in *The New Yorker* over the pseudonym Lee Strout White. It was suggested by a manuscript submitted to the magazine by Richard Lee Strout and was written by E. B. White. Reprinted by permission. published in book form by G. P. Putnam under the title *Farewell to Model T,* in 1936. Reprinted under its original title in *The Second Tree from the Corner,* by E. B. White, Harper & Brothers, 1954.

when the Ford gadget section was larger than men's clothing, almost as large as household furnishings. The last Model T was built in 1927, and the car is fading from what scholars call the American scene—which is an understatement, because to a few million people who grew up with it, the old Ford practically *was* the American scene.

It was the miracle God had wrought. And it was patently the sort of thing that could only happen once. Mechanically uncanny, it was like nothing that had ever come to the world before. Flourishing industries rose and fell with it. As a vehicle, it was hardworking, commonplace, heroic; and it often seemed to transmit those qualities to the persons who rode in it. My own generation identifies it with Youth, with its gaudy, irretrievable excitements; before it fades into the mist, I would like to pay it the tribute of the sigh that is not a sob, and set down random entries in a shape somewhat less cumbersome than a Sears Roebuck catalogue.

The Model T was distinguished from all other makes of cars by the fact that its transmission was of a type known as planetary—which was half metaphysics, half sheer friction. Engineers accepted the word "planetary" in its epicyclic sense, but I was always conscious that it also meant "wandering," "erratic." Because of the peculiar nature of this planetary element, there was always, in Model T, a certain dull rapport between engine and wheels, and even when the car was in a state known as neutral, it trembled with a deep imperative and tended to inch forward. There was never a moment when the bands were not faintly egging the machine on. In this respect it was like a horse, rolling the bit on its tongue, and country people brought to it the same technique they used with draft animals.

Its most remarkable quality was its rate of acceleration. In its palmy days the Model T could take off faster than anything on the road. The reason was simple. To get under way, you simply hooked the third finger of the right hand around a lever on the steering column, pulled down hard, and shoved your left foot forcibly against the low-speed pedal. These were simple, positive motions; the car responded by lunging forward with a roar. After a few seconds of this turmoil, you took your toe off the pedal, eased up a mite on the throttle, and the car, possessed of only two forward speeds, catapulted directly into high with a series of ugly jerks and was off on its glorious errand. The abruptness of this departure was never equalled in other cars of the period. The human leg was (and still is) incapable of letting in a clutch with anything like the forthright abandon that used to send Model T on its way. Letting in a clutch is a negative, hesitant motion, depending on delicate nervous control; pushing down the Ford pedal was a simple, country motion—an expansive act, which came as natural as kicking an old door to make it budge.

The driver of the old Model T was a man enthroned. The car, with top up, stood seven feet high. The driver sat on top of the gas tank, brooding it with his own body. When he wanted gasoline, he alighted, along with everything else in the front seat; the seat was pulled off, the metal cap unscrewed, and a wooden stick thrust down to sound the liquid in the well. There were always a couple of these sounding sticks kicking around in the ratty sub-cushion regions of a flivver. Refuelling was more of a social function then, because the driver had to unbend, whether he wanted to or not. Directly in front of the driver was the windshield —high, uncompromisingly erect. Nobody talked about air resistance, and the four cylinders pushed the car through the atmosphere with a simple disregard of physical law.

There was this about a Model T: the purchaser never regarded his purchase as a complete, finished product. When you bought a Ford, you figured you had a start—a vibrant, spirited framework to which could be screwed an almost limitless assortment of decorative and functional hardware. Driving away from the agency, hugging the new wheel between your knees, you were already full of creative worry. A Ford was born naked as a baby, and a flourishing industry grew up out of correcting its rare deficiencies and combatting its fascinating diseases. Those were the great days of lily-painting. I have been looking at some old Sears Roebuck catalogues, and they bring everything back so clear.

First you bought a Ruby Safety Reflector for the rear, so that your posterior would glow in another's car's brilliance. Then you invested thirty-nine cents in some radiator Moto Wings, a popular ornament which gave the Pegasus touch to the machine and did something godlike to the owner. For nine cents you bought a fanbelt guide to keep the belt from slipping off the pulley.

You bought a radiator compound to stop leaks. This was as much a part of everybody's equipment as aspirin tablets are of a medicine cabinet. You bought special oil to prevent chattering, a clamp-on dash light, a patching outfit, a tool box which you bolted to the running board, a sun visor, a steering-column brace to keep the column rigid, and a set of emergency containers for gas, oil, and water —three thin, disc-like cans which reposed in a case on the running board during long, important journeys—red for gas, gray for water, green for oil. It was only a beginning. After the car was about a year old, steps were taken to check the alarming disintegration. (Model T was full of tumors, but they were benign.) A set of anti-rattlers (ninety-eight cents) was a popular panacea. You hooked them on to the gas and spark rods, to the brake pull rod, and to the steering-rod connections. Hood silencers, of black rubber, were applied to the fluttering hood. Shock-absorbers and snubbers gave "complete relaxation." Some people bought rubber pedal pads, to fit over the standard metal pedals. (I didn't like these, I remember.) Persons of a suspicious or pugnacious turn of mind bought a rear-view mirror; but most Model T owners weren't worried by what was coming from behind because they would soon enough see it out in front. They rode in a state of cheerful catalepsy. Quite a large mutinous clique among Ford owners went over to a foot accelerator (you could buy one and screw it to the floor board), but there was a certain madness in these people, because the Model T, just as she stood, had a choice of three foot pedals to push, and there were plenty of moments when both feet were occupied in the routine performance of duty and when the only way to speed up the engine was with the hand throttle.

Gadget bred gadget. Owners not only bought ready-made gadgets, they invented gadgets to meet special needs. I myself drove my car directly from the agency to the blacksmith's, and had the smith affix two enormous iron brackets to the port running board to support an army trunk.

People who owned closed models builded along different lines: they bought ball grip handles for opening doors, window anti-rattlers, and de-luxe flower vases of the cut-glass anti-splash type. People with delicate sensibilities garnished their car with a device called the Donna Lee Automobile Disseminator—a porous vase guaranteed, according to Sears, to fill the car with a "faint clean odor of lavender." The gap between open cars and closed cars was not as great then as it is now: for $11.95, Sears Roebuck converted your touring car into a sedan and you went forth renewed. One agreeable quality of the old Fords was that they had no bumpers, and their fenders softened and wilted with the years and permitted the driver to squeeze in and out of tight places.

Tires were 30 × 3½, cost about twelve dollars, and punctured readily. Everybody carried a Jiffy patching set, with a nutmeg grater to roughen the tube before the goo was spread on. Everybody was capable of putting on a patch, expected to have to, and did have to.

During my association with Model T's, self-starters were not a prevalent accessory. They were expensive and under suspicion. Your car came equipped with a serviceable crank, and the first thing you learned was how to Get Results. It was a special trick, and until you learned it (usually from another Ford owner, but sometimes by a period of appalling experimentation) you might as well have been winding up an awning. The trick was to leave the ignition switch off, proceed to the animal's head, pull the choke (which was a little wire protruding through the radiator) and give the crank two or three nonchalant upward lifts. Then, whistling as though thinking about something else, you would saunter back to the driver's cabin, turn the ignition on, return to the crank, and this time, catching it on the down stroke, give it a quick spin with plenty of That. If this procedure was followed, the engine almost always responded—first with a few scattered explosions, then with a tumultuous gunfire, which you checked by racing around to the driver's seat and retarding the throttle. Often, if the emergency brake hadn't been pulled all the way back, the car advanced on you the instant the first explosion occurred and you would hold it back by leaning your weight against it. I can still feel my old Ford nuzzling me at the curb, as though looking for an apple in my pocket.

In zero weather, ordinary cranking became an impossibility, except for giants. The oil thickened, and it became necessary to jack up the rear wheels, which, for some planetary reason, eased the throw.

The lore and legend that governed the Ford were boundless. Owners had their own theories about everything; they discussed mutual problems in that wise, infinitely resourceful way old women discuss rheumatism. Exact knowledge was pretty scarce, and often proved less effective than superstition. Dropping a camphor ball into the gas tank was a popular expedient; it seemed to have a tonic effect on both man and machine. There wasn't much to base exact knowledge on. The Ford driver flew blind. He didn't know the temperature of his engine, the speed of his car, the amount of his fuel, or the pressure of his oil (the old Ford lubricated itself by what was amiably described as the "splash system"). A speedometer cost money and was an extra, like a windshield-wiper. The dashboard of the early models was bare save for an ignition key; later models, grown effete, boasted an ammeter which pulsated alarmingly with the throbbing of the car. Under the dash was a box of coils, with vibrators which you adjusted, or thought you adjusted. Whatever the driver learned of his motor, he learned not through instruments but through sudden developments. I remember that the timer was one of the vital organs about which there was ample doctrine. When everything else had been checked, you "had a look" at the timer. It was an extravagantly odd little device, simple in construction, mysterious in function. It contained a roller, held by a spring, and there were four contact points on the inside of the case against which, many people believed, the roller rolled. I have had a timer apart on a sick Ford many times. But I never really knew what I was up to—I was just showing off before God. There were almost as many schools of thought as there were timers. Some people, when things went wrong, just clenched their teeth and gave the timer a smart crack with a wrench. Other people opened it up and blew on it. There was a school that held that the timer needed large amounts of oil; they fixed it by frequent baptism. And there was a school that was positive it was meant to run dry as a bone; these people were continually taking it off and wiping it. I remember once spitting into a timer; not in anger, but in a spirit of research. You see, the Model T driver moved in the realm of metaphysics. He believed his car could be hexed.

One reason the Ford anatomy was never reduced to an exact science was that, having "fixed" it, the owner couldn't honestly claim that the treatment had brought about the cure. There were too many authenticated cases of Fords fixing themselves—restored naturally to health after a short rest. Farmers soon discovered this, and it fitted nicely with their draft-horse philosophy: "Let 'er cool off and she'll snap into it again."

A Ford owner had Number One Bearing constantly in mind. This bearing, being at the front end of the motor, was the one that always burned out, because the oil didn't reach it when the car was climbing hills. (That's what I was always told, anyway.) The oil used to recede and leave Number One dry as a clam flat; you had to watch that bearing like a hawk. It was like a weak heart—you could hear it start knocking, and that was when you stopped to let her cool off. Try as you would to keep the oil supply right, in the end Number One always went out. "Number One Bearing burned out on me and I had to have her replaced," you would say, wisely; and your companions always had a lot to tell about how to protect and pamper Number One to keep her alive.

Sprinkled not too liberally among the millions of amateur witch doctors who drove Fords and applied their own abominable cures were the heaven-sent mechanics who could really make the car talk. These professionals turned up in undreamed-of spots. One time, on the banks of the Columbia River in Washington, I heard the rear end go out of my Model T when I was trying to whip it up a steep incline onto the deck of a ferry. Something snapped; the car slid backward into the mud. It seemed to me like the end of the trail. But the captain of the ferry, observing the withered remnant, spoke up.

"What's got her?" he asked.

"I guess it's the rear end," I replied, listlessly. The captain leaned over the rail and stared. Then I saw that there was a hunger in his eyes that set him off from other men.

"Tell you what," he said, carelessly, trying to cover up his eagerness, "Let's pull the son of a bitch up onto the boat, and I'll help you fix her while we're going back and forth on the river."

We did just this. All that day I plied between the towns of Pasco and Kennewick, while the skipper (who had once worked in a Ford garage) directed the amazing work of resetting the bones of my car.

Springtime in the heyday of the Model T was a delirious season. Owning a car was still a major excitement, roads were still wonderful and bad. The Fords were obviously conceived in madness: any car which was capable of going from forward into reverse without any perceptible mechanical hiatus was bound to be a mighty challenging thing to the human imagination. Boys used to veer them off the highway into a level pasture and run wild with them, as though they were cutting up with a girl. Most everybody used the reverse pedal quite as much as the regular foot brake—it distributed the wear over the bands and wore them all down evenly. That was the big trick, to wear all the bands down evenly, so that the final chattering would be total and the whole unit scream for renewal.

The days were golden, the nights were dim and strange. I still recall with trembling those loud, nocturnal crises when you drew up to a signpost and raced the engine so the lights would be bright enough to read destinations by. I have never been really planetary since. I suppose it's time to say goodbye. Farewell, my lovely!

Elwyn Brooks White, born in Mount Vernon, New York, received his A.B. degree from Cornell University and honorary Doctorates of Literature from Dartmouth, the University of Maine, Yale, Bowdoin, Hamilton, and Harvard. He served as a private in the United States Army in 1918 and began his career as a reporter in 1921. He was a free-lance writer and contributing editor for the *New Yorker Magazine* and a contributor to the monthly department of *Harper's Magazine* from 1938 to 1943. A recipient of the gold medal of the American Academy of Arts and Sciences and of the Presidential Medal of Freedom, he is the author of *The Lady Is Cold* (poems, 1929), *Is Sex Necessary?* (with James Thurber, 1929), *Every Day Is Saturday* (1934), *One Man's Meat* (1942), *Here Is New York* (1949), *Charlotte's Web* (1952), *The Second Tree from the Corner* (1954), and *The Points of My Compass* (1962). He revised William Strunk, Jr.'s, *The Elements of Style* in 1959 and edited *A Subtreasury of American Humor* (with Katherine S. White) in 1941.

Vocabulary Study

From the list below, select the word nearest in meaning to the italicized word in these excerpts from "Farewell, My Lovely!" The list contains extra words.

A. And it was *patently* the sort of thing that could only happen once.

B. Mechanically *uncanny,* it was like nothing that had ever come to the world before.

C. My own generation identifies it with Youth, with its gaudy, *irretrievable* excitements

D. a shape somewhat less *cumbersome* than a Sears Roebuck catalogue

E. a certain dull *rapport* between engine and wheels

F. Persons of a suspicious or *pugnacious* turn of mind

G. self-starters were not a *prevalent* accessory

H. Dropping a camphor ball into the gas tank was a popular *expedient;* it seemed to have a *tonic* effect on both man and machine.

I. one of the vital organs about which there was *ample* doctrine

J. amateur witch doctors who drove Fords and applied their own *abominable* cures

admirable	cunning	accord
unwieldy	common	kindly
irrecoverable	detestable	quarrelsome
weird	sufficient	bracing
clearly	device	cure-all

Questions on Form and Content

A. How does Mr. White begin his essay?

B. What tone does he establish in his introduction?

C. What distinguished the Model T from all other makes of cars?

D. What were some of the accessories, the "almost limitless assortment of decorative and functional hardware," that most owners purchased?

E. What did the dashboard of the early models contain?

F. Why was the Number One Bearing particularly vulnerable?

G. Mr. White personifies the Model T throughout the essay. What gender or genders does he use for it? Go through the essay again to see how many examples you can find of this extended, and mixed, personification.

H. How does Mr. White conclude the essay?

Suggestions for Writing

A. Mr. White writes with nostalgia about the demise of the Model T. We are witnessing the diminishing use and gradual elimination of another form of locomotion: the passenger train. If you have fond recollections of train rides and regret that future generations may have no opportunity for similar experiences, write a farewell to the locomotive.

B. Mr. White recalls that the section of the Sears Roebuck catalogue devoted to parts and accessories was once longer than the section on men's clothing. What gadgets are available for today's automobiles? How do they differ in purpose and appearance from those Mr. White describes? Which car accessories do you consider essential, which desirable, which merely decorative?

C. Concerning the Model T, Mr. White writes: "As a vehicle, it was hardworking, commonplace, heroic; and it often seemed to transmit those qualities to the persons who rode in it. My own generation identifies it with Youth. . . ." Do you associate certain human characteristics with certain cars? If so, give some examples and state your reasons.

D. The Model T owner could invest thirty-nine cents in radiator Moto Wings and give a Pegasus touch to his automobile. Discuss some subsequent and more current fads in radiator and hood ornaments.

E. "The lore and legend that governed the Ford were boundless," writes Mr. White. Do you have a favorite anecdote about a car you have driven? If so, relate it.

F. The dashboard of the early-model Fords contained only an ignition key, according to Mr. White. Describe the dashboard of a contemporary automobile with which you are familiar.

G. In the title and subtitle, Mr. White refers to the Model T as "My Lovely" and "an old flame." Does he maintain the personification throughout? If so, how? Does the car sometimes seem to have masculine characteristics?

ANTIQUE

Moulin Studios, S.F.

Recollections of the Gas Buggy

James Thurber

Footnotes to an Era for the Future Historian

Now that the humorous magazines have taken to printing drawings of horses rearing at the sight of an automobile, and of children exclaiming as a car goes by, "What is that thing, Mamma? Mamma, what is that thing, huh, Mamma?," it is perhaps not out of place to prepare some small memorial in advance of the passing of the motor car. It appears to have reached, on its way backward to oblivion, what corresponds roughly to the year 1903.

I think that no one has drawn a darker or more vivid picture of the approaching doom of the gas engine than Mrs. Robertson, the aged colored washerwoman whose prophecies and pronouncements I have the privilege of listening to every

□James Thurber, "Recollections of the Gas Buggy," in *The Thurber Carnival* (New York, 1945), pp. 36-40.

Monday morning. Mrs. Robertson is, for my money, an extremely sound woman, although admittedly my judgment of soundness has sometimes been questioned.

Some of the opinions of Mrs. Robertson which I recall offhand are these: "If you don't pay no mind to diseases, they will go away." "The night was made partly for rest and partly as a punishment for the sinful." And "The government only allows you to keep furniture for two months." This last conviction grows out of Mrs. Robertson's habit of buying furniture on the installment plan and failing to keep up her payments longer than six or seven weeks, with the result that the things are repossessed. She looks upon this recurring ritual in her domestic life as a form of federal taxation.

Mrs. Robertson's beliefs and feelings about the future of the automobile (which I have been leading up to) go like this: the oil supplies of the world are being dried up in order to prevent future wars. This will also put an end forever to pleasure driving, but that is all right because, if people kept on riding in cars, they would soon lose the use of both legs, and the life of Man would pass from the earth.

If Mrs. Robertson is right in her predictions, I should like to set down my own few unique experiences with gas-driven vehicles before I forget them. They may possibly serve as footnotes to the work of some future historian, lightening a little the dolorous annals of the automobile.

Let me admit, to begin with, that the automobile and I were never in tune with each other. There was a fundamental incompatibility between us that amounted at times almost to chemical repulsion. I have felt the headlights of an automobile following me the way the eyes of a cat follow the ominous activities of a neighbor's dog. Some of the machines I have owned have seemed to me to bridle slightly when I got under the wheel. Neither the motor car nor myself would greatly mourn if one of us were suddenly extinguished.

Years ago, an aunt of my father's came to visit us one winter in Columbus, Ohio. She enjoyed the hallucination, among others, that she was able to drive a car. I was riding with her one December day when I discovered, to my horror, that she thought the red and green lights on the traffic signals had been put up by the municipality as a gay and expansive manifestation of the Yuletide spirit. Although we finally reached home safely, I never completely recovered from the adventure, and could not be induced, after that day, to ride in a car on holidays.

When I got an automobile of my own and began to drive it, I brought to the enterprise a magnificent ignorance of the workings of a gas engine, and a profound disinterest in its oily secrets. On several occasions, worried friends of an engineering turn of mind attempted to explain the nature of gas engines to me, but they succeeded only in losing me in a mechanical maze of terminology. I developed the notion that the gas engine was more soundly constructed than I was. I elaborate this point only to show you on what unequal terms the motor car and I were brought together.

Out of my long and dogged bouts with automobiles of various makes, there comes back to me now only one truly pleasurable experience. There may have been others, but I doubt it. I was driving in the British Isles in 1938, and came one day to a sudden, coughing stop in a far and lonely section of Scotland. The car had run out of gas in the wilderness. This car's gasoline gauge had a trick of mounting toward "Full" instead of sinking toward "Empty" when the tank was running low, one of many examples of pure cussedness of which it was capable. There I was, miles from any village, with not even a farmhouse in sight. On my left was a thick woods, out of which the figure of a man suddenly appeared. He asked me what was the matter, and I said I had run out of petrol. "It just happens," he told me, "that I have a can of petrol." With that, he went back into the woods, and came out again with a five-gallon can of gasoline. He put it in the tank for me, I thanked him, paid for it, and drove on.

Once when I was telling this true but admittedly remarkable story, at a party in New York, a bright-eyed young woman exclaimed, "But when the man emerged from the lonely woods, miles away from any village, far from the nearest farmhouse, carrying a five-gallon can of gasoline, why didn't you ask him how he happened to be there with it?" I lighted a cigarette. "Madam," I said, "I was afraid he would vanish." She gave a small laugh and moved away from me. Everybody always does.

Another experience I had in England the same year helped to shake the faith of at least one Briton in the much-vaunted Yankee affinity for machinery. The battery of my car had run down in a village about twenty miles from York, my destination. I put in a call to a garage and a young mechanic showed up presently in a wrecking car. He said he would give me a tow for a few yards. I was to let the clutch in and out (or out and in, whichever it is) and start the engine that way. It is a device as old as the automobile itself, and years before I had managed it successfully. Any child or old lady can do it.

So he attached a rope to the back of his car and the front of mine, and we were off. I kept letting the clutch out and in (or in and out) madly, but nothing happened. The garage man kept stopping every 500 yards or so and coming back to consult with me. He was profoundly puzzled. It was farther than he had ever dragged a car in his life. We must have gone, in this disheartening manner, about a third of the way to York. Finally he got out for the seventh time and said to me, "What gear have you got her in?" I didn't have her in any gear. I had her in neutral. She had been in neutral all the while.

Now, as any child or old lady knows, you have to have her in gear. If she is in neutral, it is like trying to turn on the electric lights when there are no bulbs in the sockets. The garage mechanic looked at me with the special look garage mechanics reserve for me. It is a mixture of incredulity, bewilderment, and distress. I put her in low gear, he gave me a short haul, and she started. I paid him and, as I drove off, I could see him in the rear-view mirror, standing in the road still staring after me with that look.

After I had got back to America (safe and sound, to the surprise of my friends), I produced this same expression on the face of a garage man in Connecticut one afternoon. I had driven the same car from Newtown to Litchfield on a crisp October day. It happened that I was just getting over an attack of grippe, and still running a temperature of a couple of degrees. The car, out of plain deviltry, began to run one, too. The red fluid in the engine gauge on the dashboard started to rise alarmingly. It got to the point marked "Danger." I drove into a garage in a pretty jumpy state of mind. A garage man looked at the gauge and said the thermostat was clogged—or something of the kind. I was standing outside the car, staring at the dashboard and its, to me, complicated dials, when I noticed to my horror that one of them registered 1560. I pointed a shaking finger at it and said to the mechanic, "That dial shouldn't be registering as high as all that, should it?" He gave me the same look I had got from the man in England. "That's your radio dial, Mac," he said. "You got her set at WQXR."

I got into the car and drove home. The garage man stared after me until I was out of sight. He is probably still telling it around.

My temperature rose a degree that night, and I developed a theory about my automobile. The thing possessed, I decided, a certain antic intelligence, akin to that of a six-months-old poodle. It had run a temperature that afternoon out of mischief and mockery, because I was running one. It had deliberately betrayed me in the Scottish wilderness that other afternoon, by running its gasoline gauge toward "Full" instead of "Empty." I began to wonder what I had done to the car to arouse its malice. Finally I put my finger on it. The car had probably never forgiven me for an incident that had occurred at the border between Belgium and France one day in 1937.

We had stopped at the Belgium customs on our way into France. A customs man leaned into the car, glanced at the mileage recorded on the speedometer, and said something in French. I thought he said I would have to pay one franc for every kilometer the car had travelled. I was loudly indignant in French and in English. The car had gone about 35,000 miles. I figured this out in kilometers, and it came roughly to 55,000. Changing that figure into francs and then into dollars, still loudly and angrily, I estimated I would have to pay around $1800 to the Belgian customs. The customs man kept trying to get a word in, and so did my wife, but I roared on to my peroration. I shouted that the car had not cost one half of $1800 when it was new, and even then it hadn't been worth a third of that. I announced that I would not pay as much as fifty dollars to drive the car into Oz or Never-Never Land *(Jamais-Jamais Pays).*

The engine, which had been running, stopped. The customs man finally got in a word. Dismissing me as obviously insane, he spoke to my wife. He shouted that he had said nothing about $1800 or even eight dollars. He had simply made some small comment on the distance the car had gone. As far as he was concerned, we could drive it to *Jamais-Jamais Pays* and stay there. He turned on his heel and stalked away, and I started the motor. It took quite a while. The car was acting up. The night my fever rose, I thought I knew why. It had resented the slighting remarks I made about its value and had determined to get even with me.

It got even with me in more ways than I have described.

Whenever I tried to put chains on a tire, the car would maliciously wrap them around a rear axle. If I parked it ten feet from a fire plug and went into a store, it would be only five feet from the plug when I came out. If it saw a nail in the road, the car would swerve and pick the nail up. Once, driving into a bleak little town in the Middle West, I said aloud, "I'd hate to be stuck in this place." The car promptly burned out a bearing, and I was stuck there for two days.

If Mrs. Robertson is right in her prophecy, and the gas engine is really on the way out, it will be no dire blow for me. I will move within roller-skating distance of a grocery, a drugstore, a church, a library, and a movie house. If the worst comes to the worst, I could even walk.

JAMES THURBER (1894-1961) was born in Columbus, Ohio, and attended Ohio State University. He was a reporter in the United States and abroad before joining the staff of the *New Yorker,* to which he contributed sketches, essays, and drawings for over thirty years. He is remembered for the irony, satire, and whimsical humor of his essays, short stories, sketches, drama, and cartoons. Co-author with E. B. White of *Is Sex Necessary?* in 1929, he later wrote *My Life and Hard Times* (1933), *Let Your Mind Alone* (1937), *My World—and Welcome to It* (1942), and *Fables for Our Times* (1940-1956).

Vocabulary Study

A. Much of James Thurber's humor results from his combination of words not ordinarily occurring together. Comment on the meaning of the individual words in the italicized phrases; then on their meaning in combination.

1. I brought to the enterprise a *magnificent ignorance* of the workings of a gas engine, and a *profound disinterest* in its *oily secrets.*
2. one of many examples of *pure cussedness* of which it was capable

B. From the list below, select the word nearest in meaning to the italicized word in the following excerpts. The list contains extra words.

1. on its way backward to *oblivion*
2. the *dolorous annals* of the automobile
3. She enjoyed the *hallucination,* among others, that she was able to drive a car.
4. the much-*vaunted* Yankee *affinity* for machinery
5. It is a mixture of *incredulity,* bewilderment, and distress.
6. The thing possessed, I decided, a certain *antic* intelligence, akin to that of a six-months-old poodle.
7. I began to wonder what I had done to the car to arouse its *malice.*
8. I roared on to my *peroration.*

petulant	derided
sad	delusion
boasted	natural liking
unbelief	yearly records
spite	ludicrous
conclusion	pertinence
state of being forgotten	

Questions on Form and Content

A. How does Mr. Thurber begin his recollections? How does he conclude them? What is the purpose of the framework?

B. Comment on the soundness of Mrs. Robertson's observations. How do they reflect her personal experiences?

C. Who is the chief target of Mr. Thurber's humor? Do you consider the essay funny? Why or why not?

D. What was his one truly pleasurable experience in his innumerable bouts with automobiles? Why was it pleasurable?

E. To what did he ascribe the malice of one of his automobiles?

F. How does he view the projected demise of the gas vehicle? How will he manage without it?

Suggestions for Writing

A. If you, like Mr. Thurber, are fundamentally incompatible with the automobile, recount some of your experiences.

B. The author says that his father's aunt "enjoyed the hallucination, among others, that she was able to drive a car." If you have ridden with a similarly deluded individual, relate your adventure.

C. Write a paper based on one of Mrs. Robertson's opinions.

D. Relate one of your truly pleasurable experiences with the automobile.

E. "He is probably still telling it around," says Mr. Thurber of the garage mechanic in Connecticut before whom Mr. Thurber had confused the radio dial with the temperature gauge. Relate a comparable episode, on any subject, which you consider worth repeating.

F. Mr. Thurber's difficulties with the Belgium customs official resulted from a linguistic confusion. Describe an incident caused by a similar type of misunderstanding.

G. How important is the automobile to you? How would you cope with a world without cars?

H. Write an essay, using Mr. Thurber's as a model, on the passing of the motorcycle—or the airplane.

I. Analyze the humor in "Recollections of the Gas Buggy."

J. Compare and contrast Mr. White's view of the automobile with Mr. Thurber's.

Handles with Care

Harland Manchester

Dr. William Haddon, Jr.,
Administrator,
The National Traffic Agency

Dear Mr. Haddon:

As a taxpayer and motor vehicle driver I wish to thank you for your interest in the safety of my vehicle. It is nice of you to invite comment, and I have an idea which may help. It seems to me that you have neglected one of the most dangerous components of today's automobile. This single feature, fraught with deadly peril, has probably caused more highway deaths than all other faulty parts rolled into one. And unlike other booby traps concealed in the car's vitals, it is visible, highly publicized, and can be easily corrected at trifling expense.

I refer to the names of cars. What good are grim warnings about safety when you put a man behind the wheel of a Fury, a Sting Ray, a Tempest, a Thunderbird?

□ Harland Manchester, "Handles with Care," from "The Phoenix Nest," *Saturday Review* (December 24, 1966), 2.

Why bother with seat belts when you blast off at the controls of a Comet, a Polara, a Galaxie? We can double the State Police forces and they will be helpless before the wild zeal of the man who owns a Mustang, a Wildcat, a Spyder, or a Barracuda.

The wise men tell us that these names are chosen not only to stimulate man's urge for speed and power: they are also designed as aphrodisiacs to incite old men to act younger and to make children act older. In any case it is crystal-clear that drivers of all ages, most of them sane and sober before they turn the key in the switch, are automatically transformed into Monte Carlo maniacs with James Bond syndromes.

This grave situation can be corrected in thirty days flat. All you have to do is pass a law to make the manufacturers call back all the cars and rename them. To help you out, I have compiled lists of pre-tested names, all guaranteed not to increase the pulse rate, blood pressure, or amorous appetite. For example, a Mustang becomes a Dobbin, a Sting Ray becomes a Sand Flea, a Tempest becomes a Teapot, a Spyder becomes a Fly, a Wildcat becomes a Kittycar.

For future models, I have pre-tested names according to the age brackets of potential drivers. For the late teens and early twenties I recommend the names of pleasant, unexciting but noble little beasts, like Lamb, Ant, Burro, Beaver, Tortoise, or Commuter.

For middle-aged marrieds, names symbolizing domestic bliss, like Peace, Moderation, Meat Loaf, Rocker, Stroller, or PTA.

For the moneyed prestige-seekers, there are solid names: Cashier, Teller, Security, Debenture, Bookkeeper, and Dow-Jones.

For senior citizens the category could include: Medicar, Myopia, Thrombosis, Mayo, Mt. Sinai, and Forest Lawn. I had included Sexagenarian in this category, but early testings indicated confusion in the potential market: teen-agers outnumber senior citizens ten to one.

It has been proved conclusively by computer trial runs that this single change in the American auto will reduce traffic fatalities by several per cent.

I certainly hope you get busy on this.

Respectfully yours,
HARLAND MANCHESTER

HARLAND MANCHESTER, born in Barnet, Vermont, is a graduate of Phillips Exeter Academy and Dartmouth College. After serving as a reporter for the *Boston Post* and *Boston Herald,* he became a free-lance writer and, since 1943, a roving reporter for *Reader's Digest.* The author of approximately two hundred articles, mainly on science and technology, for periodicals including *Scribner's, Harper's Magazine, Atlantic Monthly, Saturday Evening Post,* and *American Mercury,* he has also written numerous play and book reviews and two books, *The New World of Machines,* 1945, and *Trail Blazers of Technology,* 1962.

Vocabulary Study

Mr. Manchester's letter is a study in what Paul Roberts calls colorful, and colored, words. The names of most cars are designedly both colorful and colored. They are "calculated to produce a picture or induce an emotion." They are "loaded with associations, good or bad," depending on one's point of view.

A. What associations do the following names of cars, aside from the automobiles they represent, have for you?

Fury	Galaxie
Sting Ray	Mustang
Tempest	Wildcat
Thunderbird	Spyder
Comet	Barracuda
Polara	

B. How do the following pairs of words, representing name changes for cars which Mr. Manchester would make mandatory, reflect contrasting associations and situations? What familiar sayings do some of them invoke?

Mustang—Dobbin	Sting Ray—Sand Flea
Tempest—Teapot	Spyder—Fly
Wildcat—Kittycar	

C. What are the connotations of the following "pleasant, unexciting but noble little beasts" which Mr. Manchester suggests as names for cars to be driven by people in their late teens and early twenties?

Lamb	Burro	Tortoise
Ant	Beaver	Commuter

Questions on Form and Content

A. Mr. Manchester casts his material in the form of an open letter. To whom does he address it? In what role is he writing? What is his topic? What does the term "open" imply?

B. What is the tone of the letter?

C. Mr. Manchester suggests names "guaranteed not to increase the pulse rate, blood pressure, or amorous appetite." What importance do you attribute to the names of automobiles? As a selling device, to what instincts or motives are manufacturers appealing?

D. Why did Mr. Manchester omit the name Sexagenarian from his category? In what two groups of the general market did confusion over the meaning of the word arise? What does the word mean?

E. By what method, according to Mr. Manchester, has it been proved that his suggested change will reduce traffic fatalities by several per cent?

F. Discuss the significance of the title "Handles with Care."

Suggestions for Writing

A. Write an open letter in answer to Mr. Manchester, in the vein in which you think Dr. Haddon might reply.

B. Write the reply you think a representative of General Motors might make to Mr. Manchester's idea.

C. Write a reply to Mr. Manchester as a member of the late-teens or early-twenties set.

D. Some names of cars not mentioned by Mr. Manchester have now attained associations, either pleasant or unpleasant, in addition to their original meanings. Antoine de la Mothe Cadillac (1657?-1730) was a French explorer who founded Detroit. What connotations does the word Cadillac now have? Edsel Bryant Ford (1893-1943) was the son of Henry Ford and served as President of the Ford Motor Company from 1919 until his death. Edsel was the name selected, after much pondering, for one of the Ford automobiles—no longer in production. What associations does the word Edsel now have?

E. Discuss the names and connotations of some of the antique cars, such as the Stutz Bearcat and the Stanley Steamer.

F. Write a paper on the names of some cars not mentioned by Mr. Manchester. You might consider the Dart, the Rambler, the Charger, the Country Squire, the Estate Wagon, and the Lincoln among others.

G. Discuss the car as a status symbol.

H. Henry Ford was the largest automobile manufacturer in the world. He designed his Model T in 1909 and over 15,000,000 cars were sold before the model was discontinued and the Model A was created, in 1928, to meet growing competition. The Model T is now a part of American folklore and is known by more nicknames than any other automobile: Baby Lincoln, bouncing Betty, dehorn, flivver, Henrietta, Henry's go-cart, Michigan mistake, perpetual pest, Spirit of Detroit, Model T-Pot, Tin Lizzie, and Tin Lizzard are among the number. Discuss nicknames you have used or have heard used for other automobiles. What is their significance?

I. What is a clunker? A jalopy? Are they terms of opprobrium or praise? Define each term, using examples.

J. Suggest, in all seriousness, your own list of appropriate names for cars. Defend at least some of your choices.

K. Shakespeare wrote, in quite another context, "What's in a name? That which we call a rose/By any other name would smell as sweet." What is in a name?

The Truth and Soul Car

Jack Viets

The Department of Motor Vehicles' austerely efficient office at 1377 Fell street was briefly transformed into a living museum of modern junk art yesterday.

"Oh, God," moaned engine and body verification expert Wenico Fresnoza when he stepped outside to do his duty.

"What is it used for?"

"To blow people's minds," answered Steve Gillman, carefully directing Fresnoza around the yellow apparition he created from a junked 1957 DeSoto and an abandoned Volkswagen body.

Inspection

While Fresnoza clambered up to the vehicle's "flying bridge" to do a registra-

□Jack Viets, "Art on Wheels / The Truth and Soul Car," *San Francisco Chronicle,* July 1, 1970, p. 3.

tion inspection of the safety glass in front of its elevated driving center, Gillman tried to answer the single, insistent question of onlookers—"What is it?"

"It's a piece of art," the 24-year-old San Francisco State College graduate student said. "There is art outside a museum."

"You drive this thing?" someone asked.

"It sways a little but it's fun," said Gillman's wife, Bonnie.

Scramble

Kids scrambled inside the apparition's bomber-like plastic nose bubble and swung from its flying bridge, fashioned from two of its original DeSoto doors.

Gillman said his auto sculpture started out as "revived junk"—a 1957 DeSoto which had been towed away and sold at an auction of abandoned and junked cars for $23.

He spent eight long months adding its plastic bubble nose, its VW mid-section, the flying bridge, and an elevated rear deck strangely reminiscent of a Spanish galleon.

Now he wants to enter it in the approaching Civic Center Art Festival.

And, of course, he hopes to register it so he can share his auto sculpture with drivers on California's freeways.

"The California Highway Patrol is coming to my house to give the car a road test," he said almost proudly. "They want to determine its stopping distance."

The dilemma of the Department of Motor Vehicles was quickly solved with the disclosure of this vital intelligence.

"We'll wait and see what the Highway Patrol decides," agreed the band of anxious DMV workers who had gathered alongside the sculpture.

"If you don't have any trouble with them, you won't have any with us."

JACK VIETS is a general-assignment reporter on the staff of the *San Francisco Chronicle,* a Bachelor of Arts from the University of Vermont who majored in political science but enjoyed creative writing.

SCULPTURE

Gordon Peters; © Chronicle Publishing Co., 1970

Vocabulary Study

From the list below, select the word or phrase nearest in meaning to the word italicized in each of the following excerpts. The list contains extra words.

A. The Department of Motor Vehicles' *austerely* efficient office
B. the yellow *apparition* he created
C. Fresnoza *clambered* up to the vehicle's "flying bridge"
D. the *dilemma* of the Department of Motor Vehicles
E. the disclosure of this *vital* intelligence

heinous
climbed with difficulty
extremely important
severely
concern
phantom
ran noisily
nonsensical

Questions on Form and Content

A. This brief article appeared as a feature story in the San Francisco *Chronicle.* Newspaper leads traditionally answer the questions *who, what, when, where,* and *why.* Which of these questions are answered in the initial sentence of this story?

B. Where are the remaining questions answered?

C. What was the single insistent question of the onlookers at the Department of Motor Vehicles? What did the creator reply?

D. How did officials of the Department of Motor Vehicles solve their dilemma?

E. What is art?

Suggestions for Writing

A. "There is art outside a museum." Comment.

B. Do you think Mr. Gillman should have been given a license to drive his art-sculpture? Why or why not?

C. Describe the most unusual car you have ever seen.

D. What is the primary purpose of an automobile? What should it be? What secondary factors help determine the car one buys?

E. What reasoning and evidence do you think the graduate student would have to present to convince the Highway Patrol and the Department of Motor Vehicles that he should be permitted to drive his sculpture on the highways?

F. In a television interview, Mr. Gillman later revealed that he had made his sculpture even more artistic by planting an avocado tree and other greenery in its plastic nose bubble. Comment.

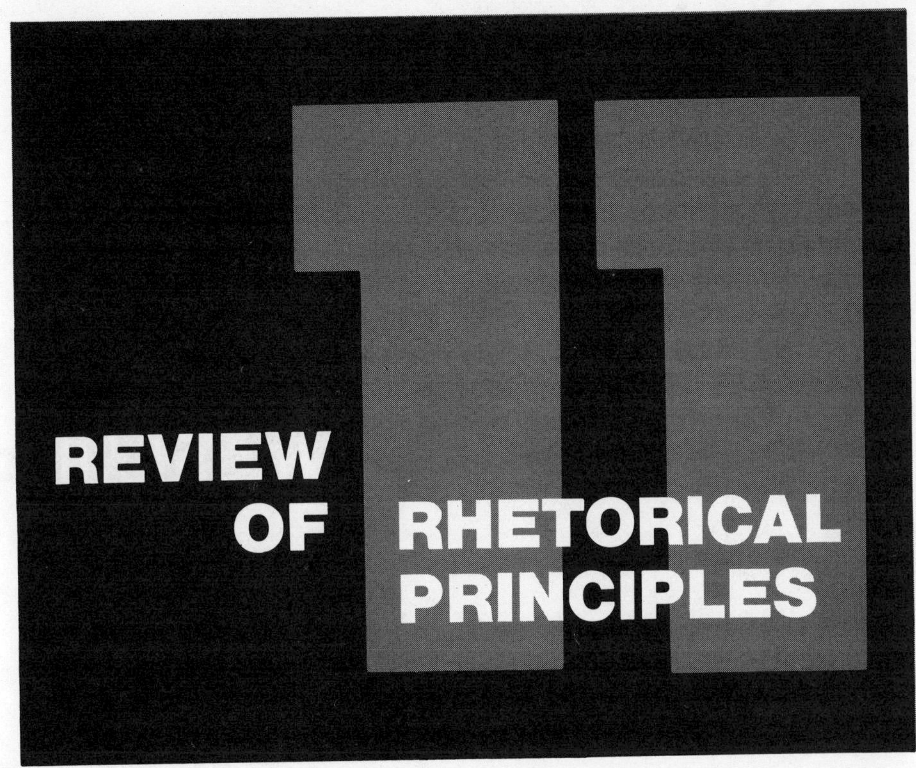

11 REVIEW OF RHETORICAL PRINCIPLES

John Ciardi's "The Unfading Beauty: A Well-Filled Mind" serves admirably as a review of the principles of composition that have been called to your attention throughout this text. You will probably profit by reading the essay first for a study of its content only. A second, more thorough reading should then reveal to you the excellent style of the author.

The questions which follow this essay are designed to help you both in analyzing it and in reviewing your work for the whole course. If you have difficulty answering any of the questions on form, perhaps you will find a review of the introductory section in the earlier chapter where that question was considered helpful.

The Unfading Beauty: A Well-Filled Mind

John Ciardi

Anatole France once observed of his countrymen that they raised ther daughters in convents and then married them to pirates. Most of today's college girls will find themselves married not long after graduation, and whether or not they later think of their college days as having been passed in a convent, few of them will find themselves married to anything quite as dramatic as a real pirate, or quite as revolting as a late-nineteenth-century French pirate of finance. The present-day standard model husband is more likely to come out as a serious suburban gardener who flies his week-end flag from the patio of a split-level, and who does his daily cruising in a car pool or on the 7:45 local in the morning and on the 4:40 in the afternoon. The girls are headed for a well-advertised and basically well-padded way of life, but the gist of Anatole France's observation may still apply: it may still be that what the girls do in school is no real preparation for what they will be doing after graduation.

□ John Ciardi, "The Unfading Beauty: A Well-Filled Mind," the commencement address Professor Ciardi delivered at Wells College, reprinted from *Glamour,* 1959.

What a liberal arts college is supposed to do in theory is certainly clear enough and can be summarized in the single phrase: "To see life steadily and see it whole." The college exists to teach some sense of the dimensions of a meaningful life. Were our colleges infallibly fulfilling that purpose, there would be nothing to say to college girls, today's or yesterday's, except to congratulate, to admire them, and to envy them happily.

World as it is, however, being in college is no occasion for unreserved congratulation. Hundreds of bachelor's degrees are being conferred annually by American colleges, and not one of them serves as any real evidence in itself that a reasonably adequate education has taken place, or that the holder of the degree has some viable sense of the whole dimension of the life that starts next.

True, it is still possible for an able and willing student to get something like an education in almost any college in the land, but the fact seems to be that no college any longer insists upon it. The educational insistence of a college is defined by its minimum standards, and the minimum standards of American colleges are everywhere too low. Even Harvard, proud as it is of its scholarly tradition, will grant a bachelor's degree on a four-year scholastic average of three C's and a D. "Three C's and a D and keep your name out of the papers," the rule runs: practical sounding, certainly, but a bit smaller in scale than "To see life steadily and see it whole."

The colleges, for their part, can educate only up to the level permitted by society, and our society has been reluctant as a general thing to support "egghead institutions" that think Aristotle is more important than a well-rounded social life that somehow develops a quality called "leadership," a quality that seems to be best developed by doing exactly the same thing everyone else does.

I do not know by what confusion of the national mores we are so insistent on this idea of leadership, but I have received hundreds of application forms in the last year or two, and there is hardly a one that does not contain a dotted line labeled "Leadership?" Certainly as things are, no man need be an intellectual explorer to do well in American business. The chances are, in fact, that he will go further on a little common sense and a lot of social manner than he will on an enthusiasm for Chaucer. No salesman who has made the mistake of acquiring a Phi Beta Kappa key can afford to make the mistake of wearing it when he goes to call on a customer.

Nor is it likely that the affable young man with his destiny in an attaché-case is going to scour the *summa cum laude* list when he starts looking for a wife. He wants her pretty, easy to get along with, a good mixer, a good dancer, and without any freakishly high-brow ideas. Besides, there really isn't room for more than a small decorative bookcase in the rumpus-room of a split-level—not once you have put in the bar, the TV set, the TV chairs, and the card table.

The girls know all this very well, and to the extent that they know it, they have before them no such transition as Anatole France saw from the convent to the pirate's bed. They know the advertised standard and most of them will slip into it eagerly and without a hitch. The chance they must take, however, is that the dreary gist of that advertised standard will eventually trap them into dullness. A few years ago one of our largest corporations prepared for distribution in the Ivy League colleges a pamphlet advising the boys how to behave as undergraduates if they wanted a corporation career after graduation. One sentence from that pamphlet could not be improved as a summary of the necessary intellectual tone. "Personal opinions," it read, "can cause a lot of trouble." The student editor of the Princeton newspaper assaulted the pamphlet and especially that sentence as a desecration of the free mind, and the corporation sent down as trouble-shooters the man who had written the pamphlet and a vice-president in charge of public relations. As I have the story, the pamphlet writer could not see what there was to argue. Personal opinions *can* cause a lot of trouble; everyone knows that. The vice-president, on the other hand, granted the student's point and the pamphlet was withdrawn and later rewritten. Victory for the free mind, perhaps, but there still remains one speculation: did the vice-president really see that a great principle was involved, or was he simply acting as a good public-relations man soothing a possibly troublesome crackpot?

Wherever the speculation comes out, the girls are reasonably well aware of what is required of a successful corporate wife, and while they have enough public-relations sense of their own to get along with the fuddy-duddy faculty, they are certainly not going to ruin their chances by getting themselves reputations as bookworm intellectuals.

So it happens that our colleges are divided into two cultural groups whose values tend to meet only in the most tangential ways. The faculty group is made up of men and women not particularly distinguished as smooth dancers but, rather, dedicated to books; so dedicated, in fact, that they are willing to live on academic salaries in return for the freedom of having their reading interfered with by students, most of whom are only taking the course because they have to. The student group does share the same campus with the faculty group, but tends to center around the jukebox in the snack bar rather than around the library. Professor Jones is eager to explain the Greek aorist and to show its connection with the Latin ablative absolute, but what the girls really want out of Greek Week is a good date for the dance. Let the faculty praise great minds; the girls are there to get married, most of them as per the advertised standard.

And were that advertised standard a sufficient and a lasting truth, the colleges would be more than justified in becoming finishing schools of the minor social graces. And may the graces flourish: the least thing the world needs is ungainly and ungracious women. The trouble with the advertised standard is that it simply is not true enough. It does to lounge in; it cannot do to live by. Its plot starts well, but the later chapters have an alarming tendency to fall to pieces.

It is those later chapters the girls generally fail to foresee, and it is that failure that still gives point to Anatole France's observation. For it may well be argued that we are raising our daughters in some sort of illusory heaven and then turning them loose to be mortal. Americans have always tended to be a bit surprised at their own deaths; it all seems so unprogressive. It almost seems that the Constitution, or at least General Motors, should have taken care of that.

But why should the girls be thinking of mortality? They have better things to foresee, glorious things. They see the excitement of the wedding, of the honeymoon, of setting up housekeeping, of the children arriving, and of the busy happy years of raising a family. It seems a paradise, and it is. It seems an eternity, and it is not. But who needs Plato among the nursery babble? As Yeats put it, beginning with what might very reasonably be taken as a reference to the faculty:

> That is no country for old men. The young
> In one another's arms, birds in the trees
> —Those dying generations—at their song,
> The salmon-falls, the mackerel crowded seas,
> Fish, flesh, or fowl, commend all summer long
> Whatever is begotten, born, or dies.
> Caught in that sensual music, all neglect
> Monuments of unaging intellect.

The faculty has no place in paradise. Their monuments of unaging intellect are meaningless to those caught up in that sensual music. The monuments have point only in the silence that follows the music.

And that silence comes. By the time today's college girl has reached thirty-five and forty, having spent fifteen or twenty years busily and happily rearing a family that has needed her, she will find that the children have grown free. There will come a morning after the last of them has moved out to his own life. She will get up at 7:30 for a strangely silent breakfast with her husband who eight years ago was promoted from the 7:45 local to the 8:50. She would like to talk to him, but through her busy years she will have lost touch with his business affairs. And he, doggedly working away at his thrombosis, has his own thoughts to think.

By 8:30 he will have left, and there is the day stretching ahead. Dawdle as she will, the breakfast dishes are in the dishwasher by 9:00. The cleaning woman will be in tomorrow to do the house, which is immaculate anyhow. And the ironing woman will be in the day after to do the clothes. She could write that letter to Mary, but 10:00 o'clock is still a long way off. And 11:00. And is lunch worth bothering with just for herself? Well, maybe a really fancy dinner. But that is hours ahead and the push-button oven will do most of that anyhow. And what is there to do? Today, tomorrow, and the next day? What will there ever be to do?

She will have entered the First Loneliness. Statistically, too, she will have entered the circle of possible widowhood. The years that follow are those in which her husband is more and more likely to achieve the final thrombosis of his success. American women outlive their husbands by an average of six years. Six years is perhaps not an alarming figure, but to begin with it is a bit higher among the wives of professional men. And if the average for all is six years, it must follow that the average for half will be more nearly twelve, and that for a quarter of them it will be more nearly twenty-four. May it be later rather than sooner, but there can be no doubt that the unadvertised years also lie ahead.

And what will today's college girls take into those long, well-padded, and lonely years? There is touring, of course. And there is bridge. And there is TV. And there are community projects, and gardening, and gay little shopping trips with the other girls. But is it enough? Ernest Hemingway once said to Marlene Dietrich, "Daughter, never confuse motion with action." Our better suburbs—and by this time most of the girls will have graduated from the split-level to the custom-built house—are full of little organizations devoted to making motions for the girls to go through. But there still remains that force at the core of the unstultified psyche that cries for a more meaningful and more human thing to do, that cries for action rather than motion.

Many such women make sudden awkward gestures of turning to the arts again. They used to play the piano rather well. Or they used to write for the college magazine. Now that they no longer have the P.-T.A. on their hands, why not start again?

Many of them turn to poetry; and because a poet is easily taken as some sort of summonable clergyman, many have sent their poems to me, as if I had no more to do than to spend a day reading and criticizing them. At that, one would somehow make the time if the poems were not so hopeless. For invariably it is too late. There is that about an art form that will not survive being held in abeyance for a decade or two. They should have had enough devotion to have kept it alive. If only in a stolen hour of the day. If only at the expense of sleep. It can be done. As Salvador Dali once declared: "One always has time to do what he really wants to do." One may have to pay a price for it, but one does pay the price for his true hungers. It is not easy, but to quote Yeats once again:

> To be born woman is to know,
> Though it's not taught to us at school,
> That we must labor to be beautiful.

No, it is not easy. It is something better than easy: it is joyous. It is as Frost put it, "The pleasure of taking pains." That gracious lady, distinguished biographer, and my good friend, Catherine Drinker Bowen, raised her family and managed her household for years while turning out a series of meticulously researched biographies, stealing one piece of every day at whatever cost, putting herself through the routine busyness of her day on the excitement of anticipating that hour at her own particular work. She had, in fact, had two books selected by the Book of the Month Club before she dared label her income-tax form "author" rather than "housewife."

A human being is finally defined by what he does with his attention. It is difficult to keep one's attention in order; difficult and demanding. How much easier it is to let one's mind into a lawn chair of the advertised life and to tune it there to Hollywood scenarios, or to let it drift into what Aldous Huxley called "the endless idiot gibberish of the reverie." It is easier to be inane; but the price is boredom, emptiness, and finally the inability to communicate meaningfully with any human being. How many mothers are there in America today who have begotten sons of their own body and pain and are now unable to speak to them except in the stereotype of "Mom" and "Dicky-boy," rather than as human being to human being, open to both joys and distresses but bound together by a love that includes understanding. It was a better thing than stereotypes that Adam and Eve began, and whoever allows that better thing to be lessened in himself lessens the possibility of the race.

It is what one does with his attention that defines him, and because art is the best ordering we have of human attention, there can be no truly meaningful life without the dimension of art. The arts—and I take them to include religion, philosophy, and history at those points where they are least dogmatic and most speculative—teach us not only ideas but the very dimension of possibility in ideas. There is a resonance in a great line of poetry without which the mind cannot truly tune itself. Listen to your own mind. Think the best thing you know. Then measure it against such a line as Wallace Stevens' "The major abstraction is the idea of man." Who can permit himself to think that what was in his mind before he read that line was as good as what was in his mind as he read it? Or listen to John Donne: "And now goodmorrow to our waking souls / Which watch not one another out of fear." Those lines may take a bit of mental focusing, but what a concept of love they speak! Whatever mental effort they require is indistinguishable from joy, and what the effort leaves behind it is a better human being.

Art is the resonance of inseeing joy, but that resonance is only the beginning. Every work of art is a piece of life one may have for the taking. It is not a thing said about an experience, it is the experience itself, not only re-enacted but given form, and therefore, value. Art is the best memory of the race. Art stores up in everlasting form the most meaningful experiences of the most perceptive minds of the past, and because there is such a thing as vicarious experience any man is free to relive those experiences, which is to say, he is free to take those lives into his life. May heaven defend those people who live no lives but their own. Imagine being only Susie Jones when one could also be Penelope, and Cleopatra, and Ophelia, and Madame DuBarry, and Emma Bovary, and Anna Karenina. And may heaven defend the man married to the woman who has not tied all those other necessary lives into herself. Nothing will defend monogamy sooner than a wife who—this side of schizophrenia, to be sure—contains her pluralities. "Age cannot wither her, nor custom stale / Her infinite variety."

And that finally is what any good book is about. A good book offers the reader a life he has no time for on the clock-as-it-ticks, and a world he may enter *as if* in actual fact. A great book is distinguished from a good book only by the size of the life and the world it offers, but no novel or book of poems is worth the reading unless it has that basic fact of experience to offer.

Art cannot fend loss and loneliness from any life. Loss and loneliness will fall as they must, and for many people they will fall inevitably. But let the meaningful woman look at the statistical probability of that loss and loneliness that lies before her, and let her ask what she will take into those years. Can a mind with Mozart in it ever be as lost as a mind with nothing in it? If girls now in college, just out of college, or even several years away from it do no more than set themselves a twenty-year program of reading meaningfully and carrying alive in their minds one passage a day from the English poets, can they fail to see that they will be more valuable to their families as mothers, and more valuable to themselves as widows?

One of Hemingway's characters in "Winner Take Nothing" is told that so-and-so is a coward and he answers, "He didn't invent it." The line is underplayed but a great understanding and a great mercy shine through it. One could do worse than to store a bit of that understanding and mercy for himself. So stored, one may learn in time that whatever happens to him is not his own invention. He may learn to see then that there is such a thing as the experience of the race on this planet, and learning that he will learn that one who takes that experience into himself has joined himself to the ever-uncertain but ever-hopeful and sometimes glorious continuum of man-and-woman born of man-and-woman.

It is that one must say to today's college girls. That they are beautiful, and ignorant, and illusory. And that only as they learn to shape their attention to the long memory we call the humanities, can they be beautiful after the bloom is off, and understandingly compassionate as time furrows them, and real to the lives they labor to make shapely.

JOHN CIARDI—poet, editor, and educator—received his M.A. degree at the University of Michigan, where he was awarded the largest Avery Hopwood Award ever given for poetry. He has taught English at the University of Kansas City, at Harvard, and from 1954 to 1961 at Rutgers University. He has been a lecturer in poetry at Bread Loaf Writers Conference since 1947 and director since 1955. He also has been poetry editor for *Saturday Review* since 1956. Among his books are *Other Skies,* which interprets his experiences as gunner on a B-29 during World War II; *Live Another Day,* a report of his return to civilian life; *As If: Poems New and Selected, How Does a Poem Mean?,* and *You Read to Me, I'll Read to You.* He has translated Dante's *Inferno* and edited an anthology of mid-century American poets.

Vocabulary Study

Select ten words you were not familiar with before reading the essay and explain how Mr. Ciardi uses them. Be able to use the words in sentences of your own.

Questions on Form and Content

A. Identify the topic sentence and the transitional words in the fourth paragraph. By what means other than the obvious linking words does the author gain coherence in this paragraph?

B. How many examples are used to answer the initial question in paragraph 18 ("And what will . . .")?

C. What comparisons are made in paragraph 1?

D. What contrast is developed in paragraph 10 ("So it happens . . .")?

E. What pattern of development is used in the first four paragraphs? How is coherence attained between these paragraphs?

F. Discuss the author's use of analysis in paragraphs 15 ("And that silence . . .") through 17.

G. Mr. Ciardi quotes Anatole France, Yeats, Frost, Hemingway, Salvador Dali, Aldous Huxley, Wallace Stevens, and John Donne. For what purpose?

H. Why does the author use the anecdote about Catherine Drinker Bowen?

I. What is the purpose of the essay? What theme idea is expressed?

J. Discuss the effectiveness of the introduction and conclusion. What functions, in addition to the obvious ones of beginning and ending the essay, do they fulfill?

K. Notice the variety in length and pattern and the skillful use of inversion and subordination in Mr. Ciardi's sentences. Can you find good use of parallelism in paragraph 13 ("But why . . .")?

L. Mr. Ciardi's language is noteworthy. Read paragraph 7 ("Nor is it likely . . .") for examples of exact, specific words and expressions.

M. Mr. Ciardi uses a short, simple explanation to tell what he means by the word *leadership.* He uses the extended method of definition to explain his use of the word *art,* however. Do you understand what he means by each word? Which form did you find easier to understand?

N. What are the rewards that lifelong awareness and worthwhile learning offer to any woman? Would they be the same for a man?

Suggestions for Writing

A. Comment on Mr. Ciardi's belief that "it may still be that what the girls do in school is no real preparation for what they will be doing after graduation."

B. If you could live the life of another—someone alive now or someone who lived in the past—who would you prefer to be? Why?

C. Discuss a book you have read recently, using as a guide for your remarks Mr. Ciardi's comment: "A good book offers a reader a life he has no time for on the clock-as-it-ticks, and a world he may enter *as if* in actual fact. A great book is distinguished from a good book only by the size of the life and the world it offers, but no novel or book of poems is worth the reading unless it has that basic fact of experience to offer."

D. Mr. Ciardi says: "The college exists to teach some sense of the dimensions of a meaningful life." Evaluate your college experiences in the light of his statement.

E. According to Mr. Ciardi, "minimum standards of American colleges are everywhere too low." What are the minimum standards of your school? Are they too low? Why or why not?

F. In his discussion of "leadership," Mr. Ciardi describes it as a "quality that seems to be best developed by doing exactly the same thing that everyone else does." How would you define leadership? What are the qualities of a leader?

G. If, because of lack of space, you had to omit a bar, a bookcase, a television set, or a card table and chairs from your rumpus room, which would you omit? Why?

H. Comment on this sentence that Mr. Ciardi discusses from the corporation pamphlet: "Personal opinions can cause a lot of trouble."

I. Do you agree with the author that a reputation as a bookworm intellectual can be ruinous? Why or why not?

J. Comment on Ernest Hemingway's advice to Marlene Dietrich: "Daughter, never confuse motion with action."

K. Relate to your own experience Salvador Dali's statement, "One always has time to do what he really wants to do."

Since Edith Hamilton's "The Lessons of the Past" is your last selection for analysis, neither hints for writing assignments nor other student aids are supplied.

You should profit by analyzing the material yourself and making your own lists of study aids for this final essay. Using those exercises supplied throughout the book as patterns, formulate questions on the vocabulary and on the form and content of "The Lessons of the Past." Then write a list of eight of ten writing suggestions based on Miss Hamilton's material.

Is there an ever-present past? Are there permanent truths which are forever important for the present? Today we are facing a future more strange and untried than any other generation has faced. The new world Columbus opened seems small indeed beside the illimitable distances of space before us, and the possibilities of destruction are immeasurably greater than ever. In such a position can we afford to spend time on the past? That is the question I am often asked. Am I urging the study of the Greeks and Romans and their civilizations for the atomic age?

Yes; that is just what I am doing. I urge it without qualification. We have a great civilization to save—or to lose. The greatest civilization before ours was the Greek. They challenge us and we need the challenge. They, too, lived in a dangerous world. They were a little, highly civilized people, the only civilized people in the west, surrounded by barbarous tribes and with the greatest Asiatic

☐ Edith Hamilton, "The Lessons of the Past," *The Saturday Evening Post* (September 27, 1958), 24-25⁺.

power, Persia, always threatening them. In the end they succumbed, but the reason they did was not that the enemies outside were so strong, but that their own strength, their spiritual strength, had given way. While they had it they kept Greece unconquered and they left behind a record in art and thought which in all the centuries of human effort since has not been surpassed.

The point which I want to make is not that their taste was superior to ours, not that the Parthenon was their idea of church architecture nor that Sophocles was the great drawing card in the theaters nor any of the familiar comparisons between fifth-century Athens and twentieth-century America, but that Socrates found on every street corner and in every Athenian equivalent of the baseball field people who were caught up by his questions into the world of thought. To be able to be caught up into the world of thought—that is to be educated.

How is that great aim to be reached? For years we have eagerly discussed ways and means of education and the discussion still goes on. William James once said that there were two subjects which if mentioned made other conversation stop and directed all eyes to the speaker. Religion was one and education the other. Today Russia seems to come first, but education is still emphatically the second. In spite of all the articles we read and all the speeches we listen to about it, we want to know more; we feel deeply its importance.

There is today a clearly visible trend toward making it the aim of education to defeat the Russians. That would be a sure way to defeat education. Genuine education is possible only when people realize that it has to do with persons, not with movements.

When I read educational articles it often seems to me that this important side of the matter, the purely personal side, is not emphasized enough; the fact that it is so much more agreeable and interesting to be an educated person than not. The sheer pleasure of being educated does not seem to be stressed. Once long ago I was talking with Prof. Basil L. Gildersleeve of Johns Hopkins University, the greatest Greek scholar our country has produced. He was an old man and he had been honored everywhere, in Europe as well as in America. He was just back from a celebration held for him in Oxford. I asked him what compliment received in his long life had pleased him most. The question amused him and he laughed over it, but he thought too. Finally he said, "I believe it was when one of my students said, 'Professor, you have so much fun with your own mind.' " Robert Louis Stevenson said that a man ought to be able to spend two or three hours waiting for a train at a little country station when he was all alone and had nothing to read, and not be bored for a moment.

What is the education which can do this? What is the furniture which makes the only place belonging absolutely to each one of us, the world within, a place where we like to go? I wish I could answer that question. I wish I could produce a perfect decorator's design warranted to make any interior lovely and interesting and stimulating; but, even if I could, sooner or later we would certainly try different designs. My point is only that while we must and should change the furniture, we ought to throw away old furniture very cautiously. It may turn out to be irreplaceable. A great deal was thrown away in the last generation or so, long enough ago to show some of the results. Furniture which had for centuries been foremost, we lightly, in a few years, discarded. The classics almost vanished from our field of education. That was a great change. Along with it came another. There is a marked difference between the writers of the past and the writers of today who have been educated without benefit of Greek and Latin. Is this a matter of cause and effect? People will decide for themselves, but I do not think anyone will question the statement that clear thinking is not the characteristic which distinguishes our literature today. We are more and more caught up by the unintelligible. People like it. This argues an inability to think, or, almost as bad, a disinclination to think.

Neither disposition marked the Greeks. They had a passion for thinking things out, and they loved unclouded clarity of statement as well as of thought. The Romans did, too, in their degree. They were able to put an idea into an astonishingly small number of words without losing a particle of intelligibility. It is only of late, with a generation which has never had to deal with a Latin sentence, that we are being submerged in a flood of words, words, words. It has been said that Lincoln at Gettysburg today would have begun in some such fashion as this: "Eight and seven-tenths decades ago the pioneer workers in this continental area implemented a new group based on an ideology of free boundaries and initial equality," and might easily have ended, "That political supervision of the integrated units, for the integrated units, by the integrated units, shall not become null and void on the superficial area of this planet." Along with the banishment of the classics, gobbledegook has come upon us—and the appalling size of the Congressional Record, and the overburdened mail service.

Just what the teaching in the schools was which laid the foundation of the Greek civilization we do not know in detail; the result we do know. Greek children were taught, Plato said, to "love what is beautiful and hate what is ugly." When they grew up their very pots and pans had to be pleasant to look at. It was part of their training to hate clumsiness and awkwardness; they loved grace and practiced it. "Our children," Plato said, "will be influenced for good by every sight and sound of beauty, breathing in, as it were, a pure breeze blowing to them from a good land."

All the same, the Athenians were not, as they showed Socrates when he talked to them, preoccupied with enjoying lovely things. The children were taught to think. Plato demanded a stiff examination, especially in mathematics, for entrance to his Academy. The Athenians were a thinking people. Today the scientists are bearing away the prize for thought. Well, a Greek said that the earth went around the sun sixteen centuries before Copernicus thought of it. A Greek said if you sailed out of Spain and kept to one latitude, you would come at last to land, seventeen hundred years before Columbus did it. Darwin said, "We are mere schoolboys in scientific thinking compared to old Aristotle." And the Greeks did not have a great legacy from the past as our scientists have; they thought science out from the beginning.

The same is true of politics. They thought that out, too, from the beginning, and they gave all the boys a training to fit them to be thinking citizens of a free state that had come into being through thought.

Basic to all the Greek achievement was freedom. The Athenians were the only free people in the world. In the great empires of antiquity—Egypt, Babylon, Assyria, Persia—splendid though they were, with riches beyond reckoning and immense power, freedom was unknown. The idea of it never dawned in any of them. It was born in Greece, a poor little country, but with it able to remain unconquered no matter what manpower and what wealth were arrayed against her. At Marathon and at Salamis overwhelming numbers of Persians had been defeated by small Greek forces. It had been proved that one free man was superior to many submissively obedient subjects of a tyrant. Athens was the leader in that amazing victory, and to the Athenians freedom was their dearest possession. Demosthenes said that they would not think it worth their while to live if they could not do so as free men, and years later a great teacher said, "Athenians, if you deprive them of their liberty, will die."

Athens was not only the first democracy in the world, it was also at its height an almost perfect democracy—that is, for men. There was no part in it for women or foreigners or slaves, but as far as the men were concerned it was more democratic than we are. The governing body was the Assembly, of which all citizens over eighteen were members. The Council of Five Hundred which prepared business for the Assembly and, if requested, carried out what had been decided there, was made up of citizens who were chosen by lot. The same was true of the juries. Minor officials also were chosen by lot. The chief magistrates and the highest officers in the army were elected by the Assembly. Pericles was a general, very popular, who acted for a long time as if he were head of the state, but he had to be elected every year. Freedom of speech was the right the Athenians prized most and there has never been another state as free in that respect. When toward the end of the terrible Peloponnesian War the victorious Spartans were advancing upon Athens, Aristophanes caricatured in the theater the leading Athenian generals and showed them up as cowards, and even then as the Assembly opened, the herald asked, "Does anyone wish to speak?"

There was complete political equality. It was a government of the people, by the people, for the people. An unregenerate old aristocrat in the early fourth century, B.C., writes: "If you *must* have a democracy, Athens is the perfect example. I object to it because it is based on the welfare of the lower, not the better, classes. In Athens the people who row the vessels and do the work, have the advantage. It is their prosperity that is important." All the same, making the city beautiful was important too, as were also the great performances in the theater. If, as Plato says, the Assembly was chiefly made up of cobblers and carpenters and smiths and farmers and retail-business men, they approved the construction of the Parthenon and the other buildings on the Acropolis, and they crowded the theater when the great tragedies were played. Not only did all free men share in the government; the love of the beautiful and the desire to have a part in creating it were shared by the many, not by a mere chosen few. That has happened in no state except Athens.

But those free Greeks owned slaves. What kind of freedom was that? The question would have been incomprehensible to the ancient world. There had always been slaves; they were a first necessity. The way of life everywhere was based upon them. They were taken for granted; no one ever gave them a thought. The very best Greek minds, the thinkers who discovered freedom and the solar system, had never an idea that slavery was evil. It is true that the greatest thinker of them all, Plato, was made uncomfortable by it. He said that slaves were often good, trustworthy, doing more for a man than his own family would, but he did not follow his thought through. The glory of being the first one to condemn it belongs to a man of the generation before Plato, the poet Euripides. He called it, "That thing of evil," and in several of his tragedies showed its evil for all to see. A few centuries later the great Greek school of the Stoics denounced it. Greece first saw it for what it is. But the world went on in the same way. The Bible accepts it without comment. Two thousand years after the Stoics, less than a hundred years ago, the American Republic accepted it.

Athens treated her slaves well. A visitor to the city in the early fourth century, B.C., wrote: "It is illegal here to deal a slave a blow. In the street he won't step aside to let you pass. Indeed you can't tell a slave by his dress; he looks like all the rest. They can go to the theater too. Really, the Athenians have established a kind of equality between slaves and free men." They were never a possible source of danger to the state as they were in Rome. There were no terrible slave wars and uprisings in Athens. In Rome, crucifixion was called "the slave's punishment." The Athenians did not practice crucifixion, and had no so-called slave's punishment. They were not afraid of their slaves.

In Athens' great prime Athenians were free. No one told them what they must do or what they should think—no church or political party or powerful private interests or labor unions. Greek schools had no donors of endowments they must pay attention to, no government financial backing which must be made secure by acting as the government wanted. To be sure, the result was that they had to take full responsibility, but that is always the price for full freedom. The Athenians were a strong people; they could pay the price. They were a thinking people; they knew what freedom means. They knew—not that they were free because their country was free, but that their country was free because they were free.

A reflective Roman traveling in Greece in the second century, A.D., said, "None ever throve under democracy save the Athenians; *they* had sane self-control and were law-abiding." He spoke truly. That is what Athenian education aimed at, to produce men who would be able to maintain a self-governed state because they were themselves self-governed, self-controlled, self-reliant. Plato speaks of "the education in excellence which makes men long to be perfect citizens, knowing both how to rule and be ruled." "We are a free democracy," Pericles said. "We do not allow absorption in our own affairs to interfere with participation in the city's; we yield to none in independence of spirit and complete self-reliance, but we regard him who holds aloof from public affairs as useless." They called the useless man a "private" citizen, *idiotes,* from which our word "idiot" comes.

They had risen to freedom and to ennoblement from what Gilbert Murray calls "effortless barbarism"; they saw it all around them; they hated its filth and fierceness; nothing effortless was among the good things they wanted. Plato said, "Hard is the good," and a poet hundreds of years before Plato said,

> Before the gates of Excellence the high gods have placed sweat.
> Long is the road thereto and steep and rough at the first,
> But when the height is won, then is there ease.

When or why the Greeks set themselves to travel on that road we do not know, but it led them away from habits and customs accepted everywhere that kept men down to barbaric filth and fierceness. It led them far. One example is enough to show the way they took. It was the custom—during how many millenniums, who can say—for a victor to erect a trophy, a monument of his victory. In Egypt, where stone was plentiful, it would be a slab engraved with his glories. Farther east, where the sand took over, it might be a great heap of severed heads, quite permanent objects; bones last a long time. But in Greece, though a man could erect a trophy, it must be made of wood and it could never be repaired. Even as the victor set it up he would see in his mind how soon it would decay and sink into ruin, and there it must be left. The Greeks in their onward pressing along the steep and rough road had learned a great deal. They knew the victor might be the vanquished next time. There should be no permanent records of the manifestly impermanent. They had learned a great deal.

An old Greek inscription states that the aim of mankind should be "to tame the savageness of man and make gentle the life of the world." Aristotle said that the city was built first for safety, but then that men might discover the good life and lead it. So the Athenians did according to Pericles. Pericles said that Athens stood for freedom and for thought and for beauty, but in the Greek way, within limits, without exaggeration. The Athenians loved beauty, he said, but with simplicity; they did not like the extravagances of luxury. They loved the things of the mind, but they did not shrink from hardship. Thought did not cause them to hesitate, it clarified the road to action. If they had riches they did not make a show of them, and no one was ashamed of being poor if he was useful. They were free because of willing obedience to law, not only the written, but still more the unwritten, kindness and compassion and unselfishness and the many qualities which cannot be enforced, which depend on a man's free choice, but without which men cannot live together.

If ever there is to be a truly good and great and enduring republic it must be along these lines. We need the challenge of the city that thought them out, wherein for centuries one genius after another grew up. Geniuses are not produced by spending money. We need the challenge of the way the Greeks were educated. They fixed their eyes on the individual. We contemplate millions. What we have undertaken in this matter of education has dawned upon us only lately. We are trying to do what has never been attempted before, never in the history of the world—educate all the young in a nation of 170 millions; a magnificent idea, but we are beginning to realize what are the problems and what may be the results of mass production of education. So far, we do not seem appalled at the prospect of exactly the same kind of education being applied to all the school children from the Atlantic to the Pacific, but there is an uneasiness in the air, a realization that the individual is growing less easy to find; an idea, perhaps, of what standardization might become when the units are not machines, but human beings.

Here is where we can go back to the Greeks with profit. The Athenians in their dangerous world needed to be a nation of independent men who could take responsibility, and they taught their children accordingly. They thought about every boy. Someday he would be a citizen of Athens, responsible for her safety and her glory, "each one," Pericles said, "fitted to meet life's chances and changes with the utmost versatility and grace." To them education was by its very nature an individual matter. To be properly educated a boy had to be taught music; he learned to play a musical instrument. He had to learn poetry, a great deal of it, and recite it—and there were a number of musical instruments and many poets; though, to be sure, Homer was the great textbook.

That kind of education is not geared to mass production. It does not produce people who instinctively go the same way. That is how Athenian children lived and learned while our millions learn the same lessons and spend hours before television sets looking at exactly the same thing at exactly the same time. For one reason and another we are more and more ignoring differences, if not trying to obliterate them. We seem headed toward a standardization of the mind, what Goethe called "the deadly commonplace that fetters us all." That was not the Greek way.

The picture of the Age of Pericles drawn by the historian Thucydides, one of the greatest historians the world has known, is of a state made up of people who are self-reliant individuals, not echoes or copies, who want to be let alone to do their own work, but who are also closely bound together by a great aim, the commonweal, each one so in love with his country—Pericles' own words—that he wants most of all to use himself in her service. Only an ideal? Ideals have enormous power. They stamp an age. They lift life up when they are lofty; they drag down and make decadent when they are low—and then, by that strange fact, the survival of the fittest, those that are low fade away and are forgotten. The Greek ideals have had a power of persistent life for twenty-five hundred years.

Is it rational that now when the young people may have to face problems harder than we face, is it reasonable that with the atomic age before them, at this time we are giving up the study of how the Greeks and Romans prevailed magnificently in a barbaric world; the study, too, of how that triumph ended, how a slackness and softness finally came over them to their ruin? In the end, more than they wanted freedom, they wanted security, a comfortable life, and they lost all —security and comfort and freedom.

Is not that a challenge to us? Is it not true that into our education have come a slackness and softness? Is hard effort prominent? The world of thought can be entered in no other way. Are we growing slack and soft in our political life? When the Athenians finally wanted not to give to the state, but the state to give to them, when the freedom they wished most for was freedom from responsibility, then Athens ceased to be free and was never free again. Is not that a challenge?

Cicero said, "To be ignorant of the past is to remain a child." Santayana said,

"A nation that does not know history is fated to repeat it." The Greeks can help us, help us as no other people can, to see how freedom is won and how it is lost. Above all, to see in clearest light what freedom is. The first nation in the world to be free sends a ringing call down through the centuries to all who would be free. Greece rose to the very height, not because she was big, she was very small; not because she was rich, she was very poor; not even because she was wonderfully gifted. So doubtless were others in the great empires of the ancient world who have gone their way leaving little for us. She rose because there was in the Greeks the greatest spirit that moves in humanity, the spirit that sets men free.

Plato put into words what that spirit is. "Freedom," he says, "is no matter of laws and constitutions; only he is free who realizes the divine order within himself, the true standard by which a man can steer and measure himself." True standards, ideals that lift life up, marked the way of the Greeks. Therefore their light has never been extinguished.

"The time for extracting a lesson from history is ever at hand for them who are wise." Demosthenes.

Edith Hamilton (1867-1963), a classical scholar and author, wrote her first book, *The Greek Way,* at the age of sixty-three. Born in Dresden, Germany, she was reared in Fort Wayne, Indiana, studied at Miss Porter's School, Bryn Mawr College, and the Universities of Leipzig and Munich. The first woman ever admitted to classes at the latter, she had to sit on the platform beside the teacher. From 1896 to 1922, she was director of the Bryn Mawr School in Baltimore, where despite the censure she could have received, she once walked in a suffrage parade. She approached the ancient world primarily through literature, and particularly wished to make clear the relevance of the Greek ideal to modern civilization. She received honorary D. Litt. degrees from Yale and the Universities of Pennsylvania and Rochester, and at ninety was made an honorary citizen of Athens.

Appendices

Cartoon reprinted by permission of Dick Bibler. Reprinted from the syndicated panel *Little Man on Campus,* Box 1533, Monterey, California.

Appendix A.

How to Say Nothing in Five Hundred Words

Paul Roberts

Nothing About Something

It's Friday afternoon, and you have almost survived another week of classes. You are just looking forward dreamily to the week end when the English instructor says: "For Monday you will turn in a five-hundred word composition on college football."

Well, that puts a good big hole in the week end. You don't have any strong views on college football one way or the other. You get rather excited during the season and go to all the home games and find it rather more fun than not. On the other hand, the class has been reading Robert Hutchins in the anthology and perhaps Shaw's "Eighty-Yard Run," and from the class discussion you have got

□Paul Roberts, "How to Say Nothing in Five Hundred Words," from *Understanding English* (New York, 1958).

the idea that the instructor thinks college football is for the birds. You are no fool, you. You can figure out what side to take.

After dinner you get out the portable typewriter that you got for high school graduation. You might as well get it over with and enjoy Saturday and Sunday. Five hundred words is about two double-spaced pages with normal margins. You put in a sheet of paper, think up a title, and you're off:

Why College Football Should Be Abolished

College football should be abolished because it's bad for the school and also bad for the players. The players are so busy practicing that they don't have any time for their studies.

This, you feel, is a mighty good start. The only trouble is that it's only thirty-two words. You still have four hundred and sixty-eight to go, and you've pretty well exhausted the subject. It comes to you that you do your best thinking in the morning, so you put away the typewriter and go to the movies. But the next morning you have to do your washing and some math problems, and in the afternoon you go to the game. The English instructor turns up too, and you wonder if you've taken the right side after all. Saturday night you have a date, and Sunday morning you have to go to church. (You shouldn't let English assignments interfere with your religion.) What with one thing and another, it's ten o'clock Sunday night before you get out the typewriter again. You make a pot of coffee and start to fill out your views on college football. Put a little meat on the bones.

Why College Football Should Be Abolished

In my opinion, it seems to me that college football should be abolished. The reason why I think this to be true is because I feel that football is bad for the colleges in nearly every respect. As Robert Hutchins says in his article in our anthology in which he discusses college football, it would be better if the colleges had race horses and had races with one another, because then the horses would not have to attend classes. I firmly agree with Mr. Hutchins on this point, and I am sure that many other students would agree too.

One reason why it seems to me that college football is bad is that it has become too commercial. In the olden times when people played football just for the fun of it, maybe college football was all right, but they do not play football just for the fun of it now as they used to in the old days. Nowadays college football is what you might call a big business. Maybe this is not true at all schools, and I don't think it is especially true here at State, but certainly this is the case at most colleges and universities in America nowadays, as Mr. Hutchins points out in his very interesting article. Actually the coaches and alumni go around to the high schools and offer the high school stars large salaries to come to their colleges and play football for them. There was one case where a high school star was offered a convertible if he would play football for a certain college.

Another reason for abolishing college football is that it is bad for the players. They do not have time to get a college education, because they are so busy playing football. A football player has to practice every afternoon from three to six, and then he is so tired that he can't concentrate on his studies. He just feels like dropping off to sleep after dinner, and then the next day he goes to his classes without having studied and maybe he fails the test.

(Good ripe stuff so far, but you're still a hundred and fifty-one words from home. One more push.)

Also I think college football is bad for the colleges and the universities because not very many students get to participate in it. Out of a college of ten thousand students only seventy-five or a hundred play football, if that many. Football is what you might call a spectator sport. That means that most people go to watch it but do not play it themselves.

(Four hundred and fifteen. Well, you still have the conclusion and when you retype it, you can make the margins a little wider.)

These are the reasons why I agree with Mr. Hutchins that college football should be abolished in American colleges and universities.

On Monday you turn it in, moderately hopeful, and on Friday it comes back marked "weak in content" and sporting a big "D."

This essay is exaggerated a little, not much. The English instructor will recognize it as reasonably typical of what an assignment on college football will bring in. He knows that nearly half of the class will contrive in five hundred words to say that college football is too commercial and bad for the players. Most of the other half will inform him that college football builds character and prepares one for life and brings prestige to the school. As he reads paper after paper all saying the same thing in almost the same words, all bloodless, five hundred words dripping out of nothing, he wonders how he allowed himself to get trapped into teaching English when he might have had a happy and interesting life as an electrician or a confidence man.

Well, you may ask, what can you do about it? The subject is one on which you have few convictions and little information. Can you be expected to make a dull subject interesting? As a matter of fact, this is precisely what you are expected to do. This is the writer's essential task. All subjects, except sex, are dull until somebody makes them interesting. The writer's job is to find the argument, the approach, the angle, the wording that will take the reader with him. This is seldom easy, and it is particularly hard in subjects that have been much discussed: College Football, Fraternities, Popular Music, Is Chivalry Dead?, and the like. You will feel that there is nothing you can do with such subjects except repeat the old bromides. But there are some things you can do which will make your papers, if not throbbingly alive, at least less insufferably tedious than they might otherwise be.

Avoid the Obvious Content

Say the assignment is college football. Say that you've decided to be against it. Begin by putting down the arguments that come to your mind: it is too commercial, it takes the students' minds off their studies, it is hard on the players, it makes the university a kind of circus instead of an intellectual center, for most schools it is financially ruinous. Can you think of any more arguments just off hand? All right. Now when you write your paper, *make sure that you don't use any of the material on this list.* If these are the points that leap to your mind, they will leap to everyone else's too, and whether you get a "C" or a "D" may depend on whether the instructor reads your paper early when he is fresh and tolerant or late, when the sentence "In my opinion, college football has become too commercial," inexorably repeated, has brought him to the brink of lunacy.

Be against college football for some reason or reasons of your own. If they are keen and perceptive ones, that's splendid. But even if they are trivial or foolish or indefensible, you are still ahead so long as they are not everybody else's reasons too. Be against it because the colleges don't spend enough money on it to make it worth while, because it is bad for the characters of the spectators, because the players are forced to attend classes, because the football stars hog all the beautiful women, because it competes with baseball and is therefore un-American and possibly Communist inspired. There are lots of more or less unused reasons for being against college football.

Sometimes it is a good idea to sum up and dispose of the trite and conventional points before going on to your own. This has the advantage of indicating to the reader that you are going to be neither trite nor conventional. Something like this:

> We are often told that college football should be abolished because it has become too commercial or because it is bad for the players. These arguments are no doubt very cogent, but they don't really go to the heart of the matter.

Then you go to the heart of the matter.

Take the Less Usual Side

One rather simple way of getting into your paper is to take the side of the argument that most of the citizens will want to avoid. If the assignment is an essay on dogs, you can, if you choose, explain that dogs are faithful and lovable companions, intelligent, useful as guardians of the house and protectors of children, indispensable in police work—in short, when all is said and done, man's best friends. Or you can suggest that those big brown eyes conceal, more often than not, a vacuity of mind and an inconstancy of purpose; that the dogs you have known most intimately have been mangy, ill-tempered brutes, incapable of instruction; and that only your nobility of mind and fear of arrest prevent you from kicking the flea-ridden animals when you pass them on the street.

Naturally, personal convictions will sometimes dictate your approach. If the assigned subject is "Is Methodism Rewarding to the Individual?" and you are a pious Methodist, you have really no choice. But few assigned subjects, if any, will fall in this category. Most of them will lie in broad areas of discussion with much to be said on both sides. They are intellectual exercises, and it is legitimate to argue now one way and now another, as debaters do in similar circumstances. Always take the side that looks to you hardest, least defensible. It will almost always turn out to be easier to write interestingly on that side.

This general advice applies where you have a choice of subjects. If you are to choose among "The Value of Fraternities" and "My Favorite High School Teacher" and "What I Think About Beetles," by all means plump for the beetles. By the time the instructor gets to your paper, he will be up to his ears in tedious tales about the French teacher at Bloombury High and assertions about how fraternities build character and prepare one for life. Your views on beetles, whatever they are, are bound to be a refreshing change.

Don't worry too much about figuring out what the instructor thinks about the subject so that you can cuddle up with him. Chances are his views are no stronger than yours. If he does have convictions and you oppose them, his problem is to keep from grading you higher than you deserve in order to show he is not biased. This doesn't mean that you should always cantankerously dissent from what the instructor says; that gets tiresome too. And if the subject assigned is "My Pet Peeve," do not begin, "My pet peeve is the English instructor who assigns papers on 'my pet peeve.' " This was still funny during the War of 1812, but it has sort of lost its edge since then. It is in general good manners to avoid personalities.

Slip Out of Abstraction

If you will study the essay on college football [near the beginning of this essay], you will perceive that one reason for its appalling dullness is that it never gets down to particulars. It is just a series of not very glittering generalities: "Football is bad for the colleges," "it has become too commercial," "football is a big business," "it is bad for the players," and so on. Such round phrases thudding against the reader's brain are unlikely to convince him, though they may well render him unconscious.

If you want the reader to believe that college football is bad for the players, you have to do more than say so. You have to display the evil. Take your roommate, Alfred Simkins, the second-string center. Picture poor old Alfy coming home from football practice every evening, bruised and aching, agonizingly tired, scarcely able to shovel the mashed potatoes into his mouth. Let us see him staggering up to the room, getting out his econ textbook, peering desperately at it with his good eye, falling asleep and failing the test in the morning. Let us share his unbearable tension as Saturday draws near. Will he fail, be demoted, lose his monthly allowance, be forced to return to the coal mines? And if he succeeds, what will be his reward? Perhaps a slight ripple of applause when the third-string center replaces him, a moment of elation in the locker room if the team wins, of despair if it loses. What will he look back on when he graduates from college? Toil and torn ligaments. And what will be his future? He is not good enough for pro football, and he is too obscure and weak in econ to succeed in stocks and bonds. College football is tearing the heart from Alfy Simkins and, when it finishes with him, will callously toss aside the shattered hulk.

This is no doubt a weak enough argument for the abolition of college football, but it is a sight better than saying, in three or four variations, that college football (in your opinion) is bad for the players.

Look at the work of any professional writer and notice how constantly he is moving from the generality, the abstract statement, to the concrete example, the facts and figures, the illustration. If he is writing on juvenile delinquency, he does not just tell you that juveniles are (it seems to him) delinquent and that (in his opinion) something should be done about it. He shows you juveniles being delinquent, tearing up movie theatres in Buffalo, stabbing high school principals in Dallas, smoking marijuana in Palo Alto. And more than likely he is moving toward some specific remedy, not just a general wringing of the hands.

It is no doubt possible to be *too* concrete, too illustrative or anecdotal, but few inexperienced writers err this way. For most the soundest advice is to be seeking always for the picture, to be always turning general remarks into seeable examples. Don't say, "Sororities teach girls the social graces." Say, "Sorority life teaches a girl how to carry on a conversation while pouring tea, without sloshing the tea into the saucer." Don't say, "I like certain kinds of popular music very much." Say, "Whenever I hear Gerber Sprinklittle play 'Mississippi Man' on the trombone, my socks creep up my ankles."

Get Rid of Obvious Padding

The student toiling away at his weekly English theme is too often tormented by a figure: five hundred words. How, he asks himself, is he to achieve this staggering total? Obviously by never using one word when he can somehow work in ten.

He is therefore seldom content with a plain statement like "Fast driving is dangerous." This has only four words in it. He takes thought, and the sentence becomes:

> In my opinion, fast driving is dangerous.

Better, but he can do better still:

> In my opinion, fast driving would seem to be rather dangerous.

If he is really adept, it may come out:

> In my humble opinion, though I do not claim to be an expert on this complicated subject, fast driving, in most circumstances, would seem to be rather dangerous in many respects, or at least so it would seem to me.

Thus four words have been turned into forty, and not an iota of content has been added.

Now this is a way to go about reaching five hundred words, and if you are content with a "D" grade, it is as good a way as any. But if you aim higher, you must work differently. Instead of stuffing your sentences with straw, you must try steadily to get rid of the padding, to make your sentences lean and tough. If you are really working at it, your first draft will greatly exceed the required total, and then you will work it down, thus:

> It is thought in some quarters that fraternities do not contribute as much as might be expected to campus life.
> Some people think that fraternities contribute little to campus life.

> The average doctor who practices in small towns or in the country must toil night and day to heal the sick.
> Most country doctors work long hours.

> When I was a little girl, I suffered from shyness and embarrassment in the presence of others.
> I was a shy little girl.

> It is absolutely necessary for the person employed as a marine fireman to give the matter of steam pressure his undivided attention at all times.
> The fireman has to keep his eye on the steam gauge.

You may ask how you can arrive at five hundred words at this rate. Simply. You dig up more real content. Instead of taking a couple of obvious points off the surface of the topic and then circling warily around them for six paragraphs, you work in and explore, figure out the details. You illustrate. You say that fast driving is dangerous, and then you prove it. How long does it take to stop a car at forty and at eighty? How far can you see at night? What happens when a tire blows? What happens in a head-on collision at fifty miles an hour? Pretty soon your paper will be full of broken glass and blood and headless torsos, and reaching five hundred words will not really be a problem.

Call a Fool a Fool

Some of the padding in freshman themes is to be blamed not on anxiety about the word minimum but on excessive timidity. The student writes, "In my opinion, the principal of my high school acted in ways that I believe every unbiased person would have to call foolish." This isn't exactly what he means. What he means is, "My high school principal was a fool." If he was a fool, call him a fool. Hedging the thing about with "in-my-opinion's" and "it seems-to-me's" and "as-I-see-it's" and "at-least-from-my-point-of-view's" gains you nothing. Delete these phrases whenever they creep into your paper.

The student's tendency to hedge stems from a modesty that in other circumstances would be commendable. He is, he realizes, young and inexperienced, and he half suspects that he is dopey and fuzzy-minded beyond the average. Probably only too true. But it doesn't help to announce your incompetence six times in every paragraph. Decide what you want to say and say it as vigorously as possible, without apology and in plain words.

Linguistic diffidence can take various forms. One is what we call *euphemism.* This is the tendency to call a spade "a certain garden implement" or women's underwear "unmentionables." It is stronger in some eras than others and in some people than others but it always operates more or less in subjects that are touchy or taboo: death, sex, madness, and so on. Thus we shrink from saying "He died last night" but say instead "passed away," "left us," "joined his Maker," "went to his reward." Or we try to take off the tension with a lighter cliché: "kicked the bucket," "cashed in his chips," "handed in his dinner pail." We have found all sorts of ways to avoid saying *mad:* "mentally ill," "touched," "not quite right upstairs," "feeble-minded," "innocent," "simple," "off his trolley," "not in his right mind." Even such a now plain word as *insane* began as a euphemism with the meaning "not healthy."

Modern science, particularly psychology, contributes many polysyllables in which we can wrap our thoughts and blunt their force. To many writers there is no such thing as a bad schoolboy. Schoolboys are maladjusted or unoriented or misunderstood or in need of guidance or lacking in continued success toward satisfactory integration of the personality as a social unit, but they are never bad. Psychology no doubt makes us better men or women, more sympathetic and tolerant, but it doesn't make writing any easier. Had Shakespeare been confronted with psychology, "To be or not to be" might have come out, "To continue as a social unit or not to do so. That is the personality problem. Whether 'tis a better sign of integration at the conscious level to display a psychic tolerance toward the maladjustments and repressions induced by one's lack of orientation in one's environment or—" But Hamlet would never have finished the soliloquy.

Writing in the modern world, you cannot altogether avoid modern jargon. Nor, in an effort to get away from euphemism, should you salt your paper with four-letter words. But you can do much if you will mount guard against those roundabout phrases, those echoing polysyllables that tend to slip into your writing to rob it of its crispness and force.

Beware of the Pat Expression

Other things being equal, avoid phrases like "other things being equal." Those sentences that come to you whole, or in two or three doughy lumps, are sure to be bad sentences. They are no creation of yours but pieces of common thought floating in the community soup.

Pat expressions are hard, often impossible, to avoid, because they come too easily to be noticed and seem too necessary to be dispensed with. No writer avoids them altogether, but good writers avoid them more often than poor writers.

By "pat expressions" we mean such tags as "to all practical intents and purposes," "the pure and simple truth," "from where I sit," "the time of his life," "to the ends of the earth," "in the twinkling of an eye," "as sure as you're born," "over my dead body," "under cover of darkness," "took the easy way out," "when all is said and done," "told him time and time again," "parted the best of friends," "stand up and be counted," "gave him the best years of her life," "worked her fingers to the bone." Like other clichés, these expressions were once forceful. Now we should use them only when we can't possibly think of anything else.

Some pat expressions stand like a wall between the writer and thought. Such a one is "the American way of life." Many student writers feel that when they have said that something accords with the American way of life or does not they have exhausted the subject. Actually, they have stopped at the highest level of abstraction. The American way of life is the complicated set of bonds between a hundred and eighty million ways. All of us know this when we think about it, but the tag phrase too often keeps us from thinking about it.

So with many another phrase dear to the politician: "This great land of ours," "the man in the street," "our national heritage." These may prove our patriotism or give a clue to our political beliefs, but otherwise they add nothing to the paper except words.

Colorful Words

The writer builds with words, and no builder uses a raw material more slippery and elusive and treacherous. A writer's work is a constant struggle to get the right word in the right place, to find that particular word that will convey his meaning exactly, that will persuade the reader or soothe him or startle or amuse him. He never succeeds altogether—sometimes he feels that he scarcely succeeds at all—but such successes as he has are what make the thing worth doing.

There is no book of rules for this game. One progresses through everlasting experiment on the basis of ever-widening experience. There are few useful generalizations that one can make about words as words, but there are perhaps a few.

Some words are what we call "colorful." By this we mean that they are calculated to produce a picture or induce an emotion. They are dressy instead of plain, specific instead of general, loud instead of soft. Thus, in place of "Her heart beat," we may write "her heart *pounded, throbbed, fluttered, danced.*" Instead of "He sat in his chair," we may say, "He *lounged, sprawled, coiled.*" Instead of "It was hot," we may say, "It was *blistering, sultry, muggy, suffocating, steamy, wilting.*"

However, it should not be supposed that the fancy word is always better. Often it is as well to write "Her heart beat" or "It was hot" if that is all it did or all it was. Ages differ in how they like their prose. The nineteenth century liked it rich and smoky. The twentieth has usually preferred it lean and cool. The twentieth century writer, like all writers, is forever seeking the exact word, but he is wary of sounding feverish. He tends to pitch it low, to understate it, to throw it away. He knows that if he gets too colorful, the audience is likely to giggle.

See how this strikes you: "As the rich, golden glow of the sunset died away along the eternal western hills, Angela's limpid blue eyes looked softly and trustingly into Montague's flashing brown ones, and her heart pounded like a drum in time with the joyous song surging in her soul." Some people like that sort of thing, but most modern readers would say, "Good grief," and turn on the television.

Colored Words

Some words we would call not so much colorful as colored—that is, loaded with associations, good or bad. All words—except perhaps structure words—have associations of some sort. We have said that the meaning of a word is the sum of the contexts in which it occurs. When we hear a word, we hear with it an echo of all the situations in which we have heard it before.

In some words, these echoes are obvious and discussable. The word *mother,* for example, has for most people, agreeable associations. When you hear *mother* you probably think of home, safety, love, food, and various other pleasant things. If one writes, "She was like a mother to me," he gets an effect which he would not get in "She was like an aunt to me." The advertiser makes use of the associations of *mother* by working it in when he talks about his product. The politician works it in when he talks about himself.

So also with such words as *home, liberty, fireside, contentment, patriot, tenderness, sacrifice, childlike, manly, bluff, limpid.* All of these words are loaded with favorable associations that would be rather hard to indicate in a straightforward definition. There is more than a literal difference between "They sat around the fireside" and "They sat around the stove." They might have been equally warm and happy around the stove, but *fireside* suggests leisure, grace, quiet tradition, congenial company, and *stove* does not.

Conversely, some words have bad associations. *Mother* suggests pleasant things, but *mother-in-law* does not. Many mothers-in-law are heroically lovable and some mothers drink gin all day and beat their children insensible, but these facts of life are beside the point. The thing is that *mother* sounds good and *mother-in-law* does not.

Or consider the word *intellectual.* This would seem to be a complimentary term, but in point of fact it is not, for it has picked up associations of impracticality and ineffectuality and general dopiness. So also with such words as *liberal, reactionary, Communist, socialist, capitalist, radical, schoolteacher, truck driver, undertaker, operator, salesman, huckster, speculator.* These convey meanings on the literal level, but beyond that—sometimes, in some places—they convey contempt on the part of the speaker.

The question of whether to use loaded words or not depends on what is being written. The scientist, the scholar, try to avoid them; for the poet, the advertising writer, the public speaker, they are standard equipment. But every writer should take care that they do not substitute for thought. If you write, "Anyone who thinks that is nothing but a Socialist (or Communist or capitalist)" you have said nothing except that you don't like people who think that, and such remarks are effective only with the most naïve readers. It is always a bad mistake to think your readers more naïve than they really are.

Colorless Words

But probably most student writers come to grief not with words that are colorful or those that are colored but with those that have no color at all. A pet example is *nice,* a word we would find it hard to dispense with in casual conversation but which is no longer capable of adding much to a description. Colorless words are those of such general meaning that in a particular sentence they mean nothing. Slang adjectives, like *cool* ("That's real cool") tend to explode all over the language. They are applied to everything, lose their original force, and quickly die.

Beware also of nouns of very general meaning, like *circumstances, cases, instances, aspects, factors, relationships, attitudes, eventualities,* etc. In most circumstances you will find that those cases of writing which contain too many instances of words like these will in this and other aspects have factors leading to unsatisfactory relationships with the reader resulting in unfavorable attitudes on his part and perhaps other eventualities, like a grade of "D." Notice also what "etc." means. It means "I'd like to make this list longer, but I can't think of any more examples."

Paul Roberts (1917-1967), specialist in structural linguistics, received his A.B. degree at San Jose State College and his M.A. and Ph.D. degrees at the University of California. He is the author of *Cornflakes and Beaujolais,* an account of adventures in England, Europe, and Egypt while a Fulbright professor. His other books include a series of textbooks on English for elementary and secondary schools, *Patterns of English, Understanding English,* from which the preceding essay is taken, and *Understanding Grammar.*

Appendix B.

How to Be a Perfect Speller

Rudolf Flesch

Spelling is the stepchild of our scientific age. Unlike other universal problems such as the common cold or obesity, it isn't even an object of current research or scientific interest. To a scientist, spelling is simply a nuisance, the relic of a prescientific age—something that will sooner or later go away. The famous linguist Leonard Bloomfield, in his book "Language," winds up his discussion of spelling with the hope that "mechanical devices for reproducing speech will supersede our present habits of writing and printing." Another famous linguist, E. H. Sturtevant, in his "Introduction to Linguistic Science," wryly suggests that "the most efficient as well as the easiest way to improve the situation would be the complete cessation of the teaching of spelling."

So there's no hope at all from that quarter. Meanwhile, you and I and everybody else have trouble with spelling, and the man-hours lost to the nation in hunting through dictionaries and correcting errors run into millions, particularly at the level of professional writing.

□ Rudolf Flesch, "How to Be a Perfect Speller," *Saturday Review* (January 14, 1961), 41-42.

What can the ordinary person do to improve his spelling? The usual advice is to memorize spelling lists until your weaknesses are overcome. But experience shows that this is no good at all. I've stared at the words *harass* and *embarrass* on spelling lists ever since I can remember and still have to look up *harass* every time I want to use that word in writing—or rather, I had to, until I hit upon the simple method explained in this article.

The main point about spelling is that you have to use psychology. Psychology tells us that for memorizing anything we have to use the principle of association. We memorize Mrs. Farrington's name by reminding ourselves that she lives *far* away; we remember our aunt's telephone number (LYric 2-9918) by mumbling to ourselves that nine and nine makes eighteen.

So with spelling. A spelling list that tells us that a *tail* is an appendage attached to the hind part of an animal, while a *tale* is a story, is of no use at all when it comes to distinguishing between the spellings for the two different meanings. What we might be told is that a *tail ails* when it itches, whiles *tales* are told with cheese and *ale.*

On that principle I've drawn up my own little private spelling list, which is printed [on the next page]. For me, it works. But before I pass it on to you, let's first recapitulate a few general rules.

1. To be a good speller, remember the basic rules of English phonetic spelling —or, if you've never learned them, learn them now.

First, consonants: There's only one spelling for almost all consonant sounds—or rather, written consonants are usually sounded in just one regular way. The great exceptions are *c* and *g,* which are sounded hard (as in *call* and *gall*) except before *i* and *e,* when they are sounded soft (as in *cent* and *gent*).

This rule will take care of such spelling demons as *courageous, serviceable,* or *manageable.*

Also, note that the *zh* consonant sound (as in Zsa Zsa Gabor) is usually spelled as a single *s,* as in *vision, leisure, enclosure, pleasure, treasure.* Remember that when doubt assails you about such words as *occasion* or *incision.*

Next vowels: the vowels, *a, e, i, o,* and *u* are sounded as short vowels when followed by just one consonant (as in *mat, pet, kit, not, cut*) but sound "like their names" when followed by one consonant plus a vowel (as in *mate, Pete, kite, note, cute*).

This means that if you want to preserve a short vowel sound in a verb form, adjective, etc., you have to double the consonant—as in *gabby, Peggy, filling, topper, nutty.*

The other way around, you can drop the silent *e* that marks the long vowel

DR. FLESCH'S OWN SPELLING ASSOCIATIONS

ACCIDENTALLY. There's a *tally* in *accidentally.*

ACCURATE. *Accuracy* is the only *cure* for mistakes.

ADDRESS. On second-class mail, the *address* is the *ad dress.*

ADVISER. Even an *adviser* may *err.*

AGING. Drinking *gin* speeds *aging.*

ALL RIGHT—ALREADY. The two of them are *all right;* they're *already together.*

BATTALION. The *battalion* fought like *a lion.*

BOGEY. Keep your *eye* on the ball.

BRITAIN. *Britain* wanted to *retain* her empire.

BUSES. *Buses* have many *uses.*

COLLAR. A *collar* in a *large* size.

COLOSSAL. *Colossal* movies are in *color.*

COMPARISON. The *comparison* shopper went to *Paris.*

COMPLIMENT. *Compliments* flatter the ego—the *I.*

COSTUME. *Costumes cost* money.

COUNSEL. A *counsel sells* his advice.

CUSTOM. Don't *cuss* when you go through *customs.*

DEPENDENT. *Dependents* must be taken to the *dentist.*

DESCRIBE. The *description* is on your *desk.*

DIARY. In a *diary,* the *I* comes first.

DUMFOUNDED. *I* was so dumfounded I lost a *b.*

EMBARRASS. *Embarrassment* is a *barrier* to conversation.

EXHILARATING. It's ex*hil*arating to walk up a *hill.*

FORTY. *Forty* soldiers held the *fort.*

GORILLA. The dead *gorilla* was a *gory* sight.

GYPSY. *I*'m not a *gypsy.*

HANGAR. A han*gar* is an airplane *gar*age.

HARASS. *Har*assed as a hunted *hare.*

HYPOCRISY. Hypo*crisy* can produce a *crisis.*

IMMINENT. It can happen any *min*ute.

INCIDENTALLY. There's a *tally* in *incidentally.*

INDISPENSABLE. As indispen*sable* as *sable.*

LOOSE. A *moose* let *loose.*

MANTEL. There's a *tel*ephone on the man*tel.*

MORTGAGE. *Mort*als are apt to die before the *mort*gage is paid off.

MUSTACHE. His *mus*tache was *musty* and dusty.

NICKEL. It cost a nick*el* to ride the old *el.*

OBBLIGATO. A steady *obb*ligato of *b-b-b-b.*

PAID. To be *paid* is an *aid.*

PARALLEL. *All el* tracks are par*allel.*

PENDANT. My *aunt* wore a pend*ant.*

PLAYWRIGHT. Some playwrights are carpenters rather than writers.

PYGMY. *I*'m not a *pygmy.*

RESIN. They decided to *re-sin.*

SACRILEGIOUS. Sac*ril*egious is the opposite of *rel*igious.

SEPARATE. To *separate* means to set *apart.*

SIBYL. The si*by*l lived near*by.*

SIEGE. The besi*eg*ed city was down to one egg.

SIEVE. They used a si*eve* for the *eve*ning meal.

STATIONARY. He made *nary a move.*

STATIONERY. *One* pen, *one* pencil, *one* sheet of paper.

SUCCEED—SUCCESS. He *succeeded* in *doubling* his fortune.

SUPERSEDE. When you're being super*seded,* take a *sed*ative.

SURPRISE. A *burp* gives *rise* to *surprise.*

THEIR. *Their* house was left to an *heir.*

THERE. *There* is not *here.*

VILLAIN. That's the *villa in* which the *villain* lives.

sound when the word is changed so that you get another vowel after the consonant instead—as in *likable, salable, usable, competing, rosy, unruly.*

2. The second basic spelling rule is the old jingle

> *I* before *E*
> Except after *C*
> Or when sounded like *A*
> As in *neighbor* or *weigh.*

Frankly, I don't think this rule is very helpful, since there are at least a dozen exceptions: *science, financier, seize, height, weird, either, sheik, seizure, forfeit, leisure, foreign, neither, seismograph, kaleidoscope, counterfeit, weir, sleight.*

3. If you've had Latin in school, you're better off than most people, because many spelling problems don't exist for the person who has a firm grip on Latin. If you've had no Latin, you can still help yourself to some extent by looking up your favorite bugbears in the dictionary and noting carefully their Latin roots (if any). This will nail down for you such words as *accommodate, illiterate, affect* and *effect, immanent* and *imminent.* At least, I hope so.

And that—these three basic rules—pretty much takes care of all there is of rational, more or less logical spelling rules in English. The rest is wilderness—a mass of whimsical, indefensible, utterly mad spellings without rhyme or reason. There are a thousand and one historical reasons for this mess, most of them as ridiculous as someone's bright idea of spelling *whole* with a *w* so as to distinguish *whole* (entire) from *hole* (in the ground). Or Dr. Samuel Johnson's lapse of memory that made him spell *deign* and *disdain* within a few pages of his dictionary.

RUDOLF FLESCH was born in Vienna, Austria, and received his Ph.D. degree at Columbia University. He has written a syndicated newspaper column, "Conversation Piece," since 1959. Among his books are *The Art of Plain Talk, The Way to Write* (with A. H. Lass), *The Art of Readable Writing, Why Johnny Can't Read, A New Way to Better English,* and *The ABC of Style.*

Appendix C. Ideas for Themes

The following quotations are intended to stimulate writing, to be used as springboards for paragraphs or full-length compositions. They represent a period of more than two thousand years from Sun Tzu to our own contemporaries—from the young and the elderly; from the rich and the poor; from the formally educated, the self-educated, and the uneducated; from the clergyman, the scientist, the artist, the business man, the student.

You will agree with some and disagree with others. You will find some amusing; some irritating; some puzzling; a few, perhaps, inspiring; several, no doubt, boring; and a great many, we hope, interesting, or, at any rate, sufficiently so to write about.

If you are not interested in any, perhaps you should reconsider your reasons for being in college. If, on the other hand, you find a great many of the ideas worth considering, but feel that you have nothing important to say about them, you probably need only to select one quotation and think about it for a few minutes. Then start writing. Do not attempt to achieve great significance in your paper.

Just write honestly about what you have experienced or observed, or about what you believe. Do not feel that every essay must be perfectly organized and flawlessly written. Remember, however, that unsupported opinions or judgments are of little value. Use examples, anecdotes, personal reminiscences, statistics, or any illustrative or factual material to develop and support your assertions. Organize your thoughts well enough that you will not bury or lose sight of the idea you are trying to put into words. Use topic sentences, either stated or implied, so that your paragraphs will have unity. Check your work for coherence and effective transitions, and begin and conclude your paper in as effective a manner as you can. Finally, proofread for grammar, spelling, and punctuation and write so that your paper is legible.

Remember that your instructor's primary interest is in what you have to say and how well you can learn to say it.

1. If our soldiers are not overburdened with money, it is not because they have a distaste for riches.—*Sun Tzu,* 500 B.C.
2. Humor is the instinct for taking pain playfully.—*Max Eastman*
3. Religion, in whatever form, is consolation for the pain of life.—*Max Eastman*
4. Pride is equal in all men; and the only difference is in the means and manner of displaying it.—*La Rochefoucauld*
5. When you are aspiring to the highest place, it is honorable to reach the second or even the third rank.—*Cicero*
6. Applause is the spur of noble minds, the end and aim of weak ones.—*C. C. Colton*
7. Ah, don't say that you agree with me. When people agree with me I always feel that I must be wrong.—*Oscar Wilde*
8. Art is the right hand of Nature. The latter has only given us being, the former has made us men.—*Schiller*
9. Some men make fortunes, but not to enjoy them; for, blinded by avarice, they live to make fortunes.—*Juvenal*
10. Truth is as impossible to be soiled by any outward touch as the sunbeam. —*Milton*
11. Speech was given to the ordinary sort of men whereby to communicate their mind; but to wise men, whereby to conceal it.—*Robert South*
12. Those marriages generally abound most with love and constancy that are preceded by a long courtship.—*Joseph Addison*
13. A man should always consider how much he has more than he wants, and how much more unhappy he might be than he really is.—*Joseph Addison*

14. I never knew any man in my life who could not bear another's misfortunes perfectly like a Christian.—*Alexander Pope*
15. Human felicity is produc'd not so much by great pieces of good fortune that seldom happen, as by little advantages that occur every day.—*Benjamin Franklin*
16. Curiosity is one of the permanent and certain characteristics of a vigorous mind.—*Samuel Johnson*
17. Sir, your levellers wish to level *down* as far as themselves; but they cannot bear levelling *up* to themselves.—*Samuel Johnson*
18. People will not look forward to posterity who never look backward to their ancestors.—*Edmund Burke*
19. There is not a passion so strongly rooted in the human heart as envy.—*Richard Brinsley Sheridan*
20. All men feel something of an honorable bigotry for the objects which have long continued to please them.—*William Wordsworth*
21. Every reform, however necessary, will by weak minds be carried to an excess, that itself will need reforming.—*Samuel Taylor Coleridge*
22. No young man believes he shall ever die.—*William Hazlitt*
23. A decent and manly examination of the acts of Government should be not only tolerated, but encouraged.—*William Henry Harrison*
24. Everything nourishes what is strong already.—*Jane Austen*
25. Those who do not complain are never pitied.—*Jane Austen*
26. The greatest pleasure I know is to do a good action by stealth, and to have it found out by accident.—*Charles Lamb*
27. I have heard something said about allegiance to the South. I know no South, no North, no East, no West, to which I owe any allegiance.—*Henry Clay*
28. When a person dies who does any one thing better than anyone else in the world, it leaves a gap in society.—*William Hazlitt*
29. The office of government is not to confer happiness, but to give men opportunity to work out happiness for themselves.—*William Ellery Channing*
30. The surrender of life is nothing to sinking down into acknowledgment of inferiority.—*John C. Calhoun*
31. Your true dull minds are generally preferred for public employ, and especially promoted to city honors; your keen intellects, like razors, being considered too sharp for common service.—*Washington Irving*
32. The barrennest of all mortals is the sentimentalist.—*Thomas Carlyle*
33. I am certain of nothing but the holiness of the heart's affections, and the truth of Imagination. What the Imagination seizes as beauty must be Truth. —*John Keats*

34. We can do without any article of luxury we have never had; but when once obtained, it is not in human natur' to surrender it voluntarily.—*Thomas Chandler Haliburton*
35. Age is the most terrible misfortune that can happen to any man; other evils will mend, this is every day getting worse.—*George P. R. James*
36. Free trade, one of the greatest blessings which a government can confer on a people, is in almost every country unpopular.—*Lord Macaulay*
37. It is as impossible for a man to be cheated by anyone but himself, as for a thing to be, and not to be, at the same time.—*Ralph Waldo Emerson*
38. We do not count a man's years until he has nothing else to count.—*Ralph Waldo Emerson*
39. Individualities may form communities, but it is institutions alone that can create a nation.—*Benjamin Disraeli*
40. Wherever there is a human being, I see God-given rights inherent in that being, whatever may be the sex or complexion.—*William Lloyd Garrison*
41. The highest possible stage in moral culture is when we recognize that we ought to control our thoughts.—*Charles Robert Darwin*
42. Selfishness is the greatest curse of the human race.—*William Ewart Gladstone*
43. In giving freedom to the slave we assure freedom to the free,—honorable alike in what we give and what we preserve.—*Abraham Lincoln*
44. Those who dream by day are cognizant of many things which escape those who dream only by night.—*Edgar Allan Poe*
45. None can be an impartial or wise observer of human life but from the vantage ground of what *we* should call voluntary poverty.—*Henry David Thoreau*
46. It is by presence of mind in untried emergencies that the native metal of a man is tested.—*Herman Melville*
47. O brave new world
    That has such people in 't.—*Shakespeare*
48. It is as fatal as it is cowardly to blink facts because they are not to our taste. —*John Tyndall*
49. The rarer action
    Is in virtue than in vengeance.—*Shakespeare*
50. If poetry comes not as naturally as leaves to a tree it had better not come at all.—*John Keats*
51. Labor disgraces no man; unfortunately you occasionally find men disgrace labor.—*Ulysses S. Grant*

52. It is much better to want a teacher than to want the desire to learn.—*Thomas Henry Huxley*
53. The man who lets himself be bored is even more contemptible than the bore. —*Samuel Butler*
54. Work consists of whatever a body is *obliged* to do, and Play consists of whatever a body is not obliged to do.—*Mark Twain*
55. Ascend above the restrictions and conventions of the World, but not so high as to lose sight of them.—*Richard Garnett*
56. He who has contempt for poetry cannot have much respect for himself, or for anything else.—*William Hazlitt*
57. To be what we are, and to become what we are capable of becoming, is the only end of life.—*Robert Louis Stevenson*
58. Individuality is the salt of common life. You may have to live in a crowd, but you do not have to like it, nor subsist on its food.—*Henry VanDyke*
59. The test of a man or woman's breeding is how they behave in a quarrel.—*George Bernard Shaw*
60. Children begin by loving their parents; as they grow older they judge them; sometimes they forgive them.—*Oscar Wilde*
61. What we call "morals" is simply blind obedience to words of command.—*Havelock Ellis*
62. A perfect husband is one who goes along with his wife's efforts to improve him.—*Franklin P. Jones*
63. Let parents, then, bequeath to their children not riches, but the spirit of reverence.—*Plato*
64. Let love come last, after the lesson's learned;
Like all things else, love must be earned.—*Plato*
65. Ill fares the land, to hastening ills a prey,
Where wealth accumulates and men decay.—*Oliver Goldsmith*
66. And this our life, exempt from public haunt,
Finds tongues in trees, books in the running brooks,
Sermons in stones, and good in everything.
I would not change it.—*Shakespeare*
67. Our concern with any man is not with what eloquence he teaches, but with what evidence.—*St. Augustine*
68. I tell you, you must have chaos in your soul if you would give birth to a dancing star.—*Friedrich Nietzsche*
69. Love one another, but make not a bond of love;
Let it rather be a moving sea between the shores of your souls.—*Kahlil Gibran*

70. Poetry is the record of the best and happiest moments of the happiest and best minds.—*Percy Bysshe Shelley*
71. Only a lack of imagination permits the pride of certain fools. True intelligence very readily conceives of an intelligence superior to its own; and this is why truly intelligent men are modest.—*André Gide*
72. Every kind of discrimination is a protection of the incompetent against the competent, with the result that the motive to become competent is taken away.—*Goldsworthy Lowes Dickinson*
73. In spite of the large population of this planet, men and women remain today the most inaccessible things on it.—*Frank Moore Colby*
74. Public opinion's always in advance of the law.—*John Galsworthy*
75. True kindness presupposes the faculty of imagining as one's own the sufferings and joy of others. Without the imagination, there can be weakness, theoretical or practical philanthropy, but not true kindness.—*André Gide*
76. Except in street cars one should never be unnecessarily rude to a lady.—*O. Henry*
77. No one can expect a majority to be stirred by motives other than ignoble. —*George Norman Douglas*
78. It is preoccupation with possession, more than anything else, that prevents men from living freely and nobly.—*Bertrand Russell*
79. The power of words is such that they have prevented our learning some of the most important events in the world's history.—*Sir Norman Angell*
80. Absolute freedom of the press to discuss public questions is a foundation stone of American liberty.—*Herbert Hoover*
81. People ask you for criticism, but they only want praise.—*Somerset Maugham*
82. Vanity as an impulse has without doubt been of far more benefit to civilization than modesty has ever been.—*William E. Woodward*
83. Education . . . has produced a vast population able to read but unable to distinguish what is worth reading.—*George Macaulay Trevelyan*
84. To the man with an ear for verbal delicacies—the man who searches painfully for the perfect word, and puts the way of saying a thing above the thing said—there is in writing the constant joy of sudden discovery, a happy accident.—*Henry Louis Mencken*
85. All successful newspapers are ceaselessly querulous and bellicose. They never defend anyone or anything if they can help it; if the job is forced upon them, they tackle it by denouncing someone or something else.—*Henry Louis Mencken*

86. Injustice is relatively easy to bear; what stings is justice.—*Henry Louis Mencken*
87. The only limit to our realization of tomorrow will be our doubts of today. —*Franklin D. Roosevelt*
88. Let there be spaces in your togetherness.—*Kahlil Gibran*
89. The responsibility of the great states is to serve and not to dominate the world.—*Harry S. Truman*
90. Each honest calling, each walk of life, has its own elite, its own aristocracy based on excellence of performance.—*James Bryant Conant*
91. Humor is emotional chaos remembered in tranquility.—*James Thurber*
92. It is a part of probability that many improbable things will happen.—*Agathon*
93. With the decline of the religious life, neuroses grow more frequent.—*Carl G. Jung*
94. A house without a woman and firelight is like a body without soul or spirit. —*Benjamin Franklin*
95. It is woman who saves what man needs if he is to remain man.—*Alain*
96. If you love, you must needs become wise; be wise and you surely shall love. —*Maurice Maeterlinck*
97. Marriage is the alliance of two people, one of whom never remembers birthdays and the other never forgets them.—*Ogden Nash*
98. Girls we love for what they are; young men for what they promise to be. —*Goethe*
99. There is nothing noble in being superior to some other man. The true nobility is in being superior to your former self.—*Hindu Proverb*
100. The obvious is that which is never seen until someone expresses it simply. —*Kahlil Gibran*
101. There's beggary in the love that can be reckoned.—*Shakespeare*
102. Neither gods, nor men, nor bookstalls have admitted mediocrity in poets. —*Horace*
103. Knowledge without integrity is dangerous and dreadful.—*Samuel Johnson*
104. If I had to make a choice between a month of playing football and month of reading Marcel Proust, I'd take Proust.—*Ronnie Knox, quarterback of the Toronto Argonauts*
105. This Johannesburg is the city that imperial money and brains made with republican gold, and the black man sold his labor at a price that made it all possible.—*Alan Paton*
106. You can lose most of your formal education by just coasting for a year or two.—*Laurence M. Gould, President of Carleton College*

107. The great virtues are within reach of all the people.—*Laurence M. Gould*
108. At least half of the sins of mankind are caused by the fear of boredom.—*Bertrand Russell*
109. In this world, there is always danger for those who are afraid of it.—*George Bernard Shaw*
110. The destiny of any nation, at any given time, depends on the opinions of its young men under five and twenty.—*Goethe*
111. I doubt that what is ordinarily called "travel" really broadens the mind any more than a cocktail party cultivates the soul.—*Joseph Wood Krutch*
112. I don't want Negro faces in history books. I want American history taught. Unless I'm in the book, you're not in it either.—*James Baldwin*
113. Whether he wants to or not, whether he is conscious of what he's doing or not, man is in point of fact determining the future direction of evolution on this earth.—*Julian Huxley*
114. Our military, like Trotskyists in reverse, dream of permanent revolution requiring agencies of suppression.—*I. F. Stone*
115. Faith, to my mind, is a stiffening process, a sort of mental starch, which ought to be applied as sparingly as possible.—*E. M. Forster*
116. When citizens of the same state are in arms against each other, and the constituted authorities unable to execute the laws, the interposition of the United States must be prompt, or it is of little value. The ordinary course of proceedings in the courts of justice would be utterly unfit for the crisis. —*U.S. Supreme Court in Luther v. Borden, 7 Howard 1 (1849)*
117. For an idea to be fashionable is ominous, since it must afterwards be old-fashioned.—*Ascribed to George Santayana*